THIS BOOK,

LIKE ALL BOOKS, IS FOR SOLITARY
ENRICHMENT AND HUMAN
CONNECTION.

From Your LEMURIA BOOKSTORE
EST. 1975

Something in the Water

Macon, Georgia, has a surprising and amazingly deep, diverse, and incredibly rich history of music. Throughout that history Macon has produced every genre of music from minstrel to vaudeville to jazz; from blues, soul, r&b to rock, rap, hip-hop, and beyond; from primitive to classical and everything in-between, Macon has been in the middle of it all. The Georgia Minstrels, Reverend Pearly Brown, Little Richard, James Brown, Otis Redding, Charlie Daniels, The Allman Brothers Band, and so many more have strong connections to the city. In *Something in the Water*, Ben Wynne explores and chronicles all of this in a riveting read...

—Chuck Leavell

Strike a tuning fork on Macon's piedmont, and you will hear the enduring sounds that revolutionized and defined American music. Ben Wynne has thoroughly researched an under-sung subject and given it the spotlight it richly deserves. A must for audiophiles!

—Candice Dyer, author of *Street Singers, Soul Shakers, Rebels with a Cause: Music from Macon*

Ask the average music fan who they associate with Macon, Georgia, and they will probably say Little Richard, James Brown, Otis Redding, and The Allman Brothers Band, but there's more, much more. In *Something in the Water*, Ben Wynne comprehensively chronicles the city's musical history covering minstrel, gospel, popular, country, blues, r&b, and rock. Meticulously researched and incredibly detailed, it is a fascinating read.

—Willie Perkins, former tour manager and co-personal manager of The Allman Brothers Band, and author of *No Saints, No Saviors: My Years with The Allman Brothers Band*

Exploring the music of Macon, Georgia, from the early 1800s all the way up to 1980, *Something in the Water* is a wonder to behold. For music historians like myself, it is a virtual goldmine. Ben Wynne tells the whole story—warts and all. A simply outstanding, well-researched, and richly detailed history of the impact of one small Southern town on the history of popular music.

—Michael Buffalo Smith, author of *The Road Goes on Forever: Fifty Years of The Allman Brothers Band Music, 1969–2019*, and publisher of KUDZOO music magazine

MUSIC AND THE AMERICAN SOUTH

Something in the Water

A HISTORY OF MUSIC IN MACON, GEORGIA,

1823–1980

Ben Wynne

MERCER UNIVERSITY PRESS

Macon, Georgia

2021

MUP/ H1008

25 24 23 22 21   5 4 3 2 1

Books published by Mercer University Press are printed on acid-free paper that
meets the requirements of the American National Standard for Information
Sciences—Permanence of Paper for Printed Library Materials.

Printed and bound in the United States.

This book is set in Adobe Caslon Pro and Cambria (display)

Cover/jacket design by Burt&Burt.

Library of Congress Cataloging-in-Publication Data

Names: Wynne, Ben, 1961– author.
Title: Something in the water : a history of music in Macon, Georgia,
    1823-1980 / Ben Wynne.
Description: [1st.] | Macon, Georgia : Mercer University Press, 2021. |
    Series: Music in the American South | Includes bibliographical
    references and index. |
Identifiers: LCCN 2021026543 | ISBN 9780881468021 (hardback)
Subjects: LCSH: Music—Georgia—Macon—History and criticism. | Popular
Music—Georgia—Macon—History and criticism. |
    Musicians—Georgia—Macon.
Classification: LCC ML200.8.M23 W96 2021 | DDC 780.9758/552--dc23
LC record available at https://lccn.loc.gov/2021026543

For Malcolm and Edna Mullican,

and George E. Wynne

MERCER UNIVERSITY

MERCER UNIVERSITY PRESS

Endowed by

TOM WATSON BROWN
and
THE WATSON-BROWN FOUNDATION, INC.

Contents

Acknowledgments

This book was made possible through the help of many people. Macon, Georgia, is fortunate to be the home of Mercer University Press, and I would like to thank the staff there for all that they have done to encourage this work. It is my third book with Mercer, and director Marc Jolley, Marsha Luttrell, Mary Beth Kosowski, Heather Comer, and Jenny Toole are always a pleasure to work with. The research for this book could not have been completed without the assistance of the staffs of a number of archives and libraries. A special thanks is due the staff of the John Harrison Hosch Library on the Gainesville Campus of the University of North Georgia. With cheerful professionalism they expressed interest in this project while guiding me toward appropriate collections, books, and databases. They are a great group that includes Christopher Andrews, Allison Galloup, Sarah Grace Glover, Cheryl Hawkins, Austina Jordan, Monique Martinez, Christine Oslin, Harley Palmer, Kristine Stilwell, Emily Thornton, and Sheila Waldrep. I would also like to thank Muriel McDowel Jackson and the staff at the Middle Georgia Archives at the Washington Memorial Library in Macon. It is ground zero for information on the history of Macon and the surrounding area. Also very helpful were the staffs at the Hargrett Rare Book and Manuscript Library, University of Georgia, Athens, Georgia; the Center for Popular Music, James E. Walker Library, Middle Tennessee State University, Murfreesboro, Tennessee; the Lucy Lester Willet Memorial Library at Wesleyan College, Macon, Georgia; the Jack Tarver Library at Mercer University, Macon, Georgia; the Georgia State Archives, Morrow, Georgia; the Library and Archives, Rock & Roll Hall of Fame and Museum, Cleveland, Ohio; the Robert W. Woodruff Library at Emory University, Atlanta, Georgia; the Library of Congress, Washington, DC; and the Jean and

Alexander Heard Libraries, Special Collections and University Archives, at Vanderbilt University, Nashville, Tennessee.

While notes and a full list of sources are contained within, I would like to acknowledge several authors whose work was very helpful as I prepared the latter chapters of the manuscript. Candice Dyer's book, *Street Singers, Soul Shakers, Rebels with a Cause: Music from Macon* (Indigo Custom Publishing, 2008), provided a great road map for research on some of Macon's most colorful music personalities. Peter Guralnick's classic *Sweet Soul Music: Rhythm and Blues and the Southern Dream of Freedom* (Little, Brown and Company, 1986) and Preston Lauterbach's *The Chitlin' Circuit and the Road to Rock 'n' Roll* (W. W. Norton and Company, 2011) were also very helpful. Parts of the final two chapters of this book include material on performers with international reputations about whom much has already been written. In this regard, I benefitted greatly from the work of Charles White, Jonathan Gould, Alan Paul, Alan Light, Randy Poe and R. J. Smith. Michael Buffalo Smith's detailed research on Southern rock was an invaluable resource related to the Capricorn Records era in Macon, and it is must-read material for anyone interested in the subject. Anyone intrigued by Macon's music history would also benefit by visiting the website of Rock Candy Tours, an interesting company that offers tours showcasing many of the city's most important music sites.

I am fortunate to work at the University of North Georgia in Gainesville, Georgia, where the administration at every level is very supportive of my teaching and publishing pursuits. Along with many other members of our university community, I have benefitted from the generosity of our president, Bonita Jacobs, who is always quick to provide encouragement and resources for all types of scholarly activity. I also owe a great debt of gratitude to Chris Jespersen, dean of the College of Arts and Letters; Ric Kabat and Tim May, associate deans of the College of Arts and Letters; and Jeff Pardue, department head for the History, Anthropology, and Philosophy Department, all of whom have provided me with great support. I would also like to recognize my colleagues in the History, Anthropology, and Philosophy

Department who have, throughout my entire tenure at the university, blessed me with their friendship and fostered a warm and collegial work atmosphere conducive to academic ventures of all kinds.

While I was working on this project, I was fortunate to meet and talk to many people who were knowledgeable, friendly, and helpful. I am grateful to those from Macon and beyond who were nice enough to communicate with me about this book either in person, by telephone, or through email. This includes Newton Collier, John H. Darlington, Candice Dyer, Willie Perkins, Paul Hornsby, Leon Kennington, Wayne Pierce, Charles Reynolds, Chuck Leavell, Shawna Dooley, Jared Wright, Ben Sandifer, Richard Brent, Peter Guralnick, Dr. Debi Hamlin, Jessica Walden, Michael Buffalo Smith, Robin Duner-Fenter, Larry Brumley, Lisa and Barry Darnell, Bob Konrad, and Kristin Oren. Friends John and Julie Leggett, Marty and Kris Lester, Alan and Leigh Vestal, and Johnny Greer were also instrumental in helping me get this project off the ground.

Last but certainly not least, nothing I do is possible without the support, love, and comfort of my family, Carly Wynne, Lily Wynne, Cotton Wynne, Patricia Wynne, and Noelle Wynne. I dedicate this book to my late grandparents Malcolm and Edna Mullican and to my late father, George E. Wynne.

Introduction

"If I had to be born all over again, I'd want to be born in Macon."[1]
—Little Richard

"There's something in the water." It is a cliché often used to account for an important occurrence that defies easy explanation, or to flippantly explain away a mystery. Residents of Macon, Georgia, have been using the phrase for decades in a lighthearted effort to give better definition to their city's culture. Macon is known as a music city, and for almost two centuries, talented musicians have been born in or passed through its city limits. Some lived and died in obscurity while others achieved international stardom. From its pioneer origins to the modern era, Macon has produced waves of talent with amazing consistency, representing a wide range of musical genres. As a result, the city's influence stretches far beyond the borders of Georgia, and its musical imprint on America's cultural heritage, unnoticed by many, is significant. Many Macon residents call this historical concentration of talent in their city a phenomenon while others chalk it up to nothing more than coincidence. The truth of the matter is elusive, lying somewhere between those two points of view. In the meantime, crediting the drinking water is as good an explanation as any.

It is an overstatement to say that there would have been no rock and roll, or music labeled Southern rock, without Macon's musical energy, or that rhythm and blues, funk, and rap would not have evolved as they did without the city's influence, but there are grains of truth in the assessment. Little Richard was born and raised in Macon, where he faced his first audiences. He would go on to become a global celebrity whose intense, outlandish, and raucous musical delivery made his self-proclaimed status as "the Architect of Rock and Roll" hard to argue with. For James Brown, another true original, Macon was the springboard to a stellar career that saw him honored worldwide as "the Godfather of Soul" and "the Hardest Working Man in Show Business." After he became famous, many performers copied Brown's dance moves, but no one could ever effectively replicate the intensity of his act. Echoes of the music he created and arranged can still be heard in contemporary rhythm and blues, funk, and rap circles, as well as rock and roll.

Singer, songwriter, and arranger Otis Redding, one of the most dynamic performers of the 1960s, was also a product of Macon. Redding's rise to fame was meteoric. A rock and soul music pioneer, he wrote or cowrote a number of classics, including "I Can't Turn You Loose," "These Arms of Mine," "I've Been Loving You Too Long," and the Aretha Franklin signature song "Respect." His recording of "Sittin' on the Dock of the Bay," released posthumously after his death in a plane crash, routinely appears in opinion polls and on music media lists as one of the greatest songs of the rock era. His 1967 performance at the Monterey Pop Festival was the stuff of legend, and even the Beatles sought him out for autographs. Like Little Richard and James Brown, he started out in Macon with no way of knowing that he would one day become an icon.

A group of Macon transplants calling themselves the Allman Brothers Band eased into the city in 1969. They were the crown jewel of Phil Walden and Frank Fenter's Capricorn Records, the famous Macon-based label responsible for bringing a great deal of rock talent into the city during the 1970s. While Capricorn recorded a number of well-known artists, the Allman Brothers Band was special. If there was indeed something in the Macon water supply that produced talent, members of the group must have consumed gallons of it. They took the foundational formula for rock and roll—a blues base with some country music sprinkled in—to a whole new level. Record executives, critics, and many fans labeled their music "Southern rock," although it was popular all over the country. The band played and recorded old blues standards and innovative original material, the sounds of which were mesmerizing. They called Macon their home for years as they altered the history of rock music in America.

While Little Richard, James Brown, Otis Redding, and the Allman Brothers Band are among the most prominent names associated with Macon's music history, they are not alone in shaping the city's musical heritage. The history of music in Macon is long and layered. It stretches back to the 1820s, when volunteers formed the city's first militia unit, complete with a small drum and fife corps, and when entrepreneurs such as Lemuel Newcomb and Alexander Shotwell first began selling musical instruments in their shops on the banks of the Ocmulgee River. Amateur musicians flourished in Macon from its founding, and touring musical artists passed through the city with great consistency after the coming of the railroad in the 1840s. Venues such as Washington Hall and the Floyd House—both razed long ago—hosted musical soirees on a regular basis. During the antebellum period, enslaved musicians, such as John Brooker, Henry Fields, Lucius Griffin, and Andrew Gospel, played the guitar, banjo, fiddle, and flute at social occasions on plantations and in the community. Phillip Guttenberger, a German immigrant and the patriarch of a musical dynasty in Macon, moved to the city in 1845. The era also produced flutist and poet Sidney Lanier, who many consider Macon's first music celebrity, and prominent Confederate-era music publisher Hermann L. Schreiner also called Macon his home.

After the Civil War, Macon produced the Georgia Minstrels, an unusual African American singing and dancing troupe consisting of former slaves who toured the United States and Europe. Vincent Czurda, who came to Macon during the war years, became a fixture on the city's music scene. He taught at the Georgia Academy for the Blind and provided the music for innumerable social occasions in the city during the last three decades of the nineteenth century.

As the war's guns fell silent, Macon's streets continued to ring with church music. All the city's congregations organized choirs for Sunday services and frequent "community sings." The music departments at Wesleyan College and Mercer University contributed many well-trained musicians to Middle Georgia's music culture. After the war, Macon became an even more frequent tour stop for national acts, and local musicians and singers formed groups like the Macon Harmonic Society to entertain at formal and informal gatherings. In 1882, the Macon Academy of Music, a spacious new entertainment venue, opened its doors to the public, hosting all types of musical events. Two major music stores, J. W. Burke and Company and the Georgia Music House, outfitted the city's musicians and dominated the music marketplace.

During the 1890s, the Macon Railway & Light Company established a new system of electric streetcars in the city and created "streetcar parks," including Crump's Park, Ocmulgee Park, and North Highlands Park, that hosted concerts. Bands led by Henry Card and Ferdinand Guttenberger routinely performed at these outdoor venues. In 1896, local entrepreneur Michael G. Putzel opened "Putzel's Vaudeville Palace" on Mulberry Street, which advertised "the best vaudeville entertainment in the

South." Edouard Hesselberg, a nationally known music professor, mentored students at Wesleyan, organized concerts, and provided music for civic events. African American street performers Ike Brown and Joe Gordon plied their trade for nickels and dimes as examples of the type of rambling bluesmen whose music would lay the foundation for rock and roll.

Just after the turn of the century, Macon entered a new era as the Academy of Music gave way to a new venue, the Grand Opera House, billed as the finest entertainment center in the South. The new structure drew more national acts and bigger crowds. African American impresario Charles Douglass started his career in the entertainment business with the construction of the Douglass Theatre, an important stop on the "chitlin circuit," where he hosted innumerable local events in the African American community. In 1912, a dozen socially prominent Macon women founded an organization "to cultivate a taste for the highest and best in music, and to assist others to a broader knowledge of the same." They christened their group the Saturday Morning Music Club, and it still meets today. The Chautauqua movement came to Macon during the World War I era, exposing residents to different forms of music from all over the world.

As the 1920s roared, Macon produced Jazz Age diva Lucille Hegamin, who was among the first wave of jazz and blues artists to make records. Hegamin toured with her band, the Blue Flame Syncopators, and had fans across the country. The city was also home to Emmett Miller, a "burnt cork" minstrel performer whose recording of "Lovesick Blues" greatly influenced Hank Williams. An early "hillbilly" trio, the South Georgia Highballers, were locally popular and recorded several songs, including numbers oddly accented by a musical saw. Charles Collier headquartered "The Silas Green Show" in Macon, where it flourished as one of the most famous African American entertainment revues in the nation. Country music pioneer Riley Puckett and blues legend Willie McTell both received musical training in Macon at the Georgia Academy for the Blind, and Emory O'Hara, another local resident, became a prolific songwriter. Macon's stylish new city auditorium opened to the public in 1925 with a highly anticipated concert by organist Henry F. Siebert.

Macon contributed singing talent to the big band era as well, including the Pickens Sisters, who forged a productive national career for themselves. Signed by the Victor Recording Company, they made more than two dozen singles for the label during the 1930s, mostly popular or jazz-based numbers. The press took note of their Southern roots, often pinning on them nicknames, such as "The Georgia Peaches" and "Three Little Maids from Dixie." For a time, they were a radio staple on NBC and appeared on Broadway and in films. Another Macon singer, Beatrice Carter, moved to New York, took the stage name Betty Barclay, and caught the attention of Sammy Kaye, one of the biggest stars of the big band era. She sang with Kaye's group and had a national hit with the song "I'm a Big Girl Now." The most successful instrumentalist from Middle Georgia during the era was probably trumpet player Emmett Berry, who was born in Macon in 1915. Berry played with bands led by Fletcher Henderson, Benny Goodman, Count Basie, Earl Hines, Lucky Millinder, and Lionel Hampton, just to name a few, and for a time was a member of the formidable CBS Studio Orchestra in New York.

Key personalities in the evolution of Macon's music culture after the Second World War were a tough-talking promoter named Clint Brantley and a just-as-tough bandleader named Gladys Williams. Both were keen judges of talent who for decades helped guide and develop young musicians in the city. Brantley booked musical acts in Macon and elsewhere on the chitlin circuit. He advanced the career of an unknown Little Richard during the 1950s, and a very good case can be made that he discovered James Brown. Known for being strict but encouraging, Williams was unusual in that she was a female bandleader in a profession dominated by men. The parade of Macon talent that she influenced was significant, including singers Little Richard and Otis Redding, and musicians who toured with bands all over the country. Macon's African American nightclubs, such as Club 15 and Adams Lounge, hosted some of the chitlin circuit's biggest names as well as local artists who excelled at their craft.

Macon's more modern era produced Phil Walden, who was by far the city's most committed white advocate for African American music. He managed black artists and began building a musical empire with his friend Otis Redding before Redding's untimely death. Many called Walden a genius, though some had names for him that were not nearly as flattering. In the late 1960s, he turned his attention to promoting mostly white rock acts, recruiting the Allman Brothers Band and other groups to the city, beginning a process that earned Macon the title "the Cradle of Southern Rock." Walden and Frank Fenter ran Capricorn Records, Macon's legendary label that for a decade was a force in the music industry and whose influence can still be felt today.

These personalities, along with many more in the pages of this book, have contributed to Macon's music history over the last two centuries. They make up a great, melodious, multigenerational chorus of talent that collectively forged the city's reputation as a creative center. From a musical standpoint, the question of whether the city made the artists, or the artists made the city, is open for debate, but one element of the story is clear. All involved apparently took at least one sip of the area's magical water and, in so doing, helped create a colorful, complicated, and not easily explainable culture. "If I had to be born all over again," Little Richard said many times, "I'd want to be born in Macon."[2]

1

SOUNDS ALONG THE FRONTIER
1823–1865

"The singers went on, the musicians after them, in the midst of the maidens beating tambourines."

—Psalm 68:25

In July of 1824, the aging Marquis de Lafayette, staunch American ally and Revolutionary War hero, embarked on a fourteen-month tour of the United States at the invitation of President James Monroe. Celebrated at every stop, the general finally reached Georgia in the spring of the following year. On his journey through the state, Lafayette arrived first at Savannah, then moved on to Augusta, Warrenton, and Sparta before finally reaching Milledgeville, which was at the time the state capital. On the morning of March 27, 1825, he and his entourage left Milledgeville and traveled west, further into Georgia's rugged interior on a route designed to take them across the state and into Alabama. After several hours, the group reached a significant but rough-hewn backwoods village that at first glance seemed unaccommodating, though in reality it was the nucleus around which a thriving city would one day grow. Residents gave Lafayette a warm reception, and though the recently founded settlement was primitive by the standards of eastern cities, its location on the banks of the Ocmulgee River and the enthusiasm of its residents seemed to evoke a spirit of limitless potential. The community left a favorable impression on Auguste Levasseur, the general's secretary, who was chronicling the trip. "Macon, a pretty little town, had no existence eighteen months ago," he later wrote. "It has risen from the midst of the forests as if by enchantment."[1]

Despite Levasseur's magical interpretation of Macon's origins, the genesis of the settlement actually lay in treaties signed between the Creek Indians and the United States government in the years following the American Revolution. These agreements ceded vast tracts of Creek land to the United States and opened central Georgia for development. In 1807, the Americans built Fort Hawkins on the Ocmulgee River, and a trading post opened nearby that drew settlers into the area. On December 9, 1822, the Georgia legislature created Bibb County, naming it for recently deceased physician and statesman William Wyatt Bibb. Two weeks later, the same body appointed commissioners to establish a town across the Ocmulgee River from Fort Hawkins that would serve as Bibb County's seat of government. The legislature chose the name Macon for the new settlement, after Nathaniel Macon of North Carolina, a prominent national politician of the period. In early 1823, officials surveyed Macon and the sale of lots commenced. Streets were laid out on a grid, with those running north and south named numerically (First through Eleventh) and most of those running east and west given the names of trees (Walnut, Mulberry, Cherry, Poplar, Plum, and Pine).

Once Macon was surveyed and lots were sold, building commenced and within an amazingly short time the town began to take shape. During the first six months of 1823, seventeen new frame buildings were completed and Macon was officially incorporated on December 10. Just a year later, the town had "twenty respectable stores, sixteen on the west side of the river and four on the east, four large taverns, a warehouse for cotton, [and] upwards of sixty families." Throughout the 1820s, the town continued to take on the trappings of a growing frontier settlement. Two newspapers, the *Messenger* and the *Telegraph*, began publication, more businesses sprang up, the town's first school opened, and local men organized a Masonic Lodge. In 1825, a new wooden courthouse was constructed, only to be replaced a short time later by a three-story brick structure. Almost immediately after its founding, the town became a hub of commerce not just for Bibb County, but for all of central Georgia. By the end of the decade the cotton trade was in full bloom and flatboats loaded down with cotton bales left the town's docks on a regular basis. The Federal Road, which ran through Macon and into south Alabama, also stimulated commerce and the cotton trade, so much so that the section running through the town was sometimes called "Cotton Avenue." As in the rest of the South, the bulk of the cotton trade in Macon rested on slave labor, and the number of slaves in the town and surrounding area increased as the cotton trade flourished. By 1830, 1,183 (approximately 45 percent) of Macon's 2,635 residents were slaves, and ten years later, slaves outnumbered whites in the town 3,952 to 2,291.[2]

Music penetrated the Georgia wilderness early on as Macon's residents created a collective culture for themselves on the frontier. Periodic community celebrations and special events usually included some type of music as part of the program, especially after 1825 when the fledgling town organized a volunteer militia unit—the Macon Volunteers—that included a company band. Patriotic songs and martial music were the order of the day whenever the band performed. Independence Day celebrations were particularly festive, with residents eager to display their patriotism and, in general, make a lot of noise. On July 4, 1827, the town sponsored an all-day affair to celebrate the fifty-first anniversary of American independence, complete with an abundance of food and drink. According to one report, "Toasts were drunk, interspersed with songs and martial music." Two years later, town fathers planned an even grander celebration that literally began with a bang around dawn as men from the local militia discharged a cannon. During this event, "flags were displayed from the cupola of the new courthouse and other places during the day. Martial music was heard in our streets and all business was suspended." The founding of the Macon Volunteers was commemorated each year with a daylong event that featured music and dancing. Citizens held similar celebrations to commemorate the American victory at New Orleans during the War of 1812 and George Washington's birthday. As Macon was the county seat for Bibb County, political gatherings during presidential election seasons were common and usually included "music and banners" promoting candidates.[3]

The strains of martial music echoing through the wilderness in recently settled Middle Georgia were part of Macon's formative process. Far from an unusual occurrence, the presence of a military band in the town reflected a time-honored tradition transplanted from Europe and Americanized over time. The Militia Act of 1792, passed by the Second United States Congress, required every "free able-bodied white male citizen" between the ages of eighteen and forty-five to serve in militia units in their state, giving rise to the creation of resident militia outfits in towns, villages, and hamlets all over the country. Filled with local men, these groups promoted neighborhood cohesiveness and generated a great deal of community pride as they marched in holiday parades and held public drill events. As music had been a part of the military since ancient times, both on the battlefield and in a ceremonial context, most militia units in the United States included a band. Local militia bands of the early nineteenth century were not uniform from state to state, but most functioned as a traditional fife and drum corps consisting of five to eight woodwind instruments and at least one drum, with brass instruments later becoming standard. They drew their material from circulating sheet music of the period, such as Samuel Holyoke's *The Musical Assistant*, published in 1800. Holyoke's work was one of the first comprehensive music manuals published in the United States. In addition to popular tunes, it included "a selection of favorite airs [and] marches, progressively arranged" that became the foundation of militia band music in many parts of the country.[4]

In Macon, the 1827 Fourth of July celebration was typical of a frontier gathering featuring music from a local militia band. Interspersed between speeches and toasts, the band of the Macon Volunteers entertained a large, boisterous crowd with a variety of instrumental selections. The rustic ensemble began with "The Star-Spangled Banner," the famous Francis Scott Key poem that was adapted to the melody of a popular British tavern song that would become the national anthem of the United States, followed by the familiar Scottish farewell lament "Auld Lang Syne." They played a tune called "Macon's March," an old military marching song adapted especially for the occasion, and "Hail Columbia," another patriotic tune originally written in 1789 for the inauguration of George Washington. In addition to martial music, the band entertained with popular songs that reflected the northern European heritage of most local whites, such as the Scottish ballad "John Anderson, My Jo," a musical adaptation of a Robert Burns poem, and the lively Gaelic jig "Haste to the Wedding." Other crowd favorites were the bawdy Irish folk tune "The Scolding Wife" and traditional tavern songs with murky origins, such as "The Landlady of France," "The Glasses Sparkle on the Board," and the upbeat novelty song "A Light Heart and a Thin Pair of Breeches." To locals, the most interesting song that the band played was probably "Cumming and McDuffie," a typically Americanized tune with new words set to an old English melody. The song told the story of two feuding politicians, Georgian William Cumming and George McDuffie of South Carolina, who had recently met one another in a widely reported duel.[5]

The band of the Macon Volunteers flourished during the 1830s under the direction of Theodrick L. Smith. In addition to the traditional fife and drum, the group boasted a variety of brass instruments by the middle of the decade. The band functioned as a part of the military company, but also operated independently, performing concerts in Macon and elsewhere. Composed of "respectable young gentlemen of the city," the band was with the militia company when it was deployed to Florida during the Second Seminole War in 1835 and was apparently present at the Battle of Withlacoochee Swamp. By late July of the following year, they were back in Macon about to depart "on a musical excursion up the country" to Athens to celebrate commencement week at the University of Georgia. The band gave two concerts at the university and "in the intervening villages on the way up." In addition to Smith, other musicians who were part of the Macon Volunteer Band during this period were Andrew J. Hurd, Francis A. Jones, Giles Tucker, Seth Hart, George Horn, George Damon, and Edwin Ives.[6]

In Macon, there was also demand for musical instruments among the local population outside the military band, at least to the extent that some of the town's earliest merchants carried instruments in their shops. As early as 1827, Lemuel Newcomb advertised two pianos for sale in his shop, and not long afterwards Alexander Shotwell opened a store that sold books, stationery, and "pianos of a rich description, and a variety of other musical instruments, with instruction books, and music adapted to the same." A merchant named Bruno opened the first store dedicated exclusively to the sale of music and musical instruments during the 1830s. Like Shotwell, he sold many instruments, but his advertising focused on high-end pianos "of various patterns of rosewood and mahogany, with grand action...embracing the latest fashion of furniture." In 1840, Bruno partnered with brothers Samuel and Jonathan Virgin, two New Hampshire transplants, to create an even larger music store to serve Macon's growing population. The new enterprise sold pianos and also carried "guitars, violins, flutes, flageolets, clarinets, Kent bugles, trumpets, trombones and drum fifes." In newspaper advertisements, the entrepreneurs claimed that they could import any instrument and "sell them as low as they can be bought in New York." Two years later, Jonathan B. Morrell opened yet another music store in Macon that had "as complete an assortment of musical merchandise as can be found in the southern country," including a wide range of sheet music both domestic and foreign.[7]

As the town began to prosper, organized entertainment became more common, requiring the use of public spaces for a wide variety of gatherings. The new courthouse served as one gathering place, playing host to a Christmas gala in 1829 that was the first major public celebration of the holiday in the area. According to reports from the Macon *Telegraph*, "The best music within a hundred miles of the place was procured," and partygoers danced by candlelight into the late hours. "We had hardly ventured to hope," the newspaper stated, "that so many of the fair patrons of the harpsichord could be found in this vicinity." Soon, new hotels with large public rooms for entertainment began to spring up. Many of the earliest were simple boarding houses with taverns attached. Among the first were Beasley's Tavern, sometimes referred to as the Pealicker Hotel, which advertised "Entertainment for Man and Beast," and the "Yellow House," opened by Lucinda Bird and her partner William Bivens. Two substantial hotels operating in Macon beginning in the late 1820s were the Washington Hall on the south corner of Mulberry and Second streets, and the Mansion House, which advertised itself as "as good a house of entertainment as the country affords." Washington Hall was owned for a time by Sterling Lanier, the grandfather of poet Sidney Lanier, who upon purchasing the building promised the residents of Macon that they "may rest assured of good entertainment at this house." Of all the early hotels, it was the most active with regard to hosting concerts, plays, and a wide range of other social events. Macon's first brick hotel, the Central Hotel, was built in 1833 a block away from Washington Hall. It burned after only a few years and was replaced by the Floyd House, another fixture of Macon's social scene during its formative period.[8]

Beginning not long after the town's founding, caravans of traveling performers passed through Macon giving concerts or presenting plays that included music. In May of 1828, the Lafayette Equestrian Company came to town with a group of actors and musicians in tow. It was a circus of sorts that specialized in riding exhibitions. The show featured feats of "expert horsemanship" that were "interspersed with songs, recitations, theatrical representations and accompanied with good music." The exhibition apparently pleased the editor of the *Telegraph*, who later gave a review that reflected both his enjoyment of the performance and the disconsolate nature of life in a pioneer setting. "In these gloomy times," he opined, "something of this sort is needed to raise our spirits and drive away the melancholy." Not long after the equestrians left town, Washington Hall hosted a traveling acting troupe that performed the farce "How to Die for Love," which was peppered with traditional music and "comic songs." In 1832, Solomon "Old Sol" Smith, a theatrical producer and actor, purchased a lot on Second Street and built a makeshift theater that periodically hosted his touring troupe. Smith was originally from New York, but he became a well-known personality in the South after years of traveling through the region. His productions ranged from Shakespeare to slapstick and always included "songs, duets, recitations and instrumental music." While professional touring troupes were an exciting diversion in a frontier town like Macon, they were not the sole outlet for those seeking theatrical entertainment. In 1836, a group of local amateurs formed the Macon Dramatic Corps, which presented plays at public events.[9]

Music in early Macon was not limited to performances at secular occasions. The rapid growth of the town led to the equally rapid growth of its religious institutions. By the end of the 1830s, the Baptists, Methodists, Episcopalians, and Presbyterians had all built significant permanent structures to house their flocks. Naturally, music was an integral part of weekend worship, with all the denominations organizing their own choirs. They sang standard hymns of the day during services, and all of Macon's music stores carried hymnals for use in the home. The hymns themselves were mainly of European origin, with those of Isaac Watts and John Wesley being in most of the standard hymn books of the day. Alexander Shotwell prominently displayed copies of *Watts' Psalms and Hymns* for sale in his store as well as Methodist hymnals and *The Cluster of Spiritual Songs, Divine Hymns, and Sacred Poems* by prominent Baptist minister Jesse Mercer. Congregations also sponsored choral events to raise funds and apparently competed with one another for the limited dollars available on the frontier. In April of 1837, the Presbyterians hosted "A Concert of Sacred Music" in their building featuring "hymns, trios, solos, anthems and choruses," and charged an admission price of fifty cents per ticket. Around the same time, the Episcopalians organized their own concert, promising the public "a splendid night of music featuring hymns by the most celebrated authors." They were particularly aggressive in promoting their event, seeming to claim that their choir was superior to any of the others in town. "Feeling a desire to improve the standard of music in our churches," their advertising material read, "and believing that they have contributed in some degree toward so desirable an object, the choir have been induced to give a public performance, believing that all who honor them with their presence will be pleased."[10]

Macon emerged as the commercial center of Middle Georgia—and one of the state's fastest growing communities—during the 1840s. The town prospered as the cotton economy took hold, and a number of significant cotton planters made Bibb County their home. "Macon, since its first existence," one early town historian boasted, "has been one of the largest interior cotton markets in the South." Barges loaded down with cotton bales left the Macon wharf on the Ocmulgee on a regular basis bound for Savannah and Darien. Cotton brokers and slave dealers prospered. For an antebellum cotton hub, the city's economy was also remarkably diverse. Macon was filled with mercantile establishments, several foundries were in operation, and two factories manufactured furniture. Roads connected Macon with most of the other important cities in Georgia, and stage lines ran from Macon to Savannah and Columbus on a regular basis. This commercial activity helped produce a moneyed class in Macon that had the time and the resources to promote the arts, and the money to purchase tickets to significant cultural events. Those with wealth built nice homes and cleaned up Macon's streets in an attempt to help the town move on from its pioneer origins. "The streets run at right angles with each other, and are from 100 to 120 feet in breadth," one observer of the period later wrote describing the town. "The houses are mostly wood; many of these are spacious and elegant; and some of the private dwellings are of brick, well-built and in good taste. The public edifices are large, well-proportioned, and indicative of a rising and prosperous city."[11]

As some in Macon flourished, more and more traveling performers passed through the town. This was especially the case with the coming of the railroad to Georgia's interior. The first railroad connecting Savannah to Macon began service in 1843, effectively creating an early Georgia entertainment circuit for singers and musicians, who typically worked Savannah first, followed by Macon and Augusta. Traffic through Macon increased as new lines connected the town to Columbus and ran north toward the Tennessee border. While regional balladeers, minstrels, and instrumentalists visited Macon, many of the performers who passed through the area were Europeans who had come to the United States at the height of the Romantic movement. These included opera singers and classical musicians who traveled the country introducing the American public to Beethoven, Mendelssohn, and Wagner. Among the first European performers to stop in Macon were a husband-and-wife team, the Keppells, who had come to the United States from England. Mr. Keppell was an actor and singer of questionable ability who was routinely savaged by the reviewers in London. In contrast, his wife had a stellar reputation as a pianist and "an excellent contralto," and the Keppells designed their act to showcase her talents. She usually accompanied herself on the piano, and her repertoire included English ballads, such as "Rise Gentle Moon," "My Pretty Page," "Look Out Afar," and "Banks of the Blue Moselle," all popular tunes of the period. "Madame K. has chanted a variety of beautiful songs in her own witching way," one Macon observer gushed after seeing her performance. "She has sung our favorite airs and we thank her for it.... [Her] performance on the piano is sweet and scientific beyond our capacity to describe." Not long afterwards, another English performer, Henry Phillips, came to Macon and performed to a standing-room-only crowd at the Floyd House. Phillips, who some called "the best bass singer in England," was born into an acting family in Bristol, but he eventually abandoned the theater to concentrate on a singing career. He toured Europe a number of times before finally coming to the United States during the 1840s. Phillips was well received in Middle Georgia, with locals praising "the plaintive melody of his voice" as he sang period standards, such as "Molly Bawn" and "Light of Other Days." One local journalist later wrote that Phillips's delivery was "plain and simple, but perfectly natural, displaying a manly sensibility and energy in expression."[12]

In January of 1846, a popular national act billed as "The Orphean Family" came to Macon for multiple performances at the Floyd House, creating a great deal of excitement in the town. While reviews from the 1840s state that the group included four siblings—two brothers and two sisters—the lineup changed over the years. In Macon, their program consisted of twelve songs, most of which were recently penned, including the Victorian parlor song "The Old Arm Chair," by English pianist Henry Russell, and a maritime ditty, "Our Boat Sets Lightly on the Wave," by William Clifton. In the middle of the program, the quartet sang two more subdued tunes, "Funeral of Napoleon" and "Grave of Napoleon," that paid tribute to the former French emperor. Originally from Maine, the Orpheans ended their show with "We Left New England's Sunny Hills," a song written especially for them by Alfred Wheeler. "We have enjoyed the charms of these delightful vocalists," the editor of the *Telegraph* wrote of the troupe after the Macon performance, "and have indulged the hope that our citizens would be relieved for a short moment from the leaden dullness of the city by these enchanting voices." Another reviewer was equally effusive, stating, "As a whole, we have never heard a band whose voices in singing were in such perfect harmony." While most who heard the group sing seemed to enjoy their performance, not everyone was equally enchanted by their physical appearance or their Northern lineage. Future South Carolina governor Benjamin Franklin Perry saw the Orphean family perform around the same time and included an unvarnished account of the experience in a letter to his wife. "Last night I went to hear the Orphean Family sing, and was very much pleased," he wrote. "They are two men and two women, brothers and sisters—big, awkward Yankee people, and ugly withal—but they have wonderful voices."[13]

Not long after the Orpheans' visit, another prominent family of entertainers stopped in Macon for multiple performances at the Floyd House. The English actor John Sloman led the troupe, which included his two daughters Ann and Elizabeth, who sang and played the harp and piano. The Slomans had come to New York from England in 1839, and since then had toured the country playing venues large and small. The elder Sloman was a veteran of the English stage and specialized in musical comedy. His eldest daughter Jane, who toured separately, was a well-known pianist and composer. The Floyd House promoted the Slomans' appearances as "a series of entertainments of vocal and instrumental music containing solos and duets for the harp and piano, with ballads and vocal compositions from the great masters by the Misses Sloman, interspersed with original [comic] songs by Mr. Sloman." Their eclectic show was as grand as advertised, with most of the focus on the Sloman daughters. It began with instrumental pieces from two Italian operas. Both young women played piano on a selection from *La Sonnambula*, followed by Elizabeth performing a selection on the harp from *Norma*. In a dramatic change of pace, the daughters sang a pair of ballads, "Auld Robin Gray," a Scottish tale about lost love, and the romantic Irish lament "Kathleen Mavourneen," which "won every ear and every heart" in the room. John Sloman offered an interlude "in the burlesque" that included comedic songs loosely based on the old French folktale Blue Beard, and the show ended with more music by his daughters. At the end of the evening, the

Slomans received hearty applause for their "truly rich feast for lovers of fun and melody."[14]

Increased railroad traffic in Middle Georgia during the 1840s and 1850s brought even more singers and musicians through Macon. Some of the acts were well known, traversing a circuit that took them through many of the major cities east of the Mississippi River. At least a week in advance—and sometimes as much as a month, depending on the artist— newspaper announcements and broadsides appeared in town announcing upcoming shows. Many of the visitors were foreign-born artists attempting to advance their careers by ceaseless touring. English acting troupes remained common, along with singers from Scandinavia, Germany, Italy, or eastern Europe, and their performances introduced Macon's population to a diverse range of classical music. Included in the parade of talent that performed in Macon during the late 1840s and 1850s were the renowned Swedish vocalist and pianist Emilie Hammarskjöld, Moravian pianist Maurice Strakosch, German violinist Conrad Charles Reisinger, and Austrian pianist and composer Henri Herz. One act, a couple billed as "Mr. and Madame Leati," came to Macon in the spring of 1849 and apparently altered the performance that they usually gave in larger, Northern cities to meet the tastes of their rural patrons. The Leatis specialized in Italian opera and works by the classical masters, but in Macon they based their repertoire in "selections from the most admired songs, duets, and ballads of America, England and Scotland." Around the same time, a group of nineteen German musicians, billed as the Steyermarkische Musical Company, performed at the Floyd House. Their repertoire included polkas and waltzes by the notable Austrian composers Johann Strauss, Joseph Lanner, and Joseph Gungl.[15]

In June of 1850, the celebrated English soprano Anna Bishop appeared in Macon as part of a grand tour of the United States, accompanied by French harpist Nicolas-Charles Bochas. She performed at the Lanier House a mix of classical tunes and ballads, including "Home Sweet Home," which was considered her signature song. Other selections ranged from the comic aria "Oh Light of All My Joys, Alone" to the Spanish-inspired "The Banks of the Guadalquiver" to "Anna Bolena," an operatic tribute to the doomed second wife of Henry VIII. Bishop was a popular singer of the period, celebrated for her voice as well as the scandals attached to her personal life. She was married to the English composer Henry Bishop, with whom she had three children, but she abandoned him and took up with Bochas, who became her manager. Regardless of the behind-the-scenes drama, her performances drew large crowds wherever she went, and the day after her Macon performance, a local reporter complimented the appearance. "We never beheld a more gratified and enthusiastic audience.... Everything she did, every note she sang, displayed the artiste in the highest perfection." The correspondent was also generous to Bochas, who, in addition to being a harpist, was well known as a musical arranger. "The harp in his hand," the reporter wrote, "gives utterance to such sweet sounds, that you lose sight of Bochas, and only hear and see the instrument."[16]

To meet the entertainment demand in Macon, a new theater opened in a recently constructed building on the corner of Mulberry Street and Cotton Avenue, across the street from Washington Hall. Referred to as the "Macon Concert Hall," or simply "the Concert Hall" by locals, the theater was on the second floor of the structure, which also housed local chapters of the Odd Fellows and the Sons of Temperance. One of the first events held in the new theater was billed as a "musical festival" featuring "distinguished artists of the Italian Opera." Among the performing company were the well-traveled contralto Carolina Vietti along with baritone Antonio Avignone and Antonio Sanquirico, whom many considered "a legend in comic opera." The troupe played two sold-out shows in Macon. Not long afterward, another veteran of the Italian opera, soprano Teresa Parodi, appeared at the Concert Hall with pianist Maurice Strakosch and violinist Miska Hauser. Parodi was a true diva who had maintained an impressive career touring both Europe and the United States. "In the operatic scene," one onlooker wrote, "Parodi's magnificent powers as a tragic actress combine with her ability as a vocalist to give her a decided advantage over all her Italian compeers." The concert began at 8'oclock on the evening of May 12, 1852, and lasted well into the night, offering patrons an eclectic mix of "gems from the great masters of classical, sacred, popular and miscellaneous music, English ballads and songs, Italian airs, duets and fantasies."[17]

Traveling musical troupes stimulated local interest in the arts that already existed among Macon's population. During the town's formative period, private individuals and fledgling educational institution offered pupils instruction in music, the first being a short-lived "Singing School" organized by R. E. Brown in August of 1824. As early as 1829, Macon Female School offered girls and young women in the area classes in "music and the ornamental branches of female education," while Macon Academy began offering instruction in music during the 1830s. Both sponsored "monthly soirees" to highlight the accomplishments of their students. Two sisters, Maria and Helen Lord, were among the first to open a school specifically dedicated to musical pursuits when they rented two rooms at the Central Hotel in 1833 and began seeing pupils. Not long afterwards, a man named Matthews started a singing school that met at the Presbyterian church, where he also taught piano and organ. Tuition rates were three dollars per quarter for children and five dollars for adults. In 1839, G. R. Hurlburt, who had taught at Macon Female School, opened his own music school in a building across the street from the Central Hotel. Hurlburt offered students a wide range of course options that "embrace the study of the piano, organ, thorough bass, singing, and musical elocution." He also started a "juvenile singing school for lads and misses" and scheduled two recitals for his pupils each month. Tuition for Hurlbut's school was twenty dollars per quarter. Washington Hall was also home to an Englishman named Swain, who came to Macon in the spring of 1845 and began seeing students and occasionally giving vocal performances to supplement his income. Swain was well-traveled and offered instruction in "piano, sacred music, [and] French, English and Italian singing." He stayed through the summer before moving on to Nashville.[18]

One of the most influential music teachers to pass through the Macon area prior to the Civil War was a German expatriate name Ernst Grimme. Born in Brunswick in 1822, Grimme came to the United States as a young man, apparently due to political persecution. He once told a friend that he was "an exile to this country on account of sympathy toward the uprising in the year 1848, which threatened to overthrow the German empire." He settled temporarily in Wilmington, North Carolina, and then made his way to Macon, arriving around the first of the year in 1850. A talented musician, he offered classes in singing as well as "piano, guitar, and other instruments." He taught first at a recently established girls school run by Uriah and Henrietta Wise, and then moved to Macon Female Seminary where he taught both music and French. He was popular and touted by a local newspaper as a "highly accomplished professor" whose "qualifications have been satisfactorily tested by this community." Grimme stayed in Macon for several years before moving to Laurens,

South Carolina, and later to Danville, Kentucky, where he died in 1905 at the age of eighty-three.[19]

One of the highlights of the Macon social season of 1853 was a concert including several of Grimme's students who sang and played instruments. "Grimme's Soire," as locals called it, took place at the Concert Hall and was well attended. According to one enthusiastic spectator, the event "gave the most convincing evidence of Mr. Grimme's superior ability as a teacher, while it exhibited a musical genius in the performers of no ordinary character." The event also reflected the subtly increasing class divisions within the white population of Macon. Grimme's students were from families that could afford to pay the tuition for classes, meaning that they were from what passed at the time as the area's elite. The three students whose singing was featured most prominently during the concert were Mattie Bond, whose father was a member of the city council; Ann Wiley, whose father was a prominent physician; and Mary Ann Cotton, whose father was a successful merchant. Among the songs performed were "We Met by Chance," a romantic ballad of German origin, and two selections from Verdi operas, "To Dream of Peace" and "Thou Who Know'st Each Human Feeling." The concert also included instrumental piano performances by other students, but it was the singing that drew the most praise in the next issue of the *Telegraph*. "The singing was exquisite," the correspondent wrote, "and we do not recollect having seen an audience on any former occasion, so much delighted.... We think Mr. Grimme has just cause to be highly pleased with the performance of his pupils." The reporter went on to praise the singers by comparing them to some of the professional performers who had recently passed through town.[20]

Around the same time, three musicians from Boston arrived in Macon, claiming that they were about to permanently relocate to Georgia. William Bennet and Claude H. Clarke had been part of a touring company called the American Musical Society that featured singing and a wide range of instrumental music. The company also included Clarke's wife, described as "a beautifully full-toned soprano," along with tenor J. Q. Alexander and his wife, and William Mathews, who sang bass. In October of 1852, the group launched an ambitious tour of the Southern states. "In addition to the vocal department," one reporter wrote of the troupe, "they will introduce into their performance music for two cornets, baritone-tuba, flageolet, violin, and piano, consisting of solos, duets, trios, quadrilles waltzes [and] polkas." Life on the road apparently took its toll on the American Musical Society, and the group quickly splintered, with the Clarkes and Bennet landing in Macon, where they opened the Macon Musical Institute. "Wm. Bennet and C. H. Clarke," their advertisement in the local newspaper read, "respectfully announce to the citizens of Macon their intention to become permanent residents of this city, and will be happy to give instruction in every department of vocal and instrumental music." The curriculum of their new music school included voice lessons as well as lessons on the organ, piano, guitar, violin, flute, cornet, flageolet, violin, and cello. Classes met in the Concert Hall, and fees for pupils were fifteen dollars per quarter, "invariably in advance." The school was open for a little more than a year before the Clarkes and Bennet decided to return to Boston. In the meantime, the trio performed at local events and occasionally accompanied visiting artists who passed through town.[21]

In December of 1836, Georgia Female College, the first degree-granting college for women in the United States, was founded in Macon, expanding educational opportunities for women, including opportunities for a musical education. Within two years the first college building was completed, an imposing, fifty-six-room structure that included a dining hall, chapel, standard classrooms, and one room dedicated as the "music room." The goal of the founders was "to furnish to females an opportunity for as thorough and as extensive an education as was afforded to the other sex by our colleges," and in 1840 the college granted its first degree. Among the first music professors hired at Georgia Female College was John H. Euhink, who had taught previously in Columbus and Monroe, Georgia. The college also hired two young women, Maria Lord and Martha Massey, as his assistants. Music classes included vocal lessons as well as instruction on the piano, harp, and guitar. Euhink stayed at the college for six years before moving on and paving the way for university officials to hire a man who would become a great pillar of the Macon music community.[22]

Phillip Gerhart Guttenberger was born in Frankfurt, Germany, on November 1, 1799, the son of a prosperous merchant. A gifted painter and musician from an early age, Guttenberger graduated from the University of Heidelberg before studying at the Académie des Beaux-Arts in Paris. He came to the United States in 1824, and eventually made Georgia his home, spending time in Athens and Savannah, where he made a modest living painting portraits and giving violin and guitar lessons. He married Emily Antoinette Muse in 1834, and while the couple would go on to raise six children, their life together was almost immediately touched by tragedy. Not long after their marriage, Guttenberger's vision began to deteriorate, and he was soon left permanently blind. Unable to make a living as a painter, he focused all of his energies on teaching music, and by 1840 he had secured a position teaching piano, guitar, and violin at Emory College in Oxford, Georgia. He was an excellent instructor, and five years later he accepted an offer to head the music department at Macon Female College, which by that time had been renamed Wesleyan Female College. Guttenberger's eldest daughter, Francesca, a child prodigy on the violin and piano, usually went to work with her father, and by the time she was fifteen, she was serving as his official assistant in the music department. Father and daughter also gave popular recitals in Macon and elsewhere to supplement the family income.[23]

Under Guttenberger's leadership, and with the help of his daughter, the music department at Wesleyan flourished. In 1850, a group of educators from across the state visited Wesleyan to review the college's programs. "With regard to the music department," their report later stated, "we are of the opinion that this institution is second to none in the Union." The group complimented Guttenberger and his daughter specifically for their "artistic skill," and gushed over the student examination exercises that provided "interludes of rich and varied music, both vocal and instrumental."[24] Guttenberger also organized the music for the college's commencement exercises, including an array of hymns for the graduation ceremony, and a collection of "opera arias, popular songs and a few instrumental works" for celebratory concerts at the end of each school year. The 1852 year-end program was typical. The concert took place in the college's chapel, with the professor's pupils performing the following songs:

WESLEYAN COLLEGE CONCERT[25]

July 14, 1852

"Overture," from John of Paris

"Oh! Haste Crimson Morning," from the opera *Lucia Di Lammermour*

"La Diademe," Brilliant Variations

"It Was Here in Accents Sweetest," song from the opera *I. Puritani*

"O Dolce Concent"

"Scenes That Are the Brightest," ballad from the opera *Maritani*

Variations to "Nel Cor Piu" from the comedy *La Molinara*

"A Governess Wanted"

The Celebrated "Medley Overture" of Aldridge

"While My Thoughts Still Turn to Thee," from the opera *Giovanni di Napoli*

Intermission

"L'elagante fantaisie, pour la Harpe"

"Salut a l'amerique"

"National Scottishe"

"The Wildflowers Soon Will Shed Their Bloom," from the opera
     Lucia Di Lammermour

"Friendship Polka"

"I'll Be No Submissive Wife"

"Emerald Waltz"

"For Our Queen and Liberty," from the opera *Giovanni di Napoli*

"Battle of Resaca de la Palma"

"Fare-Thee-Well"

Guttenberg's personal tastes and popular tastes of the period influenced his musical choices for the event. Touring opera troupes were usually well received in Macon, and circulating sheet music led to the dissemination of more and more recently penned popular songs. Many who attended the concert had likely heard some of the operatic selections before, sung by European artists, such as Anna Bishop and Teresa Parodi. The conventional tunes gleaned from sheet music included the works of songwriters from both Europe and America. By far the most patriotic selection of the evening was "Battle of Resaca de la Palma," penned by John Schell to celebrate the American victory at Resaca de la Palma during the Mexican War. It was one of several popular "battle pieces" composed immediately following the conflict. These tunes were especially popular in the South, where many veterans lived, and where support for the war had been very strong.[26]

As Wesleyan was a Methodist School, the actual commencement ceremony was held at the Macon Methodist Church the day after the concert. The music at the graduation exercise was confined to religious works:

WESLEYAN COLLEGE COMMENCEMENT EXERCISES[27]

July 15, 1852

"Sanctus and Hosanna"

"Our Father Who Art in Heaven"

"Be Kind to The Loved Ones At Home"

"How Lovely Is Zion"

"When the Bosom Heaves a Sigh"

"Farewell Ode"

In addition to his work with the college, Phillip Guttenberger and members of his family gave public performances. All of the Guttenberger children—Francesca, Charles, Louisa, Ferdinand, Julie, and Emma—were musically inclined, but it was Francesca who usually garnered the most attention in the community. Playing the piano, violin, and harp, she was accustomed to generating rave reviews from the local press. "Those who attend her concert," a Georgia correspondent wrote about one performance, "know that they may expect a rich entertainment.... Upon her piano her touch is firm and critically exact, while her performance on the violin is wonderfully skillful and cannot fail to secure increased interest and admiration." After their father's death in 1874, all of his children carried on the Guttenberger musical tradition of teaching and performing in Middle Georgia, cementing Phillip Guttenberger's status as the patriarch of one of the region's foremost musical families.[28]

In 1852, the Georgia Academy for the Blind opened its doors in Macon, with a charge of providing instruction to blind children that would "qualify the pupils for self-support after graduation." Because music at the time was seen as an important potential career path for sightless pupils with talent, vocal and instrumental instruction was a central part of the school's curriculum. Through the years, the academy organized annual fundraising concerts featuring star pupils as well as some of their teachers. "There is a great deal of musical talent in the school, and it is under scientific cultivation," an observer wrote after seeing one of the shows. "Music must be the great resource for the blind, and it is so peculiarly gratifying to see such evidence of proficiency in this department." Notable among the academy's instructors, who from time to time also graced the community with solo performances, were J. C. Van Houten, who had come to the area from New York as "a first class pianist" and organist, and M. Bennis Clark, a versatile musician who played violin, piano, guitar, flute, and clarinet.[29]

In the years leading up to the Civil War, there was certainly no shortage of private musical instruction in Macon. Some teachers came and went, while others, such as Delia A. Hall and Maria King, stayed to become community stalwarts. Hall was a native of New Marlborough, Massachusetts, and a recent graduate of the Charlottesville Seminary in New York when she came to Macon in 1852. She settled into a job assisting Ernst Grimme at Macon Female Seminary, providing instruction in vocal music, and she also gave private singing lessons. King was born in England and moved with her family to Macon around 1850. She was one of the area's most popular piano teachers, with an impressive list of pupils. "She is fully competent," a *Telegraph* correspondent reported, "pledging herself to the advancement of her pupils, and to imparting a thorough knowledge of music." King built a reputation that eventually allowed her to find employment as a music instructor at Wesleyan.[30]

The era also saw the arrival in Macon of Sterling Lanier, whose family would have a significant effect on the city. An entrepreneur of the first order, Lanier brought his clan to Macon around 1840, after living for a time in Jones County and Athens, Georgia. Hotels were his business, and he purchased Washington Hall and later opened the Lanier House, both of which were entertainment venues as well as boarding establishments. "Nature and education had qualified him well for his avocation," one acquaintance later remembered of Lanier, as he was a "landlord of a first-class hotel [with] a kind regard for the rights and feelings of his guests." Sterling and his wife, Sarah, had six children, among whom was Robert Sampson Lanier, who was born in 1819. As a teenager, Robert was sent to study at Randolph-Macon College, and while in Virginia he met his future wife, Mary Jane Anderson. The two married and moved back to Macon, where Robert practiced law. Their union produced three children, the oldest of whom was musician, poet, novelist, and literary critic Sidney Clopton Lanier, who grew up to become Macon's first native-born cultural celebrity.[31]

Sidney Lanier came into the world on February 3, 1842, at his grandfather's home on High Street in Macon. Music was a part of his life as a youngster, and many later credited his mother with instilling in him a great love of song. According to one early biographer, Lanier's mother "could play well on the piano, and frequently sang with the children hymns and popular melodies." Educated locally as a youngster, his own musical talents blossomed at an early age. "I could play passably on several instruments before I could write legibly," he once wrote to a friend, "and since then, the very deepest of my life has been filled with music." At thirteen, he provided flute accompaniment for the Presbyterian choir at a public performance where he "played admirably and was warmly applauded." Three years later, he entered Oglethorpe College, a Presbyterian school near Milledgeville, where many of his classmates and instructors immediately noticed his talents. He was particularly proficient on the flute and in great demand as an entertainer in both formal and informal settings. "He played directly and naturally from the first," Charles Campbell, one of Lanier's Macon friends, later remembered, "as one hardly conscious of effort or obstacle." Milton H. Northrup, an Oglethorpe classmate, agreed, once remarking that Lanier was "the finest flute player you ever saw. He is far-famed for it.... He runs the notes easily and smoothly." A sharp focus on music dominated Lanier's time at Oglethorpe, and his social circle was made up almost entirely of others with musical talent. "While cordial to all," one friend later recalled, "he had few associates; and they were chiefly those whose musical bias attracted his companionship. Music, rather than intellectual affinity, was the potent influence that determined his choice of comrades." With two other students, one a guitarist and the other a violinist, Lanier formed a popular trio that performed "exquisitely beautiful music" at social events. Shortly before Lanier finished his studies in 1860, he purchased a flute for fifty dollars that he carried with him everywhere, even into the army.[32]

While Lanier had refined musical tastes, he also took note of folk music, particularly African American tunes and rhythms that he heard as he came of age in a region awash in cotton and slaves. As a child, he was fond of mimicking the music of the minstrel shows, and later he became a reasonably competent banjo player. At college, he was apparently quite animated when he played the banjo for fellow students. According to one friend, as Lanier started strumming "he would begin to smile and laugh as if his very soul were tickled, while his hearers would catch the inspiration, and an old fashioned 'walk around' and 'negro breakdown,' would be the ultimate result." Later in life, Lanier occasionally commented on his interpretation of "primitive" African American folk music and the "natural gifts" of amateur African American performers whom he heard while he was growing up.[33]

With the outbreak of the Civil War, Lanier joined a local company and entered Confederate service. He ended up in the signal corps, and eventually served aboard a blockade-runner, the *Lucy*, that made runs between Wilmington, North Carolina, and the West Indies. Lanier's flute served as his musical Excalibur, and he used it during the conflict to entertain both his comrades in arms and various civilians he encountered as he moved from place to place. Confederate general Samuel G. French later remembered Lanier as "an excellent musician" who would often "come to my quarters and pass the evening with us, where the alarms of war were lost in the soft notes of [his] flute." Lanier played social occasions as a matter of routine during his off hours. At Petersburg, Virginia, he and several other musically inclined soldiers were given "honorary freedom of the town" after one performance, and after serenading a group of young ladies, the men reportedly returned to their quarters "laden with bouquets." Late in the war, Lanier was captured and shipped—with his flute concealed in his uniform sleeve—to a prison camp at Point Lookout, Maryland. Even there, among twelve thousand suffering Confederates living in squalor, his instrument would not be silenced. John B. Tabb, a fellow prisoner who was sick at the time, later remembered his first meeting with Lanier. "Here in this hell hole," he wrote, "while I was lying on my cot, ill with a fever, the distant notes of a flute reached my ears. I said to myself, 'I must find this man.' When I got out of my bed I commenced searching, with the result that I found the flutist in the poet Sidney Lanier." While Lanier was only at Point Lookout for three months, it was long enough for him to contract tuberculosis, and as a result, poor health plagued him for the rest of his life.[34]

Despite his illness, Lanier survived the war, but as the next chapter of his life unfolded, he struggled to find a permanent profession. Music was his first love, but at the time it was not seen as a stable career path. "His devotion to music rather alarmed more than pleased his friends," Lanier's wife later wrote, "and while it was here that he first discovered that he possessed decided genius, he for a time shared the early notion of his parents that it was an unworthy pursuit." Frustrated, Lanier studied law and briefly worked as a clerk at one of his grandfather's hotels. He sought out teaching positions at the university level, but few were available. Finally, he accepted the fact that he was destined for a life in the arts. "I am more than perplexed," he once reflected, "that the prime inclination, that is the natural bent of my nature is to music; and for that I have the greatest talent; indeed, not boasting, for God gave it to me." Unable to find work in or around Macon, he moved north and eventually joined the Peabody Orchestra in Baltimore as first flutist. He began composing flute pieces and also gave private lessons to supplement his income. He composed for publication musical poetry that gained him significant notoriety. Among his most famous works were "Corn" (1875), "The Symphony" (1875), "Centennial Meditation" (1876), "The Song of the Chattahoochee" (1877), "The Marshes of Glynn" (1878), and "Sunrise" (1881). At the time, one critic claimed that Lanier's poetry resonated because it "is absolutely dependent on melody—that the poet is first and last a singer.... It was written to be sung, not to be read. Its words were meant to lend themselves to music." Lanier lectured at the Peabody Institute, and in 1879 took a position at Johns Hopkins University teaching English literature and poetry. Unfortunately, his health took a turn for the worse. He fell seriously ill as a result of his tuberculosis, and teaching became a struggle. His condition deteriorated and he finally succumbed to the disease September 7, 1881, at age thirty-nine. Upon hearing the news of Lanier's death, the *New York Times* praised the Macon native as a man who "understood music thoroughly and loved it dearly." In his home state, the *Atlanta Constitution* lamented, "The untimely death of the late Sidney Lanier removed from the sphere of American letters one of the rarest spirits and most accomplished and lovable of men."[35]

As Macon grew, the procession of touring acts passing through its confines never ceased. During the 1850s, two musical families, the Derworts and the Columbians, played to full houses at the Concert Hall within weeks of each other. Veterans of the road, the Derwort family included German immigrant George Henry Derwort and his four talented children—called a "tribe of prodigies" by the newspapers—all of whom sang and played instruments. Among the popular tunes they performed were "Yankee Doodle Dandy," "The Pilgrim Fathers," "Gentle Lady," and "Homeward Love, Homeward." The Columbians, a quartet made up of two brothers and two sisters, played multiple shows that included "a choice selection of songs, glees duets, trios, etc." In addition to the family acts, the Scottish composer William Richardson Dempster made a well-publicized appearance in Macon in May of 1854. Dempster specialized in "parlor singing" and "original ballad entertainment" that featured his own compositions. Among his most popular songs were "Lament of the Irish Emigrant," "The Blind Boy," "The May Queen," "The Rainy Day," and "Footsteps of Angels."[36]

The renowned Norwegian violinist Ole Bull came to Macon in April of 1856, creating a great deal of excitement. Bull was a world-class performer who, at the time, was touring the nation to great acclaim. "On Ole Bull's arrival from Europe," the *New York Herald* trumpeted shortly after the violinist's initial appearances in the United States, "the tide rose to its highest point—theaters, churches, every place in which he appeared was crowded." After a string of successful appearances in the Northeast, Bull came South and eventually into Georgia. His traveling party included singers Anna Spinola and Anna Vail, pianist Franz Roth, and Louis Schrieber, a popular entertainer in his own right whose primary instrument was the cornet. "We need not say," a correspondent for the *Telegraph* wrote on the eve of Bull's performance, "it will be such an entertainment as the Macon public are not often invited to." During the performance, each of the musicians had a chance to showcase their talents by performing popular tunes and more complicated operatic pieces. There were solos and duets by Spinola and Vail, and instrumental interpretations from Roth and Schrieber, but it was Bull who drew the most attention and the greatest audience reaction. According to one witness, "His violin was his pet—almost his idol. He held it caressingly, as a mother holds her child, and smiled fondly as dulcet notes came vibrating forth, so smooth, so clear."[37]

As was the case with other well-known performers, the audience drawn to Bull's appearance included many of Bibb County's more affluent citizens—those who could afford to pay for concert tickets and had the leisure time required to attend the show. In the upper reaches of Macon's developing social system there were many who felt a responsibility to help the town develop culturally. They supported the arts and were genuinely excited when a notable performer came to town. These same individuals also sought to create social outlets where the well-heeled in the community could gather and enjoy the finer things in life without being disturbed by their social underlings. This attitude was reflected in a review that appeared in the *Georgia Citizen* following Bull's Macon concert, which happened to take place on the same night that a traveling circus was passing through town. Heaping flattery on the local gentry who saw Bull perform, the review also reflected growing social divisions within the white community. "The concert of Ole Bull last evening was attended by one of the most brilliant assemblages of the elite of the city," the reviewer wrote. "The circus being in full blast in another part of town, there were no disturbers of the peace to annoy the lovers of sweet sounds of music on the ears."[38]

The "disturbers of the peace" that the newspaper referred to in Macon were many, and they were perfectly capable of finding their own musical amusements apart from the strains of Ole Bull's violin or the sophisticated deliveries of Anna Bishop or Teresa Parodi. For those citizens, the circus not only offered acrobats, animals, and "human oddities," but also musical performances designed to draw and animate crowds. Most traveling circuses that passed through Macon carried bands with them. The Spalding and Rogers North American Circus brought its "Renowned New York Cornet Band" to town to entertain crowds between acts, while Yankee Robinson's Circus maintained a full band that "paraded through the streets making most delicious music." Robinson and Elred's Menagerie and Circus came to Macon in 1854 with a band under the leadership of veteran touring musician Joseph Nosher. Nosher was well known in New York and Boston as a "celebrated E Flat bugle player and violinist" and had traveled for years on the performing circuit as a solo artist and with large groups. Three years later, the Great Southern Circus entered Macon in a grand procession, led by Henry Able's Brass Band, a twelve-piece unit. As townspeople gawked, the musicians rolled into town playing on the back of a large, gold-plated wagon designed to look like a chariot.[39]

Another form of "primitive" entertainment that was available to Macon's growing antebellum population was the minstrel show. This was a form of entertainment that had been growing in popularity in the United States for the last two decades. A manifestation of acute racism, a minstrel show was usually some form of variety show that included comedy and a great deal of singing and dancing. The shows were primarily performed by white men who used burned cork or some other substance to blacken their faces, and who imitated and parodied black forms of music and dance. While the musical performances could be genuine, the shows promoted every negative stereotype that many whites held toward African Americans, lampooning blacks as loud, simpleminded, and lazy. In many cases, they also presented a fictional and extremely romanticized version of plantation life in the Old South, steeped in race-based paternalism and complete with characters including the kind master and the ignorant, ever-loyal "darkie." The typical minstrel show consisted of several players "armed with an array of instruments, usually banjo, fiddle, bone castanets, and tambourine." The shows varied in length, but in general included animated singing, satirical monologues, slapstick comedy, and narrative skits. Ironically, following the Civil War some minstrel shows became outlets for African American performers who, despite the deep racial overtones, found performing in such a manner preferable to making a living as an impoverished agricultural laborer. Because these shows were almost always performed by a traveling troupe, minstrel shows affected musical culture in the South by exposing residents of the region to many songs that they had never heard before. Many traditional tunes associated with the South first became popular as minstrel songs, including "Oh! Susanna," "Old Dan Tucker," "The Blue Tail Fly," "Old Folks at Home (Swanee River)," and, of course, "Dixie." One of the most famous minstrel songs of the pre-Civil War era, "Jump Jim Crow" lent its name to the so-called Jim Crow laws of the twentieth century that codified segregation in the southern United States.[40]

While it seemed to some an uncouth form of entertainment, the minstrel show was also of great importance in the South because it represented a vehicle for the blending of white and black musical styles. As such, it helped advance the complicated musical culture of the region. Minstrel skits and music highlighted interaction between whites and blacks in both exaggerated and subtle contexts. White pretension was a common theme in concert with black clowning. Minstrel performances in the South never challenged white authority, but those portraying the African American subordinates in skits were sometimes able to win the day, outsmarting their white antagonists using nonthreatening foolishness and an ability to "make an art of talking back under cover of playing stupid." The music that was part of these spectacles had a distinct racial mix that affected what would later be labeled "blues" and "country music" in the region. It was a key ingredient in the musical melting pot that made Southern music distinct and had an immeasurable influence on American popular culture in general as time wore on.[41]

During the 1850s, the Campbell Minstrels, one of the most popular troupes of the period, made multiple stops in Macon. The original Minstrels were organized in New York in 1847 under the leadership of John Campbell and included seven members. From that point forward, different incarnations of the group toured constantly, sometimes carrying a roster of up to fifteen men. According to one observer, early shows "were very simple, consisting of songs, solos on the banjo or violin...champion jigs, double polka, solo on a comb, jewsharp, snare drum or kitchen bellows." In Macon, the group titled their blackface performance "Plantation Darkies of the South" and dressed as field hands in checked shirts, striped pants, and large shoes. The company's advertisements claimed that their "delineations of Negro characters are taken from natural scenes and incidents in African life, and aim at presenting the musical and comical peculiarities of the southern negro." Among the songs in their repertoire were traditional minstrel tunes, such as "Old Bob Ridley," "Lucy Long," "Banjo Lesson," "Negro Traveler," "Miss Julia Tanner," and the Stephen Foster compositions "Dolly Day" and "Gwine to Run All Night" (popularly known as "Camptown Races"). The performances of the Campbell Minstrels were well attended in Macon, and the local press always lauded the group as "the best Negro delineators and comedians; the most pleasing and best vocalists and balladeers; the most distinguished and best instrumentalists and dancers at present engaged in the Ethiopian profession."[42]

Not long afterwards, another group, the Double Minstrel Troupe, made a stop in Macon for multiple performances. Veteran performers Charles H. Duprez and J. Edwin "Mocking Bird" Green led this group.

Born in France, Duprez came to the United States as a young man and began his career in New Orleans. Green, whose nickname was an homage to the birdcalls that were part of his act, was a native of New Hampshire who had been touring the country with multiple groups for a decade. Duprez's and Green's blackface outfit claimed to be "the original New Orleans and metropolitan burlesque opera troupe and brass band," promising their audience "chaste, elegant, laughter-provoking and irresistible Ethiopian Entertainments, introducing the greatest variety of new songs, ballads, duets, quartettes, overtures [and] burlesque opera pieces." Their appearance in Macon was quite a spectacle. "This is certainly, beyond a doubt, the best group of negro delineators and comics, that is now in existence," one newspaper correspondent crowed. "Their performance last night met with the approbation of everyone in attendance."[43]

In January of 1861, George Christy's Minstrels passed through Macon for two shows at Ralston Hall. This troupe had roots going back to a blackface group founded by Edwin P. Christy in Buffalo, New York, in 1843. Various incarnations and offshoots of Christy's Minstrels had toured for years to widespread acclaim, relying heavily on Stephen Foster's catalogue to the extent that they helped give Foster a great deal of national exposure. Some credit the original Christy's Minstrels with establishing the basic three-part format for minstrel shows nationwide. This included an initial round of popular songs performed either as solos or as a group, followed by a hodgepodge of comedic recitations and slapstick routines, and finally a major burlesque skit usually set in the South. Instrumental music on the fiddle, banjo, or accordion also played a prominent role in most shows. The group that came to Macon had recently toured Europe as well as the Eastern Seaboard of the United States, and they were on their way to New Orleans when they passed through Middle Georgia. They delivered to the Macon crowd "all the gems of Ethiopian minstrelsy" with an admission price of fifty cents for adults and twenty-five cents for "children and servants." One audience member who saw their show during the tour later reflected, "There is something in the performance of these accomplished musicians and delineators of negro peculiarities that is sure to find them popularity and patronage everywhere."[44]

Of course, music related to the African American population in antebellum Macon was not limited to contrived blackface performances by whites. Despite their difficult existence before the Civil War, Macon's slave community, like Southern slaves in general, created their own vibrant culture, which included authentic forms of musical expression rooted in a collective heritage. Beginning in the early seventeenth century, slaves brought the rhythms and vocal styles of their African homeland to America, where an evolutionary process began that filtered the music through the circumstances under which they lived. The West African tradition of "call and response" during communal labor gave way to the "field holler" and other chants that were heard on cotton plantations throughout the South during the eighteenth and nineteenth centuries. Among the West African tribes, from which many American slaves descended, music was an integral part of most activities, particularly those involving strenuous labor, and it would be an integral part of the existence of the American slave.[45]

For the bondsmen, the field holler was far more than a primitive form of musical expression that helped them pass the time as they worked. It had a much deeper function. In the slave community, the music of the fields allowed slaves to exert limited control over their situation. In a world where they were under scrutiny and did not fully control their day-to-day lives, slaves developed subtle ways of influencing their environment through song. Whites equated singing in the fields with contentment and were therefore less likely to discipline a field full of what they believed to be peaceful laborers. In a way, the music allowed members of the white community—most of whom were constantly concerned about potential slave uprisings—to relax. In turn, they might be more relaxed in their treatment of the slaves, potentially exerting less direct control over a slave population they believed was docile. Because whites mainly heard only the rhythm of the slave music and rarely listened carefully to the words, slaves in the field could also communicate with one another through their music. As political tensions over slavery in the United States grew, one white Macon observer in 1850 commented that "the abolitionists of the North are sighing and groaning and praying and raving over the miseries of negro slavery, while the 'victims' of their sympathy are at this very moment singing away in the sunny hours among the pleasant fields." Although slaveholders generally linked the slaves' singing with passiveness, the slaves actually used music to communicate with one another, pass messages, or articulate social comment, and in the process, they created an art form that would reverberate in one form or another through the passing generations. By 1860, Southern slaves had created the foundation of a music that would later be popularly labeled blues.[46]

In addition to the work song, religious music was a significant part of the slave world. By the nineteenth century, most had converted to Christianity as either Baptists or Methodists, the South's two largest denominations. Masters imposed Christianity on enslaved persons in large part as a means of social control, but it did not take long for slaves to create their own special brand of American religion. While masters saw religion as a positive force in the slaveholding world, many slaves who embraced Christianity had a different perspective than whites on the Bible and its teachings, though they could not reveal this perspective to members of the white community. Slaves were particularly interested in stories from the Old Testament, with Moses being by far the dominant figure. The story of Moses delivering his people from bondage in Egypt was the story that slaves seized upon to give them hope for a better future. Enslaved individuals could relate well to the stories of the Israelites, who faced many trials and tribulations before finally gaining their freedom, and who eventually smote their enemies with the help of God. For whites, deliverance to the promised land meant saved souls and the prospect of eternal life in heaven. For slaves, however, the promised land reflected their dreams of freedom. The slaves took the spiritual music of the whites, based in large part on hymns and other songs of European origin, and added their own words, phrasings, and rhythms to make the music their own. This music would evolve and later be broadly labeled "black gospel music," and in its own way it would move people unlike any other form of American song. Religious music gave the enslaved the right to express themselves openly under the guise of worshipping the same God as the white masters they served, but the musical style of their spirituals remained unique to their community.[47]

In Macon, as in other parts of the South, many white observers of the antebellum period commented on the "hymns or religious chants" of the slave community. One of the earliest public references in Macon related to slavery and religious music was an 1832 notice in the *Telegraph* about a runaway slave named "July." In addition to a general description of the young man, who was twenty years of age, the notice stated that July was "remarkably fond of singing and whistling Methodist songs and tunes." In 1849, a correspondent from the newspaper listened from afar to a hymn sung at a slave funeral, insisting later that "the southern negroes are proverbial for the melody and compass of their voices, and I thought that hymn, mellowed by distance, the most solemn yet sweetest music that had ever fallen upon my ears." On her travels through the South in 1850, Swedish author Fredrika Bremer attended a camp meeting in Macon that included a segregated audience of whites and slaves. She was particularly impressed by the music offered by both the slave choir and the African American congregants at the event. "They sang hymns—a superb choir," Bremer later wrote. "Strongest of all was the singing of the black portion of the assembly, as they were three times as many as the whites, and their voices were naturally pure and beautiful." Around the same time, Virginia journalist Edward A. Pollard visited Macon and attended a slave church service, and likewise felt compelled to comment on the music. "The words are generally very few, and repeated over and over again," he stated later, "and the lines, though very unequal, are sung with a natural cadence that impresses the ear very agreeably." He went on to list some of the lyrics of one of the hymns that he heard performed at the Macon gathering:

> Oh carry me away, carry me away, my Lord
> Oh carry me away, carry me away, my Lord
> The green trees a-bowing, Sinner, fare you well!
> I thank the Lord I want to go,
> To leave them all behind,
> Oh, carry me away, carry me away, my Lord,
> Carry me to the burying ground.[48]

Whites who either lived in or passed through Macon before the Civil War also commented on the secular music of the slave community and on the prowess of those slaves who played musical instruments. One local resident recalled watching a talented slave fiddler in town who "sat in a chair with a violin to his shoulder which he scratched with great vigor," performing an old fiddle tune called "The Devil Bream." Sidney Lanier seemed fascinated by the unusual beats and rhythms—syncopations—that characterized the music of the slaves as well as the slaves' abilities to take standard tunes of European origin and make them their own. "The negro shows that he does not like the ordinary accentuations nor the ordinary cadences of tunes." Lanier later wrote, "I have heard negroes change a well-known melody by adroitly syncopating it...and nothing illustrates the negro's natural gifts in the way of keeping a difficult tempo more clearly than his perfect execution of [songs] thus transformed from simple to complex accentuations." When the English musician Henry

Phillips made a tour stop in Macon, he visited one of the local plantations and heard a group of enslaved musicians. Later, he wrote about the experience, emphasizing that their authentic performance bore little resemblance to the minstrel shows that depicted "typical" plantation behavior. Of the ten slaves he saw, Miller wrote that "two of them played the banjo [and] the way they preluded their songs was diametrically opposite to the representations given us in England by those gentlemen who black their faces, and who, clever as they certainly are, do not represent the mode in which the negroes execute their songs."[49]

As Macon's social strata became more clearly defined, so did the nature of social interaction between the planter elite and the community in general. On large plantations, slave musicians sometimes played for white audiences at structured social events and for their peers in the slave quarters at informal gatherings. These same musicians might also be "hired out" to entertain elsewhere. Their exact repertoire would depend on the audience, but usually included versions of contemporary standards or traditional songs at which the musician had become proficient. In general, musicians held a special position in the slave community as their talents usually won them special privileges. Because they entertained at functions for both races, they could move, at least to an extent, between black and white social spheres in a way that other slaves could not. Those who were hired out also enjoyed greater freedom of movement within the larger community.[50]

Plantation owners routinely kept fiddlers on their property to entertain at picnics or parties, and these same musicians were popular in the slave quarters where they entertained their peers in the evening, or at social events that the planters sometimes allowed workers to organize during slow periods. The same was true for musicians proficient on the banjo, another popular instrument. While the fiddle was European in origin, the long lineage of the banjo traces back to Africa, where strings stretched across drumlike instruments were strummed and plucked for centuries. These more primitive offerings evolved over time into string instruments made from hollowed-out gourds. Slaves brought these instruments into America during the seventeenth century, where they were called by many names, including the banza, banjil, banjar, and banshaw. Soon variants of these instruments were in widespread use. In describing slave music in his own state, Thomas Jefferson wrote in 1781, "In music they [slaves] are generally more gifted than the whites with accurate ears for tune and time.... The instrument proper to them is the banjar, which they brought with them from Africa."[51]

In Macon, there were a number of slave musicians who routinely entertained at both plantation and community functions. Accounts from after the Civil War state that most of these musicians worked in town or in the plantation houses rather than in the fields. "They were natural born musicians," one white observer stated, "and by being of a high grade of slavery, the majority of them trusted servants around the poker rooms and club rooms, they had ample time to practice and were encouraged by their owners." An 1885 article from the *Atlanta Constitution* lists the names of several former enslaved musicians from Macon who ended up in a minstrel troupe after the war, including John Brooker, Henry Fields, Lucius Griffin, Aleck Jacobs, Neil Rogers, Andrew Gospel, Jeff Kiner, Austin Brighthaupt, Riley Covington, Albert Slaughter, and Phil Lamar. Of these, Lamar, Brighthaupt, and Covington were said to be very proficient fiddlers, while others excelled on the banjo, guitar, "bones," or flute.[52]

During the 1850s, a number of Bibb County slaves were recruited to form a "colored brass band." This group was attached at one point to Macon's white volunteer militia unit and to the all-white Macon Fire Brigade, performing at ceremonial functions and other events. Their first public showcase was a "Firemen's Parade" held on April 15, 1856. The following week the *Telegraph* offered muted praise to the group, stating that "the colored band, which made its first public demonstration with the Fire Department last Tuesday, ought to be encouraged. A band of music is a very essential adjunct to any parade—military or civic, and we were equally surprised and pleased at their general harmony." By this time, the Macon Volunteers had apparently ended the practice of local whites serving as musicians in the unit, passing that function on to slaves. Many of the musicians involved in the firemen's event also performed at Fourth of July celebrations and militia drill sessions that were open to the public. A year after their formation, the band played during an unusual funeral procession honoring an elderly slave called "Old Albert," who was something of a community fixture. The man had at one time served as a drummer for the Macon Volunteers, and his passing resulted in a more elaborate send-off than the typical slave usually received. According to one white witness, "A formidable array of colored musicians, bearing their instruments in mourning, led the sable procession—drums and fifes preceded by the hearse playing a melancholy strain, and a long train of the colored population brought up the rear."[53]

Also among the African American musicians in antebellum Macon was a free man named Charley Benger, who had a long association as a fifer with the Macon Volunteers. Benger was born of free parents around 1792 in Camden County on the Georgia coast. According to one account, he served as a fifer for American troops at Point Peter before it was overrun by the British during the War of 1812. Benger came to Macon around 1831 and served as a fifer for the Macon Volunteers, accompanying the group to Florida during the Seminole War. He moved to Marietta for several years but returned to Macon and continued his association with the local militia. When the Macon Volunteers left home for the Civil War, Benger was apparently allowed to accompany them as a musician, but because of his advanced age—he was almost seventy—he was with the unit only a short time after they were deployed to Virginia early in the war. Though Benger was free, the men he served later referred to him in the same derogatory manner that they would a slave, calling him a "faithful negro," and they seemed to view him more as a source of amusement than a true comrade. The Volunteers offered typically paternalistic praise of "Old Charley, the fifer," when he left them in July of 1862, stating in a resolution that they "all have learned to respect and love this faithful old fifer, despite his dark skin and humble position." Benger returned to Macon and eventually found work as a mattress maker. He died in 1880 at the age of eighty-eight.[54]

In late 1857, Macon witnessed the unusual and bittersweet performance of Tom Wiggins, better known to the public as "Blind Tom." Wiggins was born a slave on a plantation in Harris County, Georgia, and as an infant was sold to Columbus attorney and newspaper editor James Neil Bethune. Blind from birth, Wiggins could not work in the fields and was allowed to stay in his master's house during the day, where he was treated like a family mascot or pet. Bethune's daughters discovered that Wiggins was a prodigy who could play the piano and memorize almost any song after only hearing it once. By age six, Wiggins was composing his own music, and his master saw the opportunity to exploit the child's ability for financial gain. Bethune hired out Wiggins to concert promoters who took him on endless tours around the United States. He was treated shabbily by his handlers and called "an idiot" and "an indifferent sample of a Georgia nigger" in the newspapers, but his musical abilities were undeniable.

He had a huge repertoire and even an ability to play the melody of two songs simultaneously, one using his left hand and the other his right. The novelty of his performance, as well as the music, drew large crowds, although Wiggins himself never saw any of the profits.

Wiggins was only eight years old when he came to Macon. His performance was typical, and the review that it received in the Macon newspaper was similar to those from other Southern newspapers that routinely disparaged the slave as some sort of freak of nature rather than an artist. "He patterns [himself] strictly after the ape in all his movements, contortions, and grimaces," the correspondent from the *Telegraph* reported. "Tom can, in consequence, sing after a fashion and thrum the piano with great facility. Without any instruction at all, he has caught by ear all the popular airs—plays them readily and can even give a tolerable counterfeit to more difficult music upon once hearing it played." Wiggins continued touring after the Civil War, "managed" and further exploited by Bethune and his family. While he generated a great deal of money and notoriety during his career, he was never allowed to enjoy the fruits of his labor. Wiggins died in 1908, leaving behind original compositions including "Oliver Galop" (1860), "Virginia Polka" (1860), "Battle of Manassas" (1861), "The Rainstorm" (1865), and "Water in Moonlight" (1866).[55]

Macon's cultural life was enhanced a great deal in the early months of 1858 with the opening of Ralston Hall, a large theater named for its owner, James A. Ralston. Ralston was a wealthy planter and entrepreneur who already owned several downtown buildings. He had previously built a smaller theater to service the area, but Bibb County's status as a cotton center, and its growing population—more than sixteen thousand residents, including almost seven thousand slaves—created the need for a larger entertainment venue. Civic leaders celebrated the new venue, as did the local press. "This hall will seat an audience of 1,200," one correspondent wrote, "and its internal arrangements are patterned after the most modern style, with parquet and gallery.... The access to the hall is spacious and easy, and care has been exercised to have everything about it secure and strong.... We believe that Macon can boast the finest and most commodious public hall in the state."[56]

The new concert venue was "auspiciously inaugurated as a place of public amusement" on February 5, 1858, with the appearance of Swiss composer and pianist Sigismund Thalberg, accompanied by Belgian violinist Henri Vieuxtemps. Both men were well-known musical personalities of the era. They were on the southern leg of a grand American tour, and their stop in Macon followed well-received concert performances in Savannah and Augusta. Soprano Bertha Johansen and several members of the New York Academy of Music were also on the bill as vocalists. Thalberg specialized in the works of Beethoven, Chopin, and Bach, and also performed some of his original compositions. "Ralston's Hall was handsomely filled Friday night at the Thalberg Concert," one excited spectator later reported. "The great pianist is, of course, a marvel of efficiency. So also, is the great violinists [Vieuxtemps].... Both were entirely successful in winning rapturous applause from the audience."[57]

The appearance of touring artists in Macon continued to encourage interest in the arts. In 1858, local teenagers from some of the town's first families formed the Macon Harmonic Society, a "club of young ladies and gentlemen who meet for the practice of operatic and sacred music." There were twenty-three original members of the group, and Virginia Lamar, the daughter of a prominent local merchant, served as the organization's first president. The Harmonic Society performed at private parties in Macon, usually sponsored by the parents of one of the members. At one gathering during the 1858 Christmas season, two music teachers from Wesleyan, one a pianist and the other a violinist, accompanied the group through a series of selections from popular operas. "These difficult choruses were rendered in perfect time and harmony," one observer wrote, "and with great spirit and expression."[58]

By the end of the 1850s there was no shortage of music in Macon. Touring opera troupes, minstrel shows, local musicians, and church choirs filled the air with song. Multiple stores sold sheet music and instruments of all sorts. "Macon," one excited local resident wrote at the time, "with her railroads to every section of the state, her growing population, and highly intelligent, refined musical society, possesses every advantage over her sister cities." The culture of the town was evolving at a rapid pace, but outside events were about to alter Macon's musical climate. Music stores that stocked sheet music standards such as "Listen to the Mocking Bird," "How Sweet Are the Roses," and "My Cottage Home" would soon sell music tied to current events. Sentimental ballads and lively dance numbers would give way to songs that were celebratory but resolute, reflecting a new brand of patriotism that was sweeping the region. Among those new titles that would find their way into stores were "The Bonnie Blue Flag,"

"Confederate Grand March," "God Save the South," and "Beauregard's Manassas Quick Step."[59]

On January 19, 1861, the Georgia Secession Convention voted to sever political ties with the United States, and within a month Georgia was part of the Confederacy. Over the next four years, the state would be involved in a massive military undertaking as the Southern slaveholding states struggled unsuccessfully to achieve independence. While the Civil War ultimately devastated Georgia, in Macon the conflict never completely silenced the music. This was due in large part to the fact that for much of the war the town was not directly threatened by Union advances. It became a safe haven for refugees from other parts of the South, a weapons manufacturing center for the Confederacy, and even served as the temporary state capital late in the conflict. Because several railroad lines serviced Macon, the city was also a transportation center for troops and supplies. On the eve of the war, one visiting newspaper correspondent described Macon in effusive terms. "The different factories and machine shops were all in full blast," he wrote. "The sound of the hammer can be heard in every direction. Quite a number of large business houses have been erected here within the past twelve months. The shelves of the merchants seemed filled with splendid, beautiful stocks of goods. Macon is rapidly improving.... She has the means and the will, and these two combined will accomplish anything."[60]

Touring groups passed through Macon during the war years, and local musicians did their part by giving performances inspired by Confederate patriotism, particularly during the conflict's first two years. If anything, music was even more important during this time of great crisis than it had been during peacetime. It served as a morale booster and a diversion from the anxiety that the war produced among the white population. "Music is a great humanizer," a correspondent for the *Telegraph* opined at the time, "It sways the soul as if with a magic wand.... If we devote our time to music, what change would be wrought!" Musical performances also served as a vehicle for raising money for the war effort. The music department at Wesleyan College organized fundraising affairs to aid departing soldiers, and during the summer of 1861 performed the popular operetta *The Flower Queen* to a large and enthusiastic audience. During the same period, the musical Guttenberger family raised almost seventy-five dollars for the recently organized Soldiers' Relief Society by performing a well-attended benefit concert.

In late 1861, an "Amateur Club" was formed by what one effusive observer described as "ladies and gentlemen who, though not aspiring to the stage, are yet equal to any [performer] that ever promenaded the country." The group gave concerts almost weekly to raise money for the war effort and to raise the spirits of Macon's white population. "Let the public show their appreciation not only of good music, but of the laudable and patriotic purpose in which these entertainments are conceived," one Macon newspaper correspondent wrote after listening to the group. "Public amusements now are few, and we ought to be glad of some who serve the double end of amusement and patriotism." A March 21, 1862, performance was typical, featuring a mix of Italian opera and popular tunes with accompaniment on flute and piano. Among the opera selections were pieces from *Norma* and *La Sonnambula* by Vincenzo Bellini, and the popular tunes included the Stephen Foster composition "Come Where My Love Lies Dreaming" and "The Brightest Eyes" by Giorgio Stigelli.[61]

Macon hosted fewer touring acts as the war progressed, as was the case in the rest of the South. "It is much to be regretted," one observer wrote in 1863, "that in the present condition of things...audiences capable of appreciating highly artistic performances are so much scattered." Still, there were a handful of notable performances in Macon during those years. The fall of New Orleans in 1862 caused an exodus of many artists from that city. Some went north, while others toured the Confederacy. Situated as it was, away from major military activity, Macon was an attractive stopover point for some traveling outfits. Violinist and composer Carlo Patti left Louisiana and toured the South, stopping briefly for a show in Macon in 1863. Two opera singers, Bertha Ruhl and Eliodora Camps, accompanied by pianist G. A. Gnospelius, appeared in town in the summer of 1864 for a show at the Concert Hall. All three were "cultural refugees" from New Orleans who had passed through Georgia before. Ruhl received top billing and entertained her audience with selections taken from Italian operas as well as a number of tunes for "admirers of English song." Another group, billed as Taylor and Company, performed in Macon not long afterward. This was an acting troupe made up of two couples, J. B. and Nellie Taylor, and J. J. and Bella Wallace, all veterans of the Southern stage circuit. They offered "parlor entertainment" that featured "comedy, farce, music, singing and dancing." John Sloman brought his musical family back to Macon for multiple shows during the war years, and Blind Tom also made several more appearances.[62]

Probably the best known performer to pass through Macon during the war—at least in the Confederacy—was Harry Macarthy. Born in England in 1834, Macarthy came to the United States as a teenager, and in his twenties established himself as a passable comedian and singer on the New York stage. As a touring performer he was well received in the South and developed an affinity for the region. With the outbreak of the war, he toured the Southern states incessantly, performing in theaters and occasionally in military camps. He was best known for composing "The Bonnie Blue Flag," which became an unofficial national anthem in the Confederacy, and established him in the minds of many as a great Southern patriot. Macarthy visited Macon several times, and at his July 15, 1864, show, the performance of his signature tune was still the highlight. "His is a natural genius and has no competition," one reviewer wrote after seeing Macarthy perform. "His song of the 'Bonnie Blue Flag,' whose single star has grown to eleven, is nightly encored and deservedly. In the first place it is a good song, and, in the next, he sings it with infinite spirit and effect."[63]

If there was one individual who personified Macon's musical transition to a war footing, it was probably Hermann L. Schreiner. A talented composer and musician, Schreiner came to the United States from Germany with his family in the late 1840s. They settled briefly in Delaware and then moved to Wilmington, North Carolina, where Hermann's father, John, opened a music store. By the mid-1850s, the family had relocated to Macon, where the younger Schreiner worked for his father selling pianos and sheet music. In his spare time, he gave singing lessons and taught piano and guitar. Within a very short time, Schreiner became a familiar community presence. He organized his music students for charity concerts and helped form the German Musical Club. As the name implied, the club was a group of musicians of German heritage who performed German music, billing themselves as the "Macon Liedertafel." The Schreiners began a music publishing enterprise in Macon with Hermann leading the effort. Before the war, he made many trips North to procure sheet music, and he began publishing his own compositions. The business flourished, and with the start of the war, Schreiner began writing music with a decidedly Confederate flavor, including the tunes "When

Upon the Field of Glory," "The Mother of the Soldier Boy," and "General Lee's Grand March." Two of his more well-known compositions were "The Wearing of the Grey," a patriotic number adapted from the old Irish tune "The Wearing of the Green," and a reworked version of the "Battle Hymn of the Republic" praising the Confederacy. His firm published "Somebody's Darling," by Marie Ravenal de la Costa and John Hill Hewitt, which became one of the most popular songs produced in the South during the war years. Schreiner also organized benefit concerts for the Soldiers' Relief Society using local musicians as well as players brought in from neighboring communities.[64]

After the fall of New Orleans, Schreiner had one of the only fully functioning music publishing businesses in the South. He continued operating for the duration of the war, and even opened branches in Augusta and Savannah. His success was the product of sheer persistence and a dogged commitment to his own financial survival. "During the war all musical supplies from the North were cut off," one postwar account of the publisher's activities stated, "and Mr. Schreiner ran the blockade, crossing the Blue Ridge Mountains on foot to Nashville, Tenn., thence by rail to Cincinnati, where he purchased a font of music type, which he safely brought back to Macon. His grit and determination were two of his chief qualities." After the war, Schreiner left Macon and relocated to Savannah, where he continued publishing music and selling instruments. He died while on a trip to Germany in 1891.[65]

During the first months of 1865, a theatrical troupe led by actor and impresario W. H. Crisp made several appearances in Macon, performing plays ranging from silly comedies to dramas designed to pull at the heartstrings, all of which included "Dancing, Singing and Music." On Friday, March 24, 1865, the group performed *Dream at Sea*, a three-act play billed as "a good old fashioned melodrama of the strongly sensational order." The singing and instrumental music included in this performance were likely the last musical arrangements heard in Confederate Macon in a commercial context. Less than a month later, General Howell Cobb surrendered the city to United States forces.[66]

Minstrel Shows, Music Schools, the Grand Opera House, and the Douglass Theatre, 1865–1920

"Music is love in search of a word."
—Sidney Lanier

While the Civil War devastated many parts of the South, Macon sustained relatively little damage to its infrastructure as the city was not a major focal point of Federal advances. General William Tecumseh Sherman bypassed Macon on his famous "March to the Sea," and when the time came in 1865, the city surrendered to United States authorities without significant incident. As a result, it was somewhat easier for Macon to reestablish itself in the years following the conflict, although the human cost of the war was certainly high. Within a year of the war's end, the *Telegraph* optimistically boasted that "our business establishments, in every department of trade, are creditable."[1]

Macon suffered economic ups and downs through the Reconstruction period and afterwards, but commercial growth was steady, and a class structure ultimately emerged that in many ways mirrored that of the antebellum period. "The city early became the residence of many old families of social rank and wealth," one observer opined, "[and] this character it keeps." The elite social strata represented a small minority of the city's white population, but those in it controlled Macon's commercial activity and politics. The rest of the whites in the area struggled to varying degrees, as did African Americans—half the city's population in 1880—who were eventually stripped of their civil and political rights and relegated to the bottom rungs of society by the implementation of Jim Crow segregation.

The city remained a major transportation center, and within twenty years of the war's end Macon was again a commercial hub connected by rail to other significant Southern cities. Cotton and peaches were the region's chief commercial crops, but by the end of the nineteenth century Macon's business roster also included a host of mercantile establishments, foundries, lumber yards, and factories.[2]

After full railroad service was restored in Macon, touring troupes began passing through the area once again. The city's upper crust was particularly keen on promoting opera performances in an attempt to recreate the cultural environment that they had enjoyed before the war. The opera was, they believed, a perfect form of entertainment for "cultivated people" and "the intelligent classes," and a great agency for "mental and moral improvement." In 1866, musical impresario Max Strakosch led one of the first opera troupes into postwar Macon. It included more than twenty performers, many of whom had passed through the region before. The troupe performed four different operas—*Il Trovatore, La Traviata, Martha*, and *Faust*—on four consecutive nights at Ralston Hall, for a crowd that paid up to two dollars per ticket. The appearances by Strakosch's troupe apparently spurred plans by Macon's moneyed citizens to "beautify and increase the importance of our city." This included the construction of a new music venue for major performances "on such a scale that it will be an honor to the city." The effort picked up steam, and the local press did its best to encourage the project. "We are pleased to learn," a correspondent from the *Messenger* wrote at the time, "that a company of gentlemen are seriously suggesting the building of an opera house, or academy of music,...let our wealthy men put their heads and purses together to give a practical effect to the suggestion." Unfortunately, the price tag for such an undertaking was estimated around sixty thousand dollars, a tidy sum in the post-Civil War South. This doomed the effort, at least for the moment.[3]

As wealthy whites contemplated construction of a new opera house that might bring more culture into the region, a unique group of African American performers was organizing in Macon. In 1865, William H. Lee, a white United States soldier and part-time entrepreneur serving with the occupying force in Macon, and George W. Simpson, a white printer working for a local newspaper, organized area African American musicians into an "all-colored minstrel troupe" that was reportedly the first of its kind in the United States. Lee was the driving force behind the project, apparently hoping to make money entertaining local whites and his fellow soldiers. Many of the musicians had performed for Macon whites before and during the war on plantations, at community picnics, and at a few loosely organized theater shows. They were not strangers to the stage, but they were also not familiar with typical minstrel performances structured to include skits and comedy routines along with the music.

Lee and Simpson rehearsed the group for several weeks before the "Georgia Minstrels" gave their first performance in Macon on July 4, 1865, at Ralston Hall. Tickets for the show were fifty cents each, and according to one handbill, patrons were promised that "through the kindness of the Provost Marshal, a sufficient guard to maintain order will be in attendance." The music at the show included the usual array of minstrel tunes that were popular at the time, including "Darling Minnie Lee," "Plantation Jig," "Stop Dat Knockin,'" "Poor Old Joe," "Whole Hog or None," "Gypsy Davie," and "Lucy at the Ball," and the performance concluded with a rousing version of "Dixie." Two days later, a correspondent from the *Telegraph* gave the performance a positive review, writing, "We listened to the performance of the minstrel troupe on Tuesday night....Their jokes are fresh and new, their singing is excellent." According to other press reports, there were at least fifteen performers who took part in this first show, including John Brooker, Lewis Slater, Henry Fields, Lucius Griffin, Aleck Jacobs, Neil Rogers, Joe Clay, Andrew Gospel, Jeff Kiser, Aleck Mallory, Phil Mallory, Austin Brighthaupt, Phil Lamar, Riley Covington, and Albert Slaughter.[4]

The show was so well received that when Lee left the service later that summer, he took the minstrels on the road. With Lee serving as manager and Simpson as "business agent," the Georgia Minstrels were booked into many of the larger cities east of the Mississippi River. While members of the group sang and played instruments, much of their appeal stemmed from the novelty that they were African American players rather than traditional white minstrels who took the stage with artificially blackened faces. Lee marketed the group as "Genuine Darkie Minstrels" who spoke in "pure negro dialect," and "The only original, Simon-pure Negro troupe now traveling the United States." After one stop in Cleveland, Ohio, a reviewer wrote, "The fact that the performers had formerly been slaves piqued curiosity, and the singing, dancing, and comicalities had a certain grotesqueness and native extravagance which made the show relish. It is one of the best troupes which ever visited us." In Chicago, one audience member had a similar opinion, writing that "their entertainment was without a doubt one of the very best ever offered to the Chicago populace.... The troupe is composed entirely of colored men, all freed from the bonds of slavery during the recent war.... From beginning to end the program is a good one, replete with whimsicalities and oddities of the first order."[5]

While the Georgia Minstrels drew crowds as a group, their fame was fleeting. Individual members of the troupe were likely paid very little, with their management keeping most of the profits from the tour. This was particularly the case after a stop in New York, during which Lee and Simpson met Sam Hague, a veteran British blackface performer and producer who believed that the group would do well in England. Hague purchased controlling interest in the troupe and took them overseas. More concerned with the Georgia Minstrels brand than with the individual performers, Hague gradually replaced the original members with more seasoned players, both black and white, and by 1870, none of the Macon men remained with the group. With the exception of Neil Rogers and Lucius Griffin, who reportedly stayed in England, and John Brooker, who ended up in New York, most of the original minstrels returned to Georgia. While several ended up playing in the "Macon Colored Band" that performed occasionally at social events around town, most made a living working menial jobs. Eventually, in an effort to capitalize on the Georgia Minstrels' initial popularity, other African American and mixed performing groups toured the United States under the same name even though they had no connection to the original group.[6]

Many of the musical events held in Macon in the years following the Civil War involved philanthropic efforts. Locals gave concerts to raise money for construction of a library and a hospital as well as for causes aimed at aiding the poor and, in general, helping the region recover from the conflict. In late 1866, the city's "Orphan Education Society," led by some of Macon's socially prominent women as well as the city's religious leaders, sponsored a concert for the local orphans' home "to pay the expenses incurred in bestowing upon indigent and helpless orphans that schooling and care so essential to their welfare." This included children who lost their fathers during the war. Among those who performed were members of the Guttenberger family, who were always willing to pitch in and help any cause aimed at bettering the city. In addition to highlighting the purely philanthropic mission of the society, local reporters framed the concert in the language of Confederate patriotism. After the show, a correspondent from the *Telegraph* gave a positive review, crowing, "Let it be seen that Macon knows how, in taking care of the children, she remembers those who fought and died for Southern independence. Let it be seen that she appreciates the honors and sacrifices that the fathers made by educating the orphan children."[7]

Not long afterwards, female members of some of Bibb County's wealthier families organized a series of concerts for the Georgia Memorial Association. Also created in the spirit of Confederate patriotism, this group's mission was to identify and reinter the bodies of fallen Georgia Confederates who had been hastily buried on the battlefield. The association organized shows in the state's major cities, and performers from all over Georgia took part. Two of the project's principal organizers were sisters Virginia Bacon, wife of a Macon attorney, and Ellen Ogden, whose husband was a successful insurance man. The women were members of the Lamar family, who had deep roots in Bibb County, and both possessed outstanding singing voices. Richard K. Hines, a lawyer also from Macon, served as the group's manager, and his wife, Georgianna, was a performer. Local pianist and music teacher Alfred Schmidt also participated. Probably the best-known member of the group was Sidney Lanier. He had published his signature work *Tiger Lilies* in 1867 and recently moved back to Macon.[8]

The performers held the first memorial concert in Macon in January of 1869, with most of the city's upper crust in attendance. "As we anticipated, Ralston Hall was crowded with the elite of Macon Tuesday evening to hear the memorial concert," the *Telegraph* reported three days later. "It was a magnificent performance, and the delight of the audience was almost boundless. Every piece was encored." The group performed an eclectic collection of pieces ranging from classical to popular. Schmidt treated the crowd "with great effect on the piano" and performed selections from Schubert as well as the famous minstrel tune "Old Folks at Home (Swanee River)." Sidney Lanier performed a series of flute pieces, and Georgianna Hines sang "The Brightest Eyes" and "How Can I Leave Thee." Ellen Ogden apparently stole the show and received the lion's share of praise in the press for her renditions of the Scottish ballads "Auld Robin Gray," "Comin' Thro' the Rye," and "Twas Within a Mile o' Edinboro' Town." "Mrs. Ogden has a soprano voice of more than ordinary compass," one reviewer wrote. "It has great power of expression, rendering equally well strong passion and delicate pathos....Mrs. O. is wonderfully gifted."[9]

Another well-attended series of charity soirees held in Macon during the mid-1870s involved amateur performances at Ralston Hall to benefit a local militia unit, the Jackson Artillery. A unit of the same name had been organized in 1861 to fight in the Civil War, and in 1874 a movement began to reform the outfit. Surviving members of the old group and others tried unsuccessfully to acquire funding from the state, but the following year the legislature passed a bill approving the project if funds were raised locally. The legislation also created "a board of trustees with the privilege of holding a series of gift concerts, whereby it is expected that an amount will be raised sufficient to equip the company thoroughly, and thus add a valuable organization to our citizen soldiery." William A. Huff, Macon's mayor, led the effort, and he and others quickly went to work organizing the concerts. The shows went well, according to a review of one of the performances by the local newspaper:

> Indeed, many persons were surprised that such excellent music could be rendered by the local talent of this city. The overture, "Crown Diamonds," was especially well executed and immensely popular. The other pieces were as follows: Tenor solo by Mr. William Lee Ellis; violin duet by Messrs. T. Coley and J. Burkes; vocal duet by Mrs. J. E. Wells, Jr., and Mr. W. W. Carnes; bass solo by Mr. George Reynolds; vocal duet by Mrs. C. Hunter and Mr. A. L. Wood; and a vocal duet by Mrs. C. Hunter and Mrs. J. E. Wells, Jr.

One of Macon's most visible postwar charity events was an annual concert to benefit the Georgia Academy for the Blind. By the 1870s, these performances by pupils from the school were well publicized in Middle Georgia and well attended, usually taking place at the end of the spring semester. "The exercises at the Georgia Academy for the Blind closed Tuesday afternoon," a witness wrote after one of the shows, "with a fine vocal and instrumental concert. The chapel was crowded to the utmost capacity." Another attendee reported that the audience was treated with "solos, duets, quartettes, choruses and performances of instrumental music which produced a fine impression." These benefits usually included a half dozen singers and a band "numbering seven or eight violins, several flutes, bass violin, etc.," with the typical program featuring a mix of simple opera selections and popular tunes. While the students ably displayed their talents each year during the concerts, the key to the event's lasting success was the work of Vincent Czurda, the dedicated professor who led the academy's musical instruction for decades.[10]

Vincent Czurda was more than just a music teacher. He was a pillar of Macon's musical community for thirty years during the latter half of the nineteenth century. Czurda was born in Germany on May 12, 1824, and came to the United States at the age of twenty-three. An excellent pianist and violinist, he began his career as a music instructor and performer in Baltimore before moving to Raleigh, North Carolina, and then Charlottesville, Virginia, where he joined the staff of Albemarle Female Institute in 1858. With the outbreak of the Civil War, he enlisted in a Virginia militia unit but was discharged "for reason of defective sight." He gravitated to Macon, where, during the summer of 1861, he took a position as a music instructor at the Georgia Academy for the Blind. His association with the school and the city of Macon would last for more than thirty years. "From the very start his sympathies went out to the sightless children, and he was as much a father as a teacher," one observer later wrote. He supplemented his income giving private music lessons and for several years taught piano at Wesleyan College. Czurda's reputation as a musical educator grew with each passing year, and in 1874 state senator George R. Black, chairman of the committee that oversaw the Georgia Academy for the Blind, publicly noted that "Professor Czurda, the musical instructor [at the academy], has brought many of the pupils up to a high degree of musical excellence, and the performances of the pupils, both in vocal and instrumental music, are alike truly wonderful."[11]

In addition to his yeoman's service arranging concerts by his pupils to benefit the academy, Czurda helped organize innumerable musical events in Macon for the community at large. He served as the longtime organist for Christ Episcopal Church, and at one time or another helped raise money for all of the churches in the city. He was a mainstay at social events for more than a generation, providing the music for countless christenings, debutante balls, birthday parties, weddings, and funerals. Speaking of Czurda, one newspaper columnist wrote at the time that "the professor is perhaps the highest musical authority in Macon, and enjoys the love and esteem of all." In 1878, he recruited and played with "the best musical talent in the city" during a benefit for victims of the yellow fever epidemic. Through the years, Czurda also helped organize a number of musical societies and clubs in Macon, and he occasionally performed the music of his homeland with an informal band of fellow Germans from the area who "loved music for music's sake." In ill health toward the end of his life, he elected to return permanently to Germany in 1896, a decision that saddened many Macon residents. "Next week Professor Czurda leaves for his old home in Germany to remain," one observer lamented after hearing the news. "[He] is a musician of rare talent and proficiency.... His place will be hard to fill." Another sad Maconite called him "so good a man, so fine a musician, and one who contributed so much to the music-loving people of Macon." Czurda never returned to Georgia and died in Germany on May 14, 1905. In addition to his students, some of whom went on to become professional musicians, Czurda's legacy included a number of original compositions—primarily polkas and waltzes—that circulated for years via sheet music.[12]

During the last quarter of the nineteenth century, much of the music in Macon continued to revolve around the city's churches. Full or partial choirs from all of the denominations performed at public occasions in addition to weekly services. The larger congregations—Baptists, Methodists, Episcopalians, and Presbyterians—had a history of lending their voices to the community, and by the postwar period, St. Joseph Catholic Church had built a solid choir. With roots going back to Macon's origins, the church's first pastor arrived in 1841, and by the 1890s the congregation had grown to the extent that an impressive new house of worship was under construction downtown. St. Joseph's was also well known for its musical contribution to the city. Its congregation included gifted singers as well as a talented band, managed by a man who, like Vincent Czurda, was a major presence in Macon's musical community for many years.

James Geramus Weisz was born in Cambridge, Pennsylvania, in 1857. He studied music at Saint Vincent College in Latrobe and later completed his education at the Boston Conservatory of Music. In 1876, he accepted a position teaching music, as well as Latin, German, and mathematics, at Pio Nono College, a short-lived institution established in Macon in 1873 by the Catholic Church. A well-rounded and proficient musician, Professor Weisz, as he was known around the city, gave private music lessons after leaving the college and established a healthy list of pupils, in large part, because he was so versatile. He offered instruction in "voice culture" and reading music in addition to teaching piano, violin, clarinet, cornet, and flute. In 1882, he became the choir director and organist at St. Joseph Catholic Church, a position he held for sixty years until his death in 1942. There he recruited, organized, and rehearsed musicians for a church choir capable of interpreting complicated musical arrangements both sacred and secular. "The music rendered yesterday morning by the St. Joseph Catholic Church was by long odds the best I have heard anywhere since I have lived in Macon," one excited congregant wrote. "Professor Weisz's great ability as a director is an acknowledged fact, and when he has such material to handle as he had yesterday, he is given all the opportunity he needs to show his skill." Easter and Christmas services were an annual musical highlight at the church, garnering high praise from those in attendance as well as from the community. Just before the 1894 Easter service, a local columnist summed up the progress that Weisz had made with the choir since arriving in the city, stating, "On Easter Sunday it will be twelve years since the young organist, J. G. Weisz, organized the choir at St. Joseph's church. Since then, his motto has been 'excelsior,' and the music this Easter will supersede all previous efforts."[13]

Weisz organized interdenominational musical events for the general public and regularly sponsored shows for charitable causes. In 1889, he promoted a major concert benefitting victims of the Johnstown flood in his native state of Pennsylvania, and he regularly raised money for the orphan's home in Macon. Not long after the turn of the century, he organized a symphony orchestra in the city, and later, as the First World War loomed on the horizon, he organized musical events for the soldiers at nearby Camp Wheeler. Like Vincent Czurda, he performed regularly at social events in Macon and the surrounding communities for years. The entire city mourned when Weisz passed away on January 21, 1942, at the age of eighty-four. "The people of Macon of every religious denomination and all walks of life sincerely mourn the death of Prof. James G. Weisz," the editor of the *Telegraph* wrote upon hearing the news. "He was known and loved by two generations of Macon citizens, for his gifts as an artist, and for his many fine qualities as a man. He will be held in affectionate remembrance through the years to come."[14]

In April of 1874, members of Macon's musical community came together to raise funds for the construction of a new house of worship for the city's growing Jewish population. Founded in 1859, Congregation Beth Israel had been struggling for several years to build a new facility, and its members hoped to raise enough money to complete the project through a public "Temple Concert." Members of the Harmonic Society took part, and the congregation brought in a featured performer, nationally known vocalist and author Octavia Hensel, specifically for the occasion. "The music selected for this concert is as good as could have been selected," one observer stated, "and all of it will be well rendered. Some of the most skillful musicians and most accomplished vocalists in the city will take part in it." The event was held on April 14, and from all accounts it was a great success. The first part of the program featured popular songs of the day, such as "The Two Roses" by Hildegard Werner, "Hear Our Prayer" by J. M. Abbot, and Felix Mendelssohn's "I Would That My Love," while the second part focused more heavily on opera. The event raised "a snug sum," which was apparently enough to complete the temple's construction. The building was dedicated the following October, and afterwards a correspondent from the *Telegraph* who attended the ceremony wrote, "The temple was beautifully decorated, and the music on the occasion excellent.... We congratulate our Jewish friends on their accession to so fine a building, and wish them much enjoyment of their temple."[15]

Some of the music heard in Macon also reflected the heritage of local performers. The city had a thriving German community, and as early as the 1850s, German musicians organized to play the music of their homeland. By the 1870s, the German Music Society had been formed under the leadership of Adolf Engelke, president; Herman Spahr, vice president; and Charles Dryfous, secretary and treasurer. In 1874, the group had thirty-four members who gave public and private performances that usually consisted of "waltzes, polkas and marches" and other "gems of German song." Likewise, Irish celebrations took place in the city during which musicians played and sang a host of "Irish airs." St. Patrick's Day festivities drew especially large crowds for banquets, parades, and musical programs that featured "heart-touching songs of the Dear Old Isle." Typical of these were the popular standard "Kathleen Mavourneen" along with "Come Back to Erin," "The Harp That Once Through Tara's Hall," "Off in the Stilly Night," and the patriotic anthem "God Save Ireland."[16]

Traveling shows and musicians continued to make Macon a regular stop during the last quarter of the nineteenth century. Opera and classical music remained popular and drew audience from Macon's upper crust, though the city welcomed its share of balladeers and musical theater troupes that appealed to broader audiences. These performances continued to inspire local musicians as the city's culture evolved. Talented Maconites formed several mostly short-lived musical associations and performing groups during the period, some of which even toured the state. The Macon Musical Association, the Mendelssohn Quartette Club, the Tattnall Square Music Association, and the Macon Choral Club were among the organizations designed to provide entertainment for "cultured audiences." They included mostly local music instructors and part-time musicians and singers who were related in one way or another to prominent families in the city.[17]

While musical societies functioned as social outlets for some of Macon's citizens, they were also a product of their environment. Following the Civil War, Atlanta began to grow in status as a symbol of the "New South." The city expanded economically and also as a social and cultural center for the state. Many Maconites, accustomed to their city being the hub of Georgia's interior, seemed somewhat jealous, or at least mildly annoyed, with all of the attention lavished on their northern neighbor. During the 1870s, Atlanta established its own music societies, and cultural leaders in Macon were suddenly desperate to keep up. The result was a resurrection of the Harmonic Society that had existed in the city before the Civil War.[18]

The Macon Harmonic Society of the Reconstruction era, like its predecessor before the war, was an undertaking of the city's wealthy class. Only dues-paying members could perform for the society or attend concerts, with most shows being closed to the general public, at least initially. "This is not a public show to which tickets can be purchased," the society announced before its first concert in 1873, "but one to which only active and associate members of the society are to be admitted, together with such guests that they are entitled to invite." This policy effectively made the society a social club made up of only those who were willing to pay dues to join. A committee within the group was established to oversee the handing out of memberships.[19]

With regard to their musical mission, the society pledged to offer programs that were "varied, and calculated to please all shades of taste, and the entire membership will no doubt be entirely entertained." In a testament to his standing in the community, the group recruited Vincent Czurda as their musical director. Performances were often divided into two parts, separated by an intermission. The first part was usually dedicated to classical works, with the second including modern tunes, such as

"Moonlight, Music, Love and Flowers" by John Barnett and Harry Stoe Van Dyke, "The Rover's Joy" by Franz Apt, "The Grand Ocean" by D. C. McCullum and Harrison Millard, "See the Pale Moon" by Fabio Campana, and the Stephen Foster composition "Come Where My Love Lies Dreaming." Depending on the occasion, the performance might also include hymns, especially around Easter and Christmas. The society was most active between September and May, usually taking June, July, and August off to escape the heat and humidity of a typical Macon summer. Among the members who performed at shows at one time or another during the 1870s and early 1880s were Sophia E. Gustin, Florence Roberts, W. A. McLendon, Mary North, Arthur L. Wood, Virginia Bacon, Ellen Ogden, Sallie Wells, Elizabeth Crowe, Jesse Hardeman, Loyola Hardeman, William W. Carnes, Charles Volger, Marion Wells, G. H. Martin, William Volger, G. E. Sussdorff, Thomas S. Lowry, Samuel Everett, I. R. Branham, Goode Price, Ethel Crippeu, J. R. Branham, Ben C. Smith, Julian Price, Mrs. S. A. C. Everett, Georgia Stroberg, Tochie Williams, Annie Powers, Sallie Anderson, Viola Rogers, and Tacie Daniel.[20]

Although many viewed the Macon Harmonic Society as a positive community enterprise, it also generated controversy. The group's patrons and performers were members of the city's prominent families, and its exclusivity smacked of elitism. Most of the society's membership did little to combat this image, regularly taking a stand that the organization was dedicated to admitting to its concerts "none but persons of such a class as will appreciate the music, or respect the proprieties of the occasion." It was an attitude that did not sit well with some other Macon residents, who chafed under the idea of a small group assuming that it had a monopoly on the arts in the city. In an 1874 letter to the editors of both the *Messenger* and the *Telegraph*, one annoyed man complained that "the object of the society is undoubtedly musical improvements and entertainment, but not improvement for a large majoring, [only] a very small minority."[21]

There were also occasional squabbles among the membership and event attendees over the type of music the society should perform. Older members and observers promoted classical music, while younger members liked more upbeat, popular tunes. A generational divide was also apparent when members discussed what they considered proper behavior at a show. "I would remind those who attend these concerts that they are very different from the ordinary public concert," one older member complained.

"Certain youths who attend these concerts very regularly, and, while sitting in the back of the hall, disturb the audience by very noisy demonstrations of applause...it is hoped that they will applaud with due decorum hereafter." Despite these occasional frictions, the Macon Harmonic Society sponsored performances in the city for about a decade before disbanding. It is unclear why the organization ceased to exist, but its exclusivity and the growing availability of other forms of entertainment likely played a role. One of the society's last major events was a March 9, 1882, concert honoring the memory of Sidney Lanier, who had recently passed away. Several years later, some of the society's members created a similar organization, the Macon Musical Association. It lasted for around five years and gave performances that mirrored those of the Harmonic Society.[22]

During the three decades following the Civil War, minstrel shows remained a popular form of entertainment in Macon, and traveling minstrel companies frequently visited the city. They were similar to the touring groups that passed through prior to the Civil War, though in most cases they included more members. These outfits performed traditional "plantation" material like their predecessors. Among the troupes that drew the largest crowds were Colonel Wagner's Minstrels; Haverly's Minstrels; the McNish, Johnson, and Slavin Troupe; LaRue's Minstrels; the Hi Henry Minstrels; and Thatcher, Primrose, and West. In addition to these groups, made up primarily of whites in blackface, the Colored Cotton States Minstrels, an all-African American troupe, also made stops in the city, as did Madame Rentz's Female Minstrels, considered a novelty because, as their name suggests, the cast included female members.[23]

The popularity of minstrel shows in Macon and elsewhere led a group of local white performers to create their own "burnt cork outfit" in 1877. Like the national groups, their shows included singing, dancing, and racially driven comedy routines. Several members of the Macon Amateur Minstrels, as they were known, were fixtures on the local music scene and had performed with other music clubs and organizations. Among those who took part were Arthur L. Wood, Banks Winter, Julian Price, Arthur E. Boardman, Floyd Ross, James Iverson, Burr Brown, R. D. Clancy, Arthur P. Findlay, David Mackey, Abe Barnett, Bridges Smith, Mike Donahue, John Donahue, and Tim Donahue. While the players hoped to draw crowds to cover their expenses, most of their performances were for charity. They routinely raised money for local schools, orphanages, and the city's public library. After a show to benefit Macon Female

College, the school's grateful president, William C. Bass, praised the group in a letter to the newspaper. "Their native talent and chaste performances will always win the approbation of a Macon audience," he wrote, "and the noble objects for which these gentlemen are devoting their talents must ever redound to their honor." The Macon Amateur Minstrels performed in the city for approximately two years before disbanding. For most in the group, the enterprise had been a part-time hobby, but some remained associated with music to one degree or another for the rest of their lives.[24]

Arthur L. Wood and Bridges Smith were among the most musically inclined of the minstrels. In addition to having good voices, they wrote songs together and even a short opera that was "staged both in Macon and Atlanta...and was a big social event." Typically, Wood wrote the music and Smith the words, and among their popular published works were "The Lessons the Cherries Taught," "Dreamy Brown Eyes," and "The Little Low Hut," the sheet music of which all sold modestly. "These two gentlemen are beginning to be looked upon as a second Gilbert and Sullivan," a local newspaper exaggerated in 1880. "Their songs sell readily in every part of the country and are very popular among the minstrel men." Wood wrote several songs on his own that were published by major music houses, and he played the organ for both the Presbyterian and Baptist churches. While both men pursued music as a hobby, neither made it a career as they grew older. Wood owned a music store for a time but eventually purchased a funeral home in Macon, and owned the business at the time of his death in 1902. Smith pursued a career in journalism and printing before being elected mayor of the city, a position he held for several years. He died in 1930.[25]

Banks Winter was perhaps the most talented singer in the Macon Amateur Minstrels, and his experience with the outfit was a springboard to a significant career in music. Bridges Smith, one of his closest friends in the group, later reflected that Winter "possessed a fine tenor voice and was a star.... He used the organization of those [Macon] minstrels to develop his voice...and blossomed forth as a full-fledged professional." Winter was born in Macon on February 8, 1857. He attended school in the city and eventually got a job as a machinist on the Georgia Central Railroad. He began performing with the amateur minstrel troupe at the age of nineteen and quickly emerged as one of the leading members of the group. His voice attracted a great deal of attention, and in 1879 he began a professional career after securing a spot with a national touring company, Haverly's Mastodon Minstrels. Two years later, he joined Billy Arlington's Minstrels, and during a thirty-year theatrical career also performed with Skiff's California Minstrels; Leavitt's Gigantean Minstrels; and Thatcher, Primrose, and West. "Winter was one of the best ballad singers of his day," one observer reflected in 1909. "[He] possessed a commanding presence and a strong, resonate tenor voice. He never failed to receive rounds of applause." While he became a well-known theatrical presence on the minstrel circuit, Winter achieved his greatest success during the 1880s as the composer of "White Wings," one of the most popular songs of the era in the United States. During the first decade of the twentieth century, as minstrel shows began to fade, Winter toured as a vaudeville performer, at times with his daughter Winona, who became a well-known player in her own right. He retired around 1910 and for a while lived in North Carolina before moving to Los Angeles to be near his daughter's family. He died there in 1936.[26]

As the procession of out-of-town performers continued through Macon, locals began to push for the construction of a new, more modern concert facility. For years patrons had complained about the condition of Ralston Hall, believing it was antiquated. The venue was called "the coldest place in town" during winter performances, and its inadequate number of doors and windows, narrow aisles, and tight staircases raised safety concerns in the event of "a fire or any other sudden panic." Other factors driving discussions of a new facility were Macon's expanding population and a spirit of competition with other Georgia cities that were already building new halls.[27]

In 1882, a group of Macon businessmen and other interested parties, including John F. Hanson, James M. Johnston, Samuel Coleman, Solomon Waxelbaum, Samuel Jaques, William B. Johnston, Virgil Powers, and Henry Horne, met and formed a joint stock company to finance an elaborate new entertainment venue called the Academy of Music. They raised funds through the sale of stock and private donations, and construction began the following year. Architect Alexander Blair, who had an office on Cherry Street, designed the building, which everyone involved promised would be the finest concert facility in the state. By the summer of 1884, there was a great deal of anticipation in Macon related to the grand opening. The brick exterior was complete, and a team of theatrical contractors were brought in to complete the delicate work on the interior.

At the time, Henry Horne, who supervised the construction, reported that "the scenic artist and the stage carpenters will arrive from Chicago and immediately go to work on the stage fixtures. The scenery will be equal to the finest in the South, while the drop curtain will be of beautiful design and elegant in every particular. The interior will be papered with the latest and nicest designs, and no part of the building will be slighted." Upon completion, the structure would seat almost 2,500 patrons and boast a huge stage measuring fifty-eight by ninety feet.[28]

The Macon Academy of Music opened to the public with a special concert on September 22, 1884. A large orchestra under the direction of Albert Wurm was brought in to accompany local singers. The band opened the program with "the grand overture to the 'Caliph of Bagdad,'" after which Julian Price sang two standards of the period, the sentimental "Thy Sentinel Am I" by Edward Oxenford and William Michael Watson, and "British Man-of-War," a traditional love song couched as a naval ballad. Loyola Hardeman and Marion Wells sang a duet, "Thine Alone," that "brought forth the most rapturous applause," and Carrie Tarver followed with another love song, a rendition of "Mendelssohn's Zuleika, No. 1." During the course of the evening, Ferdinand Guttenberger—Phillip Guttenberger's son, who also taught at Wesleyan—Arthur L. Wood, and Margaret Smith performed piano solos, as did Charles Austin, a blind pianist who was a pupil at the Georgia Academy for the Blind. The program was a great success and a fitting grand opening for a venue described by one onlooker as "a model of elegance and a triumph of good taste." Illustrating the cultural rivalry that had developed between Macon and other Georgia cities, a correspondent from the *Telegraph* could not resist bragging about the new theater, which was among the largest and most elaborate in the South at the time. "Our country cousins from Atlanta, Augusta, and other rural places can enjoy a treat by coming to see our new opera house," he wrote. "The bicyclers will not run over you and we won't let our street sprinklers throw water on you."[29]

The Academy of Music enhanced Macon's reputation as a music center, drawing more traveling theatrical and musical companies from out of town. The first full opera production at the venue was a performance by the Milan Italian Opera Company in May of 1885. Around the same period, the academy welcomed the Madison Square Theater Company for a production of the comedy *May Blossom, The Fisherman's Daughter*, complete with "original music and effects." Not long afterwards, the

Mendelssohn Quintet from Boston drew "the largest crowd that ever greeted a concert troupe in Macon." Other major concert events of the period included performances by the Belgian violinist Ovide Musin, who appeared with a vocal ensemble, and the popular Austrian soprano Emma Juch. While the new theater was the focal point for major plays and concerts, it was not the only venue that hosted events. Macon's Masonic Hall, constructed in 1871, was a less ornate but comfortable room that attracted many acts, and several smaller recital halls and area hotels sometimes hosted entertainment. As for Ralston Hall, the opening of the academy rendered it obsolete, and in January of 1886 a large fire destroyed the building, along with several adjacent structures.[30]

Cultural activities in Macon created an increasing demand among the population for musical instruments and sheet music. During the 1880s, two stores, J. W. Burke and Company and the Georgia Music House, dominated the city's music market. The former was founded by John W. Burke, a Methodist minister and entrepreneur. Born in Watkinsville, Georgia, Burke came to Macon in 1858 and opened his business immediately following the Civil War. In addition to selling music and art supplies, he was a successful printer and publisher. In 1883, Edward D. Irvine opened The Georgia Music House, which was affiliated with a major wholesale music distributor, Ludden & Bates, in Savannah. Irvine started his career selling books and then branched out to become a successful dealer in sheet music and instruments. His store's slogan was "A Musical Home Is a Happy Home." Both Burke and Irvine were heavily involved in civic affairs, particularly Burke, who became an alderman, served on the Wesleyan College Board of Trustees, and held leadership positions in many local organizations. Irvine was a great promoter, and the Georgia Music House included a recital hall that hosted special events, including "parlor concerts" designed to encourage local musicians and singers.[31]

In 1882, the Georgia Music House hosted an event that celebrated both amateur music and Macon's continuing evolution as a modern city. The telephone had come to Macon two years earlier, ushering in a new era of mass communication. After the opening of the Macon telephone exchange, workers immediately strung wires all over the city, first to local businesses and government buildings, and not long afterwards to private homes. In addition to transmitting the human voice, many initially viewed the telephone as an excellent vehicle for disseminating music. By the time the telephone reached Middle Georgia, musicians in cities across America were already participating in "telephone concerts" during which they used the new medium to transmit their performances to eager listeners miles away.

In May of 1882, E. D. Irvine sponsored the first of several telephone concerts originating from his store. The logistics were challenging. The Macon Volunteers Band, a recently reorganized group of fifteen musicians attached to the city's militia unit, were asked to perform, and Irvine set up two hundred chairs in his recital hall to accommodate a live audience. He passed out printed programs so that the audience in his shop, as well as those listening on their telephones, could follow the show. At exactly 8:30 P.M. on the night of May 22, every telephone in the city rang as a signal for those who wanted to hear the music, and the band began their performance. The band played nine songs, including "Gypsy King," "Second Andante Waltz," "Spring Greeting," "Andante Religioso," "Castles in the Air," "The Lover and the Bird," "Captain Dalton's March," "She Sleeps Beneath the Daisies," and "Fire Spirits." According to the *Telegraph*, "People all over the city sat quietly at home and heard the concert with greatest ease."[32]

More advances in technology, in the form of an efficient electric streetcar system, increased the availability of musical entertainment in Macon beginning in the 1890s. In addition to constructing the lines, the Macon Railway & Light Company established "streetcar parks" to boost traffic on weekends and in the evenings during summer months. These types of parks were common in cities with streetcar systems, and they routinely hosted concerts and other forms of entertainment. Prominent among the parks in Macon were Crump's Park, Ocmulgee Park, and North Highlands Park. Originally called Macon Suburban Park, Crump's Park was named for Stephen A. Crump, secretary and treasurer of the Macon Railway & Light Company, who originally owned the land. The company aggressively developed the site to include "picnic grounds and a casino, containing a ballroom, theater and restaurant" as well as "a dance pavilion, shooting gallery and performing arts theater." North Highlands Park and Ocmulgee Park were smaller in scale, but still hosted social occasions and concerts. They were popular for a time, but could not compete with what Crump's Park offered. Fewer and fewer events were held at the smaller venues as time wore on, and in 1910 a fire destroyed the dance pavilion in North Highlands Park. Abandoned as "a summer

resort," Ocmulgee Park found new life in 1907 when it was "set apart for
the use of the colored people" as a venue for African American entertainment.[33]

Crump's Park hosted some national touring acts, but regional and
local bands provided the music for most of the occasions held there.
Henry W. Card and Ferdinand A. Guttenberger conducted two of the
bands that appeared frequently at the park. Card was born in 1855 in
Massachusetts and migrated to Columbus, Georgia, when he was in his
twenties. An accomplished musician, he organized an orchestra and
taught music in Columbus until 1883, when he and several members of
his group relocated to Macon. The city's music community welcomed
them with open arms, as did the local press. Trumpeting the group's arrival, an excited correspondent from the *Telegraph* wrote, "Macon will indeed have fine music, not excelled by any band in the South. They are
educated gentlemen and good citizens, as Columbus will vouch." For the
next twenty years, various incarnations of Card's orchestra served as "the
mainstay of all the big blow outs, all the church fairs and all the social
outdoor entertainment in the city." Typically, his band numbered around
twenty members, several from Macon, and others recruited from Savannah, Columbus, Atlanta, and elsewhere. One early twentieth-century version included two cornets, five clarinets, two trombones, a baritone horn,
two tubas, four alto horns, one base drum, and one snare drum. Card's
bands specialized in martial music but also performed popular tunes and
included a smaller ensemble of six to eight pieces that played more intimate gatherings. One notable occasion when the orchestra was on full
display was Admiral George Dewey's visit to Macon in March of 1900.
The group provided the ceremonial music for the occasion, including
rousing versions of "Hail to the Chief" and "Stars and Stripes Forever"
and led a parade through the city in honor of the war hero. Card remained
a fixture on the Macon music scene until 1904, when he moved back to
Columbus. He later relocated to Atlanta.[34]

As the son of Phillip Guttenberger, Ferdinand Guttenberger was a
member of one of the first families of Macon music. He was perhaps the
most versatile musician in the city during the last quarter of the nineteenth
century, having mastered the piano, organ, violin, guitar, mandolin, and
cornet. For decades, he was known for performing at local nuptials "the
sweet strains of Mendelssohn's matchless wedding march" on the organ,
or "Love's Old Sweet Song" on the violin, and for several years he taught

organ and cornet at Wesleyan College. More than just a musician, Guttenberger was an entrepreneur. Around 1887, he went to work managing John W. Burke's music store, and in 1894 purchased Burke's interest in the business, rechristening it F. A. Guttenberger and Company. He carried sheet music and a variety of instruments in his store at 422 Second Street, and he was the city's leading distributor of Steinway pianos.[35]

Guttenberger was also a superb organizer. He put together groups for all sorts of occasions including "parlor soirees," casual dances, formal balls, and large outdoor production. His turn-of-the-century orchestra was one of his best, and it played regular weekly concerts "enjoyed by hundreds of people" at Crump's Park. As with Card's band, Guttenberger's group included musicians recruited from Macon and elsewhere. According to one observer, "This excellent orchestra is composed of artists trained to perfect cadence, and they play with great sympathy." While Guttenberger was not averse to his group playing classical music, many of their shows centered around popular tunes, such as "The Jolly General" by American composer Neal Moret; "King Dodo," a dance number from a play of the same name; a two-step called "Down on the Farm" by Harry Von Tizler and Raymond Browne; and "Alabama Blossom," a ragtime tune by Charles Lawrence Van Baar. The band was also comfortable playing marching tunes, and Guttenberger composed special music that they regularly played at Wesleyan Female College commencement ceremonies. When Guttenberger died in 1905, his funeral was one of the most widely attended in the history of the Macon. His heirs took over the music store and kept the name F. A. Guttenberger and Company as a tribute to their father.[36]

Another local entertainer who performed at the city's streetcar parks and elsewhere was Dan Holt. Holt was born in Macon in 1875 and was drawn to the theater at an early age. As a teenager, he worked as an usher and stage manager at the Academy of Music, where he was able to see, and be influenced by, all types of entertainment. By the time he was twenty, he was organizing minstrel performances using local talent to raise money for all sorts of causes. He produced minstrel shows for the local Elks Club and became known as "one of the best negro impersonators around." In addition, he regularly appeared on the bill as a singer and musician—sans blackface—in variety shows at Crump's Park. After one performance, the *Telegraph* reported, "Mr. Dan Holt, a strong Macon favorite, performed superbly on various sweet sounding and difficult musical instruments and wound up by capturing the whole pavilion with his eccentricities."[37]

In 1903, Holt joined actress Mabel Paige's touring theater company, likely hooking up with the group after it made an appearance in Macon. Paige was a popular stage actress who would go on to star in motion pictures. Holt became one of the most versatile performers in the troupe. "This clever mimic and monolinguist is said to be one of the funniest men on the vaudeville stage," one Pennsylvania correspondent reported. "His musical act, in which he plays twenty-four different instruments, being rated as the best of its kind in America." Though he achieved a great deal of notoriety as a vaudeville performer, Holt's first love was the minstrel show. Tired of performing as part of a variety ensemble, he contemplated retirement after just a couple of seasons with Paige's group. "I don't like vaudeville much," he told a reporter at the time. "It is too lonesome. You do your turn, and then you are lost until the next round. I want the company of other boys." He left Paige and ended up joining Al G. Field's Minstrels, a successful touring operation. He also spent time with Coburn's Minstrels, drawing rave reviews wherever he went. "Dan Holt has to be seen, he cannot be described," a Tampa correspondent wrote after one show. "Funny is no name for Dan Holt. He is excruciating. Joke followed joke; a verse of poetry chanted in ragtime, or flung out without regard to the orchestra...until the house seemed to sway with the bodies of laughing people."[38]

While Holt was a natural as a performer, he did not always have the temperament of a touring artist. The road seemed to wear on him, and he enjoyed returning to Macon between touring seasons. As minstrel shows died out, Holt took more and more work as a more traditional singer and musician, and continued to take the stage into the 1930s. He retired from the road in 1936 and moved back to Macon for good, becoming a fixture on the local entertainment scene. At the time of his death in 1946, he was the manager of the city auditorium.[39]

While minstrel shows remained popular in Macon until the World War I era, more and more vaudeville performers passed through the city during the first two decades of the twentieth century, drawing significant crowds. The rise of vaudeville in the United States began in the 1880s, and the theatrical genre would remain popular for the next half century. Vaudeville was a general term used to describe variety shows that could include comedians, musicians, dancing girls, jugglers, acrobats, magicians, and even animal acts. These shows had no uniform program from troupe to troupe, and their quality varied based on the talents of the performers. In Macon, the Academy of Music hosted vaudeville performances, as did Crump's Park. In 1895, the Academy hosted a troupe headlined by popular singer and dancer Lottie Collins, whose signature song was "Ta-ra-ra-boom-de-ay." Not long afterward, prolific theatrical producer and writer Charles E. Blaney brought a group of "talented vocalists" to the building, along with "pretty girls, clever comedians, expert dancers, and high class vaudeville artists." At Crump's Park, nightly crowds for vaudeville shows sometimes overwhelmed the streetcar system. According to a correspondent from the *Telegraph*, "At Crump's Park, large and paying crowds attend the vaudeville every evening except Sunday. The crowds are often so large that it is with difficulty that expeditious transportation to and from the park is afforded." Among the significant vaudeville troupes that passed through Macon during the 1890s were the Corsair Company, the Herbert Cawthorne Company, Chick and Peters, and McGinley's Comedy Company.[40]

In early 1896, local entrepreneur Michael G. Putzel opened "Putzel's Vaudeville Palace" on Mulberry Street, a house that advertised "the best vaudeville entertainment in the South...new songs, new dances, new everything." A well-known saloon and restaurant owner, Putzel expanded his existing operation to include a theater with "a complete stage with scenery, drop curtain and comfortable cane chairs" for the audience. Opening night included performances by nationally known singers Mary Smith, Lillie Adams, and Effie St. Clair, along with other entertainers. While vaudeville in some instances included crude humor and burlesque performances that some considered inappropriate, Putzel promised Macon patrons that in his theater, the programs each night would be "as is seen only in the first-class shows that come to the Academy of Music." Among the performers who plied their trade at Putzel's during the 1890s were Frank Binney, G. Clayton Frye, Kittie Chapman, Bob and Eva McGinley, Eva Allen, Emma Barrett, Florence Russell, Bessie Nitram, George Mitchael, and the Peters and Green Vaudeville Company.[41]

While Putzel was able to fill seats at his establishment, the vaudeville house was open for less than three years. It was never very profitable, and the house became a lightning rod for controversy in August of 1896 when a local Methodist minister named Monk gave a fiery temperance sermon that was printed in the newspaper. In it, he called for a statewide prohibition law and singled out Putzel's theater—associated as it was with Putzel's saloon—as the town's leading den of iniquity. "Right down here on Mulberry Street," he bellowed from the pulpit, "you see it advertised in big letters 'vaudeville,' the lowest order of theatric performance with actresses composed of the lewd women of the town." Gus C. Saville, who managed the theater for Putzel, wrote to the newspaper the next day to publicly invite the minister to see a performance, arguing that "if the said Dr. Monk would visit our theater and witness our entertainment, his ideas of morality would probably run a different sphere." Even the mayor got involved, closing Putzel's temporarily. The ruckus eventually died down, but it damaged the theater's reputation. By the following year, Putzel was on the verge of closing both his saloon and theater, reporting that "expenses have been very heavy, and business not so very good, not even with the vaudeville features of the business." Despite the problems, he was able to keep his vaudeville house afloat until November of 1898, when a fire destroyed the building. Putzel never opened another theater and died on July 19, 1901, at age 46.[42]

As the nineteenth century ended, Wesleyan Female College continued to contribute to Macon's music culture, drawing into the community experienced faculty from all over the country as well as overseas, and graduating talented musicians and singers. Every summer, the Wesleyan commencement exercises included well-attended concerts and recitals, and during the school year students performed at various community events, often "enthusiastically encored by large and fashionable audiences." Wesleyan's music faculty also gave concerts to standing-room-only crowds, leading local observers to opine that the college "unquestionably possesses one of the most capable and strongest corps of instructors of any music school in the whole country." The faculty was particularly engaged in public performances from 1900 to 1904, when noted pianist and composer Edouard Gregory Hesselberg served as head of the music department. The department expanded during the period to the point that the school's 1905 annual catalogue reported, "We had quite an overflow in the department, and had to employ new teachers, buy new pianos, and build new music rooms." As a result of this expansion and "the immediate prospect of its much greater growth in all respects," the college's board of trustees in March of 1905 voted to create from the existing music department "The Wesleyan Conservatory of Music."[43]

While he was in Macon for a short time—fewer than four years—Edouard Hesselberg left quite a musical imprint on the city. Hesselberg was born in Latvia in 1870 and attended the Moscow Royal Philharmonic Conservatory of Music and Dramatic Arts. He studied under famous Russian pianist Anton Rubenstein, and afterwards toured with a number of orchestras, eventually emigrating to the United States, where he continued to perform and teach music. Hesselberg joined the faculty of Wesleyan as director of music programs in the summer of 1900 and immediately made his presence known. "Music, of all the fine arts, is the most practiced, yet the least thought of," he said. "The causes of such a phenomenon are manifold. A sweet mystery surrounds the very nature of music, with its material part quite subtle and elusive." On September 22, 1900, he gave his first public performance at the college's chapel building. Because of the pianist's lofty reputation, the event was a heavily anticipated musical event that drew a large crowd of "Macon's music-loving people." According to the *Telegraph*, "The room was crowded to overflowing with an expectant, eager multitude that left many standing, [and] the professor met the high expectation of the audience, and justified the praise bestowed on him." According to the newspaper, highlights of the "well-selected program of classical music" were Hesselberg's interpretations of "The Ocean Love Song" and "Polonaise from a Russian Suite," which he composed himself.[44]

During Hesselberg's time at Wesleyan, he oversaw the expansion of the music department and organized numerous faculty concerts that raised the department's profile in the community. Typical of these was a December 11, 1904, mix of instrumental and vocal presentations by a half dozen faculty members. Held at the Wesleyan chapel, the event was a highlight of the Christmas season. Tickets were in great demand, and on the night of the performance around five hundred people were turned away at the door. "It was a record breaker," one observer reported, "both in regard to the number of those present and those who, for lack of standing room, vainly sought admission." To accommodate the large crowds, Hesselberg hastily organized a second performance held six days later. The episode accelerated a fundraising drive that led to the building of a new, larger chapel completed in 1906. In addition to his work organizing faculty performances, Hesselberg gave recitals either by himself or accompanied by one or two of his colleagues. One reviewer reported that the pianist specialized in "Beethoven [and] in the minor compositions by

Massenet, Chopin and Tchaikovsky.... Music for the artist in the highest
sense, music for those whose love for music has gone far beyond their
fingers and reached their souls."[45]

Edouard Hesselberg left Wesleyan in 1905 to take a similar position
at Belmont College in Nashville, Tennessee. After several years there, he
moved on to other teaching jobs and established a successful career as a
touring artist. During his later years, he frequently performed on radio
broadcasts. His resignation from Wesleyan was a surprise to the college's
administration, and Macon's music community collectively mourned the
news that he was leaving the city. Hesselberg left behind a thriving conservatory that would continue to grow, as well as a legacy of talented students who benefitted from his tutelage. He also passed down his artistic
temperament to his son, Melvyn Edouard Hesselberg, who was born in
Macon on April 5, 1901, and would go on to become the prominent stage
and film actor known as Melvin Douglas. The elder Hesselberg died in
Hollywood on June 12, 1935. According to one report, at the time of his
death he had, "as a composer, some hundred vocal, instrumental and orchestral works to his credit."[46]

One of Hesselberg's colleagues at Wesleyan also played a leading role
in helping the music department expand. Maria Skidmore Connor was
born in Illinois in 1872, the daughter of a feed-store owner and granddaughter of an Irish immigrant. A naturally gifted violinist, she entered
the New England Conservatory of Music in 1892 and impressed the administration with her abilities. "I wish you had been with me and heard
her play her violin," one of the institution's board members wrote in a
letter to a friend. "With no effort at display she stands gracefully, holds
her violin at ease, and as though it was her lover, and the bow moves in
graceful lines constantly. Her performance gains the fullest applause from
both teachers and pupils." During her stay at the conservatory, she gave
many public performances and routinely provided musical interludes at
area church services and weddings. After graduation, she secured a job
teaching violin and piano in Nebraska, and around 1900 she was hired at
Wesleyan.[47]

While in Macon, Connor was active on the city's social scene. In
addition to her duties at the college, she gave solo performances and sometimes appeared with Hesselberg. At Wesleyan, she helped build up the
violin department to the point that within four years the school had to
turn away potential students because the college had reached capacity. A

SOMETHING IN THE WATER

bit of a free spirit, Connor was also known for playful banter with spectators during performances. The habit endeared her to many but annoyed
some of her more snobbish patrons, who complained about her "address-
ing the audience in witty and snappy preludes of speech, to the detriment
of and in strange contrast to the dignity of her performance." Connor left
Wesleyan in 1905, reportedly in search of better pay, and followed Hesselberg to Belmont College. She later relocated to Portland, Oregon,
where her parents had moved, and during the latter stages of her career
came back east to take a position as head of the music faculty and "instructor in violin, piano, and harmony" at Randolph Macon Institute in
Danville, Virginia.[48]

Not long after the turn of the twentieth century, a major construction project in Macon marked another chapter in its musical history. In
January of 1904, officials announced that the Academy of Music, Macon's
primary concert and theatrical venue, would be torn down and replaced
by a new, more modern theater. The DeGive family, prominent theater
promoters from Atlanta, purchased the property and hired W. R. Gunn
to design a new building that would include a theater, office space, and
small apartments. The academy closed in April, and much of the old theater was quickly demolished. Construction began on the new facility that
would be called the Grand Opera House. "The [new] building will be
constructed of gray brick and terra cotta, and will be by far the prettiest
building of its kind in Macon," the local newspaper reported, "and the
men promoting the work guarantee that Macon will have one of the most
up-to-date theaters and office buildings in the country."

The end result was an impressive theater that seated just under 2,500,
with a fifty- by ninety-six-foot stage and all the modern accoutrements of
a first-rate entertainment palace, including fifteen dressing rooms, a "ladies parlor" and "gentlemen's retiring room," glittering fixtures, wide hallways, an expansive lobby, and a state-of-the-art ventilation system. The
new theater opened on February 1, 1905, with a performance of a three-
act musical comedy titled *Glittering Gloria*, starring Dorothy Morton, and
the first music to reverberate through the theater was the orchestral arrangements that accompanied the play. After witnessing the first show, a
Macon reporter who was obviously caught up in the moment gushed,
"We doubt if, either in Europe or America, there can be found a greater
temple of art in any other city of Macon's size.... It is a pillar of strength
upholding the metropolitan character of the community." For decades,

the Grand Opera House would host all types of theatrical productions and concerts headlined by national performers as well as many notable local events.[49]

At the turn of the twentieth century, Macon, like the rest of the South, was rigidly segregated, but African American performers passed through the city regularly, playing to both black and white audiences. One of the most notable was Sissieretta Jones, a classically trained soprano who was reportedly the highest paid African American entertainer in the United States at the time. The press called Jones "Black Patti," a reference to Adelina Patti, the popular Italian prima donna. Jones made her first appearance in Macon in 1895, performing for a segregated audience at the Academy of Music. Floor seats at the venue were reserved for whites while African Americans were relegated to the upstairs gallery and balcony. "Mme. Jones is one of the most remarkable singers in any race," one Macon patron stated at the time, "and her voice is one of rare quality and power." Her repertoire included "Reminiscences of 'Faust,' 'Carmen,' 'Trovatore,' 'Grand Duchess,' 'Daughter of the Regiment,' 'Bohemian Girl,' 'Maritana,' 'Rigoletto,' and 'Lucia.'"

Several years later, Jones returned to the city as the leader and principal star of a large ensemble called "The Black Patti Troubadours," billed as "The Greatest Colored Show on Earth." While her classical selections were part of the troupe's performance, the show also included traditional minstrel performances designed to appeal to broader audiences and popular tunes, such as "My Dear Southern Moon," "Old Man Moon," and "Old Folks at Home (Swanee River)." After a 1909 performance, the *Telegraph* paid the singer and her fellow performers a somewhat patronizing compliment, with the reviewer writing, "The show as given by Sissieretta Jones and her company last night pleased those who love the Negro voice. There is a melody in his voice, whether on the wharfs rolling the cotton into the holds of steamboats, or on the stage in an opera house. There is a certain sweetness in it that falls softly on some ears."[50]

Local African American performers were an integral part of Macon's musical community dating back to the city's formative era, when Charly Benger and others played for Macon's volunteer militia. These musicians began a tradition of martial music that carried on after the Civil War with a "colored brass band" that played at community occasions and was "a very essential adjunct to any parade—military or civic." In 1874, the band gave a concert to raise money for new uniforms consisting of "felt caps, with red pompoms, grey jackets, with Georgia buttons and scarlet collars and cuffs, sky-blue pants, black patent leather music pouches bound with scarlet, patent leather pants similarly bound, gilt shoulder straps with scarlet centers and plated bugles in the middle." In the summer months during the 1880s, the band played open-air concerts in front of the Lanier House, and they also specialized in "very solemn airs" at the funerals of local dignitaries.[51]

Other African American musicians formed dance bands that played at social occasions, both black and white. These groups usually played for tips, with their income corresponding to the economic class of their audiences. According to one white patron in post-Civil War Macon,

> Music for all dances at balls and parties was furnished almost exclusively by Negro orchestras.... The usual dance orchestra was composed of first and second violins and the bass violin with occasional triangle. These orchestras, if they could be thus dignified, were hired for the occasion, there being no fixed price for their services, depending entirely on the amount of pleasure of the dancers to be liberal in filling the hat as it was passed around among the males at the close of the dance. Sometimes the hat was filled with silver quarters and halves and dollars, and sometimes the tips were disappointing.... Besides the voluntary tips of the male dancers, the musicians were always treated with refreshments.

Turn-of-the-century Macon also had its share of African American solo musicians who plied their trade any place where they might attract an audience. Some worked street corners for spare change while others were in demand to play at both white and black social functions. African American beer joints or after-hours, weekend house parties also provided a venue for these entertainers and an opportunity to make a little extra money. Among the more well-known street performers in Macon were Joe Gordon, who played the guitar and was "fond of serenades," and a guitarist and harmonica player known as "Baby Ruth." Gordon worked part time for the city but "reaped the harvest of dimes and nickels" from unsolicited outdoor performances in the evenings and on weekends. In the winter months, when the local hotels were filled with Northern tourists, he would "hang around the hotel corridors" and play for whoever would listen. Baby Ruth's failing eyesight made it difficult to find steady employment, so "thumping his guitar and blowing his harp" was his only means of supporting himself. "He is more vagabond than vagrant," one observer wrote of the entertainer in 1906, "because he makes a show of earning money by playing music. With him money comes easy and goes easy." Both Gordon and Baby Ruth fit the stereotype of the mythical rambling bluesman, the image of which would become popular decades later as blues music entered the American mainstream.[52]

Many locals lauded Ike Brown, another well-known African American performer in Macon, as the best banjo player in the city. A more polished player than Gordon or Baby Ruth, Brown usually wore a suit and "the very loudest type of necktie" when he performed. "He was in nightly demand and he was always ready," one local man later remembered. "Not only was he chief musician with serenading parties, but he cut a figure in private homes and at swell dinners and occasions." As Brown became more well known, he received invitations to play at neighborhood and civic events in other towns in the region. His repertoire of "plantation songs and banjo music" was usually well received, and for a time he toured Georgia and Florida with a traveling minstrel show. Brown died in Macon in 1896 at the age of forty-two, and the local newspaper, which at the time did not usually report in great detail on the deaths of African American, lamented his passing and ran his obituary.[53]

Some dramatic developments in the history of American music began unfolding around the turn of the twentieth century as ragtime and jazz music came of age. Many claim that music labeled "ragtime" originated with house bands and pianists in the red-light districts of New Orleans, with traveling musicians later exporting it up the Mississippi River to Memphis, St. Louis, and eventually New York and other parts of the country. Its nickname came from what many viewed as the "ragged" nature of the music's beat, a trait that drove people to either love or hate the genre with equal ferocity. Ragtime was very popular during the early twentieth century, and music publishers did their best to take advantage of what some have described as one of the earliest waves of "pop music." By far the most famous name associated with ragtime was the African American composer Scott Joplin, who in 1899 wrote "Maple Leaf Rag," a national best seller that helped broaden ragtime's appeal.

As ragtime emerged as a popular musical genre, traditional jazz also came of age in the Storyville District of New Orleans. Located two blocks off the French Quarter, the Storyville District was created by the city in the late 1890s in an attempt to regulate prostitution by limiting the practice to a specific location. The district quickly grew to include a wide variety of brothels, dance halls, and saloons that used musical entertainment as a marketing device. Musicians who played all different mixes of music with African and European origins flocked to the area, among them early jazz pioneers, such as Charles "Buddy" Bolden and Ferdinand "Jelly Roll" Morton. The musical exchange that took place in the district was rapid and electric. Because they were closely related, enthusiasts would later struggle to identify and define the musical nuances that distinguished ragtime from jazz. One general difference between the two was that ragtime performances were more often than not limited to the piano, banjo bands, and some brass bands, while jazz players improvised more on a wide range of instruments from pianos and guitars to woodwind instruments, saxophones, and trumpets. As with ragtime, jazz musicians exported their music up the Mississippi and beyond, making it one of the most popular forms of music that America ever produced.[54]

As ragtime music came of age in America, so did Ferdinand Alexander Guttenberger Jr., a member of the third generation of Macon's musical Guttenberger clan. Born in 1881, Guttenberger grew up working in his family's music store and was a talented musician and composer. In 1901, he published his first work, a piano piece titled "Hobo Days in Georgia," through the M. D. Swisher Company in Philadelphia. He published his first ragtime number, "The Log Cabin Rag," in 1908. "One of Macon's best known young musicians has joined the class of local composers with a very catchy ragtime piece," a local reporter wrote at the time. "It is the kind of music that makes you feel like dancing. You simply can't make your feet behave." He followed these up with other ragtime numbers including "Kalamity Kid" and "Shaka Foot" as well as a love song titled "Always My Own." Guttenberger stayed busy. For decades he maintained a career as a music salesman, but also led local bands and did yeoman's service playing piano at countless Macon social events. By the time of his death in 1945, he was known as the city's "Mr. Music."[55]

In early November of 1912, a dozen socially prominent Macon women who "resided along College Street in some of the finest homes in the city" founded a social organization "to cultivate a taste for the highest and best in music, and to assist others to a broader knowledge of the same." They called their new group the "Saturday Morning Music Club," and it would have great staying power in the community. They drew up a lengthy constitution, and accepted for membership only women who were "congenial," "musicians in the broadest sense," and "able and willing to sustain her share in the club's work." Mrs. J. T. Wright served as the organization's first president, and other founding members included Mrs. Charles Hall, Mrs. Arthur Codington, Mrs. John Lester, Miss Louise Singleton, Miss Philo Pendleton, Miss Florence Bernd, Mrs. T. E. Blackshear, Mrs. A. W. Lane, Mrs. Winter Wimberly, Mrs. Ben McFarland, and Mrs. I. H. Adams. "We were so young when we organized the club," Wright later said, "that we didn't know what we were doing. Perhaps we all felt like sowing a wild oat or two, and took this method of having a fling at art—for art's sake or for heaven's sake."[56]

From the outset, the women worked diligently to promote the arts in Bibb County, meeting twice a month, with the group's members presenting papers and performing a wide range of music from popular fare to classical standards. According to one report, during the group's first five years in existence, "143 papers about music and musicians were presented, along with more than double that number of selections performed." The *Telegraph* took notice of all the activity, applauding the group as "one of Macon's serious study clubs." The Saturday Morning Music Club organized very popular Christmas caroling programs and encouraged the study of music in Macon area schools. Positioned as "a leading force in elevating the public taste in music," they also sponsored performances by well-known national artists. Concerts featuring baritone Pasquale Amato of the New York Metropolitan Opera, famed Polish pianist Ignacy Jan Paderewski, and Boston's Knelsel Quartet, at the time considered one of the country's greatest string quartets, were among the first big events promoted by the Saturday Morning Music Club. The Grand Opera House hosted the events, and according to press reports, ticket prices were set low because "there is no desire to make any money, but simply a chance to give Macon people an opportunity to hear music of a class they do not often hear."[57]

Unlike similar clubs that came and went during the period, the Saturday Morning Music Club was blessed with generational longevity, lasting up to the present day (2021). Decade after decade, they have promoted scholarships, sponsored local music programs, and promoted concerts by prominent performers. The group eventually dropped "Saturday" from their name and became the Morning Music Club. In 1929, at the invitation of ardent supporter Professor Joseph Maerz, the club began meeting in the music studio at Wesleyan Conservatory.[58]

During the first decades of the twentieth century, organized enter-tainment for Macon's African American population took a great leap for-ward. The catalyst for this cultural advance was an energetic African American entrepreneur named Charles Henry Douglass. Douglass was born in a one-room cabin two miles outside Macon on February 17, 1870, and from an early age he helped support his family through a variety of jobs. "I peddled light wood and vegetables in the morning and attended school in the afternoon," he once said, reflecting on his childhood. "I went out and chopped cotton when I was so small that I had to use the short-handled hoe, and the pay was only fifteen cents a day." After his parents died, he supported his two sisters through "laboring work" until they were grown. Douglass was a natural businessman. The realities of a segregated society created a separate sphere for African American economic develop-ment, but he met the challenge head on. One of his first ventures was a successful bicycle rental and repair enterprise, and profits from the busi-ness helped him eventually branch out into real estate, banking, and the entertainment industry.[59]

In 1904, Douglass leased the Ocmulgee Park vaudeville pavilion—sometimes referred to as the Ocmulgee Park "Theater." The park imme-diately became a gathering place for African Americans in Macon and a place where African American performers could gain exposure. "The col-ored population have a separate place, Ocmulgee Park, where they can enjoy themselves," the *Telegraph* reported shortly after Douglass took charge, "and a theater has been opened up for them where they can enjoy high class vaudeville, and have all the enjoyments attendant upon a well conducted resort." Entertainment at Ocmulgee Park included prominent touring black vaudeville troupes as well as a host of variety shows. A com-pany typically came to town and settled in for several months, putting on shows and taking in money without having to pay traveling expenses. Such was the case with William Benbow's Fun Factory Company, which included actors, comedians, jugglers, and musical acts. Among the more prominent entertainers who performed in Macon with this group during the period was singer Theresa Burroughs, a "dainty soubrette" with a pow-erful voice, whose most popular rendering was a song titled "Sadie My Dusky Lady."[60]

In 1906, Douglass opened a hotel in downtown Macon that catered to African American patrons, including performers, and around the same time he sold the Ocmulgee pavilion lease to Charles Collier, another

African American entrepreneur from Macon who would make a name for himself producing vaudeville shows. Determined to remain in show business, Douglass organized a traveling minstrel troupe, the Florida Blossoms, with a partner, Peter Worthey, and headquartered the organization in Macon. Douglass later described the enterprise as a "two-car tent show...employing from thirty-five to forty people, and they were all Negroes." The troupe regularly toured more than a dozen states and reportedly "built a good reputation and made a great deal of money." Among the group was Walter H. Childs, a cornet player from Macon who became the outfit's band leader. He had toured with other shows and was part of a band that played regularly at Ocmulgee Park. While their performances included some slapstick and traditional minstrel fodder, the Florida Blossoms were known for musical comedy and having a superb band. The group's lineup changed from time to time, but the 1909 version was particularly solid, including "Walter Childs, solo cornet; George Crump, solo cornet; George Motto, clarinet; Clarence Stewart and Ed Miller, first and second altos; George Christian, baritone; John H. Tobias, first trombone; Clifford Prater, second trombone; Joe Miller, tuba; Larney Fisher, snare drum; and Cloud Glover, bass drum," along with several singers. According to contemporary accounts, musical highlights of their show were songs such as "The Honky Tonk Rag," "Lovie Joe," "Stop, Stop, Stop," and "Come Over and Love Me Some More."[61]

Douglass sold his interest in the Florida Blossoms to Worthey in 1911 and built a theater next to his hotel on Fourth Street (later Broadway and currently Martin Luther King Jr. Boulevard). The downtown entertainment venue for African Americans was a first in Macon, and it cemented Douglass's reputation as the city's leading African American businessman. The theater was devoted to vaudeville performances and early motion pictures. "My seating capacity is 350," he told a group in 1915. "We give three or four shows every afternoon, and the prices are ten to fifteen cents; running four to six reels of pictures, and using three to five acts of the best class [and] a four-piece orchestra." Pressed to offer more details about his operation, he added, "We have novelty acts, regular vaudeville bills, and other features the same as white theaters....I take particular pains to get the best [acts] obtainable."[62]

Douglass's theater flourished to the point that several years later he decided to expand, building an even larger venue on the adjacent property that became both a focal point of African American cultural activity and a Macon landmark of long standing. Patrons called it "the New Douglass Theatre." Douglass modelled the theater after the Grand Opera House, reportedly after visiting that segregated venue with his wife and "being ushered to a third floor balcony through an obscure entrance." The New Douglass Theatre was designed in a Classical Revival style and, like the Grand, it included multilevel box seats, a "graceful curved balcony," extensive ornamental plaster work, and gilt detailing. The original seating capacity was around eight hundred, and the theater could accommodate motion pictures and live entertainment. Not long before his new theater opened, Douglass became a leading member of the newly formed Theater Owners Booking Association (T.O.B.A.), an entertainment collective that quickly took control of the African American vaudeville circuit in the Southeast.[63]

The New Douglass Theatre became part of, and benefitted from, the rise of the "chitlin circuit," a network of exclusively African American performance venues that sprang up in the South and elsewhere during the first half of the twentieth century. For decades, performers on this circuit plied their trade in large tents, churches, nightclubs, or, especially in some larger cities, major black-owned theater buildings. Sometimes referred to as "Negro vaudeville," the chitlin circuit included various types of entertainment but always featured music. While the circuit nurtured young entertainers and gave experienced performers a place to showcase their talents, it also provided black audiences with an opportunity to share their collective culture away from the prying eyes of whites and among other individuals with whom they shared common societal experiences. The all-black entertainment venues promoted African American unity and allowed members of the audience to relax and, in essence, let down their cultural guard. Many early African American musicians, including jazz and blues performers, cut their teeth on the chitlin circuit, which began just before commercial recording took off.[64]

As was the case throughout the South, Douglass's status as Macon's most prominent African American businessman came at a price. Despite his position, Macon's social system still categorized him as a second-class citizen, and he still had to accept the indignities of Jim Crow. His success also bred jealousy and suspicion in some members of the white community, who viewed any successful African American as a threat. This prejudice and hatred were on full display in the summer of 1922 after a melee in one of the city's African American pool rooms left three men wounded and a white deputy sheriff dead.

On July 29, 1922, Macon police received a report that an angry and inebriated African American male named John "Cockey" Glover was waving a gun at patrons inside Hatfield's poolroom at the corner of Broadway and Wall Street alley. Three deputies, including Walter C. Byrd, were dispatched to the scene. An imposing figure, well over six feet tall, Byrd was well known around Macon as a deputy and, for years, as a bootlegger, whose past criminal activity apparently did not disqualify him from a position in law enforcement. According to published accounts, when Glover saw the officers, he began firing wildly, killing Byrd and wounding three bystanders before escaping out an open window. In an extraordinarily short time, news of the killing spread through Macon. Dozens of angry whites assembled in the streets, ready to join the manhunt for Glover, with the number eventually growing to around three hundred. Police closed the city's African American business district and began a house-by-house search of African American neighborhoods. At the Douglass Hotel, deputies roused patrons from their rooms and forced them into the streets as they searched the building. Meanwhile, someone in the mob spread the false rumor that Douglass himself was somehow behind Glover's crime and that the businessman was secretly harboring the fugitive. This led to a string of threats on Douglass's life and forced the police to provide him with protection. "C. H. Douglass, Macon's wealthiest negro," the *Atlanta Constitution* reported, "is said to have received a warning to leave Macon or he would be killed.... Douglass was threatened and twenty police formed a guard about his house during the night."[65]

Predictably, the story ended badly for Glover. He was captured at Griffin, Georgia, two days after the crime, and before Bibb County deputies could get him back to the Macon jail, a white mob intervened just north of the city. They took Glover away from the deputies and shot him multiple times, killing him. They placed the corpse in the back of a truck and drove triumphantly into Macon, parading the remains up and down Broadway. After a while, they dumped what was left of Glover at the Douglass Theatre, where there were calls to burn down the building. Police intervened, dispersed the crowd, and removed the remains before anything further happened. Within days, things calmed down in Macon, and Douglass was able to resume his business activities, but the message was clear. No matter how successful, no African American was exempt from Jim Crow "justice." It was no coincidence that the mob had chosen to deposit the lynched remains of Glover at the Douglass Theatre, a center for African American culture in Macon, owned by Macon's most prominent African American resident.[66]

As Charles Douglass built his empire in Macon, Charles Collier maintained the Oconee Park pavilion and continued to draw top talent and large crowds to the location. Collier was another African American businessman who used the profits from his successful grocery store to forge a career in entertainment management. During the summer months, the park hosted vaudeville performances, with a pit band led by pianist Locke Lee and including violinist Earl Greathouse, tap drummer Eddie Stamps, and singer Evelyn White. Two notable performers who came to the park in 1910 were William and Gertrude Rainey, known to vaudeville audiences as "Ma and Pa" Rainey. They came to Macon with their Georgia Sunbeams Company. While the troupe was a standard African American vaudeville unit that included actors and comedians, Gertrude Rainey's singing was a centerpiece of the act. Among the numbers she performed in Macon were "The Fascinating Ragtime Glide" and "Temptation Rag." In the years to come, Ma Rainey would become famous as a groundbreaking member of the first generation of blues recording artists in the United States, and blues enthusiasts for generations would lovingly refer to her as the "Mother of the Blues."[67]

Charles Collier's ambition seemed limitless. He moved on from Ocmulgee Park in 1911 and for a time managed a touring troupe called C. W. Park's Musical Comedy Company. In 1915, he founded his own group, Collier's Smart Set, and four years later latched on to an established, successful traveling company, "Silas Green from New Orleans." He bought half interest in the organization from producer Eph Williams in 1922 and took over sole ownership after Williams's death in 1935. With roots dating back to the 1880s, the show sprang from the antics of a fictional character named Silas Green, evolving over time into a revue that included singing, dancing, and slapstick comedy in a part vaudeville, part minstrel-show format. Under Collier's leadership, "Silas Green from New Orleans" became one of the most prominent African American touring revues of the period, with newspapers lauding Collier as one of America's "outstanding race producer[s]."[68]

A flurry of musical activity also took place in Macon between 1914 and 1918 thanks to the Chautauqua movement and the organization of the Macon Drum and Bugle Corps. The Chautauqua movement began in the late nineteenth century in New York and spread nationally. It was an adult-education movement designed to bring culture and entertainment to the masses, particularly in rural areas. The typical Chautauqua gathering included lecturers on education and current events, artists, musicians, and sometimes politicians, whose job it was to both inform and entertain their audiences. The movement penetrated Georgia in the 1880s, largely due to the efforts of the illustrious "New South" proponent Henry Grady, and found success in Atlanta and Albany. Macon experimented with the movement beginning in the 1890s, hosting annual gathering as part of the state fair. Eventually, local leaders decided to develop a permanent Chautauqua that would include "a full exhibit from all the colleges and schools" in Georgia, musical performances, and a host of "recitations, readings and debates." As time passed, musical events began to include national performers brought in to attract crowds from the surrounding area. Macon's civic leaders supported the movement, and local newspapers reported that "it has been given the very highest endorsement by two score or more of Macon's responsible businessmen."[69]

For several years, major musical events took place in Macon associated with the Chautauqua. Among the artists performing at the 1914 Chautauqua was the Ernest Gamble Concert Party, consisting of bass singer Ernest Gamble, violinist Verna Leone Page, and pianist Edwin M. Shonert. The group had an international reputation and was celebrated in the press and promotional literature as "an institution in the world of music" and "the only American company to tour Europe, Northern Africa and the West Indies." According to one reviewer, "Ernest Gamble's programs are so arranged as to please both musicians and laymen, the lovers of classical and the large majority which finds pleasure in ballads and folk songs." Other acts included the Neapolitan Orchestra, a group of Italian musicians who specialized in "harmonious interpretations of the great masters," and the seventeen-piece New York City Marine Band under the direction of Mario Lozito.[70]

In 1917, ambitious civic leaders welcomed the organization of the "Chautauqua of the South" in Macon, an undertaking that they hoped would make the city the permanent cultural capital of the region. "To the State of Georgia and the Southland," one official crowed at the time, "it means the establishment of a great rendezvous for intellectual, social, industrial, and civic life." Organizers had big dreams, and the move coincided with a period of significant rivalry between Macon and Atlanta for supremacy as Georgia's most enlightened city. The Chautauqua was designed to hold major events in Macon that would bring in "the best there is in American music, art, science, religious guidance, industrial experience, and political leadership." To accommodate large crowds, the city hastily constructed a large wooden auditorium to serve as a performing center. The first great meeting was held in the spring of 1917 over a three-week period and included musical talent from all over the country. While it was billed as an opportunity to expose all citizens to art and culture, the music reflected the more refined tastes of the event's prominent organizers. Among those who performed were Clarence Eddy, one of the nation's premier organists; Anna Case and Arthur Middleton of the New York Metropolitan Opera; the Russian Symphony Orchestra; Myrtle Moses and George Hamlin of the Chicago Opera Company; and the New York Artist Trio, featuring baritone Ashley Ropps, Parisian violinist Lucille Collette, and pianist John Rebarer. Despite local enthusiasm and support, the 1917 event proved to be the high-water mark for the Chautauqua movement in Macon. The city hosted meetings for the next several years, but interest in the movement waned during the 1920s, and it did not survive the Great Depression.

By the first decade of the twentieth century, the seeds of Southern mythology regarding the collective service of former Confederate soldiers were firmly planted in the states of the old Confederacy. Defeated militarily, the South in the decades following Reconstruction struggled to vindicate the ideals and decisions that had led it into the Civil War, costing so many men their lives. From the ashes of war and the turbulence of the Reconstruction period, a cultural identity took shape grounded in ideas and attitudes referred to collectively as the Lost Cause. Celebrations of the Lost Cause took many forms: annual civil and religious services honoring the Confederate dead, veterans' reunions, the deification of Confederate military leaders, the erection of Confederate monuments, and the emergence of groups such as the United Confederate Veterans (UCV), Sons of Confederate Veterans (SCV), and United Daughters of the Confederacy (UDC). Politicians on the stump used the language of the Lost Cause— language denoting moral superiority based on abstract notions of honor and chivalry—to garner votes, and ministers espoused Lost Cause virtues from the pulpit. As they entered the twentieth century, the states of the former Confederacy did their best to maintain this cultural identity by accenting the New South with many of the cosmetic trappings of an idealized Old South. From a practical standpoint, while salving the psychological wounds of defeat, such a course also helped maintain both white supremacy and the political dominance of the Democratic Party in the region.

Macon was certainly not immune to this phenomenon. In 1896, local men founded the Thomas B. Hardeman Camp of the Sons of Confederate Veterans. Named for a former Confederate officer and politician, the camp functioned as a civic organization and routinely sponsored social gatherings. In 1912, the group organized a drum and bugle corps that, through the years, would contain anywhere from twenty-five to fifty members. These types of groups were common across the country, with origins dating back to traditional drum and fife outfits in the military that predated the Civil War. One of the first events that the Macon group participated in was the city's 1912 Memorial Day parade. The parade drew a large crowd to watch an "array of uniformed men and beautifully decorated floats" making their way through the streets. According to some accounts, the drum and bugle corps established the pace of the entire affair. The next day, a correspondent from one newspaper reported that "the corps was out in full force.... The spirit of the occasion sounded forth in the Bum! Ta! Bum! Ta! of the drummers, as the thousands in the parade and on the streets fell into step at the regular cadence of the drum."

Not long afterwards, and with most of the same men, the group reorganized with help from the Chamber of Commerce as the Macon Drum and Bugle Corps, and the members became official emissaries for the city. They continued performing at local activities, but civic leaders also raised money to send them to larger events in other parts of the country. In 1913, they represented Macon at the inaugural parade for President Woodrow Wilson in Washington, and later at the national United Confederate Veterans reunion in Richmond, Virginia. "These boys have been to conventions, meetings, and even a presidential inauguration," one observer noted in 1915. "They are willing to get out and tramp through the streets of any city and advertise the fact that they are from Macon, Georgia." The group remained active to one degree or another for the next two decades.[71]

As in the rest of the nation, the years following the First World War ushered in a period of significant change in Macon. The modern world began to show itself, and the pace of life picked up speed. Like other locales in the South, Macon experienced the Roaring Twenties as a robust and sometimes turbulent decade marked by economic opportunities for some, voting rights for women, continued Jim Crow segregation, illegal alcohol, and a host of technological advances that dramatically altered the nature of entertainment. Macon's musical environment would never be the same coming out of the war years. New artists would emerge in the city, and new venues would be built to accommodate larger crowds. New devices would also bring music to the masses in unprecedented ways. While there was a great deal of stagnation in the city's political and social structures because of Jim Crow, there was no denying that by the beginning of the Roaring Twenties, Macon was on the cusp of a more modern era, and that era needed an updated soundtrack.

3

The Jazz Age, Big Bands, and Beyond, 1920–1945

"The blues craze was really upon us, and
I had to sing plenty of blues."
—Lucille Hegamin

As Macon entered the 1920s, the city's music scene became more complex. Touring troupes still passed through the region, and locals continued to perform, but two significant technological advances helped redefine the nature of entertainment in Middle Georgia, as well as the rest of the world. The first involved the ability to create, preserve, and commercialize recorded sound, and the second was the invention of the radio as a means of bringing live and recorded music to the public. As in the rest of the country, these innovations dramatically affected Macon's musical culture. The public could now hear music composed and performed in distant locations by artists they would probably never see in person, as could Macon's musicians, who were no longer isolated in the way they had been before. In the end, recorded music and the radio would have a great influence on artists and audiences alike, bringing the outside world to Macon for all to experience.

Thomas Edison began developing recording technology in the 1870s, and by the turn of the twentieth century, he and others had advanced it to the point where phonographs were coming into practical use. With regard to music, the phonograph was a transformative instrument in that it had the power to make musicians immortal. It allowed their music to be widely heard contemporaneously, but it also passed that music on to future generations. Before the invention of the phonograph, an audience could listen to a performance and, if it was good, the experience might linger for a while until the memory of it eventually faded. The echo of any performance did not last long. The music went out into the air and then dissipated in much the same way that a morning fog evaporates in the sunlight. The audience was left always wanting to hear a good performer again, and the phonograph allowed these artists to give millions of performances without physically playing a musical instrument or singing a single note. Recordings brought to life the performer to a much greater degree than a piece of formalized sheet music, which at the time was also an effective vehicle for preserving tunes. With a record, listeners could hear an artist's work as many times as they liked. They could memorize the words and the tonal qualities and inflections of the voice that set the artist's work apart, and they could hear the essence of the music's message over and over again. In short, they could take the music's message to heart.

As early as 1905, the F. A. Guttenberger Company was selling "talking machines" in Macon, and other music vendors soon followed suit. For a while, it was also fashionable for music stores to sponsor "Victrola Concerts," during which locals would gather and listen to recorded pieces as they enjoyed refreshments. By the end of the First World War, phonographs were becoming more affordable, and more people had them in their homes. The record business had become an industry, and record companies were in the process of classifying different styles of music—classical, popular, dance, instrumental, etc.—to make it easier for consumers to find the music that they preferred. In Macon in 1919, one such store, H. H. Sapp and Company on Cherry Street, advertised records ranging from dance music, such as "Texas Fox Trot" and the "Jack O' Lantern," to "operatic and standard vocals," such as "La Boheme" and "The Last Rose of Summer." "Nothing is more up to date than the VICTROLA," one period ad read, "especially when you can get the latest records, and can sit in your home and listen to the world's artists make music."[1]

As was the case with recorded music, the emergence of commercial radio revolutionized entertainment in America during the Roaring Twenties. The radio miraculously brought the outside world into family living rooms, and it quickly became a primary source of information for millions of Americans. It also revolutionized the music industry by suddenly allowing listeners to hear performances from distant places. Both live performances, and a little later recorded music, were literally at the listener's fingertips, and the entertainment industry as a whole would never be the same. "Radio is only in its infancy," one observer wrote in 1922, "but it is already a very husky and important infant."[2]

Radio in Macon had its roots on the campus of Mercer University. In the fall of 1918, Professor Claude R. Fountain, a PhD graduate of Columbia University, came to Mercer to teach in the physics department. Fountain had been interested in radio technology for some time, and in the early 1920s he led the charge for Mercer to obtain a commercial radio license. The school's student newspaper, *The Mercer Cluster*, was fully behind the effort, stating that radio transmission "has been introduced over the country with amazing rapidity, and the institution or city that is without one in the next twelve months will be old fashioned indeed." Fountain and fellow physics professor Josiah Crudup assembled and installed the necessary equipment, and Fountain began experimental broadcasts in the summer of 1921. In November of the following year, the US Department of Commerce—the Federal Communication Commission (FCC) did not yet exist—issued a license for the Mercer station under the call letters WMAZ (Watch Mercer Achieve Zenith).[3]

WMAZ broadcast sporadically during its first few years of existence, with reports stating that the station's signal sometimes carried as far as two hundred miles. While early programming included a loose mix of educational, community, and religious fare, in accordance with the Baptist university's mission, listeners could also hear special musical performances featuring locals. The broadcast facility included an upper room that housed the transmitting equipment and a "musical studio where the programs are received by the microphone and sent to the transmitter to be broadcast as electrical waves." Among the first music broadcast by WMAZ was a student chapel service that included a group of "gleeful singers" whose unusual rendition of the "Star-Spangled Banner" was performed entirely in Latin. The Lanier High School Band received airtime, and the station also broadcast an assorted mix of student recitals and fraternity music programs. Talented amateurs from Macon not associated with the university occasionally appeared alone or in small groups. Piano and guitar players were popular, as were quartets. In 1925, the station broadcast a harmonica competition featuring contestants from around the region. While most of the players and singers were white, local African American barber Alvin L. Glasco, a talented tenor whose performances in African American church and community events were always well received, sometimes appeared.[4]

Unable to afford the maintenance and equipment costs over the long term, Mercer gave up control of the station to private interests in 1927. Broadcasts became more structured and somewhat more sophisticated. Local performers continued to appear, but in 1930 the Macon station joined with several other regional broadcasters to carry common fifteen-minute and half-hour evening music programs "especially designed to appeal to southern audiences." Foremost Dairy Products and Dr. Pepper sponsored shows, which regularly featured "a selection of folk songs and modern dance music [and] also different famous southern college songs and orchestras." Macon radio crossed a major threshold in 1937 when WMAZ joined the national Columbia Broadcasting System (CBS) network. This led to regularly scheduled programming from all over the country being broadcast through the station. As big band and swing music became more popular, Macon listeners were able to hear music from bandleaders such as Anson Weeks, Ted Fiorito, Harry Owens, and Artie Shaw. These broadcasts represented an eclectic addition to the city's already rich musical environment.[5]

Music labeled as "blues" began circulating widely in the United States prior to the First World War, creating a "blues craze" during which sheet music labeled as such became very popular. Though called blues, the music was more jazz-based than the raw, country blues played by itinerate bluesmen in juke joints across the South. Composer and musician William Christopher "W. C." Handy was dubbed "the Father of the Blues," although he consistently maintained that he did not invent the genre. Some of the more polished music that he called blues was based to a great degree on the earthy, primitive music he had heard as a touring musician in the rural South. Part of what Handy and other innovators did was take this existing body of work and create a more standardized musical form that could be labeled and sold commercially. Handy's first of many big hits was "The Memphis Blues" (1912), followed by "St. Louis Blues" (1914), which became his most famous composition. Publishers producing sheet music soon noticed that music with the name "blues" in the title sold well, so it was added to as many titles as possible by other artists. While many African Americans bought these records, they were distributed mainly to white consumers, with major record companies holding fast to the belief that most whites, but few blacks, had enough disposable income to buy phonographs or records.[6]

These opinions shifted in 1920 when Mamie Smith, a veteran vaudeville performer, recorded "Crazy Blues." Some call it the first blues record, although, like Handy's music, it had more of a jazz feel. While aficionados and scholars argue over whether or not recorded blues began with Smith, there is little doubt that "Crazy Blues" helped transform the music industry. It sold around seventy-five thousand copies in its first month of release, and was the first big hit by a black artist that sold well in the African American community. These sales figures caught the attention of record company executives, who quickly made plans to exploit what they considered a raw, untapped market. Recordings by black artists—called "race records" in the industry—were soon produced and marketed to African Americans in the South and elsewhere. Hoping to emulate Smith's success, many labels promoted female performers, and among the artists who made "the first crashing wave of race recordings" after "Crazy Blues" was a talented singer from Macon.[7]

Lucille Hegamin was born in Macon as Lucille Nelson on November 29, 1894. Like many performers who made "sinful" jazz and blues recordings as adults, she grew up singing in church. From an early age, she was a versatile performer who took part in local theatrical shows in the black community. "I was what they called a natural singer who never had any formal training," she once told an interviewer. "I sang many of the popular ragtime tunes and ballads of the day." Most sources say that as a teenager she joined the Freeman-Harper-Muse stock company, an African American touring troupe that passed through Macon, eventually ending up in Chicago, where her solo career began around 1915. At the time, Chicago offered safe haven for scores of talented African American singers and musicians moving out of the Southern states, and the city's south-side nightclubs became ground zero for an emerging jazz and blues scene that would have a dramatic and lasting effect on American popular music. Billed as the "Georgia Peach," Lucille worked constantly and became a mainstay at the city's most popular clubs, including the Mineral Café, the Deluxe, the Elite #2, the Panama Café, and Bill Sneeze's Forest Inn. She also worked with many notable accompanists, including Tony Jackson and Jelly Roll Morton. "These were good years for me," she recalled. "I was an exclusive cabaret singer who sang all the popular songs.... I did more to make [the song] 'St. Louis Blues' famous in Chicago than anyone else. I worked with the best entertainers and musicians."[8]

While in Chicago, she married pianist Bill Hegamin, and in 1918 the couple moved to Los Angeles, where the early motion picture industry had created a West Coast entertainment mecca. Mingling with other performers, they eventually formed a band called the Spikes-Hegamin Orchestra that featured Lucille as vocalist, with Bill Hegamin on piano, John Spikes and Paul Howard on saxophone, and Harry Massangale on trombone. All the men were seasoned jazz players. The group was booked into some of Los Angeles's best nightclubs and also toured California and as far north as Seattle, Washington. "My biggest hits were 'Corrina,' 'Beale Street Blues' and 'Tishomingo Blues,'" she said. "The blues craze was really upon us and I had to sing plenty of blues." After only a year, the Hegamins went back east to New York, where the Harlem Renaissance was flowering and recording opportunities for African American artists were presenting themselves.[9]

As she had done in Chicago, Hegamin worked constantly in clubs, and a series of engagements at the trendy Manhattan Casino established her as one of New York's most formidable voices. "There were no mikes in those days," she later said, "and the Manhattan Casino was a pretty hard place to be heard unless you could wail. I certainly could in those days." She was also in the right place at the right time to be among the first African American "blues queens" who began recording during the period. It was an exclusive group that included Mamie Smith, Bessie Smith, Gertrude "Ma" Rainey, and Victoria Spivey, among others. Local pianist Lukie Johnson recommended Hegamin to Arto Records, a New Jersey company that had a studio in New York, and she recorded her first single, "Jazz Me Blues," in November of 1920, just months after Mamie Smith's "Crazy Blues" had help establish the blues craze. More recordings followed, including the 1921 release "Arkansas Blues," a bona fide hit that made Hegamin's reputation as one of the leading female jazz and blues performers of the era. She recorded briefly with Black Swan Records and eventually moved to the Cameo Record Company, another independent, Manhattan-based label that specialized in jazz and blues dance music. Billed as the "Cameo Girl," Hegamin recorded dozens of sides for the label during the 1920s, including "He May Be Your Man, But He Comes to See Me Sometimes," her signature song, and one of the most popular blues numbers of the period. "Hegamin has the reputation of being the greatest phonograph star yet produced by her race," one African American reviewer wrote at the time, "and her surprisingly artistic interpretations of the blues and other folk songs, combined with her very pleasing personality, make her a prime favorite."[10]

With her husband, Bill, Hegamin put together an eight-piece band they named the Blue Flame Syncopators and began a tour of East Coast cities, receiving rave reviews. "No dance orchestra gets greater enjoyment out of its work than Lucille Hegamin's Blue Flame Syncopators," one Pennsylvania reporter stated. "All lovers of dancing are urged not to miss this occasion, and as a matter of fact, those who do not dance will derive more enjoyment from this attraction than from any of the so-called big shows." Still the "Georgia Peach," she was also billed from time to time as the "Chicago Cyclone" and "Blues Singer Supreme." After touring for several months, Hegamin returned to New York and settled in briefly as the featured singer at Jack Golberg's Shuffle Inn in Harlem. Not long afterwards, she joined the touring cast of *Shuffle Along*, the successful African American musical revue written by Noble Sissle and Hubie Blake.[11]

After Hegamin's split from her husband in 1923, she worked primarily as a solo performer, most frequently accompanied by pianist J. Cyril Fullerton. She also put together a fast-paced but short-lived vaudeville revue that she called her "Jazz Jubilee" with veteran song-and-dance man "Broadway Jimmy" Parker. She had a busy recording schedule, producing a string of brisk sellers, including "Beale Street Mama," "Rampart Street Blues," "Bleeding Hearted Blues," "Dinah," "No Man's Mama," and "Reckless Daddy." Hegamin sang live on New York radio station WHN, broadcasting from the Cotton Club, where Andy Preer and the Cotton Club Syncopators provided musical backing. Through the rest of the decade, she was an in-demand performer, working frequently with other prominent artists, arrangers, and bandleaders and touring with various musical theater troupes.[12]

As the blues craze faded with the onset of the Great Depression, Hegamin's career declined. She recorded two sides for Okeh Records in 1932, and two years later, the once sought-after blues queen quit show business and became a registered nurse. After living quietly for years, she made a brief return to the music industry in the early 1960s with a few public appearances and recordings. She died in New York on March 1, 1970. "From a rising star in Macon, Georgia, her birthplace," one of

Hegamin's friends eulogized at the time of her passing, "to her final resting place, more than seventy years have passed in between which Lucille Hegamin has contributed herself to her community and to song. Her history will always be with us. Thanks to the medium of the phonograph record, her voice will be perpetuated for all time."[13]

Lucille Hegamin was not the only blues diva hailing from Macon during the 1920s. Like Hegamin, Lula Whidby was a teenager when she left the city to pursue a singing career. Along with her older sister Essie, Lula also joined the Freeman-Harper-Muse stock company at the same time as Hegamin. In 1912, the three performers were part of the cast of a musical titled "Stranded in Africa," playing at the Globe Theater, the famous African American vaudeville house in Jacksonville, Florida. Essie Whidby later married, left show business, and settled in Atlanta, but Lula continued touring with different troupes. By 1915, she had made it to New York, where she was part of Irwin C. Miller and His Mr. Ragtime Company, hailed by reviewers as "the best, biggest, brightest colored act seen in New York in a long time." Two years later, she toured with the Bruce Jazz Stock Company as one of the group's "Creole Beauties." "The Jazz band craze is now on," one observer wrote after an October, 1917, show in Indianapolis, "and the Bruce Jazz Company is presenting Jazz all the way.... Lula Whidby is a regular joy spot.... She sings 'Stepping on a Puppy's Tail' with fine support by the company."[14]

In 1920, Whidby was part of a touring musical led by actor and producer Quintard Miller titled "Broadway Gossips," and the next year she sang and danced in his production of "Darktown Scandals, 1921." She stayed with Miller for almost two years, performing on a circuit that included venues in New York, Philadelphia, Baltimore, and Chicago, all of which were run by the black-owned American Amusement Company. During the period, she also made two recordings for Black Swan Records, "Strut Miss Lizzie" and "Home Again Blues." In 1922, Miller put together a show called *The Creole Follies Revue*, a transparent attempt to copy *Shuffle Along*, in hopes of matching that landmark musical in popularity. Whidby was one of the featured performers in the show, which included "vaudeville numbers, with several new songs and dances by a large and snappy chorus." Though not as successful as *Shuffle Along*, Miller's production had a two-year run. On July 3, 1925, Whidby was on the program at a notable show for whites only in Atlanta at the Eighty-One Theater on Decatur Street. Headlined by blues queen Bessie Smith and a comedy act billed as Butterbean and Susie, the event was a "Midnight Frolic" designed to draw late-night patrons who had already attended other events in the city but were not quite ready to retire. According to one report, the show lasted "into the wee wee hours," and "the house was filled very nearly to capacity, largely with people who had attended other theaters earlier in the evening."[15]

Sadly, Lula Whidby's career was cut short, and she never achieved the same level of national notice as her fellow Maconite, Lucille Hegamin. Whidby continued touring but began having health problems in 1926. How this affected her ability to make a living is unclear, but after a show at the Hippodrome Theater in Virginia, she fell critically ill. She died on August 4, 1926, of what the doctor who signed her death certificate labeled as complications from peritonitis. Mainstream white media took little notice of her passing, but the Baltimore *Afro-American*, a prominent African American newspaper, marked the occasion by complimenting Whidby as a "prominent actress who had worked up a host of admirers with her hard work to put over the top everything in which she appeared."[16]

As blues was evolving as a quintessential American art form, so was country music, called "hillbilly" during the early years of its commercialization. This music descended in large part from the Anglo-Celtic ballads brought to America by immigrants from the British Isles. Most of these ballads were simple songs with simple melodies that were influenced over the years by a variety of other sources, particularly the music of African Americans. Most of the early Anglo-Celtic music was not written down, but came to colonial America stored in the hearts and minds of the immigrants. The songs represented an oral tradition that evolved over time, and the tunes that survived to become widely disseminated usually told a good story that reflected the environment in which the immigrants lived. As time and generations passed, many of the melodies remained the same, with new verses and words added that were more American in character.[17]

Of course, the story of country music's development in the United States was much more complicated than immigrants from the British Isles simply coming to America, bringing their music with them, and having their descendants alter the music over time to fit American sensibilities. Once in America, any music brought in from the outside by immigrants underwent a transformation due to the nature of the colonial population. American pioneers moved west very quickly, where they mingled with immigrants of different cultural origins. As the English, Irish, or Welsh immigrants moved west across the southern frontier, they came in contact with a variety of different cultural groups, such as Germans immigrants in Virginia; backcountry Native Americans all along the frontier; Spanish, French, and multi-heritage elements in the Mississippi Valley; and especially African Americans throughout the South. The result was music with an Anglo-Celtic foundation, influenced by other ethnic and racial strands of culture. Unlike later stereotypes of the genre, country music was never completely pure. That is to say, it was never completely Anglo-Celtic in origin and never completely "white."[18]

While the roots of country music are tangled in the old ballads, the ballad form of song also offered a parallel between the separate country and blues traditions. Both genres developed as forms of oral tradition in cultures with a strong reverence for the spoken word. Many Southerners, black and white, had a preference for hearing stories about real events, as well as tall tales, through a musical delivery rather than by reading a book. This was obviously the case for the many eighteenth- and nineteenth-century Southerners of both races who were illiterate. While the ballad style is more generally associated with white country music, blues ballads were not uncommon in the African American community, though they had their own special traits. Likewise, many early country music songs seemed to be constructed within standard blues frameworks.[19]

An influential but often overlooked figure in the history of country music was Emmett Miller, who grew up in Macon. Miller was an unusual artist who peaked for only a few years before passing into obscurity, yet his influence on popular music, and particularly early country music, was significant. Miller was born on February 2, 1900, the son of a cotton-mill laborer who later worked for the fire department. Little is known about Miller's early life, although in his teens he worked for a time in Macon as a mechanic and truck driver. Drawn to minstrelsy, he gave local performances billed as "Macon's Amateur Blackface Comedian." According to contemporary newspaper accounts, Dan Fitch, the leader of a traveling minstrel troupe, discovered Miller in Macon in the autumn of 1920. Miller traveled with Fitch and was an immediate hit on the touring circuit. One reporter praised his blackface performances, stating that "veteran vaudeville and theatrical men bespeak a brilliant career before the footlights for Emmett Miller, the twenty one year old comedian who scored such a big hit with Dan Fitch's minstrels.... Though he has been on the stage for less than five months, [he] has already made a name for himself on the southern circuit." Some advertisements described Miller as "a blues singing fool and harmony hound."[20]

Miller was a typical blackface minstrel performer, cracking jokes and using an exaggerated "negro dialect" when speaking, but it was his singing style that set him apart. He had what some described favorably as a "clarinet voice," and he peppered his vocals with a "crying falsetto" or "falsetto yodel" that was quick to catch the listener's attention. He eventually moved to New York City, where he worked regularly in the city's vaudeville theaters. While in New York, Miller visited the Okeh recording studio and cut his first sides, "Any Time," and "The Pickaninny's Paradise," both of which he regularly performed as part of his stage act.[21]

Not long afterwards, Miller moved to Asheville, North Carolina, and recorded several more songs for Okeh executive Ralph Peer. Peer later made country music history when he produced the first recordings of Jimmie Rodgers, dubbed by all who came after him as "the Father of Country Music." Rodgers famously used a "blue yodel" as a vocal device to punctuate many of his songs, and it became a trademark that a host of younger country performers such as Ernest Tubb and Gene Autry tried to copy. Many believe Emmett Miller's recordings influenced Rodgers to use the yodel as part of his musical presentation, and thus make the case that Miller helped lay the foundation for the development of early country music. Similarly, Bob Wills, another early innovator, lauded as the "Father of Western Swing," was a fan of Miller's work. In 1935, Wills covered Miller's 1928 version of "I Ain't Got Nobody" with the same falsetto breaks in an obvious tribute to the minstrel star. Perhaps Miller's greatest contribution to country music, and popular music in general, were his recordings of "Lovesick Blues." Miller cut different versions of the song, penned by Cliff Friend and Irving Mills, in 1925 and 1928, more than twenty years before the release of Hank Williams's wildly popular cover in 1949. For anyone listening to both the Miller and Williams versions, the influence is obvious. Miller recorded several dozen songs during his career, most backed by a band promoted on record labels as the Georgia Crackers. In reality, the Crackers were session musicians from the North, including Tommy Dorsey, Jimmy Dorsey, Eddie Lang, and Gene Krupa, all of whom would make a name for themselves later on.[22]

Unfortunately for Miller, his fame was fleeting. Popular in the 1920s, his career began a sharp decline as the Great Depression set in. Rather than change with the times, he clung too tightly to vaudeville and continued to perform in blackface long after that controversial entertainment genre was dated. He made his last recording in 1936, and toured through the 1940s, ending up primarily as a part-time nightclub performer. In 1951, he appeared in a low-budget film, *Yes Sir, Mr. Bones*, featuring other aging entertainers from the minstrel era. Returning to Macon, Miller eventually moved in with his sister on Brownley Drive. His health took a turn for the worse, and he passed away with little fanfare at a local hospital on March 29, 1962, the occupation listed on his death certificate reading simply "entertainer."[23]

Though not as influential as Emmett Miller, an energetic trio of country music players from Bibb County generated a local following and recorded six songs for Okeh Records during the 1920s. The South Georgia Highballers consisted of fiddler Melgie Ward (b. 1882), guitarist Vander Everidge (b. 1886), and Vander's nephew, Albert Everidge (b. 1899). Albert made the group particularly memorable because one of his instruments of choice was the musical saw. While its origins are up for debate, the early use of a handsaw and bow as an instrument in the United States is usually associated with the Ozark or Appalachian mountain regions. It evolved into a novel form of musical presentation that by the early twentieth century was popular in vaudeville circles. Players such as Albert Everidge produced sound from the saw by "holding the handle between the knees and bending the blade while bowing along the flat edge." The result was a sometimes mesmerizing, high-pitched ethereal wail, and many referred to the process as "making the saw sing."[24]

By the time they made their first recording, the South Georgia Highballers had been active for some time in different configurations. The two older men, Ward and Vander Everidge, had performed for a time in a group called the "Cotton Pickers," and all three men were a conspicuous presence at the "all-southern fiddlers convention" held in Atlanta in March of 1927, where Albert Everidge was also reported as being a "champion buck and wing dancer." The following October, Atlanta hosted the Southeastern Fair, which featured yet another gathering of regional fiddlers and other musicians. Taking advantage of the concentration of talent, Okeh sent representatives to Atlanta to record local acts. The South Georgia Highballers recorded six songs on October 5, 1927, including traditional folk tunes "Ida Red," "Sallie Goodwin," and "Green River Train"; an old minstrel number titled "Mister Johnson Turn Me Loose";

and two instrumentals, "Blue Grass Twist" and "Bibb County Grind." Ward handled most of the vocals, but all three men contributed playful banter to the recording that punctuated parts of the musical presentation. "Ol' Vander can win a woman's heart and make a bulldog jump a fence," one of Everidge's bandmates commented during "Macon County Grind" in response to the guitarist's nimble finger-picking. "That's the way they play it in Macon, Georgia."[25]

Okeh released four of the Highballers' songs—"Ida Red" and "Old Sallie Goodwin" were never issued—but the recording session marked the high-water mark for the band. While locally popular as a stage act that performed "a full opus of foot-tapping numbers," they never rose to national prominence, and the band eventually drifted apart as the members sought steadier incomes. Vander Everidge died in 1938 after being hit by car, and Melgie Ward passed away in 1949. Albert, the last surviving member of the group, died in 1955. All three men are buried in Macon.[26]

In the early decades of the twentieth century, the Georgia Academy for the Blind continued to provide musical instruction to visually impaired children in hopes of preparing at least some of them for careers as musicians. A 1908 assessment of the academy's curriculum stated, "In the musical department, careful instruction is given in the art of playing the piano, organ, guitar and violin, and singing." The institution was segregated, with the main campus for whites spread over twenty acres "in Macon's charming suburb, Vineville," and a less imposing facility for African Americans located in the city on Madison Street. While the school provided classical instruction, two pupils from the first quarter of the century became influential folk musicians in the country and blues genres.[27]

George Riley Puckett was born on May 7, 1894, just north of Atlanta and lost most of his sight as an infant. His father died when he was a child, and in 1901 his mother enrolled him in the Georgia Academy for the Blind in Macon, where he remained a pupil for about five years. At the school, Puckett learned to read Braille and was exposed to the guitar and banjo. He left the academy at age twelve and fell on hard times, although he knew that he wanted to make a living as a musician. He matriculated to Atlanta, and in October of 1915 wrote a desperate letter to the *Atlanta Constitution* begging for winter clothing and employment. "The afflicted boy is Riley Puckett of 694 Chestnut Street," the newspaper reported. "He only wants a chance, he says, to make a living. At present he is in need of clothing for the winter.... He says he is a musician, and if he had the help could make his living by his profession." Puckett persevered, struggling as a street musician and playing at social occasions until 1922, when he made his radio debut on WSB in Atlanta. Performing with other musicians, he developed a significant following that eventually led to a trip to New York and a recording session with Columbia Records. Among his first recordings were "Steamboat Bill" and a cover version of Fiddlin' John Carson's "The Little Old Log Cabin." He continued recording with Columbia through the 1920s, as both a solo artist and as a member of bands, most notably Gid Tanner's famous Skillet Lickers. From 1934 to 1941, he recorded more well-received sides, toured with his own tent show, and played on radio stations in Georgia, Tennessee, Kentucky, and West Virginia. Among his last recordings were "How Come You Do Me Like You Do," "Railroad Blues," and "Peach Picking Time in Georgia." One of the most popular "hillbilly" artists of his era, he continued performing until his death on July 14, 1946, in East Point, Georgia. Forty years later, he was inducted posthumously into the Georgia Music Hall of Fame.[28]

Another pupil at Macon's Academy for the Blind was William Samuel McTier, known professionally to generations of blues fans as Blind Willie McTell. McTell was born in Thomson, Georgia, on May 5, 1898, and was blind either from birth or an early age. He learned guitar as a teenager and moved with his family to Statesboro, Georgia. There, his talent and personality apparently impressed an anonymous benefactor who provided the funds for McTell to attend the Georgia Academy for the Blind. By the time he got to Macon in 1922, he was proficient on the guitar and was already making money playing on the streets, but he was also willing to absorb the formal musical training that the academy offered. According to one contemporary, McTell played by ear but "after he went to Macon to blind school, he was playing by notes. It was different, you know, [he] learned a different music there." McTell stayed in Macon for approximately three years before striking out to continue his education elsewhere. He once told an interviewer that he left Macon in 1925 and went first to New York "and went to a little independent blind school out there. And then I went with a friend of mine to Michigan, and studied over there, learning to read the Braille."[29]

McTell traveled extensively with medicine shows and carnivals and performed a good bit in Atlanta at private parties and on the streets. His abilities, particularly on the twelve-string guitar, impressed audiences as well as other musicians. In 1927 and 1928, he made his first recordings for the Victor Recording Company, including "Stole Rider Blues," "Writing Paper Blues," and "Statesboro Blues," which would become one of his most famous compositions. McTell was a commercially viable performer throughout the 1930s, recording dozens of songs for various labels, and he continued to tour, but by the 1950s his health had taken a turn for the worse. After suffering a stroke in Milledgeville, Georgia, he died on August 19, 1959. McTell's recordings later influenced a wave of younger performers during the 1960s and beyond, from blues titan Taj Mahal to rock icon Bob Dylan. In 1971, in what some still see as a moment of divine musical providence, "Statesboro Blues" became the first track on the Macon-based Allman Brothers Band's landmark live album *At Fillmore East*.[30]

The grandson of Irish immigrants, pianist and Macon resident Emory O'Hara had a brief music career in the 1920s, more as a songwriter that a performer. He was born in Bibb County on April 2, 1893, to a father who worked in Macon as a machinist, a bicycle dealer, a grocer, and, for a time, a billiard-parlor owner. As a teenager, O'Hara found quiet employment as a clerk in a clothing store, but he also received some local acclaim for writing poems and simple songs that appeared in print in the newspaper. He had his first song published in 1916, a patriotic number titled "You'll Have to Take Your Hat Off to the Red, White, and Blue." Striking out on his own, he left Macon the next year and settled in Kansas City, Missouri, where he found temporary work in a steel factory. Had the First World War not broken out, he may have remained there for the rest of his life, but instead, the war became a catalyst in his pursuit of a songwriting career. Drafted in 1918, he went to France, where he served until the demobilization of US forces the following year. There he met another musically inclined soldier, Wendell Hall, who later became a recording and radio personality. "I met Wendell Hall in France during the war," O'Hara later recalled. "He was a bugler in France, and I was in the service, too. One night I was sitting down at the 'Y' playing piano. Hall came in and asked me what it was that I was playing. I told him what the piece was, and he said he was interested in it. He told me that he was from Chicago, and that if I ever came there to look him up."[31]

Once out of the service, O'Hara settled briefly in Dayton, Ohio, and finally made it to Chicago around 1922, where he took Hall up on his offer, and the two men wrote several songs together that Hall ended up recording. Among the compositions were "Lighthouse Blues," "Blue

Island Blues," "Struttin' Hound Blues," and "Hoo Doo Blues." O'Hara had just over a dozen songs published and also worked briefly with composers Harry Geise and Gene Austin. Despite having some success as a songwriter, O'Hara apparently could not make ends meet and reenlisted in the military in late 1923. Stationed at Chanute Field, about 130 miles south of Chicago, he continued writing songs and organized a band that played local engagements both on and off the base during his spare hours. "Emory O'Hara of Chanute Field has organized a seven-piece orchestra and is now open for engagements," one local newspaper recorded in November of 1923. "Mr. O'Hara is becoming one of our foremost writers of musical hits."[32]

Despite praise from local reporters, O'Hara's career as a songwriter declined after he reentered the military. While some of the artists he worked with, particularly Hall and Austin, went on to have notable careers, O'Hara's stalled. After his second stint in the service, he moved briefly to New York but was unable to get more songs published, and by 1929 he was in Jacksonville, Florida, where much of his family had relocated. There he found work as a typist. In declining health during the 1930s due to a lung ailment, he was admitted in 1933 to the US National Home for Disabled Soldiers in Ohio, and by 1940 he was in a veterans' hospital in Gulfport, Mississippi. He died there on February 7, 1943, and was buried with fellow veterans in the National Cemetery in Mobile, Alabama.[33]

More cultural progress came to Macon in the 1920s in the form of a new municipal auditorium. The need for a new facility had been apparent for years, but city funding had not been available, at least to the extent needed to construct a truly significant building. After a number of starts and stops, construction got under way in earnest in 1924 on the corner of First and Cherry streets downtown. Architects for the project were New Yorker Edgarton Swartwout and a local firm, Dennis and Dennis. Basically square, the new building measured 175 feet on each side and 80 feet high and was built "in a style that can best be described as simplified new classical Greek revival." On top was a copper-covered dome measuring more than 150 feet in diameter. While the structure included a number of multipurpose rooms and enclosures, the centerpiece was the "Great Hall," which had an original seating capacity of around four thousand. The auditorium's interior was finished in Georgia marble and elegantly decorated with a large mural depicting "the salient features of Georgia's history," from Hernando de Soto's sixteenth-century visit through the First World War. The balcony featured "a relief design of festoons of peaches," and heavy decorative draperies hung throughout the building. Although some newspapers at the time referred to the new entertainment venue as "Macon's new million-dollar auditorium," the entire cost of the project was between five and six hundred thousand dollars.[34]

Macon's new auditorium opened to the public on November 23, 1925, with a highly anticipated concert by organist Henry F. Siebert. The event was meant to highlight not only the opening of the building, but also the large stage pipe organ that was housed within it. The organ was built at the M. P. Moller factory in Hagerstown, Maryland, and was advertised in Macon as "one of the largest in the country." Siebert, a New York native, was a well-known musician both in the United States and overseas who toured extensively and performed on radio. He did not disappoint the packed house on opening night, entertaining the crowd with selections from Mendelssohn, Schubert, Stephen Foster, Sibelius, and others. In the future, the new auditorium would host musical events of all types and for every occasion, establishing it as an iconic city structure.[35]

One of the big events held in the new auditorium not long before the onset of the Great Depression was a week of opera performances in January of 1928. Sponsored by the Grand Opera Association of Macon, a local group put together to guarantee the expenses of visiting entertainers, the San Carlos Grand Opera Company from New York came to town for a "gala week of grand opera." The large troupe included dozens of actors and musicians and featured noted singers Clara Jacobo and Myrna Sharlow. They gave eight performances to enthusiastic crowds that included many out-of-town patrons. On January 15, one newspaper stated that "a special train from Milledgeville tonight brought 1,000 young women from the Georgia State College for Women. Another special train was operated from Bessie Tift College in Forsyth." In Atlanta, the railroads advertised special rates "as a matter of accommodation and economy for the hundreds of music lovers who are planning to visit Macon for the operatic festival." The final night of the event featured a presentation of *Il Trovatore* in front of a packed house that included more than a hundred patrons who had purchase standing-room-only tickets.[36] The auditorium hosted other opera and classical performances through the end of the 1920s, but with the onset of the Great Depression, these types of events were far less frequent.

Macon had a direct connection with the San Carlos Grand Opera Company that spanned several years prior to the troupe coming to town. Fredonia Frazer, a local singer, had been a member of the company during the early 1920s. Frazer, a talented soprano, was the daughter of prominent doctor and businessman E. Powell Frazer, and the granddaughter of a former state legislator. The family traveled extensively, and her politically connected father served a brief stint in the United States diplomatic corps as a representative to Switzerland. From the age of four, it was apparent that Fredonia had a great deal of talent, and she was soon singing at neighborhood events. She studied voice with private instructors and eventually at Hollins College in Virginia. After graduation, she returned briefly to Macon, where she appeared locally, singing popular tunes at social events and recitals. In August of 1922, the twenty-one-year-old appeared on radio station WSB in Atlanta, singing "a group of entrancing melodies, familiar to everybody," including "Just A-Wearying for You," "Old Fashioned Garden," "Sunrise and You," and "One Fleeting Hour." The *Atlanta Constitution* gave Frazer's performance a good review, stating that "she backs up singularly rare natural talents with an earnestness of purpose and delicacy of expression that argue a shining future for her as an American songbird."[37]

Not long after her triumphant radio appearance, Frazer left for New York to "make a serious study of opera...having decided to dedicate her talents to the operatic instead of the [popular] concert stage." She studied with prominent vocal coach Estelle Liebling and began auditioning. In 1923, she sang for Fortune Gallo, the Italian impresario who owned the San Carlos Grand Opera Company, and won a small role, in part because of her "personality and vivacity." Well received in New York, she became a featured performer and toured with the company for almost three years. While she achieved significant success as a singer, appearing in more than a dozen different roles in cities across the country, the career of "Georgia's greatest operatic songbird" was short-lived. In 1926, she married Robert Fagar Black, a successful trucking-company executive, and gave up touring to begin a family. The couple eventually settled in Cleveland, Ohio, where Frazer died in 1986.[38]

The years following the First World War were good ones for Charles Collier. Under his leadership, "Silas Green from New Orleans"—sometimes referred to simply as "the Silas Green Show"—flourished as one of the most prominent African American touring companies of the period.

By 1939, the show included approximately eighty performers and dozens of support personnel. The African American press around the country gave Collier full credit as a promoter, sometimes referring to the production as "The Greatest Negro Show on Earth" and comparing Collier's administrative and showmanship skills to those of P. T. Barnum. "Under the sagacious leadership of Collier," the *Pittsburgh Courier* noted, "the Silas Green Show has grown to become what it is today—the best and biggest of its kind.... The show travels in its own Pullman railroad car, the only Negro institution in the world in that respect. It also owns busses and one of the biggest tents ever to house an exhibit of any kind."

While his cast and crew were African Americans, Collier employed a handful of whites whose job it was to deal with white authorities as the group toured. In every city, the show needed permits from officials who were usually wary of black strangers in their community, especially traveling performers. Whites connected to the group also helped provide security during performances. Shows drew mixed crowds of whites and blacks, who were not allowed to sit with each other, and whites in the entourage were in a better position to deal with any white patrons in case of trouble. According to one African American reporter, "It still saves considerable time and red tape in the South if you have a white man contact authorities for permits and to supervise relations with white patrons. The huge tent in which the nightly performance is given is divided in two— strait down the middle—by a rope. Whites sit on one side and Negroes on the other."[39]

After Collier took over sole ownership of the Silas Green Show, he ran it from an office in Macon. The group had a ten-month touring schedule, usually taking February and March off, but the city's black community embraced the enterprise. Collier liked to start each season with a performance in Macon, and he scheduled special performances to raise funds for local African American schools and other charitable causes. "Of course Silas Green needs no introduction to a Macon audience," a reporter for the "colored" section of the *Telegraph* wrote, shortly before a 1940 performance at the auditorium, "for the sole owner and manager, Charles Collier, was born in this city and still maintains his residence and office here.... Macon has always shown her loyalty to this organization and well she may have done so, because it represents the highest and only enduring Negro attainment of this kind on a big scale." A 1940 show was typical and included a twenty-piece orchestra, actors, acrobats, blues and jazz singers, tap dancers, more than a dozen showgirls in lavish costumes, three come-dians, and a clown in full makeup.[40]

Collier led the Silas Green show until his death in 1942 at the age of sixty-one from complications related to typhoid fever. By that time, he had established himself as one of the best-known African American show-men in the country. His funeral was held in Macon, and his obituary in *Billboard* magazine stated that the service was "marked by impressive rights, with show folk from all over the South in attendance." According to local newspapers, the family also received "telegrams and messages from almost every avenue of the business, show, theatrical and promotional cir-cles, interspersed with numerous letters from friends." Charles Collier was buried at Fort Hill cemetery.[41]

The proliferation of affordable radios and the growing number of radio stations in the United States during the 1920s and 1930s helped propel a Macon singing trio to national acclaim. Known professionally as the Pickens Sisters, Jane, Helen, and Patti Pickens were born in Bibb County with a solid musical pedigree. A fourth sister, Grace, also per-formed with the group during the early days and later became her sisters' manager. The daughters of Monte and Patti Pickens of Macon, the girls' grandfather was a gifted violinist and music teacher at Tift College in For-syth, and their mother, a pianist, was named for the popular Italian prima donna Adelina Patti. From an early age, their parents encouraged the girls' musical talents. As children, they sang regularly at family occasions, and in their teens at local events. "We used to sing everywhere, and it didn't take much coaxing," one of the sisters later recalled. "Folks were always calling on us at parties, socials, benefits, and so on. We also sang in the church choir, of course." One of the sisters' first public performances was at a variety show sponsored by the Kennesaw, Georgia, chapter of the United Daughters of the Confederacy in 1921. Although they were white, traditional African American spirituals dominated their early repertoire.[42]

The Pickens Sisters also studied music from an early age, particularly Jane, who went on to have a significant solo career after the act broke up. At the age of fourteen, Jane won a scholarship to attend the Curtis Insti-tute of Music in Philadelphia, where she studied "piano, harmony and counterpoint, eurhythmics, dancing and the languages" and received pri-vate vocal coaching. She later studied in France and returned to the United States to spend four years at the Julliard School of Music in New York. By 1932, her sisters had joined her in the city, and together they auditioned for singing engagements. At the time, sister acts were popular on the radio, and the National Broadcasting Company (NBC) was anxious to sign a good sister act to keep up with their competitors in the marketplace. The network signed the Pickens Sisters after one audition and began promoting them heavily. "One of the reasons NBC built us up," Jane later recalled, "was because CBS had the Boswell Sisters, who were already well established before we came along. They had us on every single night and on commercials around the clock. You could hardly turn the radio on without hearing us." In March of 1932, NBC gave the Pickens Sisters a nightly fifteen-minute national program slot.[43]

With the aid of constant promotion from their network, the trio gained a following that made them one of the more popular harmonizing groups of the 1930s. While Jane, Helen, and Patti Pickens were the primary lineup for the group, fourth sister and manager Grace occasionally filled in when needed. Their radio work increased, as did their number of public appearances. "The Pickens Sisters have had a good deal of publicity written about them from NBC headquarters," one reporter wrote. "After hearing them, you will think as we do, that the publicity does not do them justice. The girls are in a class by themselves." The press usually took note of their Southern roots, often pinning on them nicknames such as "The Georgia Peaches" or "Three Little Maids from Dixie." Signed by Victor, they made more than two dozen recordings for the label between 1932 and 1934, mostly popular or jazz-based numbers. Of the three sisters, Jane had the most technical musical knowledge, and she served as the group's arranger. According to one observer, "She is one of the few women in radio who can write parts for singers and produce effective orchestrations." In addition to radio, concert, and recording work, the group also appeared as a featured act on Broadway and in two films, *Sitting Pretty* (1933) starring Jack Haley and Ginger Rogers, and *Good Luck—Best Wishes* (1934), a comedy short. Despite their success, the Pickens Sisters' career as a trio ended in late 1936. Helen and Patti married and left the group while Jane struck out on her own, joining the cast of the Ziegfeld Follies of 1937.[44]

After the sister act dissolved, Jane Pickens achieved a great deal of success as a solo artist. Ambitious and indefatigable, she was a featured performer at some of New York's trendiest nightspots as she continued her radio work. In 1940, she appeared on Broadway with Ed Wynn in *Boys and Girls Together*, and during the early months of World War II, sang in hospitals for the USO. During the 1940s, she starred on the *American Melody Hour* on CBS Radio and for a time had her own show on NBC, *The Jane Pickens Show*. Touring consistently, she performed in "musical comedies, light operas and night clubs," and in 1949 starred in *Regina*, a musical adaptation of *The Little Foxes*. According to one reporter, "Jane's personal montage shows a series of stops from one end of the country to another. She sang in nightclubs, theaters, musical comedies, and every other place that boasted a microphone." In 1954, she made the transition to television with a short-lived show on ABC. On January 30, 1955, the Pickens Sisters reunited for one performance on a nostalgia-themed episode of Ed Sullivan's *Toast of the Town*. Jane began to withdraw from the entertainment business soon afterward. She married an investment banker, and after that the chairman of Tiffany and Company, spending her later years as a philanthropist and socialite. In 1974, a theater in Newport, Rhode Island, was named in her honor, and she and her sister Patti performed at the dedication. Jane Pickens passed away in 1992 at the age of eighty-four, preceded in death by her sister Helen in 1984. Patti, the last surviving member of the famed radio trio, passed away in 1995, with her obituary reminding readers that "in the 1930s she and her sisters Jane and Helen, were the toast of NBC radio."[45]

Another female singer from Macon received significant, albeit brief, national acclaim during the 1940s as the big band era peaked. Beatrice Carter was born in Tennille, Georgia, on March 12, 1924, but was raised in a Macon orphanage after her parents separated. She attended Lanier Junior High School and Miller High School in Macon, where several of her teachers recognized her talents and encouraged her to pursue a music career. Beginning in the fifth grade, Carter took piano under Mildred Donnan, and later she studied voice with Emily Craft, a gifted local singer. Encouraged by her teachers, Carter performed at civic events in Macon during her teen years and drew a good bit of recognition. She sang at talent shows and weddings, and in 1940 she was chosen to sing on a special program on radio station WSB in Atlanta honoring Bibb County.[46]

Just as it dramatically changed the lives of so many, the Second World War altered Beatrice Carter's fortunes. In 1942, she volunteered at the local USO, where she sang with dance bands for the troops at Camp Wheeler. She toured with several bands on the USO circuit, which led to an invitation for a temporary singing engagement with Al Donahue's band in New Orleans. Her tenure with Donahue's outfit, in turn, led to a whirlwind of activity that took her to Detroit, where she performed on WWJ radio, and then to New York, where she took a job with Greenwood Van's orchestra, one of the city's most popular groups. She also secured a fifteen-minute slot singing on station WSAY in Rochester.[47]

While in New York, Carter caught the attention of Sammy Kaye, one of the brightest stars of the big band era, whose catchy promotional slogan, "Swing and Sway with Sammy Kaye," had helped make him famous. Kaye's band had a national reputation as a live act and was very popular on radio. The bandleader was looking for a female vocalist, and he approached Carter about a job that would give her coast-to-coast exposure. She successfully auditioned at the open-air dance floor on the roof of the Astor Hotel in New York City. After signing her, Kaye insisted Carter change her name to something that read better in advertisements and looked better on a marquee. He chose Betty Barclay, believing that the alliteration rolled well off the tongue. From that point forward, Beatrice Carter, at least professionally, was Betty Barclay, and it was under that name that she performed and recorded. She started singing with the band and was featured on Kaye's "Sunday Serenade" program on the ABC radio network.[48]

Kaye wanted to introduce his new vocalist with a splash, so he commissioned songwriters Milton Drake and Al Hoffman to pen a song with the young singer specifically in mind. Reporters at the time described Barclay as "very small, blond, and with an attractive personality," and while she had a strong voice, there was a youthful innocence in her delivery. The songwriters came up with a quasi-novelty number titled "I'm a Big Girl Now" that lyrically, and with an underlying sexuality, tells a three-minute story of a young woman trying to convince her teenage boyfriend that she no longer wants to be treated like a little girl. It fit Barclay's stage persona perfectly. "We wrote that song to order for Sammy Kaye," Drake later recalled. "He had a new girl singer with his outfit...and wanted something special for her. She had a sweet, innocent kind of personality, and when she sang, she had a cute, syrupy little voice. I knocked my brains out to try to find just the right quality song for her, [and] came up with the idea for 'I'm a Big Girl Now.'"[49]

Barclay began performing the song with Kaye's band in late 1945 and recorded it for RCA. Not long afterwards, it came out as a single and went to the top of the *Billboard* charts, becoming one of the most popular songs in the country in 1946. It gave Barclay national exposure, and Kaye featured her with greater frequency on his radio programs. "Betty Barclay, Sammy Kaye's vocalist, has joined the charmed circle of those who achieved stardom as the result of a single hit," one reviewer wrote soon after the song's release. "[She] now receives star billing with Kaye's swing and swayers." When the band went on the road, newspaper ads sometimes featured Barclay's name just under Kaye's, along with her photograph and the title of her hit song. A January 1947 tour stop in Macon had to be particularly gratifying for Barclay, as the local press took special note of her homecoming. In the days leading up to the show, the *Telegraph* lauded her as "one of the nation's leading feminine songbirds" in a story under the headline "Macon Lassie Who Made Good as Singer to Appear with Kaye's Band." The newspaper also altered local ads for the performance by promoting the singer as "Macon's Own Bea Carter" in addition to using her stage name.[50]

While the success of "I'm a Big Girl Now" seemed to mark the beginning of a long career for Betty Barclay, protracted success never materialized. She recorded several more sides with Kaye, but none did as well as her signature song. In early 1947, she married a Florida businessman and left Kaye's band. Relocating to Miami, she sang in local clubs and recorded four songs as a solo artist, none of which sold well. She and her husband divorced in 1951, and for much of the next decade she tried to keep her solo act afloat with nightclub performances. By 1960, her career as a professional singer had run its course. Barclay stayed in Miami for several years but later remarried and moved around the country before returning to Bibb County, where she passed away in 2000. As a quiet homage to her short but intense music career, her headstone in Evergreen Cemetery in Macon includes the inscription "She's a Big Angel Now."[51]

As the Pickens Sisters and Betty Barclay vocalized during the big band era, another performer with Bibb County roots established a long and successful career for himself as a trumpet player. Emmett Berry was born in Macon on July 23, 1915. He moved with his family to Cleveland, Ohio, in the 1920s and from a young age excelled as a musician. He studied with a classical music teacher but, like many young players of the period, gravitated toward jazz after hearing Louis Armstrong. His initial break as a professional came in 1932 when, as a teenager, he was hired by a band from Toledo misnamed the Chicago Nightingales. The group canvassed Ohio and the surrounding states and performed regularly on WFBE in Cincinnati. The following year, he moved to New York, where he came to the attention of influential bandleader and fellow Georgian Fletcher Henderson. Impressed by the young man's talent, Henderson hired Berry as lead trumpet in his band. The group toured the country and performed on network radio, with Berry establishing a reputation in music circles as a skilled and dependable performer.[52]

Henderson disbanded his group to join Benny Goodman in 1939, but there was no shortage of work for Berry. He played with orchestras led by Horace Henderson (Fletcher Henderson's brother), Earl Hines, Lucky Millinder, and Lionel Hampton, just to name a few, and for a time was a member of the formidable CBS Studio Orchestra in New York led by Raymond Scott. Responding to a 1940 recording of "Ain't Misbehavin'" by Horace Henderson's band, one reviewer wrote, "Horace Henderson's crew are sly and sweet in this grand old favorite. Emmett Berry on trumpet carries the melody but rides on clouds with a riff or two, misbehavin' and loving it." Berry also recorded with other well-known jazz stars of the era, including at least three sessions with Billie Holiday. He sometimes fronted his own bands, including the Emmett Berry Five, with Don Byas, Milt Hinton, Dave Rivera, and J. C. Heard. In 1945, he began a five-year run with Count Basie and later toured the United States and Europe with Sammy Price and Buck Clayton. "I don't think Emmett ever got the credit he was due," Clayton later wrote. "He was one swingin' cat, believe me! I never enjoyed working with someone as much as I did working with Emmett on our tour of England. He used to knock me out every show."[53]

Berry continued touring the country and recording in Los Angeles and New York during the 1950s and 1960s. Along with more than fifty other jazz greats, he appeared in the iconic 1958 Art Kane photograph titled "A Great Day in Harlem." In 1970, poor health forced him into retirement, and he moved back to Cleveland. He died in 1993, leaving behind a wealth of recorded work.

As always, Macon's academic community continued to contribute to the musical well-being of the city by promoting concerts and organizing music clubs, choirs, and orchestras. The Wesleyan Conservatory continued to thrive, and musical activity on the Mercer University campus increased. Founded in 1833, Mercer moved to Macon in 1871 and for the next 135 years would be affiliated with the Georgia Baptist Convention. Following the turn of the century, the university's primary vehicle for musical presentation was the Glee Club. First organized during the 1910–

1911 academic year, the group was very popular and enjoyed sustained success at the university. The organization offered musically inclined students "systematic work in chorus and quartet singing" and from its inception gave "exhibitions in neighboring cities, besides furnishing music at the college entertainments and exercises." In 1910, students organized a small volunteer band that sometimes performed with the Glee Club at public events, and soon a larger orchestra took shape. Beginning in 1918, those so inclined could join the Mandolin Club, which also gave campus and community performances.[54]

The Glee Club's activities expanded significantly during the early 1920s when freshman trombonist Dan H. Davis arrived on campus. Davis had an interesting background. Born in 1899, he grew up in Early County, Georgia, and took up the trombone at the age of nine. As a teenager, he was in demand as a performer around his hometown of Blakely, but in 1916 he left the area and ended up touring the Midwest for a season as a musician with the Miller Brothers Wild West Show. Returning to Georgia, he served during the last months of the First World War as a musician attached to an artillery regiment stationed in France. "The band did its best work in putting new spirit in the men," one veteran later remembered. "According to schedule, when transportation was available, [they] went to each battalion one day a week...and after supper played a concert that always played to overflow houses." The experience helped Davis evolve as a musician and exposed him to music and musicians from other parts of the country.

After his discharge, Davis went back to school and eventually enrolled at Mercer for the 1921–1922 school year. He found a musical home on campus in the Glee Club and took charge of the club's band. In praising the new director, who stood over six feet tall, the campus newspaper stated that "surely no one on the campus has a more commanding appearance for the leader of the Mercer band than this man." By Davis's senior year, he led a ten-piece group considered one of the top college jazz bands in the state, and students paid tribute to Davis by nicknaming the band "Dan Davis's Shufflin' Syncopators" Some also called them the "Dan Davis Collegians." The musicians played regularly at social events and toured Georgia. "The band has been busy at practice almost daily during the past week in preparation for their first road trip," one observer noted in October of 1924. "There now being ten jazz hounds composing the band, this group of collegiate syncopators promises to be the best one yet." Local press reports frequently singled out Davis for his solo performances on the trombone. "Davis shoved that trombone all over Barnesville," one correspondent wrote during the band's tour, "and he was forced to encore before the audience was satisfied." Whether performing with the rest of the Glee Club, or as a stand-alone band, Davis and the group he led always garnered positive reviews.[55]

Davis left the Glee Club band in 1925 when he graduated, though he continued to perform around Macon. For a time, he led a group called Dan Davis and the Pilots that was popular with the college crowds at Mercer and Wesleyan. He married and began a family, which led him to abandon music as a potential career in favor of a regular and more substantial paycheck. Davis managed a music store for a time, and in 1935 began a long career with Sears and Roebuck in Bibb County, where his wife taught kindergarten. The talented trombone player, Wild West performer, and bandleader died on December 16, 1969, and was buried in Macon.[56]

At Wesleyan College, the conservatory continued to attract nationally known talent to the ranks of its faculty, including Joseph Maerz, who began a decades-long association with the school in 1914. Born in Buffalo, New York, on December 23, 1883, Maerz was a child prodigy destined to excel as a pianist. The grandson of German immigrants, he began playing the piano at age five and within a few years had already performed with an orchestra. A correspondent for the *Buffalo Commercial* fawned over the nine-year-old's abilities at a local show in 1892, stating, "His feet reached about halfway to the pedals, but his hands reached the keyboard, and that was sufficient. This boy not only plays with technical skill for one so young, but also plays with feeling."[57]

Maerz's parents recognized their son's gifts and made sure he received a musical education. "I studied at the Buffalo School of Music, giving concerts continually until [age] twelve," Maerz told an interviewer in 1921. "[Afterwards] I went to New York, and after four years of study, played again in the East for two seasons. At eighteen, I made a transcontinental tour, and for six years gave concerts in all the principal cities of America, Canada and Mexico." While he was proficient in the classics, he sometimes played his own compositions in concert. Audiences loved the young pianist and he cultivated a glowing reputation. "[The hall] was crowded to the door last evening when Joseph Maerz appeared in a piano recital," one critic wrote after an early appearance in New York. "He grew

constantly in favor with his audience, and there was great enthusiasm....
Mr. Maerz's playing was perfect." Among the touring companies Maerz
was associated with during the period was the Rosa Linde Grande Opera
Company and an orchestra featuring German-American contralto Ernes-
tine Schumann-Heink. He eventually left the road, and in 1909 married
Glenn Priest, an accomplished violinist from Boston. That same year the
couple settled into teaching positions at Syracuse University.[58]

Joseph Maerz came to Wesleyan College to direct the conservatory
in 1914, but he had apparently been aware of the institution, and of Macon, for some time. In musical circles, the school had an outstanding reputation, and he had passed through Middle Georgia years earlier with a
touring company. "The newly selected director is one of the leading musicians of this country," the *Telegraph* noted as part of the announcement
of Maerz's appointment. "He took a great fancy to Macon when he gave
a recital here when he was a young man." Maerz's talent, drive, and energy
immediately bolstered what was already a nationally recognized music
program, as did the addition of his wife as a violin instructor. His hiring
coincided with the purchase of a massive $7,500 pipe organ for the con-
servatory that Maerz and his students used for years as a teaching and recital instrument.[59]

The new director of the conservatory was also a great cultural asset
for the city of Macon. He regularly performed at community events, and
his recitals were always well publicized and well attended. His repertoire
included "practically all the old and modern classics and ultra-modern
compositions of French, German and Russian." Through his position at
Wesleyan and his musical contacts around the country, he helped organize
the musical elements of the Macon Chautauqua, and for years he was successful in bringing prominent nationally and internationally known musicians to Macon for concert appearances. During the 1920s and 1930s,
these included composer and pianist Joseph Hofman, concert pianist Mis-
cha Levitzki, violinist Jacque Thibaud, tenor Tandy MacKenzie, and soprano Florence Macbeth as well as touring opera companies from New
York, Chicago, and Cincinnati. Wesleyan's nine-hundred-seat recital auditorium hosted many of the performances. An excellent promoter, Maerz
told a national publication during the period that Macon's "newly awakened musical interest is expanding by leaps and bounds, fed by the enthusiastic work of Wesleyan College!"[60]

Under Maerz's leadership, the conservatory flourished as "an institution as will stand comparison with those now considered standards in this country." In his eighth year at the school, a local newspaper described the state of affairs at Wesleyan:

A student entering upon the course in music offered at Wesleyan takes upon herself an obligation that requires not only talent, but personal character and determination to reach the top of her chosen profession. Every branch of music necessary to the rounding out of a musical education is studied in connection with the major subjects, and the opportunity of hearing celebrated artists at frequent intervals is a part of the calculation to give students at Wesleyan all the advantages.... Wesleyan's staff of music instructors includes seven teachers of piano, three of voice, one of violin and one of pipe-organ. The class work is done by one teacher of the orchestral instruments, two theory professors, one each in the departments of History of Music, Sight-Singing, Ensemble and Chorus..... [The conservatory] has half a hundred class pianos for practice purposes and these are kept always in perfect condition. The best tuners are employed to keep these instruments in perfect tune. In the pipe organ department the same rigid care is maintained.[61]

Joseph Maerz was a fixture in Macon's music community for the rest of his life. In addition to his work at the college, he organized the Macon Symphony Orchestra and conducted the orchestra of the Macon Civic Opera Company during the 1920s. Both organizations included professors and students from Wesleyan. He led the conservatory until 1940 but continued teaching piano at the college and giving innumerable local and regional performances. His last year at Wesleyan was in 1953, and he was afterwards appointed professor emeritus in piano. After his death in 1969, the Macon Morning Music Club established and named in his honor the Joseph Maerz Award, an annual scholarship prize "to encourage and reward achievement and excellence in musical performance."[62]

Although Jim Crow segregation in Macon meant fewer opportunities for organized musical training for African Americans, Ballard Normal School, one of the city's earliest educational institutions for African Americans, offered music as part of its curriculum. Supported financially by the

American Missionary Association (AMA), the school had roots dating back to the Reconstruction era and took its name from Northern philanthropist Stephen Ballard. In 1888, Ballard donated funds for construction of a new, eight-room brick schoolhouse equipped "not only with modern furniture, but with maps, steel engravings, and even a new Steinway piano." With the original Steinway serving as the foundation, the music curriculum expanded through the decades, as did the school's population, which hovered between three and four hundred students in the years surrounding the First World War. By the twenties, Ballard's students had formed a small orchestra and male and female glee clubs that occasionally performed on WMAZ and gave programs at local churches.[63]

One of school's more accomplished graduates in the field of music was Mamie Lena Redding. Born in 1874, Redding excelled at the piano and after leaving Ballard earned a four-year degree from Fisk University in Nashville, which also had ties to the AMA. She then studied at the New England Conservatory before returning to Macon to teach school. Around the turn of the century, she married entrepreneur Jefferson Clemons, who owned a grocery store and pharmacy, and the couple established themselves as part of Bibb County's small but significant black middle class.[64]

A champion of music education for African Americans, Mamie Lena Clemons established the Lena Clemons Conservatory of Music and Arts in Macon the early 1920s. The school occupied a large house on the corner of Spring and Ocmulgee streets, and it gave black artists an opportunity to expand their knowledge base and cultivate their talents. It also served as a hub of social activity for Macon's African American community. The conservatory regularly sponsored recitals and special musical programs, and students often performed on local radio. Among those who benefitted from Clemons's guidance was her niece, Nettie Lena Chandler, who excelled at the violin and piano and after graduation toured the United States and Cuba with a nine-piece orchestra. Another notable student was Gladys Rawlins, whom Clemons tutored on the piano. Rawlins later led her own band and was a fixture of the Macon music scene for years. The conservatory survived into the 1940s, and during World War II served as a USO center for African American servicemen stationed at Camp Wheeler, Robins Field, and Fort Benning. Mamie Lena Clemons passed away on October 30, 1948, at the age of seventy-four.[65]

As the "chitlin circuit" became better defined during the 1930s and 1940s, there was no shortage of musical entertainment for African

Americans in Macon. By then, the circuit had evolved into an organized network of nightclubs and theaters throughout the East and South that catered to African Americans, offering black artists the chance to make a living in places other than major cities such as New York and Chicago. In Macon, the circuit included small clubs as well as larger venues such as the Douglass Theatre and the Macon Auditorium, where promoters staged major events targeting black audiences. The city was a profitable stop on the circuit for bands large and small, but the catalyst for bringing significant national acts to Macon was a promoter named Reece LaMarr DuPree.

Born in Bibb County in 1881, DuPree was the son of a minister, and he started his entertainment career as a singer specializing in spirituals. He eventually left Georgia, and by 1910 was in New York City, making a name for himself on the stage. He appeared in concert, mainly in New York and New Jersey, and occasionally sang on the radio. The press was kind to DuPree and quick to compliment his "fine voice that is highly cultivated." In the 1920s, he made a handful of bluesy recordings for Okeh Records, including "Long Ago Blue," "Oh Saroo, Saroo," "Norfolk Blues," and "One More Rounder Gone." Not long afterwards, he opened his own nightclub, the Tuxedo Club, in Asbury Park, New Jersey, where he started booking acts. The club burned down, but DuPree developed the property as an outdoor park that hosted music performances. He also operated the Roseland Cabaret on the corner of Springwood and Atkins avenues in Asbury Park, one of the busiest music and dance clubs in the area. Apparently not satisfied with the income he received from performing, DuPree eventually turned his full attention to concert promotion, for which he had a flair.[66]

Ambitious and willing to put in the hours, DuPree by the late 1930s had become one of the most successful African American music promoters in the country, booking many of the leading black acts of the day. He opened an office in Asbury Park and eventually Philadelphia. DuPree specialized in sponsoring dance bands and seemed to always be in the right place at the right time. He benefitted from the rise of many talented performers in New York and elsewhere during the Jazz Age and from the development of the chitlin circuit. By the World War II era, *Billboard* magazine was referring to DuPree as the "Dean of Race Dance Promoters," and the list of artists with whom he worked was long and impressive, including Duke Ellington, Ella Fitzgerald, Cab Calloway, and Jimmy

Lunceford. In 1943, one writer credited the promoter with having taken "every name colored band in the country on various tours of the South."[67]

Macon certainly benefitted from DuPree's success. While he promoted many shows in the Northeast, he paid particular attention to the Southern branches of the chitlin circuit, including his hometown. "DuPree's promotions extend deep into the Southland," one reporter wrote, "and he is rated as the biggest buyer of Negro bands on the one-night circuit." Positioned as it was as Georgia's "Central City," Macon was a natural destination for performers. It was nestled comfortably between Atlanta, Columbus, Augusta, and Savannah and tied to those cities, and the world beyond, by rail and an improving network of roads. Many of the larger shows took place in the auditorium, and they sometimes included whites in the audience. Typical was a 1939 performance by jazz great Louis Armstrong, during which "1500 negroes and 500 white people crowded the hall in order to get a glimpse and an ear full of old 'Satchmo.'" According to one account, Armstrong "made musical history in Macon with his renditions of 'My Own,' 'Old Man River,' 'You Go To My Head,' 'This Time Its Real,' and 'Blue Heaven.'"[68]

The crowd at Armstrong's show was filled with "jitterbuggers," "swing enthusiasts," and "jazz hounds," both black and white, but as usual, the races were not allowed to collectively enjoy the show. Venues large and small had different ways of enforcing segregation, depending on structural dimensions and architecture. In larger houses like the auditorium, African Americans usually occupied seats in the balcony for shows featuring white artists—if they were allowed to enter the facility at all. Conversely, and somewhat ironically, African American crowds could take floor seats at shows featuring black artists playing faster-paced blues and jazz, while white crowds sat upstairs. The prevailing attitude among the white establishment held that balcony seats for whites meant that they did not have to be too close to the black performers, and it kept them detached from the "carrying on" among the animated African American crowds enjoying the music below. In those situations, the seating represented a physical manifestation of the existing social strata and a promotion of long-standing racial stereotypes. For instance, after a 1938 DuPree-promoted concert in Macon featuring singer Ella Fitzgerald and a fifteen-piece band led by Chick Webb, the local newspaper reported the event with a headline reading, "Negroes Dance and Whites Listen to Music of Fitzgerald and Webb." The accompanying article suggested that the white crowd at the show was more refined and that somehow African American patrons were naturally primitive and more boisterous as they listened to the "dusky singer."[69]

Segregated audiences were also the norm in smaller theaters that hosted mixed crowds, as was stern treatment for African American artists. Cab Calloway later recalled on one of his trips through Georgia that "in some places...they had a rope down the middle of the dance hall, with the Negroes dancing on one side and the whites on the other." In venues that served food, African American patrons were not allowed to eat with whites, and any type of fraternization was a risky proposition. The situation was the same for band members, who were allowed to perform for whites but forbidden to socialize with them. Robert Purcell "H-Bomb" Ferguson, a rhythm and blues singer who spent a great deal of time touring, remembered harsh treatment in Macon and other Southern towns. "Macon?" he remembered later in life. "The restrooms and restaurants— BACK DOOR.... The band would play, when you got through, you get something to eat, you go to the back, you get a sandwich to go. They had 'colored' and 'white' signs. And you couldn't come in the front door.... A lot of times when we played in the Deep South the sheriff would escort you out of town [after the show]. Make sure you leave."[70]

The dynamics were obviously different in venues catering exclusively to African Americans. While seating was not an issue, law enforcement usually kept a tight lid on African American theaters and nightclubs, raiding them with greater frequency than white establishments—in Macon and elsewhere—to generate fines to fill the local coffers. Even the Douglass Theatre was not immune. In 1933, police raided the theater and arrested eighteen men, charging them with illegal gambling. According to newspaper reports, officers had stormed the theater and found the patrons playing cards with "money on the table." The men were all released after Charles Douglass came up with "$150 collateral" to pay the authorities.[71]

DuPree certainly knew all about the discrimination that his artists faced on the road and that patrons faced in theaters and dance halls. In the years after the Second World War, as civil rights organizations pressed for an end to Jim Crow, DuPree got involved, speaking out against segregated seating and the ill treatment of African American club and theater patrons. He also supported boycotts of musical performances with segregated seating, even when it cost him money. All he wanted, he said, was for African Americans to be "treated like American citizens."[72]

Age began catching up with DuPree during the 1950s. Still viewed as one of the great African American promoters of his time, he became less involved in the music business with each passing year. He died in 1963 at the home of an aunt in Macon, just short of his eighty-second birthday. It was fitting that DuPree passed away in Macon, because he had helped put the city on the map during the thirties and forties with regard to quality, African American entertainment. Writing years later about the chitlin circuit and the roots of rock and roll, author Preston Lauterbach stated that the city owed its prominence in the black music world to DuPree. According to Lauterbach, the promoter brought Macon "more consistent, high level black entertainment than a town its size deserved," allowing patrons to see "the same bands in person that fans in New Orleans, Houston, and Memphis did."[73]

As Reece DuPree promoted jazz and blues shows in Macon, other African American musical options were available in the city, particularly through the auspices of local churches. Just as in white churches, the music of African American congregations functioned as an appeal to God, but it also went much further as a musical testament to struggle, perseverance, unity, and strength. While spiritual in nature, its themes related to hope and deliverance included secular liberation from the indignities of day-to-day life in a segregated society. Despite this, public performances of African American spirituals outside of churches were palatable to the members of the white community, who saw the music only in a religious context as an expression of worship. To white authorities, the music was nonthreatening and acceptable in a social system where any public affront to segregation was not tolerated, and many whites appreciated and attended public performances by African American choirs.[74]

In 1930, Macon's African American church choirs provided much of the personnel for a large program at the auditorium sponsored by the Macon Playground Association to raise money for an African American recreation center in the city. The association brought in nationally known tenor George L. Johnson to direct the event, which included "a locally trained chorus of 250 voices." Johnson rehearsed the group for about a month and chose a handful of soloists to be featured during certain songs. The program of mostly religious music included "Steal Away to Jesus," "Oh Lord Remember Me," "Every Time I Feel the Spirit," and "Swing Low, Sweet Chariot." According to newspaper reports, tickets were fifty cents for adults and a quarter for children, with "half the auditorium reserved for Negroes." The program took place on June 13, 1930, and was so popular that organizers scheduled a second show for the following week.

One of the star performers in the show was soloist Alvin L. Glascoe. Originally from South Carolina, Glascoe was born in 1871 and lived most of his adult life in Macon as a well-known barber. Blessed with a beautiful voice, Glascoe sang at most of the important civic occasions involving African Americans, sometimes performing with a quartet or with his wife, Volie. He was one of the first African Americans to perform regularly on WMAZ and was always "in great demand around Macon" as a singer. During the 1920s, he made at least one regional tour, giving performances in North and South Carolina, where he was "greeted by large and appreciative audiences." According to reports, Glascoe had "a repertoire of one hundred and fifty songs consisting of classics and semi-classics and spirituals." At the big 1930 event in Macon, he impressed the crowd with a rendition of "The Trumpeter," a tune penned in 1904 that gained popularity during the First World War. Although he sang frequently at occasions large and small, Glascoe never made enough money to make music a full-time career. He continued styling hair in Macon until his death in 1945.[75]

In November of 1935, the auditorium hosted what newspapers billed as a "Battle of Music" between choirs from the city's African American churches. The competition was designed to raise money for African American recreational facilities, with the winners moving on to a state competition. Admission was ten cents per person, and advertisements for the event stated "a large section of the auditorium will be reserved for white patrons." While the contest participants were black, African American community leaders did not control the proceedings. Representatives from the city's white churches oversaw the event, served as judges, and awarded the prizes. According to the rules, each choir could sing one hymn and one secular song, and "only two verses and a chorus of any spiritual or hymn [would] be allowed, to give as many choirs as possible a chance to be heard." A crowd of around eight hundred African Americans and two hundred whites watched the performances and "gave the program an enthusiastic reception." Mount Moriah Baptist Church won first prize, with the choir from Macedonia Baptist Church finishing in second place. Both groups advanced to the state competition.[76]

Beginning in the 1930s, those in the Macon area interested in hearing choral music from the African American community were not restricted to live performances. In January of 1938, WMAZ began a regular weekly broadcast of the choir from Fort Valley Normal and Industrial School (now Fort Valley State University), an African American institution about thirty miles southwest of Macon. The station gave the "40-voice chorus," under the direction of Edgar Rogie Clark, a thirty-minute slot every Sunday at 5:30 P.M., for a program featuring "spirituals and plantation hymns." Later in the year, WMAZ began broadcasting parts of the Fort Valley Music Festival, an annual event that featured many of the region's most talented African American singers, folk musicians, and choral performers. The station also broadcast special holiday performances of the Fort Valley Choir on Easter, Thanksgiving, and Christmas. The relationship between Fort Valley and WMAZ lasted for more than two decades, with a regular weekly program sponsored by the Banker's Health and Life Insurance Company. "Every Sunday," one reviewer later wrote of the show, "the listener hears the very best in music brought by a finished musical group and rendered in superb style." By the mid-1940s, a Wednesday night program also featured the Fort Valley Choir singing religious and popular tunes. The appearances added to the group's already stellar reputation in the area and helped draw audiences to their regional tours and "numerous formal and informal recitals on the college campus."[77]

WMAZ also programmed gospel music by white artists, a format that was very popular, especially among rural listeners. Since the late nineteenth century, religious music had spread through the South's white evangelical community, thanks in large part to the commercial circulation of the "shape-note" hymnal. In these hymn books, different notes were represented by different shapes, making it possible for those who did not read music to sing, play, and follow the tunes of the songs. Tennessean James Vaughan, a music publisher often called "the Founder of Southern Gospel," began distributing religious songbooks in the Southern states at the turn of the century. Vaughan was a true entrepreneur with a good head for marketing. He employed traveling singing groups, usually gospel quartets, that promoted his songbooks by performing around the South. In turn, one of Vaughan's employees, Virgil O. Stamps, and songwriter Jesse R. Baxter Jr. partnered in 1926 to found the Stamps-Baxter Music and Printing Company, headquartered in Dallas. Stamps-Baxter helped blur the lines between traditional gospel music and emerging trends in popular music. The company sponsored quartet performances and all-day singing affairs at churches, schools, and county fairs around the South that included a mix of gospel and secular tunes. It also dispatched traveling singing groups to promote the company name, and by the 1930s, Stamps-Baxter was a dominant force in the Southern gospel marketplace.[78]

In 1939, one of the many groups sponsored by the Stamps-Baxter organization relocated to Macon, beginning a fifteen-year relationship with WMAZ and the listening public in Middle Georgia. The Smile-A-While Quartet was formed in 1938 in Malvern, Arkansas. It became associated with the Stamps-Baxter organization the following year, after V. O. Stamps heard them sing at a music convention. Willis Thurman "Deacon" Utley, who worked for Stamps, became the group's manager. The original members were Horace Floyd, Morgan Paul, Arvin Burrow, and Lynn Utley, Deacon Utley's son, who played piano, sang lead, and arranged much of the group's gospel and popular material. They toured the Southeast, landing in Macon in July of 1939. After securing a twice-daily time slot on WMAZ, the group made the city their headquarters. The Smile-A-While Quartet "spread the gospel" daily at 6:30 A.M. and 1:45 P.M. and were instantly popular in Middle Georgia and far beyond. "We checked our listening audience by offering a song and a picture for those who would write in," Lynn Utley later recalled about the group's first few months in Macon. "In a four-day period, we received mail from sixteen states." Once the radio show gained popularity, the group expanded, later including Clifford Thompson, Ervin Bridger, Walt Cornell, Clyde McClain, Gilbert Powell, and Oocha Sanders.

Among the biggest fans of the show were members of the Macon Fire Department, who adopted the group's members and regularly invited them for meals at the firehouse. In April of 1940, the department sponsored a successful charity concert at the auditorium featuring the Smile-A-While Quartet and two other local groups. The event reportedly attracted a standing-room-only crowd of around six thousand. "The date was April 26, 1940," Utley later remembered. "The concert that night was the largest paid program ever held at the city auditorium. Seating capacity was 5,000, but they brought in a lot of folding chairs [and] several hundred stood around the walls." According to various reports, between 800 and 1,800 individuals "were turned away when the fire department stopped allowing people to enter for safety." Virgil Stamps, who was in the audience, was so pleased with the turnout that he bought the quartet a new, spacious Buick automobile to use when they toured.

Not long before the outbreak of the Second World War, the Smile-A-While lineup began to change. Lynn Utley left temporarily to complete college in Oklahoma, and two of the men joined the service after Pearl Harbor. Throughout the war years and afterwards, the group retained a loyal following, but members frequently came and went. They toured constantly, though usually not more than a day's drive away from Macon, performing at schools, churches, civic occasions, and at "music conventions on the weekends." During the 1940s, they even recorded a handful of gospel songs for the Columbia label. After a fifteen-year run, the Smile-A-While Quartet left WMAZ in 1954. The following year Deacon Utley, the man who kept the group together all those years, passed away and was buried in Macon.

The Smile-A-While Quartet sometimes sang on the same bill with local country artists—still popularly called "hillbilly" musicians at the time—and country music was very popular in Macon. Groups such as the Melody Riders, the Southern Ramblers, and the Radio Playboys played cafés and dance halls around town and appeared at shows in the city auditorium. They were also fixtures at the Dance Arena, at Broadway and Cherry, a venue that welcomed country entertainers for years. Some of the bands were multidimensional in that they could also play popular tunes if pressed, but the "hillbilly" style was in demand at parties and square dances. While there were a number of musicians who knocked around town playing country music, the 1940s produced one performer who would be wildly popular in Macon for years. His name was Gene Stripling, but his fans called him "Uncle Ned."

Lowry Eugene Stripling was born in Jones County, Georgia, in 1915, and his family relocated to Macon when he was a child. A talented pianist, he started playing music as a student at Lanier High School, and in his early twenties formed a band that he christened Uncle Ned and His Texas Wranglers. Determined to forge an entertainment career, he moved the group to Atlanta, where they earned a regular spot on the Cross Road Follies radio program on WSB. The exposure led to regional appearances and several brief tours of the Southeast between 1937 and 1940. In March of 1938, they played one of their first big shows in Macon at the Big State Fiddler's Contest, where they shared a bill with several other regional acts. The original Texas Wranglers included Maconites Pete Arnold, Doc

Gray, Slim Lindsay, and Al Kooper and female singers Tinky and Nell Coleman.[79]

Tiring of life on the road, and having started a family, Stripling moved back to Macon with most of the Wranglers. He took a day job with the Macon Fire Department and, for a short time, the police department, but continued leading the band. The group secured a daily spot on WMAZ and made regular weekend appearances around Middle Georgia during the early forties. "Macon has a bunch of boys who whoop it up every day," the *Macon News* announced, "The gang is known as Uncle Ned and His Texas Wranglers, and it's Macon's own.... They're now on WMAZ every day for fifteen minutes just before noon and every Saturday night they meander to Thomaston where they stage a hillbilly dance. They've recently started a dance series at the YWCA on Poplar Street." Stripling's band was one of the most popular acts in Macon, and its members often shared the stage with nationally known country acts that passed through the city. One such occasion was a December 1942 show at the city auditorium featuring the band along with Bill Monroe and the Blue Grass Boys, and Uncle Dave Macon.[80]

Uncle Ned and His Texas Wranglers broke up in 1945 when Stripling entered the military during the Second World War's final year. Upon his return home, he put together a new group with several musicians who had previously performed as Dee Lee and His Georgia Ramblers. While they sometimes employed other players, the core of this new musical configuration included Stripling as the bandleader and pianist, Dee Lee on steel guitar, fiddlers R. A. "Fonzie" Gray and Homer Hudson, and drummer Bobby "Moon" Hardy. They called the new group Uncle Ned and the Hayloft Jamboree, and, as had the Wranglers, they secured a regular spot on WMAZ. While all the men had "regular" day jobs, they kept up a hectic performing pace, burning the candle at both ends. "We used to play from 9:00 P.M. to 11:45," Gray later recalled. "I guess we played about every town from Atlanta to Brunswick, from Athens and Augusta to Albany. Sometimes we hardly ever got to bed." The repertoire varied, but the band specialized in western swing music out of the Bob Wills mold.[81]

Audiences loved Stripling, and his quick-witted, homespun banter before sets and between songs was almost as popular as the tunes his band played. A big, gregarious man, Stripling was a natural entertainer who pushed himself hard to make sure his crowds got their money's worth.

During the late forties, the band seemed to be everywhere, performing at every type of venue in Macon and the surrounding area. They played organized events at the city auditorium, outdoor festivals where "they put the band up on cotton trucks," and in "gyms, roller rinks and the like." They also played some rooms that were barely rooms at all. "We played places [in the winter] where you had coal buckets sitting in the middle of the floor and ice on the building," Dee Lee recalled. "The band members had to jump up and warm their hands and then go back and play some more." In Macon, according to Lee, they were also "big at places like Durr's Lake and Ragan's Park."[82]

The band carried on for several years but eventually broke up in 1951. Interviewed years later, all the original members stated that it was an amiable split and that they had all simply reached a point where they believed the enterprise had run its course. Lee, Gray, Hudson, and Hardy, along with pianist Norman Jones, reformed Dee Lee and His Georgia Ramblers and carried on for a time. They were friendly with Stripling, who remained a popular entertainment figure in Macon and went on to form another version of the band that found success on local television.[83]

Two brothers, Charlie and Wallace Mercer, played shows with both Dee Lee's band and Uncle Ned for a about a year during the 1940s before striking out on their own. The Mercer Brothers, as they were known professionally, started playing local shows as teenagers in 1939 with guitars purchased from Sears and Roebuck. They grew up in Candler County, but jobs with the defense department during World War II drew their family to Macon. After the war, they started playing shows around town, with one of their first public appearances being a performance on the third floor of Sterchi's Furniture Store on the corner of Cherry Street and Broadway. Always in need of programming, WMAZ gave the brothers their own radio program that lasted for a year beginning in 1947.[84]

Acting on advice from members of Roy Acuff's band, whom they met while touring with Dee Lee and Uncle Ned, the Mercer Brothers picked up stakes and moved to Shreveport, Louisiana, in 1948. There they landed a fifteen-minute radio spot on Shreveport's KWKH and an invitation to perform on the *Louisiana Hayride*, a new program that later became legendary. Both men played guitar, and, according to one reviewer, their vocal harmonies had a "soft, slightly high-pitched whine" common in the bluegrass tradition. While playing on the *Louisiana*

Hayride, they rubbed elbows with well-known national acts including Hank Williams, Kitty Wells, Red Sovine, and Faron Young, and in the process developed their own following. Joining with fiddler Doyle Strickland and harmonica master Wayne Raney, they toured Louisiana, Texas, Arkansas, and Oklahoma in the late 1940s as the Mercer Brothers and the Blue Ridge Boys. They even made a handful of recordings for Columbia Records.[85]

Despite the success and tentative plans to move to Nashville, the Mercer Brothers eventually returned to Macon. They were not enamored with the business side of the music profession, and constant touring had apparently worn the two men out. "You didn't have paved roads back then," Wallace later told an interviewer. "We'd play in places that didn't have any electricity. A six-volt car battery ran the sound system. You better have a good battery or you wouldn't get home. You never knew what you would encounter." Back in Macon, the brothers took jobs at the local Air Force base in the 1950s but maintained a radio program that broadcast primarily on WMAZ for more than two decades. After the show ended in 1974, they retired from show business, with the exception of an occasional public appearance in Macon, and both men lived the rest of their lives in Bibb County. Wallace Mercer passed away in 2000, and Charlie followed him in 2014.[86]

Another group of note with Macon connections was the Sunshine Boys, a quartet that performed gospel and country music. The original group included brothers John and A. L. Smith, Ace Richman, and Pat Patterson, none of whom were from the Bibb County area. They lived in Macon briefly and had a popular radio program on WMAZ for about two years beginning in 1941. Building on that success, they moved to Atlanta, where they had a radio program and began making records. The group carried on for years, with frequent personnel changes, making records, and even appearing on television and in several films.[87]

While the list of musicians who played country music in Macon during the 1940s was overwhelmingly male, it was not exclusively male. There were a number of female artists who played in the same venues as Uncle Ned's group. Among the most popular, and most talented, was Ruby Yopp, whose name was almost as difficult to forget as her mastery of the piano. Yopp was known for playing honky-tonk style, but she could also play jazz and gospel. As a result, she was in demand at social events and played with a number of local bands, including the Starlight Swingers and the Jazz Masters. Yopp grew up in Macon, the daughter of Sam Yopp, a salesman and part-time musician who could play just about any instrument with strings. She started playing the piano at age six and began formal lessons three years later. The little girl was a natural on the instrument and had a talent for playing by ear. "I would listen to the music at the moving picture show," she once said, "and then come home and play it."[88]

By the time she was fourteen, Yopp was already making money as a musician, with a regular gig at Rock Mill Park three nights a week. She occasionally provided piano accompaniment for her father when he played the violin at social functions. Yopp graduated from Lanier High School for Girls in 1929. She married Charles Havis in 1936 and had two children. The couple divorced, and Yopp, who used her maiden name as her stage moniker, started playing piano at night to supplement the money she made doing office work during the day. She was especially active during the 1950s, when she played for the Jazz Masters, who made regular appearances at the VFW on Cotton Avenue. She also played with local country artists, and her daughter married Philip "Pee Wee" Clark, who was part of Gene Stripling's television version of the Hayloft Jamboree. "There's never been a better pop song than 'Born to Lose,'" she once told an interviewer, "and a better country song than 'Under the Double Eagle.'" Among her other favorites were "How High the Moon," "But Not for Me," "Ain't Misbehavin'," "In the Mood," and the hymn "How Great Thou Art." While she sometimes worked as a solo performer, she preferred being part of a band. "Other musicians make you do your best," she once said. "You need them." After her children were grown, Yopp made fewer public appearances as a musician, but she remained part of Macon's music community and an active participant in civic affairs until her death in 1988.[89]

Three new radio stations that went on the air during the 1940s helped disseminate country music to the residents of Macon and the surrounding area. In October of 1940, WBML began broadcasting, with studios in the First National Bank building, followed by WNEX five years later. Three years after that, WIBB went on the air. Along with already-established WMAZ, these stations provided a wide variety of programming to their listeners. Of the newer stations, WNEX and WIBB ran popular programs of country music with names like *Hillbilly Hit*

Parade, R.F.D. Jamboree, Southern Serenade, Farm Frolic, and *The Chuck Wagon.*[90]

Two early country disc jockeys on these stations were musician Charles "Peanut" Faircloth and Gordon Price. Faircloth was born in Mitchell County, Georgia. He moved to Macon and began his radio career in 1946 on WNEX. He was a small man who had survived polio as a child, but he seemed to possess boundless energy. "I ain't big, but I'm wound up tight," was an expression he often used on the radio and in his stage act. Faircloth played the guitar, mandolin, and harmonica with his own popular group, the Georgia Crackers. "He loved entertaining," one friend later remembered, "and his gang of music makers were on the go around Middle Georgia." In the late 1940s, Faircloth hosted *The Hoedown Party* on WNEX, a program of country music and banter syndicated on the Mutual Broadcasting Network. Ernest Tubb heard one of Faircloth's broadcasts and encouraged the disc jockey and musician to move to Nashville, where Faircloth made a handful of recordings before resuming a successful radio career that took him to Augusta, Georgia, and Chattanooga, Tennessee. During the 1950s, he helped launch the career of country singer Brenda Lee and rubbed elbows with many of country music's brightest stars.[91]

While Faircloth only passed through Macon, making it his home for only a short time, Gordon Price was a native of the city and a fixture on Macon radio for years. He broke into the business with WMAZ at the age of sixteen after winning an amateur radio contest sponsored by the station. He left Macon and moved to Atlanta for two years, but in 1950 returned home and got a job at WIBB. Though not particularly fond of country music, he became the host of the *R.F.D. Jamboree,* and created a humorous backwoods persona that he named "Cousin Luke." "I murdered the King's English," he once said. "A fire was a *far,* a tire was a *tar,* and a piano was a *piany.*" The marathon program ran every weekday from 9:00 A.M. to 1:30 P.M., featuring mostly country recordings with at least a half hour dedicated to gospel music. Occasionally, local bands would perform live during the show's last half hour. "Cousin Luke's familiar voice rings out over the airwaves with the best recorded music anywhere," one reviewer wrote in 1953. Price had an eight-year run hosting the program as part of a long and varied career during which he worked at almost every radio station in Macon.[92]

As part of the *R.F.D. Jamboree*, Price occasionally broadcast interviews with major country stars, from Ernest Tubb and Ray Price to Hank Williams. During one notable 1951 interview with Williams, the country music legend talked to Price about the recent release of "Hey, Good Lookin'." While the interview was recorded in Nashville, Price told Williams that the song was the number-one hillbilly record on the *R.F.D Jamboree* in Macon, to which Williams replied, "I tell you, I'm sort of partial to Macon. Been there about four or five times and have a lot of good friends there." The interview ended a few minutes later with Williams giving a homespun sign-off to his fans in Middle Georgia: "To all you folks around Macon, thanks for requesting my songs. I'd like to say that if the good Lord's willing and the creek don't rise, I'll see you again in Macon before long."[93]

As the forties turned into the fifties, bands performing popular tunes, blues, and jazz continued entertaining at social events for student organizations at Mercer and Wesleyan. While both institutions hired groups from outside Macon, they also used a great deal of local talent, both white and black. One of the most notable white bandleaders of the period was Jesse Duckworth, whose group was a familiar presence at fraternity and sorority functions. Born in 1928, Duckworth graduated from Lanier High School in 1946. He attended college, first at the University of Georgia and then at Mercer, where he earned his degree. While at Mercer, Duckworth, who played the trombone, formed a band dubbed the Jesse Duckworth Orchestra that was popular with students. He also formed a vocal quintet within the larger group, called the "Moonmisters." The original Moonmisters included Duckworth, Homer Tillery, Max Northington, Alan Northington, and Berner Heard. The Duckworth band as a whole was a jazz and swing outfit, while the Moonmisters shone on numbers with softer melodies. According to one account, while the music was certainly important, the vocalists originally came up with the idea for a vocal quintet "as a way to impress women at the Whistlestop, a college watering hole on Forsyth Road."[94]

At any given time, the Jesse Duckworth Orchestra featured between ten and twenty pieces, including members of the vocal group, who also played instruments. On the strength of their appearances at Mercer and around Macon, they received offers to play parties and dances on college campuses across the state. While promoting the university's "Spring Frolic" of 1949, a Georgia Tech student newspaper reporter wrote, "The

Duckworth Band, a 14-piece outfit hailing from Macon, has played engagements at schools and colleges throughout the state.... Featured will be the vocal quintet 'The Moonmisters,' whose renditions in close harmony have been widely acclaimed."[95]

The Moonmisters had a brush with national success in 1949, when they appeared on the Horace Heidt Youth Opportunity Program, a talent competition on NBC radio hosted by pianist and big band leader Horace Heidt. The program traveled the country auditioning young artists. The Moonmisters performed when Heidt and his entourage made a stop in Atlanta to broadcast from the Fox Theatre. The group made a positive impression and received an invitation to perform again at a show broadcast from Baltimore. They lost out on a five-thousand-dollar cash prize but did get to make one notable appearance on a radio broadcast featuring Bob Hope and Les Brown. Afterwards, the group returned to Macon and their rigorous schedule of performances in Georgia.[96]

Duckworth later expanded his band and experimented with complicated arrangements. At a 1952 concert at the Macon City Auditorium, the group featured a twenty-piece orchestra as well as a choral group recruited from music students at Mercer and Wesleyan. While the band played for a variety of different audiences, college functions remained their bread and butter as far as paying gigs were concerned. "These were the romantic post-World War II years," one local musician later recalled. "Many of the young people who crowded the front of the bandstand to hear the group were ex-GIs who were attending local college on the GI Bill, and the girls many of them would soon marry."[97] Duckworth's band remained popular for several years, but eventually dissolved as music tastes changed and its members settled down to start families. Jesse Duckworth took a job with the Bibb County school system, where he had a successful career as a teacher, coach, and counselor. He remained active in local affairs, particularly those involving music, and organized periodic reunions of his old band for nostalgia shows. After a long and fruitful life, he passed away in 2001.[98]

The Jesse Duckworth Orchestra was not the only "horn-tootin' outfit" in Macon that played jazz, swing, and contemporary popular music after the Second World War, but they were certainly one of the most popular. Others included the Cecil Walton Orchestra and bands led by Eddie Cannon, Sam Gordon, and Johnny Willis. These Macon outfits experienced a golden era for big band music in their city that began during the war but only lasted a little more than a decade.

As was the case in the rest of the country, big band music in Bibb County started to fade during the mid-1950s. A new era of cultural change was underway that included a seismic shift in popular musical tastes among the young. Many teenagers and young adults were about to embrace a new style of music that had been lurking in the shadows for years, waiting to explode. Labeled "rock and roll," this new music would change American culture forever. It was exciting to many, dangerous to some, sinful to others, and, as a cultural phenomenon, it was unstoppable. Although rock and roll would have a great effect on Macon, the relationship between the city and the music was reciprocal. Macon was destined to have a great effect on rock and roll.

4

Post-War R&B, Little Richard, and James Brown
1945–1960

"Retire from music? Honey, there's no such thing."[1]
—Gladys Williams

For African Americans in Macon, the nightclub scene expanded significantly in the 1940s. During the war, nearby military instillations guaran-
teed a substantial clientele, and the momentum carried through to the
postwar period. There were more than enough gigs available for African
American musicians, and crowds were healthy. Macon's famous musical
son Little Richard Penniman, who grew up in the city, later remember
that "Macon was a good place to live if you were in the entertainment
business....lots of nightclubs, big and small....All of them had live entertainment." These clubs were frequent stops on the chitlin circuit for artists
both prominent and unknown. The environment was lively, and the man
who controlled most of the musical traffic in and out of the clubs was a
rough, plainspoken promoter and entrepreneur named Clint Brantley.[2]

Brantley was (and is) perhaps one of the most underappreciated characters in the development of American popular culture over the last hundred years—not just in Macon, but in the United States. He certainly
deserves a place in the pantheon of promoters who helped shape the musical history of the country in the modern era. Brantley was a tough
wheeler-dealer. He advanced the careers of both Little Richard and James
Brown, who, in turn, influenced every rhythm and blues and rock performer who came after them. Whether both men would have become as

successful without the promoter is debatable, but he was an early manager of both artists. A case certainly could be made that Brantley provided both with a platform to showcase their talents at critical phases of their early careers, and without that platform they may not have become as widely known.

Clinton Eugene Brantley was born in Washington County, Georgia, on August 8, 1902, the son of a barber and a seamstress. As a youngster, he learned to play the drums and bass and formed his own band before moving to Macon in 1922. "I was playing drums," he later recalled. "I'd sing a little bit, but not too much.... We'd play little dances at the schools and so forth." Like his father, Brantley became a barber, though he continued playing music at night with local groups. Although he kept his barber shop, he entered the music-promotion business in the 1930s, booking African American acts in Macon. It was a calling for which he had a natural talent. Among the first significant entertainers that he brought to the city were Thomas Wright "Fats" Waller, who performed at the city auditorium in July of 1935, and, not long afterwards, Ruth Ellington, with her sixteen-piece orchestra. It was the beginning of a promotion career that lasted for more than three decades and saw Brantley bring to Macon a host of top stars from Louis Jordan and Sister Rosetta Tharpe to Lionel Hampton and Nat "King" Cole. He also nurtured and found employment for scores of local musicians, some of whom became nationally known.[3]

On July 4, 1941, a new African American nightclub opened on Broadway that was christened the Cotton Club, after the famous New York venue. Several days before the big opening night party, an advertising piece ran in the "colored" section of the *Telegraph* describing the club as "lavishly decorated" and "modernly equipped, further enhanced with a colorful array of soft lights that will blink." The ad went on to inform readers that in addition to a full array of dining options, the club featured "a spacious hardwood dance floor" and "music of the most enchanting type." Local musicians performed at the popular nightspot, and for a time, Brantley's group, the Sultans, served as the house band. "Clint's Sultans will furnish the smooth melodies," a newspaper reporter for the *Telegraph* noted. "If you like your music in the groove, this is the place to come." The club also hosted late-night parties and receptions for many of the national acts that Brantley brought to Macon.[4]

Several months after the Cotton Club began operation, Brantley opened the Two Spot on the corner of Walnut and Fifth streets. This club later became famous for hosting performances by the likes of James Brown and Otis Redding. Opening night included a party, with well-known Macon personality Gladys Williams and her band providing the entertainment. "The Two Spot is accommodating and well appointed," one advertisement for the place read. "Its interior is further enhanced with a green and white cocktail lounge. Centering the floor is a soft, gliding dance space fronting the confectionary, beverage and soft drink counter, and tables and chairs for those who choose to refresh and dine and hear enchanting music." Brantley had the walls decorated with "photos of many of the leading stars of the music stage and radio circles." Milt Dimmons, a musician who frequented the club, later was a bit more subdued in his description of the place, stating that it "was always a juke joint—nothing fancy ever, but it had a warm feeling" and that patrons from every social strata of Macon's black community felt comfortable there. "They feel free to walk in with their cement-stained clothes on, as well as their tuxedos," Dimmons said, "except on weekends, when they [all] dress up.... It was somewhere to let off [steam] and meet other people like you." As with the Cotton Club, the Two Spot provided employment for local musicians and occasionally hosted national acts associated with Brantley's booking activities.[5]

Most accounts state that as a promoter, Brantley was tough, profane, and as adept at pacifying the Macon police and local officials—those who had the final say in how much black nightlife would be tolerated—as he was at booking bands. He developed an iron grip on the black entertainment business in the city and cultivated contacts all along the chitlin circuit. Ralph Bass, a producer and talent scout for King Records who signed James Brown to the label, later said, "In those days, the smaller cities and towns in the Deep South always had some black cat who controlled everything across the tracks, you might say. He usually had a big nightclub. Brantley was that guy in Macon."[6]

In addition to sponsoring local events, Brantley booked statewide and regional tours for many Macon bands, although the musicians sometimes had trouble finding adequate accommodations. For local musicians of color during the period, playing in Macon was not a logistical hardship, as they lived nearby, but on the road it was a different story. "[The bands] didn't have no place to stay," Brantley, who sometimes traveled with his own group, told an interviewer in 1978. "They stayed in the car. You slept where you stopped. You didn't have no motels or facilities or nothing. We'd ride for two days and two nights without ever getting in a bed, trying to get where we're going." Some towns had "colored" hotels and restaurants that catered to African American customers, but on the road there were no guarantees. "Whenever you'd get into a town, as far as finding a decent place to live and a decent place to eat, there was no such place," Percy Welch, a musician who worked for Brantley, once recalled. "You could only just go so long without sleep and you could just go on so long without a decent meal."[7]

If Clint Brantley was an unsung hero developing postwar African American talent in Macon, then so was Gladys Williams. Williams, whom Brantley booked many times into clubs all over Georgia, was one of the most respected musicians in the city and a popular performer on Macon's music scene for more than four decades. In addition to her talents on the piano and as a singer, she occupied a unique position in Middle Georgia entertainment circles as the only female bandleader in the area. Williams was born Gladys Rawlins around 1908 and grew up in Bibb County. She spent much of her early life—from roughly the ages two through twelve— on crutches as a result of polio, but began playing the piano by ear at age four. "From the very first I could play anything I ever heard," she once recalled. "People just couldn't understand it. Neither could I." When she got a little older, her mother and father allowed her to play traditional music, classical selections, and hymns at weddings and funerals and tried without success to temper her interest in blues and jazz. "I used to sneak around and practice it when my mother was at work," she later told a reporter. "I can still hear my sister—'Mama, Gladys played the blues around here all day.'"[8]

Recognizing their daughter's talent, Williams's parents enrolled her at the Lena Clemons Conservatory, where she studied music for several years. She graduated from Hudson High School and then earned a degree from Hampton Institute. Some reports state that she received a scholarship to the school, while others say that an anonymous benefactor, impressed by both her talent and how she overcame polio, gave her financial assistance. Regardless, after she completed her studies, she returned to Macon, married Herbert Williams, and began a long, diverse, and fruitful musical career. To say that she was in demand as an entertainer would be an understatement. In addition to performing for several churches, a local funeral home, and scores of weddings and private parties, she started a nightclub career as a solo act playing the piano. According to Williams, she did not sing regularly at first, but a turning point in her career came one evening in a nightclub during the early 1930s when a patron offered her a dollar—a generous tip in those days—to play *and* sing "St. Louis Blues." "A whole dollar just for singing a song," she later said. "You'd play all night for that!" From that point forward, she was known as both a pianist and a vocalist.[9]

By the late thirties, Williams had put together her own band and began making the rounds, blazing a trail as a successful female bandleader in a rough-and-tumble business dominated by men. At any given time, she took between six and ten musicians on the road in her group. "We played everywhere," she remembered. "All over Georgia, and we were among the first bands at the leading spots in Macon and the towns around." For the next thirty years, the Gladys Williams Band would be a training ground for many of the greatest musicians Macon ever produced. "She was a great transcriber," one local player later recalled. "A great arranger. She could arrange the songs out where she could have five pieces, eight pieces, ten, whatever she needed." Among the notable members of her group were drummer Gordon Pinkston, trumpet players Lewis Hamlin Jr. and Obie Kimbro, saxophonists Hamp Swain and Jessie Hancock, and vocalist Ray Brown. "Unfortunately, Gladys came along when female musicians and bandleaders were rare," Hamp Swain later told journalist Scott Freeman. "Otherwise, she would have been a big, big, big star." Over time, players in her band came and went, had careers of their own, and, in a few cases, became some of the brightest stars in show business. When he was just starting out, Little Richard sang occasionally with the band, as did James Brown. Williams played regularly at the Hillview Springs Social Club, where she sponsored Sunday afternoon jam sessions and a talent show for the city's young musicians—"the kids," as she called them. It was one of the first places, outside of his church, that a young Otis Redding sang in public.[10]

While Williams was generous to her band members, she was also a tough taskmaster who was not shy about correcting her musicians, even on stage. She was equally stern when dealing with unruly juke joint crowds. "She had to be tough because she played all over Macon," one local musician remembered. "These guys at the time were shooting dice in one corner, playing cards for money in another corner, and had a potbelly stove in the middle of the room to heat the place. She would raise her voice, and I don't care who you were, it was 'yes ma'am' and 'no ma'am.' She ruled the place. She commanded respect." Williams's band was constantly working, playing juke joints and tamer locations, and even making a few radio appearances on WMAZ. During the war years, the *Macon News* reported that "among the popular night spots that have swung and swayed with dancers on the hardwood to the tune of Gladys's music are Rainbow Gardens, CCC camp, Cotton Club, and Lincoln Inn, along with a long list of other Middle Georgia entertainment spots." As if she were not busy enough, Williams also taught piano to youngsters in her home on Ash Street, many of whom, like her band members, went on to lively careers of their own, either in music or in other fields.[11]

While her band performed mainly in Middle Georgia, Williams developed a reputation that reached far beyond the region. "Gladys could play that piano, man," Jessie Hancock later said. "And sing like a bird. She could sing them blues and then turn right around and play a waltz, or sing a song like 'Stardust.'" She had friends up and down the chitlin circuit, a branch of which regularly took performers to Atlanta and then through Macon on their way to Savannah or Florida. Her home became a regular gathering place for African American performers on the road who, regardless of their status or popularity, had limited options in the Jim Crow South as to where they might socialize when not on stage. One of Williams's piano students, Newton Collier, never knew who he might see when he went over to her house as a youngster for his lessons. "She was my first piano teacher for years. I used to go over to her house at about 11:00 on Saturday [morning]," Collier remembered. "Any given Saturday anybody might show up there. I saw Ruth Brown, Ethel Waters, Sammy Davis, Jr., Sidney Poitier. They would come through Macon, and Ms. Gladys played the piano and they knew about her. It was unbelievable. Here you are trying to take your music lesson and they'd be there."[12]

Williams and her band remained in demand in Macon through the 1970s, and she was determined to keep playing as long as her health allowed. "Retire from music?" she once told a reporter. "Honey, there's no such thing." The combination of her natural talent, longevity as a performer, and willingness to mentor younger performers made Gladys Williams one of the most influential musicians in Macon's history. Her stamp on the Macon music scene during her era and afterwards was indelible, and her impact on the individuals whom she came in contact with through her music became her greatest legacy. "I point with pride to my boys," she once said, in reference to some of her band members and students. "They are now band masters, pianists, school principals, teachers, and businessmen. More than thirty of them finished college. And they thank me for giving them their start."[13]

Both Clint Brantley and Gladys Williams had a significant influence on another important and underappreciated Macon musical figure. Alvin Luke Gonder was born on April 21, 1918, in Hancock County, Georgia, and moved to Macon with his family as a young child. Like Brantley, Gonder's father, Willie, was a barber who operated a shop on Forrest Avenue. Luke Gonder attended Hudson High School and graduated from Beta-Etta College, a private school for African Americans in Macon that provided students with "a thoroughly practical business and literary education." A talented pianist, he was one of Gladys Williams's early pupils, and by the time he was twenty, he had his own band that played the club circuit around Macon and in surrounding towns as well as school proms and private parties. "As a protégé of Mrs. Williams," one newspaper columnist wrote in 1942, "[Gonder] learned early to break up his chords and to execute properly, and with her help he developed his present swing style." He also worked a day job driving a taxi in the city for the Colored Cab Company.[14]

World War II interrupted Gonder's professional music career for more than two years, although he led a seven-piece band while in the service. He enlisted in the army in January of 1943 and "while overseas served in France, England, and Belgium, [and] was in Germany for V-E Day." He returned to Macon after the conflict and picked up musically right where he left off. Managed by Clint Brantley, he performed as a solo act and as a valued member of Brantley's band, the Sultans, as both a pianist and arranger. Gonder's abilities and personality attracted both fans and nicknames. Locals compared Gonder in talent and temperament to Louis Jordan, to the extent that newspapers sometimes referred to him as "Macon's Louis Jordan" and "Louis Jordan #2." Others called him "Count Basic," or simply "The Count," references to popular bandleader Count Basie. A heavyset man, he also picked up the nickname "Fats" and was known professionally as Fats Gonder for most of his career.[15]

Gonder played a significant role in the early careers of both Little Richard and James Brown. He was one of Little Richard's first piano teachers, and later, during the young performer's early tours of the South,

Brantley sent Gonder along to provide both musical support and a degree of stability to what was at the time a rowdy touring company. In 1952, while traveling with Little Richard, Gonder ran into a young James Brown and was so impressed by Brown's talent that he advised Brantley to bring him to Macon. Brantley did just that, setting in motion a chain of events that launched Brown's career. Gonder went on to become part of Brown's touring entourage, playing piano, organ, and serving as an emcee for the shows. It is Gonder's booming voice that introduces *The Hardest Working Man in Show Business* at the beginning of Brown's landmark 1963 album, "Live at the Apollo." Gonder toured with Brown for years as well as with his own band, performing all over the country during the 1960s. He eventually returned to Macon, where he passed away in 1974.[16]

During the 1950s, a musical revolution began in the United States. African American blues music combined with a healthy dose of white country music and a pinch of black and white gospel to create a great hybrid, or what some would call a great bastard, that young people loved and their parents hated. Fans and the press called it rock and roll, and it represented a musical tidal wave that changed American life forever. Scholars have attempted to dissect the elements that made rock and roll what it became, but the job has always been difficult because the music's architects originally created it to be felt and not overly scrutinized. Early rock and roll, with its blues roots, evoked feelings in the young that did not lend themselves to deep discussions about style and substance.

Prior to the 1950s, blues music in the United States was popular in the black community and with a relatively small number of whites, but the blues-based rock and roll of the 1950s brought blues to the mass of white teenagers, creating innumerable social and generational tensions in the process. To teenagers, rock and roll was fun, but to many older people it seemed dangerous. Many white parents were not comfortable with their sons, and especially their daughters, listening and dancing to music that was black at its core and peppered with sexual innuendo. This tension affected politics in the South and elsewhere during the period, as the same authorities who fought to tame rock and roll also sought to check the advance of the civil rights movement. The landmark Supreme Court desegregation case, *Brown v. Board of Education of Topeka* (1954), and the rise of rock and roll music happened at the same time. Both events brought black and white young people closer together in abrupt and unprecedented ways, and rock and roll music, in a sense, began integrating American society before much of society was ready for the change.[17]

Tracing the precise origins of rock and roll is an impossible task, as it is an artistic river with many tributaries. That said, a strong case can be made that as an American cultural phenomenon, rock and roll was born, at least in part, in the mid-1950s in a Greyhound bus station in Macon, Georgia. The station included a small kitchen where an oddly extroverted African American dishwasher scrubbed pots and pans as he harbored dreams that his singing abilities might one day get him out of the Jim Crow South. His name was Richard Penniman, but fans would know him as Little Richard, and he had string of international hits in the 1950s that altered the course of history. At least one of those songs came right out of the bus station: "I wrote 'Tutti Frutti' in that kitchen," he said many years later.[18]

Richard Penniman was a musical force of nature from an early age. One of twelve children, he was born December 5, 1932, in Macon to Charles "Bud" Penniman and his wife, Leva Mae Stewart, and he came of age in the city's Pleasant Hill neighborhood. As if to foreshadow his son's later struggles with the hedonistic and the holy, Bud was both a church deacon and a bootlegger who owned a small nightclub. Richard's grandfather was also a minister, as was an uncle, and Richard harbored early dreams of being a minister. "I went to the New Hope Baptist Church on Third Street, where my mother was a member," he told Charles White in an interview for White's biography *The Life and Times of Little Richard: The Quasar of Rock*. "My daddy's people were members of Foundation Templar AME Church, a Methodist Church on Madison Street, and my mother's father was with the Holiness Temple Baptist Church in Downtown Macon. So I was kind of mixed up in it right from the start." Church music was a part of Penniman's life from the cradle, as was performing. As a child, his family formed a singing group called the Penniman Singers that performed at local worship services, and he also sang with two of his brothers and another friend in a gospel quartet called the "Tiny Tots."

As he got a little older, Penniman's love of singing, and the early rumblings of an ambition that knew no bounds, led him to contact Clint Brantley about a job. The promoter let the youngster sell bottled drinks for a dime a bucket at the shows he promoted in the Macon Auditorium. It was the boy's first exposure to show business. "That was great," he later recalled, "because I heard all the best artists and bands that were on the touring circuit then, people like Cab Calloway, Hot Lips Page, Cootie Williams, Lucky Millinder, and my favorite singer, sister Rosetta Tharpe."[19]

One night when Tharpe was in town, Penniman talked her into letting him join her for a song on stage. There are two slightly different versions of the story. Little Richard later said that Tharpe, who played gospel with a blues flair, called him up to the stage during the show to sing with her. Meanwhile, Clint Brantley, who had previously laughed at the boy's bravado, later said that Penniman actually sang a song to open Tharpe's show. "I had Rosetta Tharpe here, the gospel singer. I had her here that night at the City Auditorium," he recalled many years later. "Little Richard wasn't nothing but a boy.... He came to me before the show and said 'Mr. Clint, Sister Rosetta said I could open the program.' I said 'Boy, go on, you can't open no program.' The announcer announced the show, the curtain went up, and reckon who was there: Little Richard. I said 'Well, shit, this damn boy can sing.'" Regardless of the details about where Penniman appeared on the program, the end result in both versions of the story are the same. "Everybody applauded and cheered," Penniman remembered. "It was the best thing that ever happened to me."[20]

Despite this taste of local success, the young singer's home life soon became more complicated. From an early age, Penniman displayed characteristics that some considered effeminate, and to the chagrin of Bud Penniman, these characteristics became more pronounced as Richard entered his teen years, and a sexual ambiguity emerged in the boy's character. Richard was also born with one leg slightly shorter than the other, which gave him an unusual gate as he walked, and he became the object of ridicule on the street. "The kids would call me faggot, sissy, freak, punk," he later recalled. "They called me everything." By the time he was thirteen, Penniman had begun to embrace blues music, and this represented the last straw to his father, who threw the boy out of the house. "I came from a family where my people didn't like rhythm and blues. Bing Crosby...Ella Fitzgerald was all I heard. And I knew that there was something that could be louder than that," Penniman told writer David Dalton in a 1970 interview for *Rolling Stone* magazine. "My father didn't like loud music, so that's why he put me out, and because I dressed loud." After the episode, Penniman gravitated toward Macon's gay community in search of a place to fit in. Much speculation would surround his sexuality after he became famous, and he struggled for decades with the inevitable contradictions related to his homosexuality—bisexuality might be more accurate—and his deeply held religious beliefs grounded in evangelicalism.[21]

After leaving home, Penniman joined a traveling outfit called Doc Hudson's Medicine Show, roaming from town to town. It was his job to help draw and entertain crowds as the "doctor" sold snake oil. Penniman often sang the Louis Jordan song "Caldonia," one of the few tunes he knew in totality that was not a religious song. While performing in Fitzgerald, Georgia, he met a band called B. Brown and His Orchestra that needed a singer, and he left Doc Hudson to tour with the group, mainly singing ballads such as "Mona Lisa" and "Goodnight Irene." Penniman was by far the youngest member of the band, and the older men nicknamed him "Little Richard," a name that he would later make famous around the world. He left the band and joined another traveling show, Sugarfoot Sam from Alabam', where he occasionally performed in drag, and later the King Brothers Circus, before returning to Macon. He credited these early road experiences with helping him develop as a performer. "The jazz and blues was really like going to school, and I was in class constantly," he said. "But the carnival was an advance class in entertaining, and my personality was awakened."[22]

Penniman also made his initial recordings during this period after a blues singer named Billy Wright introduced him to influential Atlanta disc jockey Zenas Sears. Sears talked RCA into giving Penniman a contract, and he set up a local recording session at radio station WGST in October of 1951. Penniman cut three forgettable songs—"Goin' to Get Rich Quick," "Taxi Blues," and "Why Did You Leave Me"—along with a song titled "Every Hour" that received substantial airplay in Atlanta and Macon, mainly because Sears took an interest in it. Three months later, he recorded four more songs—"I Brought It All on Myself," "Thinkin' 'bout My Mother," "Please Have Mercy on Me," and "Ain't Nothin' Happening"—none of which sold well, and RCA cut him loose. It was an inauspicious beginning for one of the twentieth century's most influential musical artists.[23]

Though his early records did not sell, Penniman's talent continued to blossom back home in Macon. He never stopped singing, performing in local churches and in secular settings with a diverse repertoire of blues and gospel numbers. "He was just a natural winner," another area musician once told an interviewer. "He started singing in churches and on street corners for nickels and dimes. I've seen Richard standing on street corners, groups gathering up. I gathered up with the group to listen to him because he had that clear, compelling voice." Penniman's voice also won the respect of local bandleaders in Macon, who were always interested in vocalists who could draw a crowd. He sang with several local bands, including Gladys Williams and her group. This represented another small milestone in the singer's early development. Percy Welch, who played with Penniman during those early years, recalled, "He started singing with Gladys Williams, and she had one of the most popular groups around. She used to sing at the Young Men's club on Cotton Avenue. On Sunday nights, she used to let one of us sing and make $9 a night, and that was a lot of money. She started using Little Richard, and he started getting pretty popular." Penniman soon picked up work at other local clubs, and a group led by Welch became his primary backing band.[24]

Because Little Richard was unique as a performer, journalists for decades were curious about his early musical influences. Like rock and roll itself, Penniman's stage presence was the product of an extraordinarily diverse mix of sounds and sights. Rooted in the church, it was heavily peppered with country blues "strait out of the cotton field," the hillbilly sounds of Texas and Appalachia, and radio orchestras that played big band tunes. Somehow, he took all this music in, mixed it around in his brain, and delivered it to audiences in a wildly explosive manner that seemed completely natural even when he wore the most outlandish costumes. He also claimed that as a boy he was simply influenced by the world around him and the music he heard in his neighborhood and on the streets of Macon. "I've heard people sing with no music," he once said. "Just walking the streets, you can hear them late at night, at two o'clock in the morning. You hear somebody singing, you hear the birds, and some water running, and you hear somebody just wailing way."[25]

The list of individuals whom Penniman mentioned through the years as early influences is long and eclectic, filled with personalities ranging from the stable to the strange. On the list of gospel performers were mainstays such as Mahalia Jackson, Marion Williams, and Brother Joe May. "My inspiration for singing is Mahalia Jackson," he once said. "She sang with so much feeling, and she was so sincere; she inspired me quite a bit. I got a lot of turns in my voice from her. When you hear my show in person and if you listen closely, you can hear some of her in me." As for May, Penniman looked up to him from the first time he heard him sing, admiring his booming voice. "Oh, Boy! He was a toe-tapper," Penniman fondly recalled in a 1997 interview with Tom Snyder on *The Late, Late Show*. "He was real tall, and he had a voice like I never heard in my life. When I heard him, it sent chills through me. He was so filled with the spirit of God. He was a fantastic singer and he had a strong, powerful voice, and I wanted that." Finally, there was Sister Rosetta Tharpe, who he consistently claimed was his favorite singer. Tharpe was a very popular performer whose arrangements and delivery meshed gospel music and traditional hymns with a touch of rhythm and blues. She played the electric guitar and her work inspired not only Little Richard, but others in the first wave of rock and roll icons of the 1950s, including Elvis Presley, Johnny Cash, and Jerry Lee Lewis.[26]

Throughout his life, Penniman also lauded many of his contemporaries as early influences on his career. "I would hear Fats Domino, Chuck Berry, Ruth Brown, Faye Adams, the Clovers, the Drifters, Muddy Waters, Howlin' Wolf, John Lee Hooker, Elmore James, and I admired them," he said. "I was singing blues, the same songs that Elmore James and Sonny Boy Williamson sang. When I was a boy in Macon, Fats [Domino] used to come here...he used to play at a club in Macon. I didn't have the money to go see him, so I used to try and sneak in because I loved him. I loved his piano playing. I love his music, period." Young Richard Penniman's love of music also extended to country, which many people stereotyped as strictly white music, although it had an audience in the black community. When quizzed about country tunes later in life, Penniman told a reporter, "Back in that time black people were singing a lot of country music.... I'm a country-music lover. I think it's a true music. It's from the heart." In Macon, he was also an apparent fan of the *Uncle Ned's Hayloft Jamboree* program on both radio and television. Interviewed by David Kirby for Kirby's book *Little Richard: The Birth of Rock and Roll*, Philip "Pee Wee" Clark, who played steel guitar for the Jamboree, said of Penniman "I knew him.... We only had casual meetings, mostly on the road coming from our different places of work, mostly in the early hours of the morning. I know he had great respect for Uncle Ned and all of us on the Hayloft Jamboree gang. We were on WMAZ-TV at the time. He always had a good word for us."[27]

As far as a sense of style was concerned, blues singer Billy Wright, who helped Penniman get his first recording dates, was a great influence. Penniman crossed paths with Wright in Atlanta and was in awe of the older man's showmanship and wardrobe. Wright had a wonderful voice and he wore flashy clothes and makeup. "He was called the Prince of the Blues," Penniman said. "I've never met a man who looked like this.... He had pretty, wavy hair. He had a green suit and green and gold shoes, and I'd never seen anything like that. And so I started wearing the makeup and the cologne." Penniman's wardrobe was also influenced by a local character in Macon called Doctor Nobilio, a loud, wandering, self-professed healer and prophet who claimed to see the future. He usually wore a turban and a red cape, and his strange brand of showmanship was not lost on Little Richard, who later donned a turban and a cape as part of his act.[28]

Musically, Penniman owed a great deal to one of the more shadowy figures in rock and roll history, a musician and street hustler named Eskew Reeder Jr. Reeder was a bizarre personality who had a pronounced pompadour, loved women's makeup, and wore sunglasses even at night. He went by the name "Esquerita," a phonetic perversion of his actual name. Not much is known about Esquerita's early life other than he was born in Greenville, South Carolina, he played the piano and sang, and he met Little Richard late one night at the Greyhound bus station in Macon. He was traveling as part of a strange musical trio that included a woman called Sister Rosa, who in her spare time sold bread supposedly blessed by God, and a tiny man who sang and was appropriately nicknamed Shorty. As an act, they were going nowhere, but Penniman struck up a friendship—some claimed a relationship—with Esquerita, who taught him some fancy piano licks. "He was, and is, one of the greatest pianists, and that's including Jerry Lee Lewis, Stevie Wonder, or anybody I've heard," Penniman once said. "I learned a whole lot of phrasing from him. He really taught me a lot." After Penniman became famous, Esquerita tried to capitalize on their association. He made a handful of recordings that mirrored Little Richard's style and delivery, but his career never gained traction. He ended up in New York City, where he died penniless and forgotten in 1986.[29]

To say that Little Richard was a flamboyant performer is a hollow pronouncement. His early stage act in Macon's black clubs was the wildest thing anybody had ever seen—dancing, screaming, off-color banter, and a unique presence that was overtly sexual, yet in some ways asexual, all at the same time. He later claimed that in the early days, as he crossed over and started playing to rock and roll audiences that included excited white girls, he exaggerated the feminine components of his personality to an even greater degree as a safety precaution. "When you were a young black boy in Georgia, you didn't bother nobody, especially white women," he said, speaking about the era. "I'd be afraid for a white girl to look at me. When they looked at me I would get nervous, because you could get killed." As a result, he donned outlandish clothing and more and more makeup to promote a less threatening image. "It wasn't just a gay thing," he said. "To be black, and to work for white girls, I had to look that way. If I didn't wear make-up and look feminine I couldn't work the white clubs. So the more feminine I looked, the more they didn't mind me being with the white women.... Wasn't nobody afraid of me. I wasn't a threat to be around a white girl."[30]

Though his recording career had not yet taken off, Penniman continued working hard on the stages of Macon and at his mundane day job of washing dishes at the bus station. The station was across the street from a club called Ann's Tic Toc, where Penniman's raucous performances would become legendary. As the story goes, he would often work all day at the bus station and then cross the street after dark to put on shows. What made the performances notable, in addition to Penniman's wild ways, was that the club was by far the most unusual nightspot in Macon, Georgia, during the 1950s. Ann Howard, who was white, owned the nightspot, which was a gay club that also welcomed both black and white patrons, breaking the two most rigid social taboos of the era.

The unusual club was the perfect venue for Richard Penniman to display his talents in Macon. By then he played both piano and saxophone, and he was already developing a revolutionary stage personality. He supposedly introduced his hit song "Tutti-Frutti" there, although with famously obscene lyrics that would not make it onto the record. Howard and her husband, Johnny, took Penniman into their home for a time, and he later titled his hit "Miss Ann" in tribute to her. Howard remembered Penniman's outrageous stage act, which included multiple instruments: "He had a navy blue cape with a gold lining," she said. "He played a guitar, piano and a sax, and he would walk on the bar at night and blow his horn. Anything to add to the show. He was a good one." After he left Macon, he kept contact with Ann and Johnny Howard, once telling an interviewer, "She was just like my mother for many years.... I think they had a lot to do with me being Little Richard."[31]

On February 12, 1952, a local man named Frank Tanner shot and killed Bud Penniman outside his bar, the Tip Inn, in Macon, forever altering Little Richard's life. A definitive account of the killing never surfaced and different versions of the story later popped up in the press. At the time, the official version, accepted by police and printed in the Macon newspapers, held that both men "shot at each other with pistols" in what amounted to "a sort of duel." A Bibb County grand jury later indicted Tanner for murder, but the local district attorney did not pursue the case. A jury eventually convicted the young man of carrying a concealed weapon, and he received a six-month jail sentence. From a legal standpoint, the episode's outcome was not unusual. In the Jim Crow South of the 1950s, a black-on-black killing outside a bar with no witnesses tended to generate little interest among white prosecutors.

As to what really happened, there seems to be two versions of the story, or maybe even three. One version holds that Tanner was in the bar and annoyed Penniman by throwing firecrackers into the coal stove that heated his building. Penniman threw Tanner out in the street, and then threatened him with a gun, at which point the two men began firing at each other. This version, attributed to Little Richard, appears in the Charles White biography. In another version, Little Richard told an interviewer that Bud caught Tanner robbing the bar's peanut machine and that Tanner killed him to try to hide the crime. One rumor that made the rounds in Macon blamed the episode on some sort of jealousy or rivalry between Bud and the Tanner family, who also dabbled in bootlegging. Regardless of the truth, Bud Penniman's death had a great effect on his son. Besides the obvious psychological baggage it created, the killing strengthened Little Richard's resolve to be successful. He wanted to be famous and to make enough money to get out of Macon and take his family with him. "I really wanted to be famous so I could help my mother with my brothers and sisters," he told an interviewer. "I just wanted to get mother out of Macon.... I said I must get famous now, I've got to become a star."[32]

As Penniman grew more popular in Macon, Clint Brantley took notice. Brantley's music-promotion career by then had spanned almost two decades, and he had connections on the chitlin circuit throughout the Southern states and in several Northern cities. He knew the nuts and bolts of the business and was also a good judge of who might make it, and who would not. "He had a tremendous eye and ear for entertainers," one Brantley associate later remembered. "Everybody can't sing. He could spot those who were able to." He began booking Penniman into clubs all over the South as a solo act and then with a band called the Tempo Toppers. Little Richard and the Tempo Toppers were a hit as a live act, consistently drawing large crowds to the clubs where they performed. Their success led to another recording session for Penniman, this time with Peacock Records, headquartered in Houston. As with RCA, he cut eight tracks with Peacock that did little business. The raucously free-spirited Penniman also clashed with label president Don Robey, a strict, sometimes violent taskmaster with little patience for nonsense. Robey cut Little Richard loose, and not long afterwards the Tempo Toppers folded.[33]

Penniman did not have a record in the charts yet, but he remained as popular as ever on stage, and Clint Brantley had no trouble booking him. The singer put together a new group that included guitarist Thomas Hartwell, tenor saxophonist Charles Carmichael, drummer Charles Connor, and Wilbert Smith (known professionally as Lee Diamond), who played saxophone and piano. They billed themselves as "Little Richard and the Upsetters" and quickly established themselves as a tough act to follow. The music of Fats Domino, B. B. King, Roy Brown, and Billy Wright dominated their playlists at shows in Macon and on the road. They also played the profane version of "Tutti-Frutti," one of their show's highlights. Encouraged by Brantley, Penniman made a conscious attempt to add even more energy to his live act and to be even more outrageous, in hopes of landing another recording opportunity. According to Connor, "It was around that time that Richard's manager, Clint Brantley, was in the process of vettin' Richard for another album cycle.... A lot of his emphasis on our live setup and our energy was to make a comeback of sorts."[34]

According to both Penniman and Connor, part of the "Little Richard sound" that developed during the period came from an unlikely source—the trains that regularly ran through Macon. Specifically, the rhythm produced by the locomotives apparently created a metronome-like effect conducive to up-tempo rhythm and blues. Penniman grew up in a house near the railroad tracks in Macon, so the sounds of the trains were part of his earliest memories. "The train would shake the house in front of the tracks," he said. "Everybody would get out of the bed because the train shook the house. The train would say 'CHAKKA – chakka – chakka – chakka, CHAKKA – chakka – chakka – chakka.' To me it was a rhythm. To me it was just like a song." Interviewed later, Connor confirmed that Little Richard had an infatuation with trains that affected his music.

According to Connor, "In rhythm and blues, you had a shuffle with a backbeat, but Little Richard wanted something different...with more energy.... So Richard brought me down to the train station in Macon, Georgia, in 1954, and he said, 'Charles, listen to the choo-choo, choo-choo, choo-choo, choo-choo.' We went back to his house a couple of days later and came up with that beat." It was a beat and rhythm that laid the foundation for Penniman's early string of hits.[35]

For Penniman, the year 1955 was pivotal. He continued playing shows in Macon and elsewhere, and he mixed with other musicians on the road and at home. In Augusta, Georgia, he met popular singer Lloyd Price, who had a recent hit with "Lawdy Miss Clawdy" and drove a huge black and gold Cadillac. "When I first met Little Richard it was incredible," Price later told an interviewer. "I was in Augusta, Georgia, and Richard came over with all this make up on, and a loud suit. He was a young man, you know. I was standing by my car and he said 'I want a car just like that. I'm gonna get me a car just like that. I want to get out of Georgia.'" Later, after a performance in Macon, Price advised the young performer to send a tape to owner Art Rupe at Specialty Records, an independent label in Los Angeles that recorded rhythm and blues and gospel artists. Penniman immediately went to local radio station WBML and recorded a demo tape of two songs, "He's My Star" and "Wonderin,'" and put it in the mail.[36]

The year also included a seedy event that marked the beginning of the end for Little Richard in Macon. Penniman's personal life was as wild as his stage persona, and perhaps it was inevitable that it would one day get him into trouble. In late 1955, he was arrested for what he later called "lewd behavior," but what Macon authorities called "soliciting prostitution." Apparently, one of Penniman's curious pastimes was driving around in a car with a woman who was willing to let him watch her have sex with other men, and he would drive from place to place and accommodate the woman's partners in the back of his car. While Penniman later claimed that no money changed hands, the exercise seemed a lot like pimping, and that was certainly how the authorities viewed it. He went to court and, as the story goes, avoided significant jail time after paying a $150 fine and promising to leave the city. After the incident, Penniman was finished in the Macon clubs, although his subsequent success ended up taking him around the world.[37]

Although it took them months to respond, Specialty Records liked the demo that Penniman sent in. The company set up a recording session for him in New Orleans at J&M Recording Studio, owned by Cosimo Matassa. There he met producer Robert "Bumps" Blackwell, who paired him with Fats Domino's band in hopes of molding a sound reminiscent of Domino, or perhaps Ray Charles. The initial results were lackluster. "They wanted me to sound like Ray Charles and B. B. King, but I was tired of that, you know. Being young, I wanted to sound different. Me and the young kids, we were tired of that slow music. We wanted to boogie!" After the session, Blackwell and Penniman took a break and went to the Dew Drop Inn, the famous New Orleans nightspot on LaSalle Street. Little Richard knew the place, having performed there while touring, and he commandeered the piano for a rousing version of "Tutti-Frutti," complete with its rollicking "a-wop-bop-a-loo-mop-a-lomp-bom-bom" introduction and sexually explicit lyrics. Blackwell recognized the energy produced by the song and wanted to record it, but he knew the words needed cleaning up. He brought in local songwriter Dorothy LaBostrie to craft new lyrics, and she changed, among other things, "Tutti-Frutti, Good Booty" to "Tutti-Frutti, Aw Rooty." Blackwell took Penniman back in the studio and they cut the record in three takes.[38]

Specialty Records released "Tutti-Frutti," and it changed music history on a number of levels. With apologies to Ike Turner and Jackie Brenston's "Rocket 88," Bill Haley's "Rock Around the Clock," and all the other claimants, a strong case can be made that "Tutti-Frutti" was the first rock and roll record. It contained every element that made rock and roll wonderfully jarring to the American psyche and irresistible to teenagers, especially *white* teenagers. It was hard-charging, direct, and manic. Penniman introduced white teenagers to African American music in a more direct way than Elvis Presley, who was a great purveyor of black music but, being white, not quite the real thing. In that sense, it was a conduit for the mixing of black and white culture in an unprecedented way. "Tutti-Frutti" really started the races being together," Penniman later told an interviewer, "because when I was a boy, the white people [at black shows] would sit upstairs [in the theaters]. They called it 'white spectators,' and the blacks was downstairs. At my shows the white kids would jump over the balcony and come down where I was and dance with the blacks. We started that merging all across the country. From the git-go, my music was accepted by whites."[39]

"Tutti-Frutti" also introduced the world to Little Richard. It was the first of a huge string of hits that included "Long Tall Sally," "Good Golly Miss Molly," "Lucille," "I Hear You Knockin'," "Miss Ann," and many others. These songs anchored the first wave of rock and roll in the 1950s and, at the same time, sowed the seeds for the flowering of rock in the 1960s and beyond. The Beatles were covering Little Richard songs in their stage act as early as 1960, as were a host of other iconic bands of the 1960s and 1970s. The Rolling Stones opened for him on an early American tour, and before he became famous, Jimi Hendrix played in Little Richard's band. Without Little Richard, there would have been a great hole in early rock and roll that Elvis, Chuck Berry, and Jerry Lee Lewis would not have been able to fill, and rock and roll as a genre or musical classification would not have developed as it did without the wild singer from Macon. Throughout his long career, Little Richard would tell anyone who would listen, usually at the top of his lungs, that he was "the innovator, the emancipator, the originator, the architect of rock and roll!" It was a bold claim that was part bravado and part showmanship, but many elements of it were true.

With the success of "Tutti-Frutti" and the records that followed, Little Richard, who the authorities had already asked to vacate Macon, left Georgia for good. He moved to Los Angeles and took his mother and some of his siblings with him. His last club appearance in Macon was probably a "Midnight Ramble" at Club 15 of December 11, 1955. Not long afterward, he cancelled a Christmas appearance at the municipal auditorium that Clint Brantley had put together. After relocating to the West Coast, numerous recording sessions and tours of the United States and Europe followed, as he established himself as a founding father of rock and roll. He famously retired and unretired from the music business multiple times as he struggled to reconcile rock and roll's hedonism and his religious roots. While he visited Macon occasionally, he would not perform again in the city for years.[40] He died at the age of eighty-seven on May 9, 2020, still revered as an early rock and roll icon.

When Little Richard left Macon, the authorities may have been happy, but Clint Brantley certainly was not. The departure left a big blank spot in the list of local artists that he managed and booked, and, more importantly, it left him on the hook for around thirty regional commitments that Little Richard would not be filling. Brantley's solution was simple. He decided to substitute another singer to impersonate Penniman and sing his songs as Little Richard for the remaining dates. While Penniman had crisscrossed Georgia and the rest of the South quite a bit, Brantley surmised that much of the singer's audience did not pay attention to, or would remember, exactly what he looked like. When dressed appropriately, another singer might be able to pull off the deception, especially in the dimly lit, alcohol-soaked nightclubs that were common on the chitlin circuit. Brantley found a pretender to fill the engagements, and that should have been the end of the story. Instead, the episode generated a tale that became famous in the annals of popular music history. The singer that Clint Brantley chose to imitate Little Richard on the road was none other than James Brown, the future "Godfather of Soul," whose career Brantley was about to help launch.[41]

James Brown was born in a tiny shack in the woods of Barnwell, South Carolina, on May 3, 1933, the only child of Joseph Gardner Brown and his wife, Susie Behling. The family was poverty-stricken, and Brown's father struggled to make ends meet selling turpentine and bootleg whiskey. Brown's parents eventually split up, although there are conflicting accounts of what exactly happened. One version of the story has Susie Brown leaving the family for another man around 1937 while still in South Carolina. Another version, supported by a good deal of evidence, holds that she moved to Augusta, Georgia, with her family in the late 1930s but fled after suffering abuse at the hands of her violent husband. In his autobiography, *James Brown: The Godfather of Soul*, Brown states that his mother left when he was four years old, and he did not see her again for twenty years. However, this conflicts with city directories for Augusta that list Joseph and Susie Brown living in the city under the same roof at 1157 Norrell's Alley between 1947 and 1949, which seems to suggest that if the couple was estranged, they reconciled at some point, albeit temporarily. Also living at the same address was Joseph's aunt Minnie Walker, who had helped deliver James Brown back in South Carolina and looked after him as a child.[42]

Regardless of the conflicting accounts, James Brown's early family life was chaotic and deprived, to say the least. It was also marred by violent episodes. Brown moved with his father and Aunt Minnie—and perhaps his mother—to Augusta in the late 1930s. They lived in a large boarding house and brothel on Twiggs Street owned by another aunt, Hansone Washington, whom he called Aunt Honey. The "household" also included more than a dozen members of their extended relations as well as transients and prostitutes who were all struggling to survive. The family lived there for some time, and some sources state that this is where Brown's family actually came apart. Journalist Don Rhodes, who talked to people who knew the Browns, later reported, "The account that I got was Aunt Honey's house had two or three stories to it, and the Browns were staying on the second floor, and [Joseph] threw Susie out of a second floor window. And so it wasn't very long before she ran for her life out of Augusta." Exactly when the Browns' marriage broke up remains unclear, but by the 1950s, Susie had relocated to New York City and found work as a seamstress. Many who knew her always held fast to the claim that she "did not willingly abandon her family."[43]

Brown suffered a good deal of physical abuse as a youngster to go with the emotional wounds that inevitably came from spending his formative years in a brothel. Joseph Brown beat his son for the slightest misbehavior, as did Aunt Honey. Some of the men who visited the brothel apparently kicked James around just for fun, and many nights the boy's family allowed him to run the streets at unsupervised. It was a bleak existence that left scars he would have to deal with later in life. "There ain't but two pains, mental and physical," Brown reflected as an adult. "I think personally I'd rather deal with physical pain. I can go to the doctor and take care of that, but mental pain.... The Lord got to take care of that for me. I can't do that myself."[44]

After the United States entered the Second World War, the federal government established a huge training facility called Camp Gordon near Augusta. The post brought thousands of men into the area and helped the region economically. Even young James Brown felt the effects. His aunt Honey sent him out to tell soldiers about the brothel, earning him tips, and he also hung around the installation's front gate dancing for the men, who would throw him nickels and dimes. "We used to hustle the soldier to go get 'em a girl, cause we had to have some money," he told an interviewer. "I danced for the soldiers and I guess I picked up about six dollars [a day], and rent was five dollars. I gave all the money to Honey." James also added to the community till at home by performing "most any kind of odd job," including "shining shoes, delivering groceries, racking pool balls in local saloons, and picking cotton and peanuts." The war also took Joseph Brown away from home when he enlisted in the navy.[45]

The brothel eventually closed, and James moved with his aunt Minnie into a separate house, where his life became somewhat more stable. To his credit, Joseph Brown sent them money every month, but it was barely enough to live on. Brown attended Silas X. Floyd Elementary School, the local segregated school for African Americans, where he suffered numerous indignities. One day, school officials sent him home for "insufficient clothes" after he showed up in the morning wearing rags. His time on the streets made him combative, and he frequently got into fights. Fortunately, one of his teachers and the school's principal took an interest in Brown, especially after they noticed that he was a natural singer. They pushed the youngster to perform at school programs and talent shows, which helped bolster his confidence and self-esteem.[46]

Brown had many early musical influences. Although he was a delinquent street kid, he was drawn to local African American churches from a young age. Brown later said that he hung around Sunday services because he liked to listen to local choirs and watch the theatrics of the preachers. "At the churches there was a lot of singing and handclapping," he remembered, "and then the preacher would really get down. I liked that more than the music....He was just screaming and yelling and stomping his foot and then dropped to his knees....I watched the preachers real close. Then I'd go home and imitate them, because I wanted to preach." He also recalled doing odd jobs for whites and hearing on their radios Bing Crosby and Frank Sinatra, both of whom appealed to him, as well as classic jazz, blues, and swing by Duke Ellington, Count Basie, and Louis Jordan. While living with Aunt Honey, he learned some basic guitar from traveling bluesman Hudson Whitaker, who called on one of the girls at the house whenever he passed through Augusta. Whitaker went on to gain notoriety under his stage name, Tampa Red. Brown did his best to sneak into any traveling shows that came to town or local juke joints that thrived on live music. He soaked up the music and the atmosphere, logging everything he experienced somewhere in the back of his young mind for use in the future.[47]

Brown also started playing the piano after he met Leon Austin, another youngster interested in music who became a lifelong friend. A little less than a year younger than Brown, Austin was a prodigy as a pianist. He could play almost any tune by ear, and African American churches in Augusta sought him out because his repertoire included innumerable hymns and gospel songs. Austin invited Brown into his home, showed him a few chords, and let him practice on the family piano. Brown loved gospel music, but, according to Austin, both boys were also interested in "boogie-woogie." Brown got a job cleaning out Trinity Baptist Church just so he could practice on the congregation's piano. He also learned the drums and did his best to master a beat-up, fifteen-cent harmonica that had belonged to his father. An Augusta group led by Sammy Green was his favorite band, and he tried to see them—and *study* them—as often as possible. "There was a local man named Sammy Green who had a band of maybe ten pieces," Brown remembered, "and I tried to hear them whenever I could. They were reading charts, had a horn section, everything."[48]

The Lenox Theatre in Augusta twice served as a catalyst for Brown as his talent developed. Located in the 1100 block of 9th Street (what is now James Brown Boulevard), the Lenox was a popular African American venue that hosted live events as well as films. During the 1940s, it hosted an amateur night for local talent. By the time he was twelve years old, Brown had enough confidence in his singing abilities to enter a contest. Unaccompanied, he won first prize singing "So Long," a bluesy ballad that he later recorded. Afterwards, an emboldened Brown formed his own group with two other boys. They named themselves the Cremona Trio, because one of them played a Cremona guitar. The future Godfather of Soul later referred to this as his first band, and the group held together for the next couple of years playing for tips around the neighborhood, and for soldiers at Camp Gordon.

The Lenox was also the place where Brown first saw a film short featuring Louis Jordan and his Tympany Five. Jordan, who also influenced Little Richard, was an innovator who popularized up-tempo blues music that many consider a precursor to rock and roll. Jordan and his band made an eighteen-minute film short in 1945 that played in black theaters and featured a performance of the song "Caldonia." Brown was transfixed, and watching the performance reinforced the notion that he wanted to make entertainment a career. "'Caldonia' was a song you could really put on a show with," he later said, "and I guess that Louis Jordan short is what first started me thinking along those lines. That and the preachers."[49]

Unpredictably, another major step on James Brown's path to becoming a world-class entertainer was a jail sentence. When he was sixteen years old, Brown was arrested for burglary and sentenced to eight years in prison. The authorities shipped him to a juvenile detention center in Rome, Georgia, and eventually moved him to another facility called the Boys Industrial Training Institute in Toccoa, Georgia. Ironically, rather than stifling his creative instincts, his incarceration seemed to accomplish the opposite. The Toccoa institute was a minimum-security facility that offered little regimented supervision. In effect, the boys were given free run of the place as long as they did not make trouble for the staff or run away. "There wasn't no fence," one observer later remarked, "it was just an imaginary line. Everybody knew just how far they were supposed to go." The inmates also had access to radios, and Brown spent many of his idle hours listening to a local station, WLET, that aired a black gospel program, and WLAC, the powerful clear-channel station from Nashville that programmed rhythm and blues. Brown formed his own gospel quartet that performed for visitors to the institution, and the other boys started calling him "Music Box," the first of many nicknames he received related to his talents.

While institutionalized, Brown met two young men who would have a great impact on his life. The first was Johnny Terry, another hard case from Atlanta who was also serving time, and Bobby Byrd, whose family rescued Brown from prison. Unlike Terry, Byrd was not an inmate at the institute and was the opposite of Brown in temperament and background. He had a stable upbringing, was valedictorian of his high school, a disciplined athlete, and an active church member. Byrd performed as a pianist and singer with Toccoa bands and was a member of a popular gospel group called the Gospel Starlighters. He met "Music Box" when the Starlighters performed at the institute, and again when his local baseball team took on a team from the prison that included Brown. Byrd told his mother about the singer, and the family decided to sponsor Brown for parole. The authorities released Brown on the condition that he remain employed, lived with the Byrds, and promised to stay out of trouble.[50]

After leaving jail, Brown contemplated his future. Looking for any way out of poverty, and determined to succeed, he gave fleeting thought to becoming a professional boxer or maybe a baseball player, but it soon became apparent that music was his future. He started performing with a group that Byrd put together, and the response was positive. They sang gospel, but also performed secular tunes at clubs and for social events, adhering to a template that would launch many rhythm and blues performers of the period—raucous shows featuring popular hits for alcohol-fueled patrons on Saturday nights balanced by reverent, well-polished gospel performances in church on Sundays. They also sang for whites at social functions and during intermissions at the local movie theater. At first,

Byrd was the acknowledged leader of the group, but Brown soon took over the role. His charisma and talent were undeniable, and to his credit, Byrd allowed his friend to capture the limelight without protest. Somewhere along the line, the group took the name the "Flames." Why they chose that name is a bit unclear, but a loose consensus was later reached that it came from the members' view that the group was "hot."[51]

By the 1950s, the Flames were indeed hot, at least regionally. They played at dances for white teenagers and college students and in African American nightclubs. They even performed on the radio in Atlanta and made a handful of quickly forgotten recordings for small labels. The turning point for the group came one night in 1955 at a nightspot called Bill's Rendezvous in Toccoa. Little Richard, yet to break nationally but a phenomenon on the Southern chitlin circuit, visited for a one-nighter, and the Flames were in the house to watch the show. Between sets, they took the stage and gave an impromptu performance that both annoyed and impressed Little Richard.

There are slightly different accounts of what happened next. According to one, Little Richard told the Flames that his manager in Macon, Clint Brantley, might help the group and that he would contact Brantley on their behalf. In his book about James Brown, journalist Don Rhodes wrote that in 1996, Penniman told him, "I first met James in Toccoa, Georgia, when I was doing a show in that town. James and his group, the Famous Flames asked if they could sing at intermission of my show.... I could hear them backstage and what they were doing to the audience. I thought they weren't going to give the microphone back! They were fantastic." Brown confirmed this years later when he told an interviewer, "I was in Toccoa, Georgia. Little Richard came from Macon and saw me and told his manager about me, and I went back to Macon. I got to give Little Richard that credit."[52]

Another version has Luke "Fats" Gonder, Penniman's bandleader, contacting Brantley on Brown's behalf, but only after Richard instructed him to do so. A 1978 account left by Brantley seemed to give Gonder the lion's share of the credit for "discovering" James Brown. In the coarse language that was his habit, Brantley told an interviewer, "I sent [Gonder] up to Toccoa to play a dance [with Little Richard]. That's up in northeast Georgia...and James and them went down there to Toccoa to sing that night. Luke Gonder came back that night and said, 'Some little niggers got down and sure could sing. They call themselves the Flames. I gave them your address and how they could get you and they said they'd be down here.'" Apparently, there was enough credit to go around, as Brown seemed to confirm this account as well, stating in his 1986 autobiography, *James Brown: The Godfather of Soul*, "Fats told us about Clint Brantley, and told us to get in touch with him."[53]

While James Brown later gave Little Richard credit for helping him at this critical time, the two men had a contentious rivalry early on after Brown became popular. For his part, the flamboyant Penniman was always quick to claim that he had discovered Brown (along with Jimi Hendrix, the Rolling Stones, the Beatles, and just about every other rock act of significance from the 1960s), which made Brown uncomfortable. From the start, friction was inevitable between the two larger-than-life characters. "He wanted to punch me in the mouth," Penniman said later. "We had a rivalry thing where we would outdo each other....We were both very vain. Both of us thought we were the best that ever hit....[Brown] was not very friendly during that period, not to me anyway." Bobby Byrd also remembered that Brown "had a powerful hate for Richard there for a while," because "Richard ... was a good-looking fella and was successful. And we were like a struggling act. Richard was sharp, but all of us looked like we were strait out of the sticks.... James couldn't stand that at all." Even in 1987, after both men had become legends, the competition had not quite cooled. Interviewed by the Macon *Telegraph* for an article on Macon's music history, Brown claimed Penniman as a friend, but not before taking a shot at his rival. "[The Flames] were so hot Little Richard had to go to California," Brown said of their early days in the city. "I just beat Little Richard doing it. But I love him. Richard is a very good friend of mine."[54]

Regardless of the exact sequence of events, the Flames showed up in Macon at the Two-Spot to talk to, and sing for, Clint Brantley on a Saturday morning. According to Brantley, it was Johnny Terry, Brown's friend from the juvenile facility who had joined the group, who initially did all the talking. "Little country boys," Brantley later remembered with a chuckle. "And you could tell they were country. One of them did the talking, Johnny Terry. He said, 'We're looking for Mr. Clint Brantley.... We are the Flames from Toccoa, Georgia. We sing and are looking for someone to manage us.'" Brantley, who was nursing a hangover and probably not in the best mood, initially refused to help but changed his mind after listening to the group sing "Looking for My Mother," a spiritual.

"And goddamn man, them sons of bitches," Brantley recalled. "When they got through, I said 'Boys, y'all can sing!'" He agreed to manage the Flames and made arrangements to bring them to Macon. Brown later confirmed the story in his autobiography, stating, "We had heard that Clint really liked gospel, so instead of singing anything popular, we decided to do a sacred number. A song we could really tear up was one I taught the group at our first rehearsal, 'Looking for My Mother.'"[55]

One of the Flames' first bookings in Macon was at a popular African American juke joint called Club 15, an established chitlin circuit stop. Before the gig, Brantley added "Famous" to the group's name as a marketing ploy, and from that point forward they would be known as the Famous Flames. "We'll put 'famous' in front of it since y'all aren't from around here," he said. "We won't say where y'all *are* from, we'll just say you're the *Famous* Flames." One of the first newspaper ads promoting his new group read, "Tonight, The Famous Flames, introduced to Maconites and Bibb Countians by Clint Brantley, a top group in the entertainment world!"[56]

The Famous Flames took Macon by storm and rivaled Little Richard as the most popular act in town. Not long afterwards, "Tutti-Frutti" hit for Penniman, and he left the area for good, leaving Brantley in the lurch with a number of unfulfilled commitments on the calendar. That is when the promoter decided to substitute Brown for Little Richard for those dates. For about a month this probably caused some confusion, at least locally. "Meantime, [Bobby] Byrd and the fellas were doing the Famous Flames bookings," Brown later said. "I was getting paid as Little Richard and Bobby was getting paid as me. I guess I did about fifteen of Richard's dates. I'd come out and do 'Tutti-Frutti'.... I guess the audience thought I was really Richard." Brown returned to the Famous Flames as quickly as possible, and, with a band led by Fats Gonder backing them, the group began building local momentum. In November of 1955, they participated in a "battle of the blues" at the city auditorium on a bill that included national recording star Ruth Brown. For this appearance the group was billed as "The Famous Flames, featuring James Brown, vocalist." Gonder's band continued to back the group after the Famous Flames became nationally known and toured the country.[57]

In addition to promoting the Famous Flames as a live act, Brantley was also instrumental in helping Brown make his first significant recording, "Please, Please, Please," the song that helped establish the singer nationally. He sent Brown and at least two of the other Flames to the studio at WIBB to meet Macon radio personality Charles "Big Saul" Green. At the time, WIBB was devoting time in the afternoon to a block of "race music" popular with African American listeners. With Green serving as the engineer, Brown recorded "Please, Please, Please," a number he had been performing in the Flames' stage act for some time. Because of Brown's height, Green set up a soft drink crate for the singer to stand on so he could reach the overhead microphone. The song was related to Billy Wright's "Turn Your Lamp Down Low," which, in turn, was the musical progeny of Big Joe Turner's 1935 recording "Baby Please Don't Go." Brown and Johnny Terry shared the writing credit, although others, including Clint Brantley, later maintained that Terry alone penned the song.[58]

The record Brown cut at WIBB was strictly a demo that Brantley hoped he could use to generate interest in the Flames, and he started shopping it around to small, independent labels. He also took Brown to meet another local disc jockey, Hamp "King Bee" Swain, who worked at WBML, another station that had recently started playing the music of black artists. Swain had a large following in Macon, and he agreed to play the demo during his program. The local response was overwhelming and immediate. "It was a capella, you know—just James and his group the Famous Flames in the background," Swain later recalled. "And it just went wild. Explosive! Crazy! The harmony and the sincerity in the delivery of the song, it was just different, but it was something I thought had a chance." Suddenly, Brown's act, which already attracted good crowds, was a must-see show in Macon. He took over recently departed Little Richard's crown as the king of Macon's black nightclubs, and news of the Flames' popularity, and the energy of their front man, circulated along the chitlin circuit and elsewhere. Not long afterwards, the Flames signed with King Records, headquartered in Cincinnati, but not before one of the label's representatives made a somewhat cloak-and-dagger visit to Middle Georgia.[59]

In Macon, as in the rest of the South during the mid-1950s, many whites were wary of strangers visiting their city. As the civil rights era dawned, the Southern political community warned whites to be on guard for "outside agitators" who might come south to "stir up" the African American population to oppose the status quo. According to King Records representative Ralph Bass, this created some logistical bumps in the road as he tried to sign the Famous Flames. Bass was a talent scout and producer who first heard the "Please, Please, Please" demo while visiting an Atlanta radio station, and he immediately recognized the record's potential. "My theory as a producer," he said, "has always been, let me find someone who's different, and at least I have a chance. It might backfire, but at least I have a chance of being different, novel."

Bass, who was white, came to Macon to sign the Famous Flames and later described his visit as being "like a James Bond story." As he later said, "Macon was one of those towns. An out of town white cat could be in trouble in those days." Upon his arrival, he called Clint Brantley at home, leaving a message with his wife. Brantley called back and set up a covert meeting at his barber shop. According to Bass, the Macon music impresario told him: "Now at eight o'clock you park your car in front of the barber shop, which is right across the street from the railroad station. When the lights go up and the blinds go up and down, after they go down, you come in." Bass followed the instructions and eventually met with Brantley to make a pitch for King Records. Brantley had also heard from Chess Records in Chicago and had an unsigned contract from Chess in his hand as the two men talked. At the time, Leonard Chess was also on his way to Macon, but poor weather had grounded his flight, leaving the door open for King. In the end, Bass gave Brantley $200 cash and signed the Famous Flames, and the two men adjourned to a local club where the group was performing.[60]

Not long after the meeting in the barber shop, Bass returned to Cincinnati to get ready to record Brown's group, and Brantley made the travel arrangements. The Famous Flames, along with Luke Gonder's band, piled into one of Brantley's cars and started north. At the recording session in Cincinnati, Brown cut another version of "Please, Please, Please" with the Flames providing the backup vocals and Gonder's band the music. Syd Nathan, the head of King Records, famously hated the song and threatened to fire Bass on the spot, but Bass was able to talk his boss into releasing the record. According to one version of the story, Nathan only agreed to release the record to prove his point that it was destined to flop. Nathan misjudged the song—and Brown's performance.[61]

Federal Records, a subsidiary of King, released "Please, Please, Please," on February 4, 1956, with "Why Do You Do Me?" as the B side. Within a short time, the record began to get national airplay. "Coming out of left field," an editor at *Billboard* magazine wrote not long after the release, "is a disc that is shaping up as a sleeper to watch. Two territories— Atlanta and Cincinnati—for two weeks have reported very strong activity. Considering how quickly it has developed there, other markets are advised to keep a sharp eye on it." The record ended up peaking at number five on the *Billboard* R & B charts and was one of the best-selling R & B singles of 1956. This led to more recording sessions for the Famous Flames, although it marked the beginning of the end of Brown's association with the first version of the group.[62]

The trouble between Brown and the other singers started when the record came out labeled "James Brown with the Famous Flames," instead of giving credit to the group as a whole. From that point forward, Brown was the focal point of the act, with the Famous Flames relegated to the status of support personnel. More importantly, future financial rewards for the group would be distributed on that basis. Given the circumstances, a split was probably inevitable. In the end, Brown drew the crowds, and he understandably thought he should enjoy the benefits of his position. Despite that reality, it was still a hard pill to swallow for the rest of the group. It took about a year to occur, but the unraveling of the original Famous Flames had begun. They made several more recordings for King, but things were never the same.

After "Please, Please, Please" hit, Brown and the group signed a management deal with Universal Attractions in New York, an agency headed by Ben Bart. Bart took charge of their career, although Brantley continued to book the Famous Flames on a regional basis. Bart organized a national tour, with Gonder's band backing the group. He put the rest of the Famous Flames on a straight salary while continuing to give Brown a share of recording royalties, which doomed the relationship between Brown and his friends. Determined to make a name for himself, and interested in the money, Brown did not protest or try to alter the new arrangement. This proved to be the last straw. The Famous Flames agreed to honor any commitments that were already on the books, but after that, they wanted out. It was devastating for Bobby Byrd. "[We said] once we make a record, if we become real big, we're going to do this, we're going to do that," Byrd later remembered. "We didn't get a chance to do it, because after the records started to become big, a change came."[63]

By the summer of 1957, Brown was a solo act still performing with Gonder's group and other musicians. He maintained a heavy touring schedule and recruited some of Little Richard's former backup singers to become the new Famous Flames. Unfortunately, despite the continued exposure on the road, his recording career floundered. None of the follow-ups to "Please, Please, Please" sold well, and it looked like Syd Nathan might drop him. At the end of one tour, Brown was on the way back to Macon with the rest of the band when he approached guitarist Bobby Roach with a song he claimed he had picked up from someone on the road. As the story goes, Brown and Roach worked on the song together, and by the time they got to Macon it was ready to record. Brown, Roach, and some of the others went straight to WIBB to make a demo. Some versions of the story hold that Brown's friend "Big Saul" Green, who had first recorded "Please, Please, Please," lent Brown the money to pay for the session. The track that they laid down was "Try Me," a song that became a James Brown classic.[64]

Like many chapters of the Brown story, there is an alternate version of events surrounding the recording of "Try Me." In his 1986 autobiography, Brown, who had the sole songwriting credit, claimed that he wrote the song all by himself as a pop tune after hearing Dee Clark's "Raindrops" and "For Your Precious Love" by Jerry Butler and the Impressions. He also claimed that he cut the demo out of town and sent it to Macon so that Green and Hamp Swain could give it some airplay.[65]

Whether it was recorded in Macon or elsewhere, Syd Nathan heard the demo and was impressed enough to finance a New York recording session, where the song was polished and made presentable. The record came out in 1958 and went to the top of the R & B charts, instantly reviving Brown's career. On the strength of the new release, Brown recruited more band members and hit the road with confidence, but despite the success, drama again developed within his group. The second incarnation of the Famous Flames, and some of the supporting musicians, walked out after a dispute over money. The tension between Brown and his entourage was part of a pattern that would repeat itself again and again during the singer's career. Brown's solution to the problem was not complicated. He simply recruited some new performers and carried on.

After "Try Me" entered the charts, Brown secured his first booking at New York's Apollo Theater in April of 1959. Performing with a new batch of Famous Flames and several new band members—Gonder's and Brown's old friend Johnny Terry remained with the group—he was a hit and appeared at the famous venue numerous times over the next two years, honing his live act into something special. Brown's stage moves were incredible, and he wore a massive cape that he used dramatically as part of his routine. His crowded band and constantly dancing backup singers were a spectacle. In addition to shows at the Apollo, he toured at a feverish pace, once performing sixty-one consecutive one-nighters across the country. As Brown emerged as a national star, he maintained ties with friends in Georgia, including Clint Brantley. The promoter continued to manage local bands in Macon and booked several "homecoming" concerts for Brown at the city auditorium. Among the most notable of these events was a July 14, 1961, show that featured Brown and the Famous Flames on the same bill as Chuck Berry and Ben E. King.[66]

Brown also made a trip back to Macon in the 1960s that generated one of the most colorful stories in the annals of the city's music history. The tale revolved around bad blood that existed between Brown and R & B singer, Joseph Arrington Jr., known professionally as Joe Tex. "Joe Tex used to spend a lot of time here," local musician Newton Collier recalled. "He was being booked out of Macon.... [H]e could outdance James Brown, and knew all these tricks with the microphone."[67] The two men had apparently been friendly rivals at some point. Back in 1957, Clint Brantley promoted a successful "battle of the bands" at the city auditorium featuring Brown and Tex, but somewhere along the line the relationship soured. The genesis of the trouble may have been related to a woman named Bea Ford. She was one of Brown's backup singers and a part-time girlfriend who had once been married to Tex. Adding fuel to the fire were allegations that Brown had stolen a cowriting credit on Tex's song "Baby, You're Right" and claims that Brown also copied some of Tex's stage moves. The men traded barbs in the press for years, but the bitter feelings came to a head one night in Macon at Club 15.

According to one version of the story, the incident took place in 1963 after Tex served as the opening act for one of Brown's homecoming shows. During his performance, Tex supposedly poked fun at Brown, imitating him and waving around an old, tattered blanket as a "cape." Tex intentionally got himself tangled up in the oversized piece of fabric and then delivered the punch line for the performance, which was "Please, Please, Please, get me out of this blanket!" An excellent mimic, he would also jump up and down and fall to his knees, just like Brown did during his shows. While this makes for a good story, whether Tex and Brown were on the same bill that night is up for debate. Brown did play a homecoming concert in Macon in July of 1963, but Tex was not listed on the bill in newspaper ads for the event. It also seems curious that Brown would have asked Tex to open a show for him in Macon, or anywhere else, considering the hard feelings between the two men.

Whether they were on the same bill or not, Brown knew that Tex ridiculed him as part of his regular stage act, and that naturally made him angry. As for Tex, he seemed to relish getting under Brown's skin. The central element of the story is that one night during the 1960s, while Brown was in Macon for a performance, he and Tex ended up at Club 15, and the results were explosive. Johnny Jenkins and the Pinetoppers, including a young singer named Otis Redding, were on stage at the club and Tex was in the audience. He may or may not have done his Brown parody that night, but at some point, Brown stormed into the place with two shotguns. He started firing at Tex as the crowd and the band scattered. According to Newton Collier, who was in the building, "James was furious. Joe Tex was sitting at the table. James came in with two guns, Pow, pow, pow! Joe Tex ducked. Everybody ducked. The Pinetoppers jumped off stage. Seven people got shot. They emptied the club out and everybody that got shot got a hundred dollar bill, so they didn't call the police." Bandleader Johnny Jenkins had a similar recollection when he later told an interviewer, "Seven people got shot. They were reloading and coming back in. Me and Otis [Redding], we were hiding behind a piano. A guy went around later, and I think he gave each one of the injured $100 apiece not to carry it no further. And that just quieted it down." Tex, who was not one of the wounded, escaped out a back door, and as the smoke cleared, Brown was reportedly seen driving away behind the wheel of his tour bus. In the end, no one was arrested, and the incident would be told and retold around Macon for years, occupying a prominent place in the city's music lore.[68]

And the rest, as they say, is history. Around that time, Brown left Macon behind and moved permanently to New York City, where he continued to prosper. Another turning point for the entertainer came in 1963 when he released the landmark album *Live at the Apollo* to rave reviews. A straight recording of Brown's stage show, taped October 24, 1962, the album was a massive success that remained on the *Billboard* charts for more than a year and whet the appetites of hundreds of thousands of listeners to see Brown in person. "Soul music wasn't exactly born on October 24, 1962," *Rolling Stone* reviewer Gaylord Fiends wrote, "but on that day it took a great leap to becoming the dominant form of African-American popular song."[69]

The next year, Brown made a famous appearance in the concert film *T.A.M.I. Show*, reportedly upstaging the Rolling Stones and other up-and-coming rock acts and establishing himself as one of the greatest entertainers in the music business. He also achieved his goal of attracting a large mainstream audience, including legions of white followers, with the release of "Papa's Got a Brand New Bag" in 1965. For the next four decades, fans revered Brown as "Mr. Dynamite," "The Godfather of Soul," "Soul Brother No. 1," and "The Hardest Working Man in Show Business," and he was credited with, among other things, laying the foundation of funk and rap music. Throughout his career in show business, James Brown would have a good many highly publicized ups and downs, but upon his death in 2006 fellow performers, politicians, and the general public far and wide lauded him as one of the greatest musical performers America has ever produced.

James Brown had a reputation for being tough on the singers and musicians who worked for him, which led to a great deal of turnover in his revue. During the late 1950s and early 1960s, he ran through several bandleaders, but one stood out among the rest and remains what some describe as an unsung hero of the James Brown musical saga. Lewis Hamlin Jr. was born in Macon on October 24, 1930, the son of Lewis Hamlin Sr. and Ruby Brown Hamlin. Musically gifted from an early age, he grew up in the Tindall Heights neighborhood of Macon and attended Ballard-Hudson High School, where he played trumpet in the school band. By the age of sixteen, he was performing at church programs and social events, and was a soloist in the Young People's Choir of Friendship Baptist Church. After high school, he attended Georgia Baptist College and earned a degree in music education from Fort Valley State. At Fort Valley, he studied trumpet, saxophone, and flugelhorn under George Adams, who Hamlin later told an interviewer "was probably the most influential person on my career."[70]

Keen on giving back to the community through music, Hamlin took a job as assistant director of music at Hudson-Ballard High School after he left Fort Valley. In addition to his teaching duties there, in 1950 he organized the St. Peter Claver Drum and Bugle Corps, a church-sponsored marching outfit that included younger musicians. The corps originally included sixteen members, but within a year their numbers had grown to twenty-three, including Julius Williams, Stanley Goldsboro Jr., Roy Shanteen, Jerald Mathis, Ronald Fultz, Langston Austin, Moses Scott, William Hawkins, Ronald Thompson, Bernard Brown, Joseph Russell, Arthur Bailey, Bernard Abraham, Carlton Simmons, Carl Davis, Charles Powell, Harold Woodall, Charles Hickson, Larry Givens, Emory Billingslea, Charles Howard, Anderson Fultz, and Windell McIntosh. The group's first public performance was at a music festival at Ballard-Hudson High School, which led to an invitation to perform at a music clinic at Fort Valley State. Other civic events followed, and in 1951 they marched in Macon's annual Armed Forces Day Parade, where they reportedly "stole the show, and made quite a hit with radio commentators too, who were broadcasting during the event." While the success of the group reflected positively on Hamlin as a music instructor, it was also an early example of the focused organizational and arranging skills that defined his professional music career.[71]

While Hamlin was honing his technical expertise in classes at Fort Valley State, he was receiving a musical education of another sort in the evenings. Gladys Williams, always a discerning judge of music personnel, hired Hamlin to play trumpet in her band. He played with Williams's group for social occasions in the black and white communities and at night on Macon's African American nightclub circuit. While George Adams laid the foundation for Hamlin's career as a musician, Williams, who ran a tight ship, schooled the young trumpet player in the art of leading a band, and it was apparently quite an education. He continued to teach school during the day while keeping a crowded schedule of nighttime performances. In 1958, he became the arranger and trumpet player for a local band called the Jazz Messengers, billed as "the group that introduced 'Night Club Jazz' to Macon." Tenor saxophonist Jessie Hancock led the outfit that also included guitarist Thomas Harwell, pianist Howard Smith, bassist Benny Davis, and Little Richard's former drummer Percy Welch. For two years, they were the house band at the American Legion Post 501 on Cotton Avenue.[72]

According to Hamlin, it was a chance meeting with James Brown in Savannah, Georgia, that led him to join Brown's group. At the time, the large band that Brown carried was in disarray, mired in pay disputes and general dissension, with some old members leaving and new members coming in. Brown was looking for someone who could bring discipline to the group, especially in a musical context, to create the tight sound he needed as an energetic front man. Some of Brown's players had a hard time reading music, and the sound of the band also had to be coordinated with Brown's dance steps and those of the backup dancers. It was a large revue with a lot happening onstage. Hamlin had an excellent reputation among other musicians on the Middle Georgia circuit as an arranger, and he and Brown had crossed paths many times in Macon. "I need you to be a role model for the other musicians," Brown told him.[73]

Hamlin took the job, which was initially difficult. "The first night I heard the band I thought, 'Well, gee I can't do this. I'll never learn this,'" he recalled. "You had to memorize all the parts and the dance steps. But in a couple of weeks I could do it.... It was constant pressure, but I enjoyed it. I wanted to get on the road to prove I could do it. The road is essential to your development." Under Hamlin's leadership, the band came together to provide audiences with the foundation of the James Brown experience. Reppard Stone, a jazz musician who grew up with Hamlin in Macon and later became an esteemed professor of Jazz Studies at Howard University, told an interviewer, "Lewis, in time, grew to understand [Brown's] body language.... He could communicate with musicians when James couldn't.... James could tell them something and it would sound like criticism. Lewis could do it, and they'd go 'yeah,' and get right on board." According to Brown biographer R. J. Smith, "Hamlin was perhaps the first to understand how Brown was weaving songs into a flow that he intended to shape, and reshape, according to his reading of the crowd. Hamlin watched Brown's movements, and instructed the band to follow what he was doing."[74]

Under Hamlin's direction, the band was ready in 1962 when Brown rented out the Apollo Theater at his own expense to record his famous live album. The result was a seminal performance and record that helped make Brown's career. From the moment Fats Gonder's dramatic, one-minute introduction of the show ended, the band, according to one music critic, performed with "immaculate, fiery precision" a set that included all of Brown's hits. Recorded on Hamlin's thirty-second birthday, *Live at the Apollo* captured Brown's dynamic stage performance and changed music history. Brown had the charisma and the talent to pull off the recording, but it was Hamlin who laid the musical foundation for the show as far as crafting the sound. According to longtime Brown saxophonist St. Clair Pinckney, "Lewis is the forgotten man in setting the musical course for the band."[75]

Hamlin left the band not long after *Live at the Apollo* came out, citing Brown's dictatorial control, not necessarily of the music, but of the personal lives of the band members. The bandleader summed up the move diplomatically years later, when he told an interviewer that he simply "got tired of that rat race." He ended up in Baltimore, where he became a respected educator, teaching high school and elementary music students by day while playing in jazz bands at night. Through the years, Hamlin visited friends and relatives in Macon, occasionally performing jazz and blues at one of the local clubs. While his connection with Brown was well known, the significant role he played in making *Live at the Apollo*, a breakthrough album for the singer, is sometimes obscured by Brown's legend. Like Clint Brantley, Hamlin played an important role in accelerating the singer's career, which might not have turned out the way it did had he not encountered the two men. Hamlin passed away in 1991.[76]

It was no coincidence that James Brown's first demo for "Please, Please, Please" was recorded at a local radio station. During the 1950s, Macon's airwaves underwent an important transition as some area programmers began paying attention to the city's African American media market. The process began slowly in 1949 when WIBB, which had only been broadcasting for a year, programmed *Ebony Bandstand*. The show featured "race music," still the industry name for gospel, rhythm and blues, or just plain blues music that originated in the black community. The program originally lasted fifteen minutes, four days a week in the afternoons, but due to its popularity it later expanded to two hours. Recalling the scene during WIBB's early days, station executive Donald Frost later explained, "They did what we called block programming, which was two or three hours of one type of music, and then switch to another. We'd play Dixieland, country, etc., and we'd shut the station down with Sundown Serenade, which was soft music.... We ran what we called 'race music.' There was nothing derogatory about it. That was just the terminology of the times." *Ebony Bandstand* was an early attempt to attract African American listeners, a process that soon spawned a formidable radio triumvirate known locally as the Three Horsemen—Hamp "King Bee" Swain, Charles "Big Saul" Green, and Ray "Satellite Papa" Brown.[77]

WIBB's rival in the Macon market, WBML, also began experimenting with rhythm and blues music and in 1954 made history in the city by hiring Hamp Swain, advertised at the time as "Middle Georgia's first and only negro disc jockey." Born in Bibb County in 1929, Swain sold

170

insurance during the day and was a part-time musician at night, playing in local clubs with Gladys Williams's band and with his own group. Swain's band was popular, but it was his day job that got him on the radio. "My insurance company sponsored and ran a black rhythm and blues program on Saturday mornings at the station," he explained, "and it went over so well, they asked the company to locate someone full time for the show. They recommended me." In addition to the Saturday morning show, Swain hosted a show called "The Night Rider" that was already up and running when he signed on. It was station manager George Patton who gave him the nickname "King Bee." "It was popular for deejays to have a 'tag' in the early days," Swain said, "a funny name that people could remember." The disc jockey also held the distinction of being the first person to ever broadcast a James Brown record, the demo copy of "Please, Please, Please." Recognizing his abilities as an on-air personality, WIBB hired Swain away from WBML in 1957.[78]

Charles Green, known to his listeners as "Big Saul," was a Jones County, Georgia, native who came to Macon with his family as a child. He left the city as a young adult and worked for several years in Puerto Rico as a radio technician. In 1956, he was about to settle in New York but changed his plans after visiting family in Bibb County. "When I came through, I heard they were auditioning people for a job at WIBB," he later recalled. "So then after I won the audition, I went to New York and got everything and came back." Immediately popular, Green was a significant presence in the community, entertaining at dances, talent shows, and in local clubs on nights when there was no live music. Like Swain, Green was influential in the early career of James Brown. He was the first person to record Brown, in effect producing the "Please, Please, Please" demo session and then arranging for Brown to record "Try Me," even though the singer could not afford the session.[79]

Johnnie Ray "Satellite Papa" Brown was born on July 16, 1933, in Opelika, Alabama. He moved with his family to Macon and graduated from Ballard-Hudson High School. After serving in the Korean War, he returned home and formed a band called Ray Brown and His Red Caps, which he led as front man and vocalist. His career as a disc jockey began after he had his tonsils removed and a doctor told him that he would no longer be able to sing at high volume. "I lost my tonsils and I was kind of given the wrong information," he later said. "The doctor told me that I should talk for a living instead of sing, because it would be too much of a strain on my throat." This led to a conversation with "Big Saul" Green, who told Brown he should apply for a disc jockey position at WIBB. Brown got the job and took the nickname "Satellite Papa" as his on-air identity in tribute to the "space race" that had just begun between the United States and the Soviet Union. At the time, the Soviets had just launched the Sputnik satellite, and the United States had countered with a satellite of its own. According to Brown, "Some tried to get me to go with 'Dr. Sputnik,' but that was a communist thing, a Russian thing, and I said, 'No, I can't relate to that.' That would be an obstacle rather than an asset." Once employed at the station, Brown helped persuade Hamp Swain to come to WIBB from WBML, creating the trio that would make Macon radio history.[80]

When Green, Brown, and Swain first got to WIBB, the station had not yet made the switch to an all-African American format. The disc jockeys shared airtime with "Cousin Luke," who spun country records most days from 9:00 A.M. until noon. Then, in early 1958, station owner Thomas Maxwell decided to change the station's format to appeal exclusively to black listeners and adventurous whites, who at the time were just starting to discover rhythm and blues music. According to Donald Frost, the transition was relatively simple. "We shut down on Sunday," he said, "and on Monday morning opened up with 100 percent black appeal with the DJs on the air." The appeal of the "Three Horsemen" was immediate, validating management's decision to switch formats. According to Brown, "After we went on, everybody all the way from Dublin to Soperton to Wrightsville and Statesboro listened to us. We were the kings of this area." The men played all the latest R & B hits along with a healthy dose of gospel. For a while, Swain had a morning gospel program that he hosted as "Deacon Swain" before returning in the evenings to host his blues shift as "King Bee." Swain later laughed when he explained, "A few people asked me if I was related to the deacon, but most never linked the two personalities, since one show was gospel and the King Bee was a real up-tempo thing."[81]

While the move to an all-African American format was relatively smooth, considering the era, it was not without controversy. The station received some hostile phone calls and two sponsors pulled out. "They were sort of redneck in accusing me of promoting integration," Frost later recalled. Also, there was the issue of African American disc jockeys working in a segregated building on Mulberry Street, with separate public facilities for blacks and whites. Speaking of the separate facilities, including drinking fountains, Green later recalled, "We had some problems. I just drank enough water before I left home so I wouldn't have to deal with it."[82]

While the Three Horsemen began to dominate the R & B market on WIBB, WBML continued programming blues and R & B in the evenings with a groundbreaking personality of their own. Born March 23, 1928, Palmira Braswell was a Macon native and educator who, in 1956, became Macon's first female disc jockey. A graduate of Fort Valley State, she taught at Ada J. Banks elementary school in Macon and spun records for WBML at night. She started her radio career after hearing through the grapevine that the station was hiring. "It was before school started, and we were waiting on students to come in," she recalled, "and someone said 'I hear they're looking for a disc jockey at WBML.' I've always been interested in those kinds of things, so I said, 'Hmmm, I think I'll try out for it.'" Her professional nickname was "Honey Bee," and her evening program featuring R & B and blues was very popular. Like other Macon radio personalities, she made public appearances and emceed community events. "Black music was just beginning to be accepted as a crossover into the mainstream," she later said. "It was exciting to be part of that process.... I guess you would call it a revolution in a sense."

"Honey Bee" stayed on the air until 1960 when she left radio to focus on her education. She earned graduate degrees from Teachers College of Columbia University and the University of Georgia, and went on to have a stellar career in Bibb County as a teacher, administrator, and civic leader. She eventually served on the Georgia State Board of Education, but through it all, she never forgot her early career in radio. "Education is my heart," she later told an interviewer, "but my radio days, well, that was some good fun."[83]

While Palmira Braswell was the first female disc jockey in Macon, she was not alone for long. In 1957, a new station, WCRY, began broadcasting in the city as an "exclusive Negro programming radio station" that promised listeners "Rhythm and Blues, Tops in Pops, Progressive Jazz, Spirituals, Gospels, and Hymns." The station's ambitious management brought in disc jockeys from out of town, including Bill "The Rooster" Tunstall, who had worked all over the country and for the US Armed Forces Network; Buddy Lowe, a veteran musician and radio man from Brooklyn; and Atlanta native Winston Calloway, who specialized in gospel programming. Local personalities included Charles "The Fat Man"

173

Winn, who hosted a jazz set; trumpet player Obie Kimbro, who was familiar with Macon's club scene; and the station's most unusual hire, a teenage girl from Ballard-Hudson High School named Alice Bailey.[84]

Alice Bailey was a high school junior in late 1957 when she boldly walked into WCRY and told the station manager, "You need a woman on the air." Impressed with—or perhaps amused by—her mettle, he offered her an audition and a few days later hired her as the city's youngest radio personality. Thrown into the fray immediately, the staff trained her to do her own engineering, and management allowed her to select all the records she played on her show. Bailey took the name "Party Doll" as her professional moniker and began drawing listeners. She made public appearances around town and, because she was so young, her mother usually accompanied her wherever she went. In May of 1958, WCRY's promotional material stated that Bailey "is in direct contact with Middle Georgia's teenage set, and is always on the scene when anything of interest to this group takes place."[85]

Later in the year, WIBB hired Bailey away from WCRY, and she continued her career with the larger, more powerful station, spinning her own records that included "everything from the smooth sounds of the Platters and Tommy Edwards, to the soulful voice of Sam Cooke and the blues of Ruth Brown." She later said that one of the highlights of her career was a night at the city auditorium where she introduced a show featuring Gladys Knight, Jackie Wilson, Ruth Brown, and Chubby Checker. Bailey graduated from high school in 1959 and, like Palmira Braswell, left radio in 1960. She continued her education at Xavier University in New Orleans and gravitated toward Philadelphia, enjoying a successful career in public relations and management before returning to Macon during the 1990s. Not long after Bailey left, WCRY changed formats, becoming a country station for a short time before converting to "easy listening."[86]

What some later called Macon's "golden age of radio"—the time during which the Three Horsemen rode wild on the airwaves—only lasted three years. The beginning of the end for the trio as a collective unit came on February 10, 1960, when the Macon *Telegraph* published a letter to the editor from "Big Saul" Green condemning segregation. At the time, white authorities considered the correspondence inflammatory, crossing a line that African Americans, no matter how popular they might be, were not supposed to cross. Evoking the spirit of the times, Green's letter commented on the "gross injustices that prejudice and hate thrive on" and exposed how far Macon had to go with regard to race relations. "The issue we face is not one of integration or segregation," he wrote. "It is a question of what is right and what is wrong. To hide in the bramble bushes of tradition is no excuse for permitting or endorsing wrongness." While the letter was moderate by today's standards, the white power structure in 1950s Macon viewed it as unwanted and potentially dangerous agitation. When questioned later about why he wrote the letter, Green, who was a military veteran, told an interviewer, "I had gone overseas and seen how people lived, and got hurt and received a Bronze Star, and here I come back and they are going to put me through the same things I went through before I left? I just decided while sitting behind the board [in the studio] one day that things have to change, and I went home and wrote what I felt. I based it on my religious and moral beliefs."[87]

The fallout was immediate. The morning the letter appeared, WIBB's staff "was engrossed in it." Station owner Thomas Maxwell called Green in and tried to talk the disc jockey into retracting the statement. Green refused and was fired, proving once again the unforgiving power of Jim Crow in the South. Publicly, Maxwell stated that he agreed with the sentiments in Green's letter and that the firing was a result not of race, but of disagreements over station policy. Despite the official statement, to most observers it was obvious that "the powers that be" in Macon had branded Green as an agitator, and, as such, he had to go. To be fair to Maxwell, a white man who took the risk of establishing the all-black for-mat on his station in the first place, he was likely under a great deal of political pressure to do something about Green. In 1960, it was not unu-sual for the white establishment in Macon, or in any other Southern city, to view as a potential threat a popular African American broadcaster who had the ears of thousands of black listeners. Years later, Hamp Swain, who witnessed the events, said of Maxwell, "I can tell you this, I've never worked with a finer man in my whole life. He was what was happening in radio." Had the station owner been leading the charge to fire Green, Swain might not have been so charitable with his remarks.[88]

After receiving death threats, Green left Macon for good and moved to New York. "Satellite Papa" Brown left town not long afterwards, though he returned in 1970. Swain stayed and became one of Macon's most beloved radio personalities among both whites and blacks. He was a popular fixture on the city's entertainment scene for decades before his death in 2018. While their tenure together as the Three Horsemen was relatively short, Green, Brown, and Swain left a lasting legacy as radio pioneers in Macon, and all three later were inducted into the Georgia Radio Hall of Fame.

While radio remained the chief vehicle for listeners to hear their favorite music in Macon, the 1950s brought a new medium to the city that revolutionized entertainment. In August of 1953, television came to the city in the form of a UHF channel, WETV. The station, which was associated with WNEX and WBML radio, broadcast network programs from NBC and ABC as well as local shows and news. Among the musical acts initially featured on WETV was Dee Lee and His Georgia Ramblers, who for years had been a popular country music outfit in the region. The Ramblers show broadcast daily for an hour starting at 5:30 P.M., followed by a program of country and popular music featuring the Ray Melton Orchestra. A Griffin, Georgia, native, Melton had been one of the area's most popular bandleaders for a decade. WETV was launched with great fanfare as Macon's first television station, but it remained on the air for only short time. It ceased operations in 1955, in large part due to technical issues related to its weak UHF signal. The station also faced stiff competition from WMAZ-TV, which began broadcasting only a few weeks after WETV signed on.[89]

WMAZ first aired programs on September 27, 1953, broadcasting network content from CBS and Dumont as well as local shows. One of the station's most popular programs featured "Uncle Ned" Stripling, who made a seamless transition from radio stalwart to local television star with a new Hayloft Jamboree band. Stripling was a natural for television. He had a great, outgoing personality as well as good looks. Some said he favored Tennessee Ernie Ford, a popular country entertainer of the period, while others thought he looked a little like movie idol Clark Gable. He hosted a midday program called *Dinnerbell Time*, and most days another show later in the evening. As with his radio show, the television program featured music, homespun banter between songs, and advertisements that Stripling announced live. According to one reviewer, the bandleader had "a great talent for music and easy repartee, and a real showman's desire to entertain."[90]

Stripling assembled a top-notch band for his television show that included Al Everidge on bass and vocals, Frank Maloy on fiddle, Tom Calhoun on lead guitar, Jeanette Byrd Dukes and Bill Swain on vocals, and

Philip "Pee Wee" Clark on steel guitar. Among others who appeared with the band, either in the studio or during their innumerable public appearances, were Harry Northington, Ed Steeley, and Tony Cannon. On their first broadcast, the group opened with the Webb Pierce song "Slowly," with Al Everidge handling the vocal. During the show's run, the band played a mix of tunes ranging from Texas swing, similar to what Stripling had started with on radio, to traditional country music and hymns, and even a few "rockabilly" numbers. A sampling of their most popular covers included "Gonna Raise a Ruckus Tonight," a song popularized by Gid Tanner and Riley Puckett; Carl Smith's "There She Goes"; Slim Whitman's "There's a Rainbow in Every Tear Drop"; and an early rock and roll number, "Hot Dog Buddy Buddy," which Bill Haley and the Comets made famous. The program also featured a theme song titled "Come on Along" at the beginning and end of every broadcast.[91]

As an entertainer, Uncle Ned worked hard. In 1956, *Billboard* magazine took notice of his efforts, reporting "Gene (Uncle Ned) Stripling is currently doing nine hours of TV work a week over Channel 13, WMAZ-TV, Macon, Ga., plus five hours a week of radio time over WMAZ. In addition to his broadcasting chores, Stripling and his band, the Hayloft Jamboree, work a minimum of four square dances a week." In Macon, Uncle Ned was a bona fide celebrity, whether appearing alone or with the group, and he did a great deal of charity work. The Hayloft Jamboree also opened for national acts that performed at the city auditorium, and everywhere they played in Middle Georgia—theaters, gymnasiums, national guard armories, music halls—large crowds flocked to see the show. Reportedly, Uncle Ned's television program was for years the second-highest-rated program in Macon. Only the long-running western drama *Gunsmoke* drew more viewers.[92]

Unfortunately, Stripling's reign as a media sensation in Macon ended prematurely due to his health. After developing heart issues in the spring of 1957, doctors ordered the entertainer to slow down, but Uncle Ned refused to be sidelined. He curtailed his work schedule to an extent but remained busy. On the night of October 18, 1958, he suffered a fatal heart attack while performing at a dance in Hawkinsville, Georgia. He was only forty-two years old. Middle Georgia mourned Stripling's passing, and members of his band served as pallbearers at his funeral. "Undoubtedly he had been advised by his doctors to take it easy," an obituary in the *Macon News* read, "but Gene Stripling had too much laughter and too many songs in his heart to sideline himself for long. He and his infectious music and his informal entertainment will be missed by those who had become staunch fans of 'Uncle Ned.'"[93]

As for the Hayloft Jamboree, it carried on into the 1960s. Local bandleader Eddie Cannon took over as leader of the enterprise, and later Stripling's nephew Earl took the helm. For a while the group remained popular around Middle Georgia, but the performing dynamics were never the same. Gene Stripling's personality and showmanship were unique, and no one could adequately fill his shoes. The program still cast a long shadow, and several members of the original band performed regularly around Macon and elsewhere for years, including Al Everidge, Philip "Pee Wee" Clark, and Frank Maloy.

Al Everidge was well known in the Macon area before he joined the Hayloft Jamboree. In the early 1950s, he had his own lunchtime music program on WBML radio that competed with Cousin Luke's *R.F.D. Jamboree*. Born in Macon in 1928, Everidge was a member of a musical family. His father was one of the South Georgia Highballers, and his brothers Alton and Rubin were also talented musicians. Like many local performers, he had a day job running his own successful tree service, but he continued to perform and was a fixture on country music stages and in dance halls for decades. He was also a dedicated ambassador for traditional country music—"None of this crossover stuff," he once told an interviewer—and during the 1990s, he organized annual events celebrating the music of artists from Jimmie Rodgers to Patsy Cline. "It's the old timer's way of giving something back," he said at the time. Everidge passed away in 2008 as one of the elder statesmen of Middle Georgia's country music community.

Like Everidge, Frank Maloy was an entertainer before he became part of the Hayloft Jamboree. Born in 1927, he grew up in Milan, Georgia, and at an early age started playing the fiddle. He learned the instrument by watching one of his musical uncles and by studying a fiddle tune book purchased from Sears and Roebuck. He and his brother Joe, an excellent guitarist, played in local bands as teenagers and in 1946 landed a spot on WBHB radio in Fitzgerald, Georgia, playing with Charlie Dowdy and the Prairie Boys. Frank moved to Warner Robins in the early 1950s and played with the Ray Melton Band, then moved to Macon after receiving the call to join the Hayloft Jamboree. "I loved playing on TV," he once said, "but I never could get used to all that heavy makeup under the bright lights. They painted us up." At the same time, his brother Joe joined the Polka Dots, the WMAZ house band, and both men became sought-after entertainers in the region. The brothers later formed their own band, the Swingmasters, that performed all over the state and also toured with the Dave Mercer band. While Joe did other things, Frank's primary focus was always music, and he spent decades as a performer, arranger, and mentor for younger fiddle players. He penned countless fiddle tunes, including one for each of Georgia's 159 counties, and he appeared consistently at fairs and festivals all over the state well into his eighties.[94]

Philip "Pee Wee" Clark developed an international reputation after he left Uncle Ned. Clark was born in Macon in 1930, and by age sixteen he was already making money as a musician, playing guitar, mandolin, and fiddle. He dropped out of high school and joined a band that "played in honky-tonks along Broadway for $3 to $5 and all the beer we could drink." A little later, he mastered the pedal steel guitar, which led to better gigs. Gene Stripling invited him to join the Hayloft Jamboree in 1953, and he became a fan favorite. He played with the group even after Stripling died, but he also got the opportunity to play behind established country acts that passed through town, such as Lefty Frizzell, Tex Ritter, Gene Autry, and Hank Snow. By 1960, Clark was ready for a change. "Macon is a small town and I'd gone about as far as I could here," he said. "But I didn't want to move to Atlanta, and Nashville was too closed, too cliquish for me. I wanted to get away and make a new start." The result was a dramatic move to Australia, where there were few pedal steel guitar players and his services would be at a premium. Clark found great success there, touring constantly and recording several albums. He also started his own record label, and in 1980 was inducted into Australia's Country Music Hall of Fame. Clark retired from music in his seventies and passed away in 2015.[95]

During the mid-1950s, Elvis Presley's meteoric rise to fame helped break down barriers that for years kept white teenagers from hearing music produced in the African American community. Oversimplified, Presley's early act was blues-based but peppered with country influences, producing something new that excited teenage crowds wherever he went. The act also helped popularized the term "rockabilly" to describe energetic, young white performers, mostly from the rural South, whose musical delivery was straight out of the juke joint. Presley's career overwhelmed popular culture in America and created a musical template that influenced other performers, including a teenager from Macon named James "Sweetie" Jones.

Born in Bibb County in 1941 and given the nickname "Sweetie" by his mother, Jones grew up in the shadow of the Atlantic Cotton Mill. He sang in church as part of a gospel trio as a youngster but soon graduated to secular music. By the age of fifteen, he had formed his own band, Sweetie Jones and His Rocking Four. The group played in Macon at roller rinks, sock hops, and weekly shows at Lakeside and Ragan's Park. According to one newspaper account, the original group included musicians Jackie Etheridge, James Etheridge, Jack Dorsey, and singer Jane Darnell of Jasper, a talented performer who later carved out a career for herself as a gospel artist. Drummer Homer Scarborough also played with the band. The group changed its name to the Dixie Kats, and there were apparently significant personnel changes over the next two years. The bulk of Jones's tours included a Dixie Kats band with Darnell and Scarborough, along with pianist Billy Strom and Jackie Hobbs on guitar.[96]

Jones sang fast-paced rockabilly numbers such as "Baby, Let's Play House" along with slower ballads, and his animated delivery led local newspapers to call him "Macon's own rendition of Elvis Presley." Chuck Berry's "Johnny B. Goode" and the Lloyd Price classic "Lawdy Miss Clawdy" were also in his repertoire. He created an immediate sensation in Macon. WBML gave him his own radio program, and he and the Dixie Kats appeared on local television on Uncle Ned's program. Local managers Mel Shorey and W. W. Grant represented Jones, and he generated enough interest to spark a short tour of the East Coast and Canada, where the Presley phenomenon had created a great demand for rockabilly artists. "In Canada they were screaming and dancing in the aisles," Jones later said. "Once, in Nova Scotia, policemen were called out to restore order." Returning south, Jones made several recordings with small labels, the most popular of which was "Cheryl Ann," recorded at the National Recording Corporation (NRC) studio in Atlanta. The 1958 offering cracked the *Billboard* Top 100 list.[97]

Many people thought Jones was Presley made over. According to one reviewer, "Sweetie moves in a rocking motion and shuffles his feet to the musical beat during the song." The "youthful teenage idol" typically wore a tight-fitting red jacket on stage, with black pants and shiny black and white shoes. He and the band worked hard, playing endless one-nighters. "It was constant," Jane Darnell later recalled. "We were touring really heavy. We were somewhere every night." Jones and the Dixie Kats eventually joined a tour as the opening act for Jerry Lee Lewis, one of Sweetie's heroes, and on October 30, 1958, the show stopped at the city auditorium in Macon, where Jones got to perform for a hometown crowd. The experience gave Jones and the Dixie Kats even greater exposure, and while they were never a truly national act, they definitely developed a strong regional following. According to Darnell, "Sweetie was known pretty well, especially around the southern states. When we would get to the venues where we were going to sing and play, there were usually groups of teenagers waiting for us."[98]

Jones's musical flame burned brightly but only for only a short time. He was unable to parlay his early success into a long-term music career. Homer Scarborough later claimed that with different management Jones might have become a national star. "The only reason that Sweetie did not make it big was luck and management," Scarborough said. "[His managers] were nice guys, but they were in over their heads.... The right person never heard him." According to the drummer, Jones's managers for some reason turned down an opportunity for Jones to appear on Dick Clark's influential *American Bandstand* television program, perhaps because it would have upset Jones's touring schedule. As the 1950s ended, Sweetie Jones and the Dixie Kats folded, although Jones continued to appear locally as a solo act. By the mid-1960s, he was out of the music business and had moved on to construction work. He made a few personal appearances in the Macon area through the years but never recaptured his previous success. Jones died in Macon in 2004.[99]

Despite the outward aura of hedonism, rock and roll also had gospel music as one of its foundational elements. Many of the genre's first-generation pioneers began singing in church and at various times recorded gospel songs. As in the rest of the South, Macon's gospel tradition was always strong in both the white and African American communities. Nationally known gospel acts performed for large crowds at the city auditorium and other venues, and Macon's many churches formed the bedrock for local gospel groups. The city's radio stations also featured gospel programs of one type or another from their earliest broadcasts.

In the African American community, a group called the Flying Cloud Spiritual Singers created a template for postwar musicians and singers in Macon who were interested in gospel music. The group was founded in 1942 and included Willie Clark, James Curtis, Carl Nelson, Lewis Curtis, and Leonard Burnor. Billed as "one of Middle Georgia's most pleasing singing units," the group was in demand to perform at churches and social events by the time the Second World War ended. The group carried on for several years, disbanding around 1950.

Another group with roots in the 1940s that had greater staying power was the Silver Bell Singers, sometimes just called the Silver Bells. The vocalists convened for the first time in 1948 and carried on for decades, recording several gospel singles in the process.[100]

A citywide gospel singing event featuring groups from Macon's black churches as well as a number of touring outfits took place at the Little Rock Baptist Church in May of 1954. The event was larger than the usual "gospel sings" that took place in the city, but musically it was typical. The *Macon News* covered the event and left a record of those who participated, effectively providing a list of some of the gospel groups that were active in Macon's African American community during the period. These included "the Zion Trumpeteers, Silver Trumpet Sisters, Rhine Sisters, Mellowtone Singers, St. Luke's Baptist Gospel Chorus, the Bellaires, Miss Betty Daniel, the Bell Temple Choir, Morning Star, Little Rock Gospel Choir, Spirit of the South, New Zion Gospel Chorus, Rainbow Jubilaires, St. Luke A.M.E. Gospel Chorus, Turner Tabernacle Gospel Chorus, Vineville Baptist Gospel Chorus, Royal Travelers, Highlight Spiritual Singers, Unionville Gospel Chorus, Middle Georgia Spiritual Singers, and The Kings of Harmony." Other groups that were not part of the festivities but were also prominent in the area at the time included the Singing Crusaders, the Spiritual Eagles, and the South Winds.[101]

Local groups were plentiful in Macon's African American community, but the city also hosted major programs that included nationally known gospel artists. Clint Brantley promoted most of the shows, which he heavily advertised, drawing crowds from all over Middle Georgia. The parade of stars was endless. The Blind Boys of Alabama made their first appearance in Macon during the 1950s, as did the Soul Stirrers from Chicago. In 1961, Reverend C. L. Franklin, father of entertainment icon Aretha Franklin, led a "Gospel Feast" at the auditorium that included The Caravans and the Gospelaires. A host of other big gospel events followed, featuring the Staple Singers, the Soul Stirrers, the Consolers, the Mighty Clouds of Joy, the Pilgrim Jubilee Singers, and the Drexel Singers, among others.[102]

In the white community, gospel music was also exceedingly popular and a mainstay in local churches. The Centenary Methodist Church sponsored one of Macon's more prominent gospel quartets of the 1950s, the Centenary Quartet. They gave special radio performances and were always a highlight of the many gospel programs held in the city. Original members of this foursome were Cliff Cunningham, Lester Royal, Lonnie Tharpe, and Bill Falcon. Another popular group was the Traveler's Quartet, led by Clifford Thompson and including James B. McCook, Raymond M. McCook, and Joel Radney. Thompson and Raymond McCook were already well known in Middle Georgia, having performed with the Smile-A-While Quartet. The Powell Sisters, the Davis Trio, and the Trebles were all talented family groups who made the rounds at local churches and civic events. Ronnie Thompson, who later became Macon's mayor, had a gospel quartet of his own and later hosted a gospel radio program on WMAZ.[103]

As with black gospel, white gospel musicians and singers with national reputations also frequented Macon's municipal auditorium. Musician and promoter Wally Fowler was particularly popular in Macon. Fowler's group, the Oak Ridge Quartet, which eventually evolved into the Oak Ridge Boys, appeared frequently in the city during the 1950s and 1960s, usually as the headliner among a number of other acts. Typical was a January 1955 show that Fowler brought to Macon that included former Louisiana governor Jimmy Davis, along with the Happy Two, the Homeland Harmony Quartet, the Senator's Quartet, and the Harmony Kings. Later the same year, Hovie Lister and his group, the Statesmen Quartet, appeared at the top of the bill at a show also featuring the Blackwood Quartet and the Harmoneers. Among other popular white gospel groups who appeared in Macon during the period were the Florida Boys, the Chuck Wagon Gang, the Happy Goodman Family, and Wendell "Wendy" Bagwell and the Sunliters.[104]

By far the most nationally successful white gospel act to originate in Macon was the Sego Brothers, later known as the Sego Brothers and Naomi. The group had roots dating back to 1946, when three brothers, James, Walter, and Lamar Sego, and another singer, Charles Norris Jr., formed a gospel quartet to entertain at churches and camp meetings in Middle Georgia. Norris left the group and over the years the Sego brothers appeared with other singers. The Segos initially called their group The Harmony Kings, and their first major exposure was an appearance on

Peanut Faircloth's syndicated *Hoedown Party* on WNEX radio. This led to their own show on WMAZ radio and frequent television appearances on *Uncle Ned's Hayloft Jamboree*. The Harmony Kings disbanded in the mid-1950s, and the three Sego brothers made few public appearances until 1958, when they reformed their group with an additional member who changed the dynamics of their act and provided the spark that gave them a great deal of national success.[105]

Naomi Easters was born in Enigma, Georgia, on February 17, 1931. The daughter of a Church of God minister, she grew up singing sacred music and began performing in front of crowds when she was a little girl. She married James Sego in 1949, and when her husband and his brothers relaunched their singing group in Macon in the late 1950s, she joined the act as a full-fledged member. They called themselves "The Sego Brothers and Naomi." According to Lamar Sego, Gene "Uncle Ned" Stripling came up with the name during one of their appearances on his show. An obviously gifted singer, Naomi had a powerful voice that both blended with and stood out from those of the Sego Brothers. She was tremendously popular, and her mere presence in the group broke new ground in gospel music. "When I started singing with the Segos," she later said, "gospel music was mostly male-oriented. We were different in sound and style, and were a change of pace from the average quartet. I think that was the key reason people liked us. We established our own identity."[106]

The Sego Brothers and Naomi performed constantly, both alone and as part of gospel package tours that traveled all over the country. In 1961, they recorded "Satisfied With Me," a song that gave them their first national recognition as gospel recording artists. A year later, they released "Sorry I Never Knew You," a bona fide hit that some press reports credit as being the first million-selling gospel record. In addition to being a popular gospel number, the song briefly crossed over and made an appearance on the *Billboard* country charts in February of 1964. After "Sorry I Never Knew You," the Sego Brothers and Naomi were in demand, but the peak years of the original group lasted less than a decade. Lamar Sego left the act in 1967 to form a group with his own family, and James Sego's health began to decline. He died in 1979, the same year Walter retired. Naomi carried on and continued as one of the most famous and recognizable voices in gospel music. She passed away in 2017.[107]

MUSICAL INSTRUMENTS,
BOOKS, MUSIC, &c.
ELLIS, SHOTWELL & CO.

A RE now receiving and opening at their BOOK STORE, a number of

PIANO FORTES,

of a rich description, and a variety of other Musical Instruments, with instruction Books, and Music adapted to the same—a large collection of

NEW MUSIC,

for the Piano, embracing all the Music of the celebrated Cinderella Opera, and a variety of engravings, caricatures, prints, &c.—Also a large assortment of

BOOKS,

consisting of **1500** VOLUMES; a catalogue embracing a considerable portion of which, is published in the Christian Repertory. A great variety of

STATIONARY

and Miscellaneous Articles. A large assortment of PAPER HANGINGS, Bordering, Fire-Prints, &c.

They respectfully invite the attention of the public to the above, and request them to call and examine.   june 11   24

An advertisement for musical instruments from an 1831 issue of the *Telegraph*.

Author's collection

Musician and poet Sidney Clopton Lanier (1842–1881).

Courtesy Georgia Archives, Morrow, Georgia

Composer and Civil War era music publisher
Hermann L. Schreiner (ca. 1832–1891).

Author's collection

1876 photograph of Wesleyan Female College.

Courtesy Lucy Lester Willett Memorial Library, Wesleyan College, Macon, Georgia

Phillip Gerhart Guttenberger (1799–1874),
beloved music professor at Wesleyan College
and patriarch of a flourishing musical family in Macon.

From Kith and Kin: A Portrait of a Southern Family, 1630–1934
by Carolyn L. Harrell. Mercer University Press, 1984

1890 photograph of the Macon Academy of Music,
opened to the public in 1884.

Courtesy Middle Georgia Archives, Washington Memorial Library, Macon, Georgia

Pianist and composer Edouard Gregory Hesselberg
(1870–1935), who served as head of the music department at
Wesleyan College during the early twentieth century.

Courtesy Middle Georgia Archives, Washington Memorial Library, Macon, Georgia

The Grand Opera House, opened in 1905.
Courtesy Georgia Archives, Morrow, Georgia

Charles Henry Douglass (1870–1940),
entrepreneur and owner of the Douglass Theater.

From The National Cyclopedia of the Colored Race, vol. 1, *edited by Clement
Richardson. National Publishing Company, Montgomery, Alabama, 1919*

The Douglass Theater, ca. 1918.

Courtesy Middle Georgia Archives, Washington Memorial Library, Macon, Georgia

Interior of the Douglass Theater.

Courtesy Georgia Archives, Morrow, Georgia

Jazz Age diva Lucille Hegamin (1894–1970).

Author's collection

Lucille Hegamin with her band, the Blue Flame Syncopaters.

Author's collection

NO "KING TUT BOB" FOR HER

Photo shows Miss Lula Whidby, who has just arrived in the city from the West to join the Miller-Slater show playing a local theatre.

Newspaper clipping featuring singer and Macon native Lula Whidby (ca. 1898–1926), from the March 7, 1924 edition of the *Baltimore Afro American.*

Author's collection

The Pickens Sisters, Helen, Jane, and Patti.

Author's collection

Beatrice Carter (1924–2000), who took the stage name
Betty Barclay, received national attention while performing
with Sammy Kaye's band during the 1940s.

Author's collection

1937 photograph of students at the
Lena Clemons Conservatory of Music and Arts.

Courtesy Middle Georgia Archives, Washington Memorial Library, Macon, Georgia

Newspaper clipping from the April 17, 1927 issue
of the *Asbury Park (NJ) Press* featuring singer and nightclub
owner Reece LaMarr DuPree (1881–1963), who became
one of the most successful African American entertainment
promoters in the country.

Pianist and bandleader Gladys Williams, hailed by many as
the godmother of Macon rhythm and blues, helped countless
Macon musicians during a career that spanned decades.

Courtesy Middle Georgia Archives, Washington Memorial Library, Macon, Georgia

Luke "Fats" Gonder (1918–1974),
tutored Little Richard on piano, helped discover James Brown,
and led his own popular band for years.

Courtesy Middle Georgia Archives, Washington Memorial Library, Macon, Georgia

A caped Little Richard Penniman (1932–2020)
performing at Ann's Tic Toc in Macon, early in his career.

Courtesy Middle Georgia Archives, Washington Memorial Library, Macon, Georgia

1950s publicity photo of Little Richard.

Courtesy Michael Ochs Archives/Getty Images

Early photograph of James Brown, "The Godfather of Soul,"
who launched his career in Macon.

Courtesy Middle Georgia Archives, Washington Memorial Library, Macon, Georgia

Musician and bandleader Lewis Hamlin, Jr. (1930–1991), who led the band and crafted the sound that helped James Brown produce the landmark album *Live at the Apollo* in 1962.

Courtesy Dr. Debi Hamlin and the Bronzetone Center for Music & History

Uncle Ned and the Hayloft Jamboree, one of the most popular acts in the history of Middle Georgia music: left to right, Tom Calhoun, Philip "Pee Wee" Clark, Frank Maloy, Jeanette Byrd, Bill Swain, Eugene "Uncle Ned" Stripling, and Al Everidge.

Author's collection

Country performers Dee Lee and His Georgia Ramblers with WMAZ announcer David Reeves. From left to right: back row, David Reeves, Slim Hutcheson, Dee Lee, Homer Hudson, and Robert "Moon" Hardy; front row, kneeling: Fonzie Gray, Norman Jones, and Verge Helveston.

Courtesy Wayne Pierce

Local newspapers called rockabilly performer James "Sweetie" Jones (1941–2004) "Macon's own rendition of Elvis Presley."
Author's collection

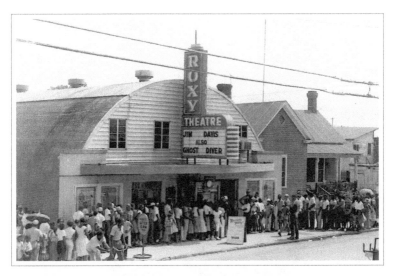

During the 1950s the Roxy Theater on Hazel Street hosted
the "Teenage Party" radio program broadcast on WMAZ.

Courtesy Middle Georgia Archives, Washington Memorial Library, Macon, Georgia

Johnny Jenkins (foreground, with guitar) and the Pinetoppers.
A young Otis Redding is in the background with the
microphone over Jenkins's left shoulder

Courtesy Mark Pucci

Percy Welch (1928–2004),
for decades one of Macon's most popular performers.

Courtesy Middle Georgia Archives, Washington Memorial Library, Macon, Georgia

Gifted guitarist and composer Eddie Kirkland (1923–2011).

Courtesy Middle Georgia Archives, Washington Memorial Library, Macon, Georgia

Street performer Reverend Pearly Brown.

Courtesy Middle Georgia Archives, Washington Memorial Library, Macon, Georgia

Publicity photo of Otis Redding (1941–1967), Macon's native
son and one of the most powerful musical voices of the 1960s.

Courtesy Bettman/Getty Images

Otis Redding onstage.

Courtesy Michael Ochs Archives/Getty Images

Music executive and Capricorn Records co-founder Frank
Fenter (1936–1983) in his Capricorn office during the 1970s.

Courtesy Robin Duner-Fenter

Phil Walden (1940–2006) served
as Otis Redding's manager and business partner,
and later co-founded Capricorn Records in Macon.

Courtesy Middle Georgia Archives, Washington Memorial Library, Macon, Georgia

The original Allman Brothers Band:
left to right, Duane Allman, Dickey Betts, Gregg Allman,
Jaimoe, Berry Oakley, and Butch Trucks.

Courtesy Michael Ochs Archives/Getty Images

The second incarnation of The Allman Brothers Band:
left to right, Chuck Leavell, Jaimoe, Butch Trucks,
Gregg Allman, Lamar Williams, and Dickey Betts.

Courtesy Redfern/Getty Images

Left to right, Robert "Pops" Popwell, Johnny Sandlin, Paul
Hornsby, Jerry "Swamp Dog" Williams, and Pete Carr. Hornsby,
Sandlin, Carr, and Popwell were the original Capricorn Rhythm
Section that backed countless artists in the studio.

Courtesy Middle Georgia Archives, Washington Memorial Library, Macon, Georgia

Phil Walden and Frank Fenter
with members of the Marshall Tucker Band.

Courtesy Robin Duner-Fenter

Sea Level: left to right, Lamar Williams, Chuck Leavell, Jaimoe, and Jimmy Nalls.

Courtesy Michael Ochs Archives/Getty Images

Phil Walden and Frank Fenter, the architects of Capricorn Records.

Courtesy Robin Duner-Fenter

5

Otis Redding,
1960–1970

"Always think different from the next person. Don't ever do a song as you heard somebody else do it. Concentrate and practice every single day."[1]

—Otis Redding

In the 1950s and 1960s, Macon's music culture entered a new era. The city's music scene was increasingly vibrant but also more complex as time wore on. Radio, records, and television were circulating songs both sacred and secular, and the airwaves were helping integrate music despite the best efforts of Jim Crow to keep the races apart. Whites could listen to music from the African American community with little effort, and vice versa, just by flipping a switch or turning a dial. Teenagers had been unleashed on the musical marketplace through the popularity of rock and roll, with large numbers of white teens for the first time coveting music based in the blues. The era also produced another powerful new music hybrid labeled "soul music," a combination of traditional blues, rhythm and blues, and jazz interacting on a strong gospel foundation. As time wore on, soul music gave Macon gravitas as a Southern music center. With rock and roll and soul added to the mix, the American music scene was percolating on a whole new level, and the effects could be felt along the Ocmulgee River in Middle Georgia. Macon had produced two national superstars of this emerging new musical world, Little Richard and James Brown, but the pool of talent in the city was much deeper.

At the dawn of the 1960s, Macon's newspapers still catered primarily to white readers, but the *Telegraph* and the *Macon News* both had a separate section set aside for "social and personal news of our colored population." There, African Americans could read news stories affecting their community and see advertisements for local entertainment. The ads of the era reflected a thriving nightclub scene, with venues such as Club 15 and Adams Lounge hosting local and out-of-town acts. As for local talent, on any given night patrons had the opportunity to see the Jazz Lads, Walter Tinsley with the Casanova Combo, Little Willie Jones, keyboardist Roye Mathis, Sonny Goss, Johnny Brown, and Oscar Mack, among others.

Melvin Colton "Percy" Welch was a significant presence on the nightclub circuit in Macon during the period, and for years to come. Born in Leary, Georgia, on May 12, 1928, he moved to Macon as a small child and eventually gravitated toward music. His first public performance in the city may have been a third-place finish at a local talent show in 1945, the year before he joined the military. He started singing and playing bass and drums in bands during his hitch, and when he got out, he joined the ranks of Macon musicians who began their careers with Gladys Williams. "I started out in music when I was in the service," he later recalled. "When I came out first in 1948, I played with Gladys Williams. She had a real tight group of the best musicians in Macon." By the early 1950s, Welch had his own band that performed at local clubs, a five-piece outfit billed as the House Rockers. He reportedly took the stage name "Percy" as an homage to rhythm and blues singer Percy Mayfield, who was popular at the time.[2]

Welch was also chummy with Clint Brantley, who took the young musician under his wing. The promoter sent Welch's band out on tour with other artists, mainly in the South, including John Lee Hooker, who for a time made his home in Macon. Hooker had already released several successful "race records," including "Boogie Chillen" (1948) and "Crawling King Snake" (1949), but because of the expense involved, he was not yet touring with his own full-time band. "I made Macon, Georgia, my headquarters," Hooker later remembered, "set up there, got a hotel or a rooming house and stay there, [went] into other states. Our booking agent was old Clint Brantley. He was a big man, and he booked us all over Georgia, Alabama, and some parts of Mississippi once in a while."[3]

After touring with Hooker, Welch moved with his group to Atlanta, where they were the house band at the Royal Peacock Club, and then back to Macon. They played all the local outlets, and Brantley again sent them out on the road, this time with Little Richard, who was just beginning to make a name for himself. "Little Richard was the star of the show and my band backed Little Richard," Welch later said. "We worked the states of Georgia, Florida, Alabama, and Mississippi, and some parts of Virginia for about two years." Welch also served as Little Richard's road manager during the period, keeping up with the money, introducing the show night after night, and even driving the band to the gigs. "I had an old Buick," he said, "and we loaded it up and went out on the road with him until 'Tutti Frutti' broke open. Then we came off the road for about two months while he was going to California." Little Richard later gave Welch credit for encouraging him during those early years, telling an interviewer, "Percy, he made me feel like I was doing something even when I wasn't."[4]

After his stint with Little Richard, Welch worked with a number of other prominent musicians, most notably Etta James, Aretha Franklin, and the Moonglows (featuring Marvin Gaye), but he always ended up back in Macon. He made appearances on WNEX radio, and in 1957 recorded "Back Door Man" on Fran Records in Louisville, Kentucky. With "Nursery Rhyme Rock" on the B side, the song was a regional hit that became his signature performance piece. "It did pretty good," he later said. "It wasn't a number one record, but it was enough to establish my name, and it kept my band working." Welch performed in local clubs and became an entrepreneur in Macon. He opened nightclubs, including the Fabulous Lounge and Welch's Jazz Lounge, along with a family-oriented entertainment venue and restaurant called the Peppermint Lounge. He also owned a wig store and a detailing shop. Probably his most notable musical configuration of the 1960s was Percy Welch and the Hornets Revue—sometimes just called the Hornets or the Hornets Band—which also featured, at various times, Macon notables Eddie Kirkland, Alice Rozier, Jimmy Robinson, Willie Goss, Walter Lee Gaston, Billy Soul, and Earl "Speedo" Sims.[5]

Welch's music career in Macon spanned decades, and he became a Middle Georgia legend as a stage act. A featured attraction at the city's Cherry Blossom Festival from its inception in the early 1980s, he was known not only for his singing, but for his stage moves. Sometimes referred to in the press as a "bluesman and dance specialist," he was a consistently popular performer. "Percy," one reviewer noted, "will teach you some very interesting dance maneuvers and positions before the evening is over." Guitarist Charles Reynolds, a veteran Macon musician who played with Welch for years and was familiar with his routine, later remembered him as a crowd favorite and committed artist, saying, "He was a good singer, not necessarily the greatest singer, but he had that ability to connect with the audience and just sell the songs. He had showmanship and everything you think of in a soul singer."[6]

Many who knew Welch later lamented the fact that he never hit nationally, but Welch seemed quite comfortable with the musical universe he created for himself in Macon. He was a family man who enjoyed being at home with his wife and children. He also enjoyed the attention he got from hometown audiences. After one especially satisfying performance, Welch told a reporter, "I don't care who you are, when you are accepted in your own hometown it's a great moment. Ain't nothing feels like that. You can go to some other town where people don't know you and put on a show, and they accept it fine and you enjoy that. But to be accepted at home is a great feeling." In 1991, the Macon *Telegraph* took the pulse of Macon's musical environment through an informal fan poll, the results of which indicated that Welch, then sixty-three, was still one of the most popular rhythm and blues performers in the city.[7]

Welch was active until the end. Despite some health issues, he spent the last months of his life recording a solo compact disc of original songs mixed with some of his favorites, including a couple of gospel numbers. He died in 2004, and Little Richard returned to Macon to attend the funeral and praise his friend. "He was a beautiful man, a sweetie pie," Penniman said. "I loved him dearly."[8]

Eddie Kirkland was one of Welch's cohorts on the Macon club circuit. A gifted guitarist, Kirkland was not a Macon native but moved to the city permanently in the early 1960s and had a very productive career. He was born in Jamaica to a single mother who took him to the United States, where they eventually settled in Dothan, Alabama. He grew up in Dothan picking cotton, and by the age of nine had squirreled away enough money to purchase a used Stella guitar. It was his first real guitar, although he had been plucking away for some time at handmade "instruments" that he cobbled together from hay bailing wire, screen door wire, cigar boxes, and empty whiskey bottles. Around the same time, his mother gave him an old harmonica.[9]

Three years later, at age twelve, Kirkland began his career in show business by stowing away on a truck belonging to a traveling medicine show passing through Dothan. Some sources say it was the Sugar Girls Medicine Show, while other say it was the famous Silas Green Show. Regardless, just before the show closed up shop after a week-long run, he made his move. "That Saturday night I went there when they closed out," he later told *Living Blues* magazine. "I waited until they got every tent in the truck except one. I got in the truck and laid the tent down. I was up under there where nobody'd see me." Those in charge of the show did not discover Kirkland was with the troupe until they were in Kentucky, at which time the young stowaway successfully auditioned to remain with them. "I got up, got my harmonica," Kirkland said, "and started goin' through my act...blow my harmonica and play, beat the hambone, you know." Whatever he did, it was enough to earn him a small spot on the show.[10]

Kirkland eventually left the traveling show and moved to Indiana. After military service and a brief career as a professional boxer, he ended up in Detroit, where he worked at the Ford plant during the day and continued to pursue music after hours, at first playing guitar on the streets for nickels and dimes, and then at house parties. He eventually ran into John Lee Hooker, who was busy making a name for himself, and Hooker hired him to play guitar. "I was popular with 'Boogie Chillen,'" Hooker later said, "but I felt that I couldn't afford a band.... I'd go out with just me and Eddie Kirkland and used pick up bands, you know? Whatever we needed, drums, bass, piano or whatever." Kirkland toured and recorded with Hooker for years and was known for occasionally upstaging Hooker at performances. In those early days, Kirkland was more than just a sideman. He was critical to the touring process, both musically and otherwise. According to Hooker's biographer Charles Shaar Murray, "Kirkland was the band, the musical arranger, the road manager, the business manager, the driver, the mechanic, the bodyguard, and anything else Hooker needed."[11]

Kirkland first came to Macon while touring with Hooker, and both men moved there while Clint Brantley booked them into Southern venues. While Hooker later left to follow a path that made him world famous, Kirkland made Macon his home. He was a regular on the Middle Georgia club circuit—where he sometimes used the name Eddie Kirk—during the mid-1950s, either backing headliners or playing and singing on the bill with local musicians, including Percy Welch. In 1955, his career took a major blow after a bar altercation in Milledgeville during which Kirkland killed a man. The guitarist claimed self-defense but served three years in prison. After his release, he continued his career, performing primarily as a featured player in different bands. He played with Otis Redding in Macon and made his last big tour with Hooker during the early 1960s. He also made a number of records. In 1962, Kirkland recorded *It's the Blues Man!* on the Tru-Sound label, an album of original blues numbers that gained him critical acclaim but little revenue. Three years later, he had a regional hit on Volt with "The Hawg," which was primarily a harmonica instrumental.[12]

Kirkland suffered another setback during the early 1970s when random gunfire in a Milledgeville, Georgia, nightclub struck him in the head. The wound caused him to lose part of his sight and would create health complications for the rest of his life. Miraculously, his energy level seemed to increase after the incident, at least as it applied to touring. He maximized his time on the road, and though he did not achieve mainstream success in the conventional sense, many blues fans and journalists were well aware of his talents. He also benefitted from a resurgence of interest in blues in the United States during the 1970s and 1980s. After a 1988 New York City performance, *New York Times* critic Peter Watrous praised Kirkland, stating that he "levelled the idea that urban blues is dust-covered music." During the period, Kirkland recorded for the Trix label and made a major television appearance on *Don Kirshner's Rock Concert*, a nationally syndicated music program. He also toured Europe, where he was very popular. "In Europe, I'm a big artist," he once said. "Here [in the United States], a whole lot of people know me, and a whole lot don't know me. But, in Europe, man, if I go over there in Europe they put up a big sign 'Eddie Kirkland is coming.' They'll come to the plane, to the airport, and pick me up in a limousine."[13]

The guitarist, singer, and composer never retired. He recorded for several smaller labels and kept a crowded touring schedule well into his eighties. "Music to me is not only the money, you know," Kirkland once told a journalist. "Music is a great love of mine. Music gives me something, really something to live for." He usually performed wearing a colorful, bejeweled turban, and his antics with the guitar were legendary. Toward the end of his life, the press continued calling him "the gypsy of the blues" and "Mr. Energy," and friends claimed he was "still trying to conquer the world one saloon or pub at a time." In 2010, Kirkland played as a guest artist on an album by Foghat, a rock band whose members he had befriended years earlier. Speaking of the experience, the group's drummer, Roger Earl, said, "We started playing with Eddie.... I don't think we stopped playing for five or six hours. It was a blast. I hope that, if the good Lord's willing and the creek don't rise, I get to 87 [with] that much energy." A road warrior to the end, Kirkland died in a car accident on February 27, 2011, the morning after he played a sold-out gig near Clearwater, Florida. He was buried in Cherry Blossom Memorial Gardens in Bibb County.[14]

Another colorful guitarist who is one of the great personalities associated with Macon's music history is Johnny Jenkins. Born Johnny Edwards Jenkins in Macon on March 5, 1939, he grew up in the rural Swift Creek community. As a child, he listened to music on a battery-powered transistor radio and later remembered that it was artists such as Bill Doggett and Bull Moose Jackson who first caught his attention. Like the rest of the rhythm and blues community in Macon, Jenkins's other great influence was the church. "I used to sing spiritual music all the time," he said. "Once I had my mother and neighbors thinking I was going to be a preacher." Because it dominated the radio airwaves in Macon when he was a child, he also took note of country music, later telling an interviewer, "I got to where I could sing just about anything Hank Williams ever put out. Hank Williams and Red Foley...just me and a guitar." Jenkins was a self-taught player who first started strumming and picking at a homemade instrument when he was nine years old. Not long afterwards, his sister's boyfriend bought the youngster a real guitar, for which he showed an immediate aptitude. Jenkins's style was somewhat unusual compared to most local guitarists in that he was left-handed and played the instrument "upside down."[15]

As he progressed musically, Jenkins played at family occasions and neighborhood parties and sometimes for tips at a local gas station. In 1957, at the age of eighteen, he became part of the Macon show business community by joining a new band called Pat Teacake and His Mighty Panthers. Organized by drummer Pat Teacake, whose real name was Charles Abrams, the heavily nicknamed ensemble originally consisted of Abrams on drums, vocalist "Little Willie" Jones, saxophonist Sonny "Hip" Goss, and guitarist Jimmie "Shhh" Barber along with Jenkins, who was billed as Johnny "Guitar" Jenkins. Others who performed with the group were Johnny "Jazzbo" Brown, Ray "Tampa" Brown, Tom "The Man" Jackson, Willie "Ploonie" Bowden, Charles "Prez" Toomer, and Samuel "Poor Sam" Davis. The band established itself as one of Macon's better rhythm and blues groups and drew big crowds at local venues, particularly after their first year, when a young singer named Otis Redding joined their ranks.[16]

Pat Teacake and His Mighty Panthers performed at all the local clubs, especially Club 15. The band also provided the music for a major show at the Douglass Theatre held in January of 1958. The event, billed as the "Big D.J. Jamboree" was a talent and fashion show hosted by WIBB, with the station's popular radio triumvirate Satellite Papa Brown, King Bee Swain, and Big Saul Green serving as emcees. A month later, WIBB hosted the first "Teenage Party" at the Roxy Theatre, another talent competition that would have great musical repercussions. Most accounts indicate that Jenkins's flamboyant stage presence was a highlight of both shows. He did splits on stage and played his guitar in fabulously contorted positions, slinging the instrument behind his back, between his legs, and even playing it with his teeth. At the time, few guitar players in Macon could match his showmanship.[17]

Jenkins's stage act was so wild and entertaining that it eventually gave rise to one of the great legends of Macon music history. Years later, Jenkins would claim that during the 1950s his guitar antics influenced a young Jimi Hendrix, creating the impression that Hendrix had gleaned at least some of his stage moves from the Macon native. The tale that the Macon guitarist was a great influence on Hendrix eventually made its way into print, and even into Jenkins's 2006 obituary in the *New York Times*. As always, there are slightly different versions of the story, but generally it revolves around Jimi Hendrix coming to Macon to visit relatives (some say an aunt) when he was young and clandestinely sneaking into nightclubs to watch the performers. One place usually mentioned in particular was Sawyer's Lake, an African American recreation center and nightspot about six miles outside of town on US Highway 80. Supposedly, Hendrix was mesmerized by Jenkins's rowdy stage act, idolized him, and later copied Jenkins on stage, famously playing the guitar in all sorts of contorted positions, complete with squealing feedback. Some people in Macon stand by the story as true, others are skeptical, and still others just break into a grin when the subject comes up.

Three heavy hitters on the Macon music scene from that era backed up the story, although not until years after the events were supposed to have taken place. Quotes attributed to Eddie Kirkland and Percy Welch during the 1990s stated that Hendrix had seen Jenkins play during the 1950s. Kirkland said, "I met [Hendrix] when he was thirteen years old, nothin' but a kid, a youngster, you understand? See, he had kin people in Macon, Georgia, some people there up on Fort Hill. He came down there in the summer, down to a place called Sawyer's Lake." While discussing both Jenkins and Hendrix, Welch said, "Both of them were left-handed guitar players. At that time, Johnny Jenkins was a better player than Jimi, because Jimi was just starting out, he couldn't play well. I remember he had a little ol' green and white guitar. He was the quiet type, didn't have a whole lot to say." Likewise, a 2006 newspaper article quoted Arthur "Bo" Ponder, another prominent Macon personality, remembering Hendrix as "a little guy who would follow us around a lot" when he was in the city. Then and afterwards, quotes like these from Kirkland, Welch, and Ponder lent gravitas to the "Jimi Hendrix in Macon" story, which naturally helped it spread.[18]

While the idea that Jimi Hendrix appropriated his Monterey and Woodstock guitar moves from a fiery but obscure local entertainer from Macon makes for a good story, it has always drawn skeptics. There seems to be a good deal of evidence that the whole scenario is nothing more than tall tale. In reality, Hendrix did not have a connection to Macon, and the narrative that Jenkins influenced Hendrix begs many questions. There is no evidence that Jimi Hendrix had any relatives in Macon or Bibb County or that he visited Macon as a teenager. His paternal grandmother was born in Georgia, but as a child during the 1880s she moved with her family to Tennessee. The story does not show up in Hendrix's lifetime and is conspicuously absent in the press for many years. A June 7, 1970, newspaper article in the *Macon News* about fledgling Capricorn Records mentioned Jenkins as a Capricorn artist but said only that he "plays in the vein of Jimi Hendrix." It made no mention of any influence Jenkins may have had on the younger man. Later that month, just before Jenkins and Hendrix both played at the second Atlanta International Pop Festival, an article featuring Jenkins appeared in the same newspaper. While the article highlighted the influence of blues on rock music and quoted Jenkins directly, there was no mention of any sort of connection between the Macon guitarist and Hendrix, who at the time was one of the most recognizable rock guitarists in the world. Jenkins later said that he realized who Jimi Hendrix was soon after the 1967 Monterey Pop Festival, so Jenkins presumably would have been aware of Hendrix at the 1970 Atlanta gathering, yet the subject never came up.[19]

Stylistically, the stage acrobatics that Jenkins supposedly passed down to Hendrix were not an innovation in blues circles or unique to the Macon guitarist. "Clowning" with the guitar was a relatively common practice in the context of the blues tradition. Generations of blues artists peppered their acts with guitar tricks and body contortions. T-Bone Walker was famous for it, and going even further back, so were Tommy Johnson and Charley Patton, who both began recording in the 1920s. Describing Patton, contemporary Sam Chatmon once said, "He'd be in there putting his guitar between his legs, carry it behind his head, lay down on the floor, and never stop picking." Chatmon could have just as well have been describing Hendrix, Jenkins, or a whole host of others.[20]

The story of Jenkins influencing Hendrix in Macon does not appear in any of the many Jimi Hendrix biographies. In a 1968 article in *Rolling Stone*, Hendrix mentions his early influences, including Muddy Waters, Albert Collins, Buddy Holly, B. B. King, and Eddie Cochran, but not Johnny Jenkins. Jenkins is absent again when Hendrix comments specifically on guitarists, adding, "The first guitarist I was aware of was Muddy Waters. I heard one of his old records when I was a little boy and it scared me to death, because I heard all of those sounds. Wow, what is that all about? It was great. And I like Albert King. He plays completely and strictly in one way, just straight funk blues." In a reference to musical influences being everywhere, Hendrix also stated, "Down south at some funky club, one cat up there starving to death, and he might be the best guitar player you ever heard, and you might not know his name." Some have taken this general statement to be a reference to Jenkins, although Hendrix does not mention Jenkins, Macon, or the name of a specific venue or club. Later, Billy Cox, an army friend and significant musical presence in Hendrix's life, said, "Jimi and I were not from the South, but our early influences were. We liked Jimmy Reed, and then we got more into a lot of B. B. and Albert King.... Albert King was a very, very powerful influence on him." Again, no mention of Jenkins.[21]

Jenkins himself did not say much publicly about Hendrix before the 1990s, but afterwards he embraced the story that he helped make Jimi Hendrix who he was as a performer. When questioned later about the facts of the matter, Jenkins sometimes added Otis Redding's name to the mix. Jenkins played with the singer in Macon and knew him well. He claimed that Redding told him about Jimi Hendrix after Redding and Hendrix performed at the Monterey Pop Festival in 1967. "Yeah, I didn't realize [Hendrix] was that into me until he got where he was," Jenkins told a journalist years later. "Otis came and told me. He said 'Hey man, there's a guy out in Monterey who looks kind of like you, who plays kind of like you, and plays left-handed upside down.' When I finally saw Jimi, I recognized him as a fellow who came out to see me play at Sawyer's Lake. He was down in front of the stage, making all the moves I was making, dancing like a crazy man." Similarly, Jenkins once told musician and noted Macon music producer Paul Hornsby that Hendrix "used to see me at Sawyer Lake. The next thing you know, he's jumping around like me, but he had his own stuff."[22]

The exact genesis of the tale about Jenkins and Hendrix is a little murky, but it may have sprouted legs after publication of Peter Guralnick's book *Sweet Soul Music* in 1986. The widely read volume mentions Jenkins and Hendrix in the same paragraph, with the relevant passage as follows: "Jenkins, a flashy guitarist and one of Macon's biggest local stars, was a light skinned black man described as 'Hollywood handsome' by all who knew him, and renowned for both the acrobatics and pyrotechnics of a style that would one day have considerable influence on Jimi Hendrix (once again via the ubiquitous Little Richard, for whom Hendrix started out on guitar)."[23]

In September of 1996, a story appeared in the Macon *Telegraph* incorrectly interpreting this passage as Guralnick, a prominent and respected music authority, blessing the idea that Jenkins had "considerable influence" on Hendrix and that somehow Little Richard was involved. It was not the first time the Jenkins-Hendrix connection was mentioned in a newspaper—the year before, an item in the *Atlanta Constitution* claimed Hendrix "based his whole look" on Jenkins—but the passage in the book seemed to accelerate the rumor. However, a careful reading of what Guralnick wrote indicates that he was actually commenting on "a" flamboyant style that both guitarists shared, rather than "the" personal style that Jenkins supposedly passed on to Hendrix directly. Some have also interpreted the reference to Little Richard as meaning that Jenkins and Hendrix first crossed paths after Little Richard's band, including Hendrix on guitar, made a pass through Macon, and the occasion set in motion the process of Hendrix taking on Jenkins's guitar moves. Again, a different and simpler interpretation seems to make more sense, that Hendrix actually learned more about flamboyant stage moves "via Little Richard" than from Jenkins. Hendrix also did not play for Little Richard's band until 1964, by which time his stage act was already drawing attention, and well after he supposedly first saw Jenkins in a Macon nightspot, a fact that throws off the chronology of that narrative.[24]

Despite all of this, the *Telegraph* account claiming Jenkins had "considerable influence" on Hendrix was picked up, quoted, and requoted over and over again for years, ultimately ending up in most of Jenkins's obituaries when he died in 2006. Both the Macon *Telegraph* and *Billboard* magazine stated in their tributes that Hendrix was visiting his aunt in Macon and that "Hendrix...saw Jenkins perform and fell in love with [his] signature acrobatic left-handed guitar style. It became part of Hendrix's act until his death in 1970." The *New York Times* obituary was similar but more succinct, stating simply, "Hendrix, whose aunt lived in Macon, saw Mr. Jenkins perform and fell in love with his way of playing."[25]

Why would Jenkins advance such an improbable story about Jimi Hendrix? One explanation might be that the story is true, but if that were the case, it means that Jimi Hendrix made a mysterious 2,700-mile trip from his home in Seattle, Washington, to Macon as a teenager to visit relatives whom no one else in Bibb County seemed to know. It also means that Hendrix, who freely discussed in the press artists whom he admired, for some reason kept his trip to Macon a secret and never mentioned a word to anyone about Jenkins being one of his early influences. It also means that Jenkins, who liked to talk, sat on the story for years without any great public pronouncement that he was a foundational influence on arguably the most famous guitarist in history. Finally, it means that Jenkins and his friends, for some unknown reason, decided to suddenly break their public silence during the 1990s, more than two decades after Hendrix's death, and begin freely discussing the story.

Another explanation could be that Jenkins enjoyed the publicity or notoriety that the story offered. A likely chronology of events was that the Guralnick book came out, newspaper reporters misinterpreted it, someone asked Jenkins about the book or the newspaper reports, and the guitarist decided to take the story and run with it, offering his own embellishments. Jenkins also claimed he bumped into Hendrix in 1969 while performing in New York and that Hendrix gave him a guitar, but

Jenkins could not produce the instrument when pressed by the interviewer. Coincidentally, around the time that the story about Jenkins and Hendrix began to appear in newspapers, Jenkins was involved in creating a "comeback album" after years of inactivity. He or someone connected with that effort may have seen the story as a promotional opportunity.

A third possible explanation is that Jenkins and some of his friends simply had fun telling a story that some people wanted to believe, which is one way that myths get started. One of the great folktales related to the history of blues music holds that in the 1920s the famous Mississippi bluesman Robert Johnson, only an adequate guitarist as a youngster, disappeared from his home for several months, only to return with magical musical powers. Where he had disappeared to, no one knew, but rumors began to circulate that he had gone down to an isolated crossroads in the Mississippi Delta and sold his soul to the devil in exchange for superhuman talent. Perhaps the Macon rumor mill simply produced a similar story. Rather than going down to the crossroads, Jimi Hendrix made a mystery-shrouded trip from Seattle to Macon, only to return home armed with abilities that would one day make him famous.

Regardless of whether Jenkins and Hendrix ever met, it was beyond dispute that Jenkins had a dynamic stage presence. Sporting a thin moustache and well-arranged pompadour, he also looked like and dressed the part of a star. Drummer Charles Davis, who played frequently with Jenkins, later summed up what a lot of people believed when he told an interviewer, "Johnny was Prince before there was a Prince. He was a real hippie. He was really laid back until he got on stage, and then he was a wild man." Likewise, Wayne Cochran, another Middle Georgia performer, once told an interviewer, "Johnny Jenkins, boy was he a freaky guy in his day.... Handsome guy. Moustache and goatee. Incredible showman. The guy could play. Left hand guitar, upside down. He'd talk with his guitar. He'd lay down on the floor and he'd hit it with his foot and dance on it." While Pat Teacake and His Mighty Panthers included other very good musicians, Jenkins's guitar work was the centerpiece of the band's show, and Jenkins became famous throughout Middle Georgia for his "eye-catching antics onstage, such as full splits, Chuck Berry-style duck-strutting across the stage, and playing on his knees."[26]

In 1958, Jenkins crossed paths with a young singer named Otis Redding. Ambitious and talented, Redding was becoming well known as the multi-week champion of "Teenage Party," a local talent show broadcast on WIBB on Saturday mornings from the Douglass Theatre. The radio station's staff designed the show as Macon's version of the famous Apollo Theater's amateur contest, with Hamp Swain and Satellite Papa hosting the event. Originally held at the Roxy, a movie theater on Hazel Street, the show moved to the Douglass as it gained popularity. WIBB hired keyboardist Roye Mathis, a veteran of the Macon club scene, to provide music, and the station publicized the event endlessly. Popular from the outset, it was one of the hottest tickets in town for African American teenagers and young adults, and hundreds flocked to the show every week.

Jenkins may have played at the event with Pat Teacake at least a couple of times, but he was in the audience when he first heard Redding sing. The guitarist later told Peter Guralnick, "I saw Otis at the Douglass, and the group behind him wasn't making it. So I went up to him, and I said, 'Do you mind if I play behind you?' And he looked at me like 'Who are you'? 'Cause he didn't know me. And I'd say 'I can make you sound good.'" It was, of course, a reciprocal musical interaction as Jenkins recognized that Redding could make the band "sound good" as well. With apparently little rancor, Otis "Rockin'" Redding, as he was billed, replaced Willie Jones as lead vocalist in Pat Teacake and His Mighty Panthers, but the association did not last long. Within a year, Jenkins had a falling out with Teacake over the songs that the band played—"creative differences" in modern parlance—and the guitarist left the band to form his own group, the Pinetoppers, with Ishmael "Ish" Moseley, Sammy Davis, and Charles Davis. Redding left as well and joined Jenkins in the new outfit as vocalist. With a dynamic guitarist/front man and a singer who would one day be recognized as one of the great voices of his generation, the Pinetoppers were in demand at local clubs.[27]

It was about this time that Jenkins met another force of nature in Macon, a young, white, would-be music promoter named Phil Walden. While no one knew it at the time, Walden was about to chart a career course that would dramatically affect the city's music culture and at the same time make him a legend in the music business. The fledgling entertainment mogul loved Jenkins and took on the Pinetoppers as a client. By association, he became Otis Redding's manager as well. He had good luck booking the group, particularly at fraternity and sorority dances around Georgia and Alabama. "Most of my shows, we'd play from eight to twelve," Jenkins later remembered. "Then, they'd have us play the breakfast dances. I played so many breakfast dances at colleges; I don't know how any damn body learned anything at college."[28]

While Walden took on other local acts, it was clear that the Pinetoppers were his first priority. He was determined to get them some sort of recording deal, hopefully to generate income, but also to establish the group as "recording artists" in promotional material. The opportunity presented itself in March of 1961 when Walden bumped in to James Newton, a part-time musician who ran a real estate business in Tifton, Georgia, about a hundred miles south of Macon. Edwards and a partner, Gus Statiris, owned a tiny label called Tifco, and they agreed to record the brash young music promoter's group. Still more enamored with Jenkins's guitar work than Redding's vocals, Walden had the group record an instrumental, "Love Twist," that sold modestly in Georgia and the surrounding states, but enough to draw the attention of Joe Galkin. Galkin was an oddly frenetic, Atlanta-based freelance record promoter who had a close relationship with Atlantic Records vice president Jerry Wexler. "Joe was a funny looking guy with a bald, pear-shaped noggin," Wexler later wrote in his autobiography. "He looked like a gremlin, drank like a fish and was absolutely adorable.... His m.o. was chaos." Galkin arranged for Atlantic to purchase the distribution rights to "Love Twist." It continued to sell, at least well enough to warrant another recording session, this time at Stax Records in Memphis at Atlantic's expense. "Joe was an irresistible pain in the ass," Wexler said, "so I put up the dough and they did it at Stax."[29]

The story of Johnny Jenkins's August 1962 recording session at Stax became part of entertainment-industry lore because it was a springboard for the career of Otis Redding, but for Jenkins himself it was a disappointment. The idea had been for the guitarist to record an instrumental track backed by Stax's studio team, Booker T. and the MGs, who had just recorded the instrumental hit "Green Onions" for the label. They were a tight group of excellent musicians that included organist Booker T. Jones, guitarist Steve Cropper, bassist Donald "Duck" Dunn, and drummer Al Jackson Jr. Unfortunately for Jenkins, after almost three hours of work, it was apparent that his blistering live stage show did not translate well onto record, and a significant instrumental hit never materialized. The Memphis session produced little other than a reworked version of "Love Twist," later retitled "Spunky" and released to little acclaim by Vox. Once the session ended, Stax's Jim Stewart told Galkin that he was not interested in cultivating Jenkins as a recording artist. What made the session notable was that with some leftover studio time Redding, who was not scheduled to sing, recorded a version of "These Arms of Mine," his first big seller.[30]

Jenkins returned to Macon with his pride bruised, but he continued playing in local clubs, where he was a popular figure. He and Redding performed together with the Pinetoppers for a short while, but the trip to Memphis was the beginning of the end of the notion that Jenkins would ever become a national headliner. He made one more brief trip to Stax for a recording session with Redding, whose career was about to soar to unimaginable heights, but afterwards, Jenkins grew increasingly bitter toward the music business. Not wishing to give up the spotlight to a singer whom he claimed he discovered, and reluctant to stay on the road for long periods of time, Jenkins remained for the most part in Macon, where many revered him. Vox released "Spunky" in late 1964, and while it did not do much business, the editor of the "Teen Tween" section of the Macon *Telegraph* predicted it would be "one of the top tunes of the day." Jenkins played with other bands as a "featured guest" and was on the bill at the second Atlanta International Pop Festival in 1970.[31]

That same year, Capricorn Records released Jenkins's first solo album, *Ton Ton Macoute!*, an eclectic collection of songs "which crossed the Delta Blues with Dr. John's New Orleans swamp rock and [Jimi] Hendrix's psychedelia." The album featured an outstanding group of supporting musicians, including several members of the Allman Brothers Band. While it was well-produced and received good reviews, it was not a huge seller and Jenkins himself said he did not care for it. Even further disillusioned with the music business, he withdrew as a performer for more than two decades. In 1996, Capricorn released Jenkins's comeback album, *Blessed Blues*, a straightforward blues album. Two more albums followed on the Mean Old World label, *Handle With Care* (2001) and *All in Good Time* (2005). Jenkins died in Macon on June 26, 2006. His obituary ran in newspapers all over the country, with most repeating the Hendrix story and mentioning his early association with Otis Redding. "I have a great deal of sentiment attached to Johnny Jenkins," Phil Walden said in 1996, after he had made his mark on the music industry. "He was my first client, and it was through him that I met Otis Redding.... I was still a teenager when I met him, and I thought my entire world rotated around Johnny Jenkins' guitar. I was convinced he could have been the greatest thing in rock 'n' roll." Jenkins was inducted posthumously into the Georgia Music Hall of Fame in 2012.[32]

While Johnny Jenkins was Phil Walden's first client, he was certainly not his last. Philip Michael "Phil" Walden was born January 11, 1940, in Greenville, South Carolina, the son of Clemiel Barto "C. B." and Carolyn Walden. The family moved to Macon when Phil was a small child, and he attended Lanier High School. Walden's devotion to African American music began as a teenager. His older brother Clark exposed him to the music of Ray Charles, Hank Ballard, and the Clovers, among others, which hooked him immediately. "I started listening to an R&B station, WIBB, and I would go to the City Auditorium in Macon and see R&B shows," he recalled with a laugh. "I would skip my Tri-Hi-Y (a youth program sponsored by the YMCA) meetings to go to the City Auditorium. It was not the type of function that I felt my parents would want me to be attending, early R&B being considered rather un-Christian." He also began scanning the "colored" section of local newspapers for entertainment news.[33]

Obsession would not be too strong a term to describe Walden's interest in R & B music. In the fall of 1957, as a senior at Lanier, he hired Hamp Swain to spin records at a party for his high school fraternity, and on Swain's recommendation hired Percy Welch's band for a live show. It was a definite break with tradition as the all-white high school typically entertained with white bands nattily dressed in sport coats or white dinner jackets. The positive response led Walden to believe that he was onto something with regard to white kids appreciating music that sprang from the African American community. As a result, he decided to try his hand at artist booking and management, and his career started in earnest the following year after he enrolled as a freshman at Mercer University in Macon.

Through the years, a host of writers would try to describe Walden in the early stages of his career, and they all commented on his drive, energy, and passion for music. In an *Esquire* magazine article, author Robert Sam Anson described the neophyte music promoter as "a popular, mouthy kid, president of his high school fraternity, a devil with his teachers, a lean-boned, green-eyed terror, as quick with a quip as he was with his fists." In his memoir, *Rhythm and Blues: A Life in American Music*, Jerry Wexler of Atlantic Records called Walden "a college boy from Macon...as wildly in love with R&B as any man who ever lived, a devotee and a businessman...the archetype of the thousands of Southern whites who'd got bitten by the funk bug." After describing Walden as "a lantern-jawed, heavy drawling freshman from Mercer," in his book *Dreams to Remember: Otis Redding, Stax Records, and the Transformation of Southern Soul*, Mark Ribowsky wrote that the young promoter "was a very strange bird, easy for some to pass off as an impressionable white kid trying to fit into black culture. While he looked like a vanilla wafer, skinny enough to break in half in a good wind, there was something compelling about him."[34]

Like a growing number of white teenagers in Macon, Walden also listened religiously to *Teenage Party* on WIBB and took a small step toward a management career by organizing a doo-wop group called the Heartbreakers to compete in the talent show. It was a ragtag group of African American youngsters described as "two carhops and a bus station employee." Walden rehearsed the group for several weeks and had them enter the competition. Ironically, he never saw them perform on *Teenage Party* because the show was segregated and for African Americans only. Instead, he parked his car outside the theater and listened to the live broadcast on the radio. Despite a game effort, the Heartbreakers didn't carry the day. The group, and others like them, were consistently upstaged by a powerful singer from Tindall Heights named Otis Redding, who would soon help shape Walden's professional and personal identity.[35]

It was around this time that Walden secured Johnny Jenkins and the Pinetoppers as clients, and it was through Jenkins that he first met Redding. Jenkins introduced the two men in the summer of 1959 at a show at Lakeside Park, a local recreation area. More than likely, Walden already knew Redding by reputation, as he had heard the singer many times on the *Teenage Party* broadcasts. "I went to Lakeside Park to hear Johnny play," Walden later recalled, "and I walked in and there was this tall, gaunt singer, and they introduced me to him, and it was 'Rockhouse' Redding. That was the first time I saw him."[36]

The association with Johnny Jenkins and the Pinetoppers helped lay the foundation for Walden's booking agency, which he started in a garage apartment behind his parents' house. At the beginning of his junior year at Mercer, he rented an office in Macon in the Professional Building (renamed the Robert E. Lee Building in 1963) on Mulberry Street. It was the same building that housed WIBB. With the help of Redding and others, he painted the place and decorated it with two used army-surplus desks. He called his business Phil Walden Artists and Promotions and enlisted the help of his younger brother, Alan, who was still in high school. "I booked [Johnny Jenkins and the Pinetoppers] for my high school dance and would often help Phil get them to their dances and parties," Alan told Michael Buffalo Smith in an interview for Smith's book *Capricorn Rising: Conversations in Southern Rock*. "I became the high school representative for Phil's new agency, Phil Walden Artists and Promotions. Also, I doubled as a Coca-Cola soda jerk at the local club where we promoted bands like Doug Clark and the Hot Nuts, the Delacardos, and Maurice Williams and the Zodiacs."[37]

While Walden picked up other acts, Johnny Jenkins and the Pinetoppers remained his focus early on. They were a very popular live act with white colleges, where fraternities and sororities kept a packed party calendar. Hamilton Jordan, who later became chief of staff for President Jimmy Carter, grew up in Albany, Georgia, and as a teenager saw the Pinetoppers play. He later described the experience in his memoir, *A Boy from Georgia: Coming of Age in the Segregated South*:

> Johnny Jenkins and the Pinetoppers were a hot, all black rock 'n' roll band we heard at a Christmas Dance at the Elk's club, which had been sponsored by a college fraternity. They made quite an impression on me that night. Arriving in a black shiny hearse, the Pinetoppers emptied out one-by-one, wearing yellow suits. Just when it looked like the last person had exited, out popped a skinny, white kid with curly hair, all dressed up in a black suit. The kid started shaking hands all around and handing out cards that read, "Phil Walden, Agent, Macon, Georgia." Smooth talking and cocky, he couldn't have been over twenty years old, but he had his own business cards! I was impressed.... The Pinetoppers played out of their minds for hours, performing current hits as well as their own songs. Everybody agreed that they were the coolest band ever to play Albany, Georgia.[38]

At the time, Jordan also noticed something very unusual about Walden, considering it was the late 1950s in the Deep South. "It was also the first time I ever saw a white person so familiar with blacks," Jordan wrote. "This Walden guy was joking with the band, whispering in their ears, and putting his arm around their shoulders. I was just not

accustomed to seeing white folks behaving that way around black folks."
It was this "familiar" feel that made Walden different—*very* different—
from most Southern whites of the period, who were brought up to believe
in black inferiority. He was never comfortable with Jim Crow segregation,
always sensing that something was amiss but having nothing else to
compare it with. "I remember asking my mother why colored people were
treated that way," he once said. "She said it's not really right, it's just the
way things are in the South."[39]

He later credited his association with the Pinetoppers as a
transformative experience. "This was my first relationship with African
American musicians," he said. "I learned so much about life from Johnny
Jenkins and Otis Redding during those early years. It was exhilarating to
say the least." Walden traveled with the musicians, ate with them, drank
with them, and sometimes stayed with them in "colored" motels.
According to Jenkins, Walden did not try to impress them or ingratiate
himself with them by using exaggerated street language, as some white
kids did. He earned their trust by simply treating them as if he cared about
their well-being and because he was all business. "Back then," Jenkins later
said, "Phil was like a brother. He was somebody that cared, and he was
somebody that would stand by you. We drank together. We played and
sung, and if we needed anything we'd go to Phil to get it. It wasn't no
'black boy' and no 'white boy'…. Phil had no racial bias; he wouldn't let
that stand in the way of what he wanted to do."[40]

Walden's relationship with black musicians did not go unnoticed in
the segregated South. Although in a much different context, he suffered
many of the race-based indignities that were an everyday part of the
African American experience in the region. Many whites viewed him with
suspicion, thought he was crazy, or in general looked on in disgust as he
disregarded long-established social boundaries. "It's so pathetic that things
can't settle down," he once said in referencing race relations, "I've seen
some of the crap that [African Americans] have to go through. I know I've
been subjected to some of the same shit by being associated with them."
Otis Redding's wife, Zelma, later said that Walden's passion for rhythm
and blues and friendships with black musicians made him "the little white
boy who everybody was waiting to beat up on," and as time wore on, his
parents even received telephone calls threatening their "communist,
nigger-loving son."

In a 1971 interview, Walden recalled one incident that took place on a freezing Christmas Eve night while he was traveling back to Macon with a carload of African American musicians. Their car broke down in Griffin, Georgia, about fifty miles from Macon, and they sought help from a local mechanic. "Christmas Eve.... It was freezing, we were all bundled up," Walden remembered. "We pulled into a repair shop, and there was this guy sitting inside behind a big stove. We knock on the door. He won't let us in, won't fix the car. That was one of those race things that always sticks out in my mind. I went to a phone to call my father and older brother to pick us up. I got into Macon about seven in the morning, just in time to open all the Santa Claus stuff."[41]

While Walden took on more clients and initially saw Jenkins as his star attraction, it soon became apparent that Otis Redding was a special talent, and it was with Redding that Walden eventually developed a special bond. "I was real fortunate to discover a new way of seeing things through my relationship with Otis," he said. "He kind of walked me through his culture, and I kind of walked him through my side of it, and we were able to absorb and learn from each other."[42]

Otis Ray Redding Jr. was born September 9, 1941, in Dawson, Georgia, the son of Rev. Otis Redding Sr. and Fannie Roseman Redding. Drawn to the wartime jobs at Warner Robins, the family moved to Macon when Redding was small, and he grew up in Tindall Heights. His first experience onstage was with the junior choir at the Vineville Baptist Church, and he also sang with a gospel quartet called the Junior Spiritual Crusaders. One of his first individual performance in front of a crowd may have taken place at a church function on May 1, 1955, when the choir director singled out the thirteen-year-old to sing a solo. Around the same time, the Reddings moved from Tindall Heights to the Bellevue section of Macon.[43]

While the church provided Redding's early musical foundation, his other influences were many and varied, driven by the times he lived in and the conditions under which he lived. He later said that some of his earliest musical memories revolved around a calypso-based Louis Jordan tune titled "Run Joe" that his parents loved. "My mother and father and I used to go to parties when I was a kid," he told an interviewer. "We used to go out to a place called Sawyer's Lake in Macon. There was a calypso song out then, called 'Run, Joe.' My mother and daddy used to play that for me all the time. I just dug the groove. Ever since then I've been playing music." As there was little black music on the radio when he was a child, Redding also heard big band music and a great deal of country music. "I know Otis liked Hank Williams," Phil Walden once said. "He liked him a lot, thought he was great." Other influences included a familiar list of African American talent who were stars during the period, including Rosetta Tharpe, Ray Charles, Fats Domino, Chuck Berry, and Sam Cooke. But there was one performer who stood out to Redding above all others, and that was Little Richard. Not only was his music fantastic, but he grew up in Macon, a hometown boy who, through music, had ascended to heights that other performers around town only dreamed about. That made Little Richard not only a star, but the personification of a dream that many African American performers in Macon shared.[44]

By the mid-1950s, Macon radio stations WBML and WIBB were experimenting more and more with "race music," and WIBB was on its way to establishing an all-black format. These developments exposed Otis Redding and his teenage friends in the African American community to an increasing amount of music based in the blues and blended with consistent doses of gospel. Significantly, it also exposed white teenagers to the same sounds, which over time helped create an integrated audience for music labeled rhythm and blues, soul, and rock and roll. The integration of the airwaves in such a manner certainly did not solve all the problems related to Jim Crow, but it did represent a cross-cultural pollination that had long-lasting effects. Musically, the pivotal year for Redding seemed to be 1955, with nothing affecting him more than the release of Little Richard's first big hit, "Tutti-Frutti." Like many other teenagers of the era, black and white, Redding was never quite the same after hearing that record.

By the end of 1956, Redding's interest in gospel music was giving way to an increased passion for more secular sounds. Much to the chagrin of his minister father, he dropped out of high school and worked a series of odd jobs, including a stint as a water well driller, all the while nurturing his show business dreams. With several friends, he formed a small, short-lived band that practiced Little Richard songs, but they never did much business. "I was almost sixteen at the time, just getting started singing," he later said. "I used to play gigs and not make any money. I wasn't looking for money out of it then. I just wanted to be a singer." He took another step in that direction when he entered a talent contest hosted by Gladys Williams at the Hillview Springs Social Club.[45]

Hillview Springs was a recreational facility built by local African American businessman Zettler Clay back in 1948. Located in a wooded area on a small lake suitable for fishing, the site included picnic tables and a clubhouse that hosted community events during the day and functioned as a dance hall after dark. On Sundays, Williams hosted a talent contest that could be both fun and intimidating for young musicians. While Williams had a reputation for taking young talent under her wing, she was also a stern taskmaster. Her band, one of Macon's finest, backed up the young musicians as they performed, and she would not long suffer any fledgling entertainer who could not produce the goods. Redding knew this when he entered the contest for the first time in 1957. During his first appearance, he reportedly stumbled through a version of Little Richard's "Long Tall Sally," unable to keep the proper time with the band. Quickly dismissed from the stage, he left dejected but not defeated.[46]

Redding went home and practiced, later returning to try again, this time taking pains to stay in sync with the band on a tight version of Little Richard's new single "Heebie Jeebies." He won the five-dollar first prize and began showing up every Sunday to enter the contest, winning consistently. "Little Richard is actually the guy that inspired me to start singing," Redding later said. "My favorite song of his was Heebie Jeebies.... That song really inspired me to start singing, because I won a talent show with it. This was at the Hillview Springs Social Club.... I won a talent show for fifteen Sunday nights straight with that song, and they wouldn't let me sing no more, wouldn't let me win that five dollars anymore." Although he won the contest multiple times, he was yet to develop the unique style that would make him an icon, trading at this early stage in his career on his ability to sing like his hero, Little Richard.[47]

Still, the exposure from his appearances at Hillview Springs eased him into Macon's music community, even earning the teenager a few appearances with Little Richard's old band, the Upsetters. Their road manager, Macon resident Henry Nash, later told Penniman's biographer, Charles White, that Redding's "impressions of Richard were word perfect and he had all of his moves down pat." Flush with increased confidence, Redding entered the *Teenage Party* talent competition, which was a major weekly event in Macon's African American community. As had been the case when he first performed with Gladys Williams, Redding did not mesh well with the house band, but he was able to put on a better show, according to Johnny Jenkins, when he started performing with Jenkins's group. With the new band, Redding won the competition on a weekly basis, just as he had done at Hillview Springs, and because WIBB broadcast the event, he became even better known in Middle Georgia. For a short time, he sang as a featured attraction in clubs with a band called Jazzbo Brown and the House Wreckers, but by the winter of 1958 he had joined Jenkins in Pat Teacake and His Mighty Panthers. In their newspaper ads, Redding was billed with Teacake as "Macon's newest Rock 'n' Roll Vocalist." By the summer of 1959, he had left that group to join Jenkins's new band, the Pinetoppers.[48]

Redding also came into Phil Walden's orbit when he joined the Pinetoppers, but not as the front man of the group. While Walden later said he and Redding had an immediate rapport, at the time, Jenkins was the acknowledged leader of the band, and it was Jenkins's career that the young promoter had his eye on. "The money wasn't behind Otis," Ish Mosely later told Scott Freeman. "The money was behind Johnny. Phil wasn't really pushing Otis. You hear that? He was pushing Johnny Jenkins." Walden did not ignore Redding, and by all accounts the two were friendly from the outset, but, initially, at least, Walden viewed Jenkins as the potential breakout star. Redding was just the singer in Jenkins's band. In these early days, the Pinetoppers' musical hierarchy was set in stone, but the situation soon became more fluid. Jenkins did not like anyone questioning his position as leader of the band, while Redding was too strong willed and too talented to be relegated to the position of perpetual second banana. In short, the association was a musical marriage of two focused performers that was destined to fail.[49]

Impatient and ambitious, Redding suddenly took a hiatus from the band in 1960 and for a brief time moved to Los Angeles, where he had relatives who provided him a place to stay. He left Macon in February, although ads continued to appear in local newspapers advertising Redding with the Pinetoppers through July—likely due to either an oversight, unwanted expenses related to changing the ads, or the fact that Redding's name still helped draw crowds. He was in California for only a few months but stayed busy. Within a few weeks of his arrival, he met some area musicians and even managed to record four songs, "Gamma Lama," "She's Alright," "Gettin' Hip," and "Tuff Enuff," during a three-hour session at Gold Star Studios in Hollywood. Later released on the Trans World label, "Tuff Enuff" with "She's Alright" did not sell well, but they represented Redding's first foray into the process of making records. On the cusp of settling down with his soon-to-be wife Zelma, who was expecting their first child back in Macon, Redding returned to Georgia. On August 14, 1960, a new Pinetoppers ad appeared in the Macon *Telegraph* promoting an upcoming club date for the band, and it once again included "Otis 'Rockin' Redding," who was "just back from L.A. California."[50]

Over the next year, the Pinetoppers played their usual schedule of fraternity and sorority functions along with shows at Macon clubs such as the Royal Palm, Club 15, Adams Lounge, and the Grey Goose. For the band, the big news of 1961 was the recording of "Love Twist," but as a vocalist, Redding was probably not overly enamored with the instrumental track. Phil Walden still seemed focused on Johnny Jenkins as the Pinetoppers' star, while the ambitious singer wanted to make a record of his own. Redding's solution to the situation was to approach James R. "Bobby" Smith, who became an early but significant character in the Otis Redding saga.

A car salesman by trade, Smith worked at a number of local dealerships in Macon before an automobile accident in the late 1950s severely affected his vision. Afterward, he decided to try entertainment management as a career and opened an office in the same building that housed Phil Walden's new enterprise. Although he had no background in the music business, Smith was able to sign a local singer, Wayne Cochran, from nearby Thomaston, Georgia. Cochran was a hybrid rockabilly performer who, though white, became moderately successful singing soul music and dancing onstage like James Brown. Cochran was an animated live performer who drew good crowds around Middle Georgia. In 1961, he wrote a song titled "Last Kiss" that Smith arranged to have released by Gala Records, a small label headquartered in Vidalia, Georgia. The song was not a big seller for Cochran, but in 1964 it was a national hit for J. Frank Wilson and the Cavaliers and, much later, Pearl Jam covered the tune. On those credentials, Smith was able to claim he was a record producer, and he started his own label called Confederate Records.[51]

Confederate Records was Macon's first significant record label, and its name reflected the times during which it was founded. By the early 1960s, the civil rights movement was gaining momentum, threatening decades of "tradition" in the South that kept the races segregated in the twentieth century just as slavery had during the antebellum era. The movement helped invigorate a revival of the Ku Klux Klan and energized those Southern politicians who were determined to fight integration. In Georgia, reaction to the movement led to, among other things, the adoption of a new state flag that prominently displayed within its design the Confederate "stars and bars." At the same time, in all the states of the former Confederacy, whites between 1961 and 1965 were celebrating the centennial of the Civil War. Confederate flags fluttered in the breeze at events throughout the region, and groups such as the Sons of Confederate Veterans marched in parades dressed in full Confederate uniforms. Cities renamed streets and buildings after Southern generals, and many new businesses incorporated the words "rebel" or "confederate" into their names. In Macon, Bobby Smith was just following a trend when he named his new enterprise Confederate Records and used the Confederate flag design in his promotional material. Unfortunately, the stars and bars had an entirely different meaning to the other half of the Southern population, as Smith later found out when he tried to get African American disc jockeys to play the records that his label produced.

Two white singers from Middle George were the first to record on the Confederate label. George Wharton Lester, who took the stage name Bobby Lee, made the first record, a rockabilly number titled "Run Fool Run" backed by "Shake Me Baby." Next up was Leon "Ken" Kennington, who recorded a ballad, "A Million Teardrops," with an up-tempo rockabilly number, "It Goes Without Saying," on the B side. Kennington had been performing almost from the cradle. He took his first music lessons and sang his first church solo at the age of four, and at age eight won a talent competition in Atlanta singing the gospel standard "Peace in the Valley." He began singing professionally at thirteen and knew Wayne Cochran, who he considered a mentor. "I was thirteen and Wayne was maybe six or seven years older," he later remembered. "I really looked up to him somewhat like an older brother, and was always impressed with his natural showmanship." Like other kids his age in Middle Georgia, Kennington grew up listening to Macon radio stations WNEX, WIBB, and WBML, and in the evenings, WLAC out of Nashville. Among his early musical heroes were Charlie Rich, Elvis Presley, James Brown, and Jerry Lee Lewis.

Through Cochran, Kennington met Bobby Smith, who agreed to listen to his demo tape. Smith liked what he heard, as did songwriter Jack Sandifer, who penned the songs that Kennington would record. Since Confederate Records at the time had no recording facility, Smith used the back room of a music store, Bibb Music on Cotton Avenue, as his "studio," with Cochran and his band serving as the session players. It was a primitive environment to say the least, with the musicians and the singer walled off from one another by cardboard boxes. According to Kennington, "The acoustics in the room were not great, and [the musicians] were arranged very loosely." Smith also suggested that Kennington adopt a stage name, with Cochran chiming in with suggestions. "Wayne changed my name to 'Ken' Kennington because he thought it sounded more rock 'n' roll than Leon," Kennington said. "It was Bobby's idea to change my name. Bobby wanted to call me Jimmy, but Wayne came up with Ken."[52]

While "A Million Teardrops" and "It Goes Without Saying" turned out well considering the less-than-stellar recording conditions, Confederate Records, like most fledgling labels of the era, did not have a sophisticated marketing infrastructure in place to push sales. "Bobby and I individually went to various radio stations to try to get air play from the program directors," Kennington said. "Also, I personally sold records to people that owned and stocked jukeboxes." Regardless of the sales figures, after his dealings with Smith, Kennington was able to bill himself as a recording artist, and he continued to play live dates. "I sang constantly in churches around the Macon and Atlanta area," he later remembered, "and as a teenager and young adult in all the nicer night clubs. One of them was The Cave, which was a great place for entertainment in Macon.... It was really cool to be one of the rotating bands performing there on a steady basis."[53]

Kennington eventually left Macon, but he never left music, forging a decades-long career touring the country. His single "It Goes Without Saying" later took on a life of its own, finding its way onto compilation works in the United States and abroad. Copies of the original 45 became collector's items. "I have performed all over the United States," he later recalled fondly when asked about his time in Macon, "but my teenage years were very exciting to me. During that time there was always a demand for live bands—high school proms, VFWs, Moose Clubs, National Guard armories. Macon was a hotbed for local music, both before and as I was growing up."[54]

Despite the Civil War imagery, Confederate Records was still the only label in town, and Otis Redding wanted to make a record. Redding approached Smith, who was impressed with both his voice and his ability to write songs. The producer took particular notice of a song titled "Shout Bamalama," a reworked version of "Gamma Lama," the song Redding had written and recorded in California. Smith decided to move forward and set up a recording date for the singer. He also began interacting with Phil Walden, who at the time had no problem with Smith recording Redding. Walden was busy promoting Johnny Jenkins, and a Redding recording would likely make the Pinetoppers a more sought-after group. At the very least, it would allow Walden to promote the singer as a "recording artist" and improve the Pinetoppers' brand. "His thing was booking," Smith later said of Walden, "mine was in the recording end." This led to a friendly relationship between Walden and Smith in the short term, but it put the two men on a collision course.[55]

Before the "Shout Bamalama" session took place, Redding visited Smith's office to show him another song he had come up with. When he arrived, he found Wayne Pierce, a local teenage musician, waiting to see Smith as well. Pierce, a talented keyboardist, got his start with a high school pickup band called the Lancers and later played organ for Wayne Cochran's band, the Rocking Capris. Smith was on the phone, so Redding, who brought along his guitar, played the song for Pierce in the waiting area. "Otis at the time had such a powerful image, I was just so impressed," Pierce remembered. Otis came in. He had his guitar with him. Bobby was tied up in the back on the phone. I introduced myself and so did he. He said he had a song he wanted to let Bobby hear, and he asked me if I wanted to hear it. I said 'sure,' and it was 'These Arms of Mine.' He played it right there." Not long afterward, Redding played it for Smith, who liked the song but at the time was concentrating on the upcoming "Shout Bamalama" session. Not realizing the potential of "These Arms of Mine," the producer ended up giving it to another group who were popular around Middle Georgia at the time, Buddy Leach and the Playboys, who recorded a quickly forgotten version that Smith released on Confederate.[56]

Wanting a cleaner sound than that produced in the back of a record store, Smith set up Redding's "Shout Bamalama" session at a public television studio in Athens affiliated with the University of Georgia. The Pinetoppers were supposed to provide the backing, but the day of the session most—and perhaps all—of the members did not show up. In his Redding biography, Jonathan Gould speculated that Johnny Jenkins may have been absent due to either his general "unreliability" or because Joe

Galkin discouraged the guitarist from playing on a record for a label other than Stax. As a result, the backing band for Redding that day was made up mostly of members of Wayne Cochran's band, with Cochran on bass. In addition to "Shout Bamalama," the session produced a B side titled "Fat Gal," and on both songs Little Richard's influence was unmistakable in Redding's vocal delivery. Smith had the records pressed and signed Redding to a one-year recording contract that later would be the subject of controversy.[57]

Record in hand, Smith and Redding went on the road to promote "Shout Bamalama." This process amounted to the two men traveling the Southeast in Smith's car trying to talk black disc jockeys at rhythm and blues stations into putting the song on their playlists. Smith quickly ran into an obstacle related to the rebel flag printed on each individual record label. Smith, like most whites in the South, never gave that type of imagery a second thought, but he quickly found out that African Americans detested it, and that black disc jockeys wanted nothing to do with anything "Confederate." He went back to Macon and created a shadow label for Confederate. He called it Orbit, with a rocket ship rather than a Confederate flag decorating the record labels. With the new label, the song started to get some regional airplay, but it never gained much traction.

Regardless of the minimal sales, "Shout Bamalama" helped raise the profile of the Pinetoppers back in Macon. Their bookings increased at the clubs around town, as did the crowds that came out to watch them perform. New Pinetoppers advertisements appeared featuring Johnny "Love Twist" Jenkins and Otis "Shout Bamalama" Redding.[58]

Redding's association with Bobby Smith caused him to cross paths more and more with Wayne Cochran, and the two became good friends. Cochran's stage show was a sight to behold, and he developed an unusual persona as the "white James Brown," complete with all the appropriate gyrations as well as a huge helmet of piled-high bleached-blond hair that made him seem a foot taller than he really was. He and Redding hung out quite a bit and even appeared together on occasion. Smith set up one of their most notable joint appearances in Macon at Lakeside Park that drew thousands. "Bobby put together a show out at Lakeside Park," Wayne Pierce, who played with the Rocking Capris, later recalled. "They called it the Battle of the Bands. It was Otis and Johnny Jenkins and the Pinetoppers, and Wayne Cochran and the Rocking Capris. There were tons of people there. It was wild. It was packed."[59]

Cochran went on to have a colorful career that for years included a breakneck touring schedule. He eventually signed with King Records, and while his songs did not generate great sales in the marketplace, his energetic live act was the stuff of legend, and he developed a cult following. He appeared on national television in the 1960s, most notably on the *Jackie Gleason Show*. Gleason, who was a big fan, contributed liner notes to one of Cochran's albums that summed up the singer's live act perfectly. "He doesn't just sing—he explodes," Gleason wrote. "He doesn't perform—he happens. And when he happens, everything in the immediate vicinity vibrates and responds." With his band, the C. C. Riders, Cochran became a popular attraction in Las Vegas, where he struck up a friendship with Elvis Presley. In 1980, the Blues Brothers, John Belushi and Dan Aykroyd, covered Cochran's signature song "Going Back to Miami" on their album *Made in America*, and two years later he made a notable appearance on the *Late Show with David Letterman*. By the mid-1980s, Cochran had backed away from the music business, and for the last thirty years of his life devoted himself to the ministry. He passed away in 2017.[60]

"Shout Bamalama" did not break Otis Redding nationally, but his career accelerated soon after he recorded it. While local bookings increased, the catalyst for a dramatic advance in the singer's fortunes was a trip to Memphis, Tennessee. Memphis was the home of Stax Records, a relatively new company run by Jim Stewart and his sister, Estelle Stewart Axton, that was destined for great things in the world of rhythm and blues. The trip took place in August of 1962, and it became the launching point for the Otis Redding legend. Naturally, as with many landmark events related to American entertainment, either as a business or an art form, there are different versions of exactly what happened. At the time, Phil Walden was busy promoting Johnny Jenkins, and Joe Galkin had gotten the guitarist an audition with Stax. That was the beginning of the story, and the only part of the story that is not in dispute.

The heavily romanticized version of the trip to Memphis has Redding occupying a minor role until the very end. As this version of the tale goes, Johnny Jenkins needed a driver for the trip, either because he had lost his driver's license or he just did not like driving. Redding, always the unassuming team player, either volunteered or was asked by Phil Walden to take Jenkins to Memphis. Jenkins arrived at Stax, but his afternoon session did not go well, and after three hours Stax co-owner Jim

Stewart called it a day, even though a half hour of studio time remained. Redding, who presumably had been dutifully waiting in the studio to drive Jenkins home, suddenly saw his chance and through shear gumption inserted himself into the situation. He begged Stewart to let him use the last half hour of studio time. Stewart hesitated, but fate gave him a nudge and he relented, allowing Redding to make a demo version of "These Arms of Mine." Redding sang into the microphone, and the Cinderella story reached full flower. Suddenly, the heavens opened, the angels sang, and a star was born.

What immediately rendered this version of events suspect was the relegation of Redding to the role of chauffeur. While the singer may have driven the car—and he later told Dick Clark on *American Bandstand* that he was paid ten dollars to do so—in reality, he was not functioning solely as hired help. Redding likely would not have made the trip unless he knew that in some way he would benefit. Stax was a recording studio, and he wanted to record, which motivated him to make the long journey from Macon to Memphis. While Phil Walden had been pushing Jenkins, he had not been completely ignoring Redding, especially after the recording of "Shout Bamalama." In Macon, the names of both Jenkins and Redding were featured in Pinetoppers ads, where previously only Jenkins's name was prominent, and Joe Galkin had also taken notice of Redding's potential as a singer. While portraying Redding as a miraculous, accidental discovery certainly makes a good story, the circumstances that led the singer to Memphis were far more calculated.[61]

While Galkin set up the Stax session for Jenkins alone, both he and Walden also hoped to get a recording deal for Redding and planned accordingly. Jenkins and Redding were supposed to drive to the session in Memphis, and Galkin was supposed to show up and convince Jim Stewart to let Redding have some of the recording time. The idea apparently was to get Jenkins's record made and hopefully get a recording contract for Redding, using whatever part of the session was left over as an audition. In his comprehensive 1997 history of Stax Records, Rob Bowman quoted Walden explaining the situation. "The plan was to make this follow-up for Johnny Jenkins, but also to give Otis a chance to sing," Walden said. "That was my understanding with Joe Galkin. I said 'Otis, if you get a shot, you got to do it just as fast as you can because you probably won't have much time.'... Thank God Joe was there because it probably wouldn't have happened if he hadn't been." Walden also told the Macon

Telegraph in 1987 that he had "requested that they give Otis the opportunity to put down a couple of things." A host of authors have echoed this version of events, including Jonathan Gould, who wrote in his Redding biography, "Together Galkin and Walden came up with a scheme designed to further the interests of both Jenkins and Redding.... Since Jenkins didn't like to drive, the plan called for Redding to chauffeur him to Memphis. The plan also called for Joe Galkin to attend the session and persuade Jim Stewart, the owner of Stax, to give Otis a chance to sing." Galkin also gave Jim Stewart half the publishing rights to what Redding recorded, apparently to clinch the deal.[62]

And there was Johnny Jenkins's version of events. Although the trip to Stax was supposed to produce a hit single for the guitarist, nothing happened for him in terms of advancing his career. Thirty-four years later, in 1996, around the time that he began taking a good bit of public credit for Jimi Hendrix's evolution as a performer, the guitarist told a reporter from the Macon *Telegraph* that *he* was the one who asked if Redding could sing at the Stax session, and that the session ended early only because *he* was so well-rehearsed. "We had already played those songs. We had them rehearsed," he said. "I did it so quickly that we got done early. Then I asked if they would let Otis record some." Quoted in the Gould biography, Jenkins was even more adamant, stating, "I had a lot of time left over, and I asked if it would be OK if my friend could sing in the spare time that I had left.... I said if you can't use him, then I won't cut any more. And they talked about it and said OK."[63]

As with the Hendrix story, there are major flaws in the Jenkins narrative that make it unlikely. First, a threat that he "won't cut any more" unless Redding was allowed to sing would have fallen on deaf ears. Jenkins arrived in Memphis wanting something from Stax—a recording deal—not the other way around. Stax did not need Johnny Jenkins and had no reason to suffer his threats or take any direction from him regarding studio time. One thing that everyone else in the room agreed on after the fact was that by the time Redding sang, Jenkins's audition had been deemed unproductive, which was another reason why he had no leverage to make demands. Jenkins's version of events was also unique. Through the years, the other witnesses never seemed to give Jenkins any credit for personally arranging Redding's audition. His name never came up in that context when others who were around on that day told the story independent of one another. Finally, as with the Hendrix story, Jenkins did not begin heavily spinning the yarn that he arranged Redding's audition until much later. If he was indeed responsible for Jimi Hendrix's wild stage act and Otis Redding's first audition, he sat on those stories for a long time.

Jenkins's later statements aside, the exact details of the Stax session differ slightly depending on who is telling the story, and exactly when they were asked about the occasion. Some of the musicians present initially mistook Redding for Jenkins's valet when the two men first drove up to the studio, because Redding was behind the wheel of the car and was the one who started unloading their equipment. Some later remembered Redding pestering them all day for an audition, and Redding himself said in a 1967 television interview that he was the one who asked to use the leftover studio time. Over the years, there has also been a bit of confusion over exactly who played what instrument during the session, although most versions have Jenkins playing the guitar. Regardless of the ebb and flow of the participants' memories, a general picture of what happened that day emerges when all the accounts are taken as a whole. Johnny Jenkins and Otis Redding showed up at Stax for an afternoon recording session in August of 1962. Backed by Booker T. and the MGs, Jenkins played for more than two hours, but it did not go well. Jim Stewart ended the session early, the musicians began packing up, and Booker T. Jones probably left the studio. Joe Galkin then made his deal with Stewart to let Redding sing. The remaining musicians stuck around, and Redding sang two songs, "Hey Hey Baby" and "These Arms of Mine."[64]

"Hey Hey Baby" was a fast number that to Stewart's ear sounded far too much like Little Richard. One Little Richard was enough, he supposedly said as he dismissed the tune. The second song had far more potential. Most accounts state that Stewart did not immediately recognize "These Arms of Mine" as a hit, but he knew that it was something he could work with. It was a slow ballad with an unmistakably heartfelt delivery from the singer, packed with emotion but not syrupy in the least. Stewart agreed to release the song with "Hey Hey Baby" as the B side. Redding signed a recording contract with Stax and, in so doing, triggered a great deal of drama back home in Macon.

As far as Bobby Smith was concerned, he had a deal in place with Otis Redding and was managing the fledgling singer's recording efforts. Ironically, Smith had lent Jenkins and Redding the car that took them to Memphis. Wayne Pierce, who knew Smith well and had driven the car before, later remembered the vehicle as "a Pontiac, a Safari I think it was called. It was a station wagon." Not savvy about the music business, Smith was unaware of Galkin's and Walden's maneuverings with Jim Stewart. After Redding returned to Memphis, and with Galkin hovering over the situation, Walden signed a management deal with Redding, despite the agreement that he already had with Smith. Samuel "Poor Sam" Davis also signed the document as co-manager. Davis was a local bass player whose many contacts with black-owned nightclubs in the region were, at the time, viewed as an asset. He later parted ways with Redding and Walden under circumstances that spawned a lawsuit.[65]

Not long before "These Arms of Mine" was released, John "John R." Richbourg, the legendary disc jockey from WLAC in Nashville, called Smith and told him he had just received an advance copy of the record on the Volt label, a Stax subsidiary. Smith and Richbourg had earlier crossed paths when Smith was promoting "Shout Bamalama." The news took Smith by surprise, and he confronted Walden and Redding. "Naturally I was upset," Smith later said. "I'd helped Otis quite a bit. Otis kinda hemmed and hawed about it, then said 'yeah, I did it.'" Smith soon talked to Galkin, who told him in a matter-of-fact way that Redding's contract with Confederate was invalid because Redding was under twenty-one years of age when he signed it, although the same could be said about the Stax agreement and Walden's management contract.[66]

Realizing too late what had happened, Smith had few choices. He could fight the whole thing in court or accept a buyout. He chose to do the latter and gave up the rights to Otis Redding's work for what he later said was a small sum. "I won't tell you how much," he once said to an interviewer, "but you can go to the Krystal [hamburger restaurant] and get ten hamburgers for it." Smith's anger at Redding dissipated and he placed the bulk of the blame on Walden and Galkin. Quoted in Scott Freeman's Redding biography, Smith said, "I didn't know the music business. I was learning. And I was mad. They knew what they were doing. They knew what was going down from the very get-go. They figured, that boy down in Macon, he don't know nothing."[67]

According to those who knew Smith, he "never got over" losing Redding but marshalled on and had a long career in the music business. While promoting Wayne Cochran, he crossed paths with Syd Nathan of King Records, who bankrolled Macon's first recording facility. Locals appropriately called it the Macon Recording Studio, and Smith built and ran the operation, recording many local acts. He later built another studio in town, where he recorded with James Brown. "James came down to record in my studio," he later recalled with a smile. "He had the studio booked for a week. And when he was here, he had them bring all of his sports cars to Macon so that he'd have something to scoot around town in." Smith continued serving as a talent manager and producer for King, opening Boblo Records in Brunswick, Georgia, and later relocating to Nashville. He returned to Macon in retirement and passed away in 2017.[68]

Phil Walden and Otis Redding marshalled on as well. After the "These Arms of Mine" session, Redding returned to Macon, but things there had begun to change. Thanks to Richbourg—who reportedly had a piece of the publishing action—playing the record consistently on Nashville's powerful WLAC, "These Arms of Mine" briefly appeared on the national R & B charts and even crossed over to number eighty-five on the *Billboard* Top 100. In Macon, Hamp Swain played the song repeatedly as well, turning Redding into a hometown celebrity. Walden continued booking Redding with the Pinetoppers, with the singer receiving top billing, but that arrangement did not last long. Redding parted ways with the group and made appearances as a solo act, or with other singers and groups. With the help of Eddie Kirkland, he put together a band and revue that made the rounds locally, and Redding even appeared at the Royal Peacock in Atlanta. The new connection with Stax allowed Walden to schedule an "Otis Redding Homecoming Dance and Show" at the city auditorium on July 20, 1963, that included Booker T. and the MGs along with Stax artists Rufus and Carla Thomas. Tickets were $2.00 in advance and $2.50 at the door, with a "special section reserved for white spectators." Redding also returned to Memphis for another recording session with several Macon musicians in tow, including Oscar Mack, Eddie Kirkland, and Bobby Marchan, a New Orleans transplant. Redding laid down another ballad, "That's What My Heart Needs," and the others also recorded songs, including Kirkland's "The Hawg."[69]

More sessions at Stax followed as Redding's career expanded, but right in the middle of all the activity, Phil Walden had to take time off for military service. "I left and went into the army for about eighteen months," he later explained. "I went to Germany and worked in special services in entertainment when I got there. I had graduated [from Mercer] with a commission in ROTC, that's why I had to go into the army."

Walden recruited his younger brother, Alan, to look after the business while he was away, and their father pitched in to work part time, which drew all the Waldens closer to Redding. "Between 4 P.M. on a Friday and 4 A.M. on a Saturday, Phil trained me to be a booking agent and the manager of Otis Redding," Alan Walden later told Michael Buffalo Smith, "Twelve hours to run a company singlehanded for the next two years! The first year it was very rough. Phil told me he left $5,000 in the bank, but failed to mention the $10,000-worth of debts."[70]

Despite any precarious financial conditions that may have existed for the company, Otis Redding's career surge slowly began. Another session at Stax produced songs including "Pain in My Heart," which also made the *Billboard* R & B charts and crossed over to the pop charts, giving Atlantic, Stax's distributor, the confidence in Redding to push for an album. On September 10, 1963, the Macon *Telegraph* ran an announcement that the first Otis Redding Fan Club had been organized in the city at a meeting at Jack's Snack Bar on Earl Street. Officers included Faye Smith, president, Johnnie Jackson, vice president, Celestine Jones, secretary, Susan Shelley, assistant secretary, Cassandra Jones, chaplain and business manager, and Winifred Lundy, assistant business manager. Other founding members included Joann Penn, David Winbush, Charlie Jackson, Terry Jackson, Larry Primus, and Johnnie Edgefield. The group adopted Redding's "That's What My Heart Needs" as their official song and chose as their motto "Go to the top because the bottom is full of holes."[71]

Atlantic Records helped Redding secure a weeklong engagement at the Apollo Theater in New York in November 1963. During his stay in the city, he crossed paths with a number of African American celebrities, including fellow Maconite Little Richard and a mouthy young boxer named Cassius Clay. Joe Galkin also introduced Redding to representatives from the Shaw Artists Corporation, a major talent agency that would promote the singer for better bookings in bigger venues in the North. Not long afterwards, Atco Records, an Atlantic subsidiary, released Redding's first album, *Pain in My Heart*. It included some of the singer's previously recorded hits and some new songs recorded at Stax, including "I Need Your Loving" and "Security." Around the same time, Decca released the title track "Pain in My Heart" in Britain, where Redding would become very popular. Incessant touring continued, including package tours with better-known performers, such as James Brown,

Solomon Burke, Joe Tex, Rufus Thomas, and Garnet Mims. Redding also put together his own band, the Otis Redding Band and Blues Revue, which reportedly featured fifteen piece, including a half dozen horns. Musicians came and went from this band, but for a time it featured Macon musicians Harold Smith, Sammy Coleman, and Earl "Speedo" Sims, who became the group's road manager. Among the stops that Redding made during the summer of 1964 was another homecoming show at the Macon City Auditorium that Alan Walden put together.[72]

At Stax, the parade of singles continued as Redding gained even more confidence. These included "That's How Strong My Love Is," written by Roosevelt Jamison, the Redding-penned tune "Chained and Bound," and "Mr. Pitiful," which Redding wrote with guitarist Steve Cropper, his chief collaborator at the studio. All three did well in the R & B and pop charts. In 1965, Redding hit his stride as he began writing and recording the songs that helped create his legend: "Respect," "I Can't Turn You Loose," and "I've Been Loving You Too Long," the latter written with Jerry Butler. He also recorded two successful albums. By the end of the year, his constant touring and his recording success had made him a national star in the R & B world, and his music began crossing over. Sales soared as he benefitted from a broad appeal among both black and white audiences. His income dramatically improved as well and, unlike Little Richard, who left Macon, Redding chose to sink his roots even deeper into Middle Georgia, purchasing a sprawling 270-acre spread for himself and his family just north of the city. He named the property the "Big O Ranch."

"Respect" was also a notable work because it became a signature song for superstar Aretha Franklin, who released her version in 1967. Exactly where the song came from is also a bit tricky to track down, and rumors about its origins have circulated for years. Although Redding received credit as the sole author, some say that he actually built on something that already existed. The prevailing theory along those lines has always been that Speedo Sims wrote at least part of the hit while he was a member of the group the Singing Demons. Sims, who traveled with Redding and knew him well, supposedly wrote the tune as a ballad and hoped to record it with his group. He was a veteran of the Macon music scene, having toured Middle Georgia consistently since the 1950s, but he was uncomfortable in the studio when he tried to cut the record.

221

Asked about the story in the 1980s, Sims said that he indeed had a hand in writing the song, but felt no animosity toward Redding. Quoted in Peter Guralnick's 1986 classic *Sweet Soul Music*, Sims stated "'Respect' was a song that came out of a group I was singing with at the time, and we were going to record it but never did. Otis rewrote the song in order for me to sing it—it had been more of a ballad type." Sims said that he "just couldn't hold the tune" in the studio and that afterwards Redding suggested that he record it instead. As for credit, Sims told Guralnick that Redding "told me I would get credit, but I never did, but I just consider that water under the bridge." A year or so after *Sweet Soul Music* came out, a newspaper reporter from the Macon *Telegraph* asked Sims about writing the song, and Sims told basically the same story. "[The song] came about during the time that I was singing," he said. "And I went into the studio to do the song, and as far as singing on stage I don't have a problem, [but] it was my first time in the studio. So I wound up not being able to sing the song. Otis said he would do the song. He made a few lyric changes and at that point told me I would get something from the song. So, him being a friend and all, I took him at his word." The credit never materialized, and after Redding passed away, some suggested to Sims that he take legal action, but he declined. "This was an agreement between me and him," Sims said. "The family was going through enough. It was done a long time ago. I don't hold Otis at fault.... It was something we both went to sleep on, you might say. I felt that when he said he was going to do these things his intentions were good. I don't have a problem with it." When asked about Redding and "Respect" by the same reporter, Alan Walden backed Sims up, stating, "Speedo gave it to him."[73]

Over the years, the Macon rumor mill produced numerous versions of the story. Some have Redding writing the song for Sims, with Sims giving it back to Redding to record, and still others suggest that Sims lifted the song from an unknown member of his band and then gave it to Redding. Some sources also say that Sims made his attempt to record the song in Bobby Smith's Macon studio, while others claim that it was elsewhere. Regardless, one thing remains clear. If Sims did write an early incarnation of "Respect," Redding significantly reworked the lyrics and altered the tempo to create the dynamic song later put on record, and in so doing he made the song his own.[74]

Phil Walden returned from military service in the spring of 1965 with ambitious plans. As energetic as ever, Walden and his brother Alan expanded their operation over the next two years. As Redding's career soared, they signed other African American artists, becoming a force in the R & B community. Alan Walden told Michael Buffalo Smith that, in addition to Redding, their roster of clients included "Sam & Dave, Percy Sledge, Clarence Carter, Johnnie Taylor, Etta James, Al Green, Booker T. and the MGs, Arthur Conley, Joe Tex, Eddie Floyd, Joe Simon, Bobby Womack, Albert King, Albert Collins, John Lee Hooker, Clarence 'Gatemouth' Brown, James Carr, Tyrone Davis, and many more." As things changed, they organized their business differently. "It was still primarily a booking agency then," Phil Walden later recalled. "I left the agency and went strictly into management. Alan ran the agency. Then we formed a publishing agency, then a record production company. And we had made plans, and optioned a building to put a studio in." The operation moved to a new building on Cotton Avenue, with Redding and the Waldens forming a publishing company called Redwal Music. Not content strictly as a performer, Redding started a company called Big O Productions, through which he produced other artists and also formed a boutique record label with Joe Galkin that they named Jotis. Ambitious and goal-oriented, Redding hoped to replicate the independent, artist-businessman model of one of his heroes, Sam Cooke.[75]

Redding continued a grueling touring schedule as he broadened his audience. He made trips to the West Coast, where white rock fans who were not overly familiar with authentic rhythm and blues heard his music for the first time. In Los Angeles, he appeared on television programs geared toward teenagers including *Shebang, Where the Action Is, Shindig,* and *Shivaree*. In the spring of 1966, he appeared on the bill at a benefit show at the Hollywood Bowl that included headliners Sonny and Cher along with Jan and Dean, the Turtles, and the Mamas and the Papas. Afterward, Redding made a storied appearance with his ten-piece band at the Whiskey a Go Go on the Sunset Strip in Hollywood, where the audience included Bob Dylan and other music luminaries. Redding was a hit with fans and with the press. On April 2, 1966, the *Los Angeles Times* gushed over his performance, informing its readers, "His material ranges from soulful moaning numbers such as 'These Arms of Mine,' 'Pain in My Heart,' and 'That's How Strong My Love Is,' to surging, belting tunes including 'Respect,' 'I Can't Turn You Loose,' and 'Mr. Pitiful.' Redding drives each number mercilessly, shouting and preaching each song with a relentless energy through the enormous sound of his band."[76]

Later in the year, Redding's reach expanded even further when he toured England and France. In England, it was a reciprocal visit of sorts. Back in 1964, the Beatles had led the "British Invasion" that forever altered the American musical landscape. Other groups followed, but the irony of the phenomenon was that much of the music they brought with them to the United States was actually based in American blues. By the time members of the Rolling Stones, the Animals, the Kinks, the Who, and others crossed the Atlantic, they had long embraced American blues and R & B music, as had many of their teenage fans. To an entire generation of young people in England, the music was raw, exotic, and irresistible. Always eager to hear the real thing, British kids purchased Redding's records and welcomed his live show with open arms. He received glowing press reviews and appeared on the popular music program *Ready Steady Go!* Eric Burden of the Animals called him "this generation's Ray Charles," and fans voted him top male vocalist in an annual poll sponsored by the influential music publication *Melody Maker.* Even the Beatles took notice. When an interviewer of the period asked the Fab Four what American artists they liked to listen to, John Lennon piped up with the short reply, "Otis Redding is one." Redding also autographed an album for the Beatles that George Harrison commandeered as a souvenir. "I don't think we ever saw Otis live," Harrison said with a smile many years later, "but I know I do have a record in my collection that's signed by him: To the Beatles, John, Paul, George, and Ringo. You've got my 'Respect'—Otis."[77]

Redding took additional steps to cement himself as a crossover star in 1967 with more recordings, live performances, and television appearances, but no show was more significant than his appearance at the Monterey International Pop Music Festival in California in June. Organized to promote pop music as an art form and, to an extent, showcase West Coast rock acts, the festival was a major event in the context of hippie culture of the period. The gathering was a seminal event of 1967's "Summer of Love," and it created a template for future large, outdoor music festivals, including Woodstock. In addition to Redding, the lineup included 1960s rock titans Janis Joplin, Jimi Hendrix, the Mamas and the Papas, the Who, Buffalo Springfield, Simon and Garfunkel, Jefferson Airplane, and the Grateful Dead, among others.

Redding not only held his own at the festival, his show was one of the highlights of both the concert and the concert film produced afterwards. Scheduled to perform on Saturday night, June 17, he followed Jefferson Airplane and quickly had the crowd on their feet with a mix of both fast and slow numbers. "Love is what he gave them—love and himself," Jerry Wexler wrote in describing the scene. "Otis simply sang his heart out...touching the hearts of the kids in a way that changed his career. He broke through, proving pure soul was strong enough to stand on its own. At that moment, Otis became a pop act." Those in attendance realized that they had seen something special, and the media responded accordingly. "Otis Redding is a hit record artist in the way that the top acts of rock 'n' roll are," formidable jazz and pop music critic Ralph Gleason wrote not long after Monterey. "In person, everything he does is an all-out powerhouse.... Each number is a crescendo of rising emotion, and Redding is an expert of a special, mass audience style." Many marked the appearance as the turning point when he became a true crossover phenomenon. Writer Stanley Booth, who interviewed Redding, told *Rolling Stone* that the singer "saw a huge crowd of white kids going nuts over him, and he began to believe he could follow in the footsteps of Sam Cooke and Ray Charles."[78]

After Monterey, Redding's explosive career trajectory seemed set. There was certainly no inkling, and no one at the time could have ever imagined, that soon it would all be over. During the months following Monterey, Redding continued to perform, though at one point he had to pause several weeks for surgery to remove polyps from his vocal cords. Once healed, he went into the Stax studio and recorded several new songs, including "(Sittin' On) The Dock of the Bay," which he cowrote with Steve Cropper. Always busy, he continued filling live dates. On Saturday night, December 9, 1967, he performed in Cleveland, Ohio, and the next day boarded his private plane to fly to Madison, Wisconsin, with members of his current backup band, the Bar-Kays. The group was scheduled to perform that evening at a Gorham Street nightspot in Madison called the Factory. Tragically, the plane never arrived, crashing on approach into Lake Monona. Everyone on board died except trumpet player Ben Cauley.[79]

Redding's death was naturally huge news in Macon. On December 11, both the *Telegraph* and the *Macon News* ran front-page stories on the plane crash. The latter included a prominent photo of the singer with several children at a charity barbecue held at his ranch the previous year. While many older whites in the city were not familiar with Redding's work, or had only a vague idea of who he was, many in the twenty-five and younger demographic, both black and white, seemed greatly affected. In a letter to the editor of the *Telegraph*, Steve McWilliams, a junior at Lanier High School, summed up the sentiments of many local white kids, who had only recently discovered his music. "I would like to express my regret, and I am sure the regret of all teenagers worldwide for this tragic occurrence. Redding was the type of singer that carried a message in his performances and a love of music in his heart.... I realize that it is probably hard for parents to understand their children's love of Redding's style and their feelings toward his death." Across the country and overseas, newspapers reported Redding's death, and disc jockeys hustled to prepare on-air tributes to his music. In Washington, DC, Vice President Hubert Humphrey issued a statement calling Redding's death "a great tragedy and a loss to the music world."[80]

Redding's funeral took place on December 19 in the city auditorium in Macon. It was a major event, drawing thousands of fans and a number of noted R & B and soul entertainers, including, Solomon Burke, Joe Tex, Percy Sledge, Dave Prater, Rufus Thomas, Carla Thomas, and James Brown, who was mobbed by screaming fans when he arrived. Various reports stated that between four and five thousand mourners packed the venue, with an equal number outside in the street. Rev. C. J. Andrews of the Vineville Baptist Church led the emotional service. "Although most of the persons attending the funeral remained composed," the *Macon News* reported, "several hundred burst into tears as Joe Simon sang slowly, mournfully, 'Jesus Keep Me Near the Cross.'" Blues singer Johnnie Taylor also choked up as he performed "I'll Stand By." Booker Jones provided musical accompaniment on the organ. Local clergy and politicians spoke, as did Hamp Swain and Jerry Wexler, who called Redding "a natural prince."[81]

The death of Otis Redding was an obvious blow to the Walden family. They were in business with the singer, but they were also personally close to him. After Redding's death, Phil Walden said he never again wanted to get that close to another act that he managed. The pain was too great. "I loved the guy," he said when asked about his relationship with Redding three years after the singer's death. "We spent an awful lot of time together. Wrapped up in him were all the dreams that we both shared, and to see it all go like that in one day. To see it happen to the one real nice guy in the whole thing, the one guy who had both feet on the ground, the one guy who had a sense of obligation. It was really tragic and unfortunate." Alan Walden, who lived close to Redding, was similarly affected. "The whole world stopped cold for me that day," he told Michael Buffalo Smith in 2002. "I had never known pain like that. He was the first man I ever loved outside my immediate family." After Redding's funeral, the *Chicago Defender*, one of the most important African American newspapers in the United States, ran a story on Redding's death that recognized the relationship between the singer and the Waldens, a relationship that was always more dramatic than it should have been because it represented pushback against the racial climate of the times. Lee Ivory, the newspaper's entertainment columnist, who attended the funeral in Macon, credited the Waldens with "showing me what love there can be between white men and black men in the God-forsaken red clay country of mid-Georgia."[82]

In Memphis, Redding had been the centerpiece of the Stax operation as well. The label continued, but nothing there would ever be the same. "The day Otis Redding died," Jim Stewart later said, "that took a lot out of me. I was never the same person. The company was never the same to me after that. Something was taken out and was never replaced. The man was a walking inspiration." Decades later, Steve Cropper, Redding's collaborator at the label, still had trouble talking about the tragedy. "That's devastating," he told an interviewer. "I don't know. It's hard to talk about. It was very emotional, and it still is. I don't know what it would be like to lose a sibling, to lose a son or a daughter, but I know what it is to lose a best friend, and it is definitely not easy. It's tough. It never goes away." Stax/Volt famously released "(Sittin' On) The Dock of the Bay" in January of 1968. It topped the charts in both the United States and England, garnering Redding two posthumous Grammy Awards. In the public mind, it was Redding's self-penned musical epitaph.[83]

Redding's music remains relevant, and in the decades since his death, he routinely makes all of the published lists of the most influential American musicians of all time. Among the more notable accolades he has received since his death are induction into the Georgia Music Hall of Fame (1988), the Rock & Roll Hall of Fame (1989), the Songwriters Hall of Fame (1994), and a Grammy Lifetime Achievement Award (1999). In 1993, the United States Postal Service honored Redding with his own postage stamp. At the Rock & Roll Hall of Fame induction ceremony, Little Richard sang abbreviated versions of "I Can't Turn You Loose" and

"(Sittin' On) The Dock of the Bay" before giving a raucous and rambling speech praising his fellow Maconite as "a pillar of rock and roll.... One of the great singers who ever lived." In addition to his musical legacy, Redding left behind his wife, Zelma, and their four children, Dexter, Demetria, Karla, and Otis III, who collectively remain the first family of Macon music.[84]

Otis Redding was only twenty-six years old when he passed away. While his catalogue of recorded work was significant, it was also limited compared to what might have been. Predictably, his premature death fueled wistful speculation through the years as to what he might have accomplished had he lived to be an old man. This was a natural phenomenon in that there has always been a magical quality surrounding artists who pass away prematurely. Those who die young do not become enfeebled by age. They do not decline in their creative production or become jaded by the ebb and flow of success and failure. Because they do not live long enough to diminish into a weakened state, they leave behind an image of creative vibrancy frozen in time and not likely to fade, which is perhaps one reason why their art holds up and transcends the eras in which they lived. On December 10, 1967, fate added Redding's name to a list of special musical talents whose untimely deaths cemented their immortality in the annals of American popular culture. The list dates from the dawn of recorded music, and includes, among others, Robert Johnson, Jimmie Rodgers, Buddy Holly, Hank Williams, Patsy Cline, Jimi Hendrix, Janis Joplin, and Kurt Cobain, all of whom died before they should have. "Otis had a voice, I don't know. It crawled up on you—such expression," Rolling Stones guitarist Keith Richards said in a 2014 interview. "Another large-hearted guy who went too soon. I always wondered what Otis would have done, *by now*."[85]

6

Capricorn
1970–1980

"Capricorn was just a place on the ground where
the lightning struck."[1]
—Paul Hornsby

While Otis Redding emerged from Macon as a great star during the 1960s, he was certainly not the only popular African American musician in town. The city remained a hotbed of talent, and while Redding's success and national impact were unparalleled, other local artists attracted good crowds at venues such as Adams Lounge, Club 15, Mann's Rendezvous, the Off-Key Club, the P.M. Key Club, Club Manhattan, and occasionally at the city auditorium, opening for national acts that passed through the area. Typical of these occasions was a July 1959 show sponsored by WIBB and headlined by Clyde McPhatter, Bo Diddley, and Chubby Checker. Among the local acts opening the show was Oscar Mack.

Mack was born in Albany, Georgia, in 1938 and moved to Macon with his family as a youngster. He started singing as a teenager and, like Redding and others, competed successfully at the *Teenage Party* talent competition. In *Sweet Soul Music*, Peter Guralnick quotes Hamp Swain as initially believing that Mack would end up making a bigger splash than Redding. "I thought Oscar Mack was *the* talent over Otis," he said. "Both of them were influenced by Little Richard initially. It was a modified Little Richard style." Mack was an animated performer, in demand as a guest vocalist along with other Macon singers such as Redding, Willie Jones, James Duncan, Walter Tinsley, and J. D. Thomas. Mack and Redding traveled in the same circles and, as they were just starting out, sang with some of the same bands. Off and on, Mack served as vocalist for Pat Teacake and occasionally for Jazzbo Brown and the House Wreckers. He later performed with the Pinetoppers after Redding left the group and as part of the James Duncan Trio along with Duncan and Carl Thomas.[2]

Phil Walden signed Mack, and the singer toured the Southeast. Mack benefitted from Redding's rise to prominence in that Redding took him on the road as an opening act and also helped him get recording time at Stax. Mack cut four songs in Memphis, including "Don't Be Afraid of Love," backed by "I See My Baby Comin'," released in 1963, and "You Never Know How Much I Love You," backed by "Dream Girl," released the following year. The association with Stax led to package tours with prominent artists from the label, including Solomon Burke, Rufus Thomas, Bobby Marchan, and Booker T. and the MGs. While his records sold locally, they did not represent a springboard to national acclaim, and Mack eventually left Macon. One of his last appearances in the city was a June 28, 1968, show at Mann's Rendezvous, billed as "An All Soul Dance and Show." He moved to Detroit, where he continued to perform with local groups, passing away in 1989.[3]

Macon's African American nightclubs and the white fraternity-party circuit continued fueling a lively R & B scene in the city as the 1960s wore on. One of the most popular live acts was the Flintstone Band, which became a clearinghouse of sorts for some of Macon's most popular musicians. Among the array of vocalists or guest vocalists who sang with the group were Thomas Bailey, Alice Rozier, and Joseph Clowers. Bailey started out, like many Macon teens with musical aspirations, as a Little Richard disciple who could sing and play piano. Before taking up with the Flintstone Band, he had stints with Pat Teacake as well as the Pinetoppers. After the Flintstones, he sang with other bands in clubs and at parties before becoming an accomplished gospel artist. For years, Rozier was one of the area's most popular female singers. Born in Parrott, Georgia, in 1942, she moved to Macon and, while still a teenager, began singing with a group called the Preptones. In demand because of her powerful voice, she sang with Percy Welch's outfit before coming to the Flintstone Band. She stayed with the group for several years, eventually moving to Massachusetts. Clowers also began singing on the Macon circuit as a teenager. Before joining the Flintstone Band, he sang for the Impalas, a local group named for the popular Chevrolet automobile. Billed in newspaper ads as "Mr. Explosive," Clowers later took a job as a disc jockey at WIBB, where he promoted Macon talent. Bailey, Rozier, and Clowers all recorded a handful of singles for small labels.[4]

The list of other African American bands of the period is long and convoluted. Musicians came and went, and groups changed their configurations sometimes weekly. For several years, the El Dorados were another clearinghouse for Macon talent. Thomas Bailey sang with the group, as did Frank Cole, Bay Bay Thomas, and Horace Williams. Among the musicians in the band were Jimmy Barberon on guitar, Willie Bowden on drums, and Harold Smith and Reggie Hall on saxophone. The Royal Vees featured vocalists Charles Burns and Arthur Johnson. Another group was the Nite Prowler Band, featuring at various times vocalists Van Fraley, Hill Lamar, Benjamin Ridley, and Early Patterson along with guitarists Ulysses Knight and Robert Coleman and drummer Willie Smith. Arthur "Bo" Ponder was one of the most popular singers on the circuit, performing with the Bossa Nova Band, the Roi Tan Band, and with his own revue. He was sometimes billed in newspaper ads as "Little Arthur Ponder, better known as Little Otis Redding." Other performers of note were Benny Davis and the Glades, the Impressions, musicians Reggie Hall, Oscar Jackson, Sonny Brown, and Clarence Roddie, and vocalists Samuel Billingsley, Jimmy Brasswell, Rose Norris, Arthur "BeBop" Moore, and Billy Young. Young was a native Texan and protégé of Otis Redding's who recorded for Redding's Jotis label.[5]

Phil Walden's operation created an explosive mingling of talent in the city, and when national acts needed musicians to fill out a band, some looked to Middle Georgia. The success of Little Richard, James Brown, and Otis Redding established Macon's reputation as a music city, and artists from Walden's stable of talent became musical ambassadors for the region. Just as Redding had taken other Macon musicians out on the road with him, Percy Sledge, Sam & Dave, Joe Tex, and other acts all used Macon players in their bands, as did Brown. Musicians from around the country viewed Macon as a place where they might advance their careers and a mini-migration ensued. Quoted in Candice Dyer's excellent book on Macon's music scene, Bo Ponder stated that "in the 1960s, every musician was trying to get to Macon to get that break. Macon was a soul capital. Lots of [musicians], they'd be getting off the bus every day with no intention of going back where they were from. With all those clubs on Broadway, it was like going to a carnival every night."[6]

While a good many musicians came to Macon looking to catch a break, the pool of local talent remained deep. Calvin Arline was born in Tennille, Georgia, in 1947 and moved with his family to Macon in 1950. His mother bought him his first guitar, and while in high school he mastered several woodwind instruments, as well as the tuba, under the watchful eye of Ballard-Hudson's legendary band director Robert Scott. As a teenager, he got a job washing dishes at Little Richard's old haunt, Ann's Tic Toc Room, and eventually hooked up as bassist with the Royal Vee Band, who occasionally played there. Clint Brantley booked the band around Middle Georgia, and as the R & B/soul scene expanded in Macon, Arline found plenty of work touring with acts such as Percy Sledge and Bobby Womack. This, in turn, led him to rub elbows with major national acts including the Temptations and Marvin Gaye. He later played with members of the Allman Brothers Band and contributed to an album by Gregg Allman's wife Cher in the 1970s. Afterwards, Arline stayed in Macon, where he raised a large family and became a mentor to younger artists. He passed away in 2016.[7]

Born in 1933, saxophonist Harold Smith, better known in Macon's music community as "Shang-a-Lang," began performing around the city as a teenager. Another member of the Ballard-Hudson band, he earned his nickname playing the cymbals, with "shang-a-lang" being a term that his bandmates used to describe the noise Smith produced with the instrument. Although the saxophone became his primary instrument, Smith also played the clarinet and piano. He toured regionally with Little Richard before the singer became a national act. "We played dumps in Milledgeville, Sandersonville," Smith later remembered. "I call them greasy spoons because most of them were holes in the wall." After service in the Air Force, Smith relocated to the West Coast for several years, where he played in jazz groups. Returning to Macon in the early 1960s, Smith was a fixture in the local clubs and signed on as a saxophonist for Otis Redding's band as Redding became popular. He later played with Percy Sledge and Joe Tex. Smith played on and off in Macon for the rest of his life and took part in several Redding tributes through the years. He maintained his status as one of Macon's best-known local music celebrities until his death in 1997.[8]

Born in Macon on May 15, 1945, Robert Lee Coleman developed into one of the best guitarists the city ever produced. He was self-taught but credited his stepfather as an early musical influence. "I had a stepfather who played the guitar," he once told an interviewer. "He didn't ever show me nothing, but every time he picked it up, I'd sit down on the floor and watch him play." Like many musicians, Coleman got his start playing at church functions, and he backed up local gospel groups including the Morning Stars and the Silver Bells. He also followed the musical course of others by transitioning from gospel to secular work. He played with the Royal Vees and later the Nite Crawlers, with some newspaper ads lauding Coleman as "Macon's own Chuck Berry." In 1964, Percy Sledge saw him play and asked the young guitarist to join his touring band. Coleman stayed with Sledge for more than three years, touring the United States, Canada, and parts of Latin America.

After touring with Sledge, Coleman returned to Macon, where he continued playing locally. In 1970, he received a telephone call from Clint Brantley, who had maintained his relationship with James Brown after Brown became an international star. Brantley's message was simple. "James wants you...James Brown wants you to play with him." According to Coleman, "James was looking for a guitar player and got in touch with Clint. Clint just picked the person he thought was best for the job." Coleman toured with Brown and played on Brown's albums *Revolution of the Mind* and *Hot Pants*. His guitar work helped the latter's title track become a hit. He returned to Macon in the mid-1970s and settled in as one of the city's most notable local performers. He later played with organist Bobby O'Dea as a member of the house band at the Rookery and toured with Larry Howard. He continued to play with local bands and recorded two albums, *One More Mile* (2012) and *What's Left* (2018), on the Music Maker label. To date, he still performs and remains one of the most revered elder statesmen of the Macon music scene. "Music ain't got no end," he once told an interviewer. "It just depends on how far your mind can take it."[9]

Newton Collier was born into a musical family in Macon in 1945 and, like many of his contemporaries, he was an early pupil of Gladys Williams. He took piano lessons with Williams for five years, starting at age seven, before deciding to take up the trumpet. According to Collier, several factors led him to switch instruments. One was a starstruck encounter he had with Sammy Davis Jr., who happened to be visiting

Williams one day when Collier stopped by for his regular lesson. In addition to his many other talents, Davis was an accomplished trumpet player, and Williams's house was a frequent pit stop for chitlin circuit performers who were touring the region. "Sammy Davis, Jr., was there and he played trumpet," Collier later recalled. "They were playing music together, playing some songs, and he let me buzz his horn and I liked it. I was hooked." At the local level, Collier's main local influences were Sammy Coleman, who was in Otis Redding's band, and Lewis Hamlin Jr., who later became James Brown's bandleader. Both men were talented players who were his neighbors in Tindall Heights. "Living in Tindall Heights I was around good musicians," Collier said. "Sammy Coleman lived up the street from me, and Lewis lived on the other side. Both were great players. I used to hear them and I loved to watch them play."[10]

Collier joined his high school band at Ballard-Hudson and volunteered to teach younger musicians in classes held at the Booker T. Washington Community Center. While still a teenager himself, he wandered into Bobby Smith's recording studio and briefly blew his horn on a recording by a local act. "I think I made 85 cents," he later recalled with a chuckle. Collier started playing in area bands, including the post-Redding Pinetoppers and a popular Augusta, Georgia, band, the Swinging Dukes. From there he hooked up with Sam Moore and Dave Prater—Walden clients known professionally as Sam & Dave—for a successful multi-year run that took him all over the world. Their hyper-animated shows were legendary, earning Moore and Prater titles such as "The Sultans of Sweat" and "Double Dynamite." Collier toured with Sam & Dave for several years and was with the group when they appeared on *The Ed Sullivan Show*. "That [show] was the top of the barrel. We met all the big session musicians in New York," Collier later remembered. "For that three minutes [on air], you rehearse about six hours for that.... You are in a little box and you don't leave that box, and those lights shine right down on you. Very intimidating, but the show went perfect."[11]

After Sam & Dave broke up, Collier relocated to Boston. In addition to being a musician, he was skilled in electronics, which allowed him to find significant day work with corporate giants such as Honeywell and Wells Fargo while still freelancing at night and on weekends as a horn player. His music career ended prematurely in 1976, the result of a street crime that remains unsolved. An assailant shot Collier in the face in what may have been an attempted robbery or a case of mistaken identity, with the bullet shattering his jaw. The incident put an abrupt end to his career as he faced several complicated reconstructive surgeries. Advances in technology—specifically the invention of the Electronic Valve Instrument (EVI) for the trumpet, an instrument that functions somewhat like a synthesizer, requiring less air pressure to play—eventually allowed him to play again. In the late 1980s, Collier moved back to Macon, opened a record store, and later found work as a taxi driver. While his days touring the country as a musician were behind him, the energetic Collier's love of music never waned, and, in fact, seemed to grow stronger over time. Armed with an encyclopedic knowledge of area musicians, he took on the task of resident historian of all things related to music in Macon. As the city's musical heritage became more prominent nationally, journalists and authors sought his counsel as they prepared books and articles on the subject. He has received a number of awards for his dedication to Macon's music scene and, as of the publication of this book, many describe him as the unofficial "mayor of music" in the city. "Music is a common denominator," he still maintains. "It's the instant magic of the soul."[12]

By the late 1960s, the Waldens had made Macon a mecca for R & B and soul performers seeking exposure. What had begun as Phil Walden's efforts to book African American bands for college fraternity parties had grown into a force in the music industry. "We actually became the biggest booker of black talent in the world," Walden later said. "It grew pretty quickly, and within a few years we were handling Sam and Dave, Percy Sledge, Clarence Carter, Al Green, Johnny Taylor, and Arthur Conley." The Waldens had gone into business with Otis Redding in hopes of building an entertainment empire that would include, among other things, a state-of-the-art recording facility in Macon. These plans were disrupted by Redding's premature death, and it took Phil Walden some time to rebound professionally and emotionally from the tragedy. When he did, he went in a different direction, opening yet another important chapter in Macon's music history.

Otis Redding's death was an indescribable blow to Phil Walden and his family, all of whom had grown close to the singer. The Waldens still managed a number of high-profile acts, but without Redding, the enterprise lost a good deal of its energy. Walden and Redding were attached at the hip from a professional standpoint, and that relationship could never be replicated with anyone else. It was a product of its time and place. "Quite honestly, after Otis's death, black music just didn't seem the same for me," Walden told the *Chicago Tribune* in 1991. "It just wasn't nearly as exciting for me. And Otis had been so much more than just a client. I guess I just felt robbed that he had been poised, ready to seize the throne, and it all just went away in the accident." Walden distanced himself from the music that he had promoted and dearly loved since he was a teenager, but he was certainly not finished in the music business. In fact, he came back with a vengeance, transforming Macon from a soul music hub into the undisputed capital of a powerful rock and roll subgenre labeled "Southern rock."[13]

While Redding's death took a toll on Phil Walden, it was not the only reason his professional interests moved from soul to rock. His career as a soul manager and promoter was also the casualty of powerful changes in society that came to a head in the late 1960s. By that time, the civil rights movement in America was developing a harder edge. Younger, more radical leaders were demanding that the wheels of change move more rapidly. The era saw the emergence of the Black Panther Party as a political force, Tommie Smith and John Carlos raising clenched fists at the 1968 Summer Olympics, the rise of the simple phrase "Black Power" as a sustained rallying cry and call to action, and the assassination of Dr. Martin Luther King. Understandably, African Americans viewed the country's white power structure with suspicion, creating innumerable social tensions within the American fabric. While music had the potential to bridge racial divides, the music *business* was another story. To say that Walden's professional move away from soul music promotion was a case study of American race relations in the late 1960s would be a bit dramatic, but the climate of the times had a great effect on the Macon impresario and other whites across the country who were in the business of promoting black artists.

The catalyst for Walden's move toward promoting rock bands over R & B acts was the annual convention of the National Association of Television and Radio Announcers (NATRA), held in Miami in August of 1968. Formed by African American disc jockeys in the 1950s as the National Jazz, Rhythm-and-Blues Disc Jockey Association, NATRA began as a vehicle for promoting and defending African American culture on the airwaves, but by the 1960s it also pressed the cause of African American media ownership. The 1968 convention, which included black media personalities as well as white music industry movers and shakers, produced a great deal of tension, in part because it took place just four months after the King assassination. The year before, the civil rights leader had addressed the group and praised its contributions to the movement. Setting the tone for the gathering, NATRA executive director Del Shields told a Miami journalist, "I don't think the white man is really interested in communicating with the black man.... All the angry voices in the black community should be heard."[14]

Shields and other leaders of the organization used provocative language at the convention related to black ownership of media outlets. They did not advocate violence, but problems developed when "rogue" activists, whom author Brian Ward later described as "a sinister group of armed, black New Yorkers calling themselves the Fair Play Committee," began demanding "reparation" money in hotel hallways and on the streets from white record company and radio executives. These miscreants injured several people who refused to comply. Atlantic's Jerry Wexler, who was threatened but not hurt, later recalled, "These shakedown artists had no program.... Under the guise of concerned citizens, hoodlums were camouflaging extortion with the rhetoric of the movement. I was hanged in effigy, the rumor went.... Phil Walden received death threats." It was somewhat ironic that Walden, once ostracized by many whites in Macon for hanging around with black artists, was suddenly coming under violent threat from African Americans for those same associations. Both Phil and Alan Walden attended the event. Alan later recalled "hiding out in his room" after several of his friends were accosted. In his Otis Redding biography, Jonathan Gould quotes Phil Walden as saying, "The Miami convention signaled the end for me. A lot of people I considered friends were suddenly calling us blue-eyed devils. It really turned me off. It was a shake down and I didn't care to be shaken down."[15]

Placing the idea of starting a recording studio back on the front burner, the Waldens made plans. When they originally purchased space on Broadway Street to build a studio, the idea had been to create a facility to accommodate R & B artists associated with the publishing company, but Redding's death and the changing times caused the Waldens to alter their course. "We began looking at the rock and roll bands," Alan Walden later recalled. "My brother and I had already purchased the building for the recording studio, and we decided to go forward with it." According to Phil Walden, the idea of starting a record label came from Atlantic's Jerry Wexler shortly after the studio was completed. Wexler and Walden were friendly through Walden's dealings with African American artists, including Redding, and his relationship with Stax, which Atlantic distributed. "I had been fishing with Jerry Wexler in Florida right after I finished the studio in Macon," Walden told a reporter for *Creem* magazine in 1972. "He told me I should have a label. I told him I didn't want a label, but he said 'Aw, come on, have a label.' I finally said OK." The idea for the label's name came from Wexler as well. "I didn't know what to call it," Walden continued. "Jerry asked me what my sign was, and when I told him Capricorn, he said 'I'm a Capricorn, too; call it Capricorn.' And that's the way it happened."[16]

While Walden would create his label with Wexler's support, and Atlantic would provide financial assistance and distribute the product, the deal was not quite as simple as a handshake on a fishing boat. Before the project reached full flower, a brotherly rift developed between Phil and Alan Walden. Years later, Alan told Michael Buffalo Smith that the two brothers clashed over managing company debts, the number of artists they needed on their roster, and an angry insult hurled one night by Phil that his brother was "riding on his coat tails." The facts of the matter are likely much more complex, but regardless of the reason, Alan Walden broke with his brother and formed his own publishing and management company, Hustler's Inc. In that capacity, he later became the first manager of the band Lynyrd Skynyrd and worked with many other artists. "Financing was short, and we were building up some very large debts again," he told Michael Buffalo Smith. "This strained my relationship with Phil.... I also felt we could take one or just a few bands and pursue every avenue, and make just as much money as handling twenty and not having time to do it all. This led to dissention, and I finally resigned in 1970."[17]

As the drama between the Walden brothers progressed, a key player in the Capricorn saga arrived on the scene. His name was Frank Fenter, and together he and Phil Walden would make Capricorn Records a major player in the American music industry. Fenter had a colorful early history, which was perhaps a prerequisite for success in the music business. He was born in 1936 to white parents in segregated Johannesburg, South Africa. He played soccer as a youngster and became a Golden Gloves boxer. In his early twenties, he left South Africa for London, drawn by the prospect of a more exciting life in the big city and harboring dreams of becoming an actor. He landed a few bit parts but earned a living primarily as a hotel porter and dishwasher at a fashionable French bistro and coffee bar called

Le Soussol. There he met and mingled with various show folk, including musicians and agents who were part of London's rapidly evolving music scene in the early 1960s. These contacts helped him get his start in the entertainment business.[18]

Like Phil Walden half a world away, Fenter gravitated toward music promotion, and he seemed to have a natural flair for the job. One British journalist later described him as "a tall, tanned, talkative South African who has a way of expression with his hands that would do credit to an Italian. When he speaks, his hands move to express a point. Quite fascinating." In 1963, Fenter became the manager of a group called Bill Kimber and the Couriers, one of the many Beatles clones that had suddenly appeared in London in the wake of the Fab Four's immense popularity in England. The group never caught on in their home country, but in what was an early testament to his determination and vision, Fenter took the group to South Africa where they developed a following. He also produced and helped direct a full-length promotional movie for the group, which was quite an undertaking at the time. Back in England, his work with other artists gained him a positive reputation in London music circles and a position as head of ARC Music, the British branch of Chess Records, a music publishing firm. His great break came when Nesuhi Ertegun, cofounder of Atlantic Records with his brother Ahmet, hired him to manage the label's business in England. In that capacity, Fenter helped make Atlantic "the hottest American label in England," according to a 1966 *Billboard* article. "Frank worked very closely with me. In those days we were signing a lot of English bands," Ahmet Ertugen later said in an interview. "He was extremely bright and very energetic, and he was very helpful to me in creating at the time the most important American label promoting English rock and roll music. We wound up with a lot of British bands." Fenter had a hand in Atlantic signing a number of groups, including Yes, Led Zeppelin, and King Crimson.[19]

In addition to his work with rock artists, Fenter also promoted rhythm and blues music in England and beyond. Like his Macon contemporary and future partner, he had grown up in a segregated environment in Johannesburg but was drawn to black music through both its rhythms and the notion of it being a forbidden fruit. Elektra record executive Clive Selwood, who met Fenter in London during the mid-1960s, later said, "Frank was born in South Africa, and either because of or despite his background, he was passionate about black music in general."[20] This made Fenter a natural fit for Atlantic, with its history of marketing of jazz and blues records. Through Atlantic's relationship with Stax, Fenter helped promote the Memphis label's artists in England, which in turn led to his first contact with Phil Walden. Fenter helped promote Otis Redding's 1966 visit to England and encouraged Walden to bring the singer back the following year. This led to what became the famous 1967 "Hit the Road Stax" package tour that brought Redding and a host of other Stax artists to Europe.

Fenter took the lead in promoting the event in London, with his enthusiasm driven by a belief that R & B would be huge in England. "Otis Redding will be bigger than he is now—throughout Europe," he told Bill Harry of the *Record Mirror* in December of 1966. "Sam & Dave will be enormous and Percy Sledge, so will Wilson Pickett. People who haven't broken yet, like Joe Tex and Don Covey." He correctly saw the Stax tour as a catalyst for an R & B explosion. "I'm sure that the tour will influence people's minds to such an unbelievable degree," he said, "that there will be no holding back soul music." Fenter was correct. The London show was a huge success, as were subsequent performances throughout Britain. "We went with them, the Stax lot, all over the country," one observer later wrote. "Everywhere they played it was a full house. They never had any bad gigs." Fenter's role in promoting the Stax tour led many to laud him as the man who help introduce R & B to England. In 1968, Atlantic promoted Fenter, placing him in charge of the company's activities in Europe. His first major assignment was to accompany Aretha Franklin on her first European concert tour.[21]

Not long after the promotion, Fenter abruptly switched gears and decided to team up with Phil Walden in Macon to form the new record label that Atlantic would distribute. It was a gamble, but a desire to work outside the corporate structure was part of his motivation. "The giant corporation is not for me," he said. "This way, you call your own shots and can be a little more aggressive and a lot more innovative." Fenter also appreciated Walden's passion for the music business and brought to the table a level of expertise and innumerable industry connections that Walden did not have. Interviewed about Fenter later, Ahmet Ertegun explained, "[Phil] wanted Frank to join him because of his expertise in the record industry, and at that point I thought it was a very good, solid partnership.... I know that we [Atlantic] were supportive of the idea of Phil and Frank creating a label that we would be involved in and we would distribute, and that they would be a very powerful and strong presence in the southern rock and roll market."[22]

While it would be an oversimplification of the division of labor to say that Walden was the charismatic face of the label, while Fenter quietly ran the business end of the enterprise behind the scenes, there was some truth in that assessment. "Capricorn was a winner, and run by as good a team as ever," Keith Crossley, who served as the label's head of production, later said. "Frank Fenter, good cop, and Phil Walden, bad cop. Together they Mutt-and-Jeffed. I remember meeting Frank shortly after I moved to town. Phil told me Frank would be working with him…. Frank ran the nuts and bolts of Capricorn. He knew everybody in the record business from the ground up."[23] Armed with confidence, ambition, and energy, Fenter moved with his family to Macon in 1969. There he joined Walden, who possessed all the same traits. It took a little time for Capricorn to come together, and of course there were innumerable naysayers who predicted gloom and doom. "In the beginning, no one believed in us at all," Fenter said later with a smile. "Who ever heard of two guys in Macon, a cracker and a South African, with a record company?"[24]

As Walden and Fenter organized the operation in Macon, a group of musicians whose work would launch the label were also organizing themselves as the Allman Brothers Band.

The principal musical players in the early history of the Allman Brothers Band at Capricorn Records were the group's original six members, Duane Allman and his younger brother Gregg, Jai Johanny Johanson, Berry Oakley, Dickey Betts, and Butch Trucks, along with a handful of other performers who would leave their mark on the band's story. Among these were Paul Hornsby, Johnny Sandlin, Pete Carr, and Reese Wynans.

Duane and Gregg Allman were both born in Nashville, Duane in 1946 and Gregg in 1947. Their father, Willis, was an army veteran and survivor of the D-Day invasion who, after the war, returned home and served as a recruiter. He was killed in a robbery in 1949, and his wife, Geraldine, was left to raise their two boys. The family moved to Daytona Beach, Florida, although Duane and Gregg spent summers back in Nashville visiting their grandmother. By the late 1950s, they had discovered music and around that time attended their first rock and roll concert, a revue of African American artists at the Nashville Auditorium.

The event was apparently transformative. Quoted in Randy Poe's Duane Allman biography, *Skydog*, Gregg Allman later remembered, "The first rock & roll show that me and my brother ever went to was headed up by Jackie Wilson. B. B. King was also on that show, and Johnny Taylor—all these incredible people. We were up in the cheap seats." Afterwards, Duane said, "Little Brother, we've got to do this," and soon the boys were getting their feet wet in local pickup bands.[25]

Jai Johanny Johanson was born Johnny Lee Johnson in 1944 on the Mississippi Gulf Coast in Ocean Springs. He was African American, which made the Allman Brothers Band an integrated band. This was significant and unusual in the South during the late 1960s. The most heavily monikered of the original Allman Brother Band members, he became internationally known by his stage name, "Jaimoe." Johanson grew up in Gulfport, Mississippi, and attended a segregated high school, where he played drums in the marching band. Drawn to music at an early age, he later credited his school's subscription to *Downbeat*, a well-known music publication, for stoking his lifelong interest in jazz and blues. "God sent *Downbeat* magazine to the 33rd Avenue High School [in Gulfport]," he later said. "He sent it to me! I read every issue from cover to cover, everything for three years." Johanson also credited nearby New Orleans radio station WBOK for turning him on to rock and roll, and a 1959 Hallmark Hall of Fame television program for introducing him to the sounds of Louis Armstrong, Gene Krupa, Duke Ellington, Oscar Peterson, and Benny Goodman, among others. As a teenager, he met saxophonist Donald "Cadillac" Henry, who was impressed enough to take Johanson under his wing. Several years older, Henry was an established musician who had played with a number of bands, including Otis Redding's touring outfit. Through this association, Johanson was drawn into Phil Walden's orbit and ended up touring with Redding, Joe Tex, and Percy Sledge. He also played regularly in Macon with artists including Johnny Jenkins and Eddie Kirkland.[26]

Raymond Berry Oakley III was the only member of the Allman Brothers Band not born in the South, but he was certainly familiar with the sounds of the region. Oakley was born in Chicago in 1948. He grew up listening to radio stations that played the "Chicago blues" of Muddy Waters and Howlin' Wolf, which, in turn, had its roots in the fertile musical soil of the Mississippi Delta. By the time he was in high school, Oakley had become a gifted guitarist and was playing in local bands, including the Shanes, who sometimes opened for national acts that passed through the area. At age seventeen, Oakley successfully auditioned for a spot as bassist in Tommy Roe's backup band, the Roemans, even though he had only recently learned to play the instrument. He toured with Roe for several months and then relocated to Sarasota, Florida, where his family had moved. Sarasota had a lively nightclub scene, where Oakley played with local musicians, including a guitarist named Dickey Betts. Oakley joined Betts's band, and the group moved to Jacksonville in search of greener pastures.[27]

Born in West Palm Beach in 1943, Forrest Richard "Dickey" Betts grew up on Florida's west coast in Bradenton. He came from a musical family—his father was a fiddler and guitar player—and he started strumming the ukulele, banjo, and the mandolin at an early age, playing country music and bluegrass. At sixteen, he picked up the guitar. He liked western swing but also had an interest in early rock and roll and the blues music from which it sprang. "At that time Chuck Berry was a big influence on my playing," he later said. "Then as I grew older and played a little while longer, I got into B. B. King. Then I started wondering where B. B. King learned to play, so I started going back into his background, and I discovered Blind Lemon Jefferson and Django Reinhardt, which was a great discovery." Betts played in teen clubs and then nightclubs around Bradenton, Sarasota, and elsewhere, making a good living for himself. He and Oakley met on the Sarasota circuit and eventually moved to Jacksonville. "Oakley and I were both young adults when we met, and we were still searching for our style of playing," Betts recalled. "He and I got together, and we started doing about half cover stuff and half original."[28]

Claude Hudson "Butch" Trucks was born in Jacksonville in 1947. He played drums in his high school band, but his Southern Baptist parents resisted the idea of him choosing music as a career. Trucks persevered and finally got his first real drum kit in the eleventh grade. He later told an interviewer that his parents allowed him to join a band with his friends only after he promised that they would never play in a place that sold liquor. At about the same time, the Beatles came to America and revolutionized the music scene. Like many other aspiring musicians, Trucks and his friends formed a band that played mostly Beatles covers. After graduating high school, Trucks enrolled at Florida State University in Tallahassee, where he formed a folk-rock trio with two other students. They modelled their sets on Bob Dylan and the Byrds, who had popularized a sound that record companies and radio broadcasters called folk rock. "We did three-part harmony," Trucks later said, "and played all the fraternity parties; ceased going to class, and grew the first long hair at Florida State." The musicians eventually left college and tried to survive on the Florida nightclub circuit. One night in a Daytona Beach club, they ran into Duane and Gregg Allman, who were trying to do the same thing.[29]

The Allman Brothers Band's story at Capricorn is well known. A musical genealogy of the group traces its origins back to a handful of other bands to which the individual members belonged in the mid-1960s. Among them were the Allman Joys, the Men-Its, Second Coming, and the 31st of February. The Allman Joys featured brothers Gregg and Duane Allman, and the Men-Its included Alabama natives Paul Hornsby and Johnny Sandlin among others. After the Allman Joys and the Men-Its broke up, these four musicians in 1967 formed a band called Hour Glass that also included Pete Carr, Mabron McKinney, and Bob Keller. They all moved to California, where Hour Glass had limited success. The band recorded two albums for Liberty Records and gained a local following in California nightclubs, but the group never quite took off nationally. Musically, the band was somewhat of a fish out of water on the West Coast at the time. Creative differences also soured the relationship with Liberty, and the experience for the band as a whole ended in disappointment. "Beach music was the thing on the West Coast," Hornsby later recalled of the band's time in California. "Here we were, a band of Southern cats with a blues-oriented sound.... The record company and producer didn't have a clue what to do with us.... By the middle of 1968 we had become disillusioned with the whole L.A. thing." Hour Glass disbanded in August of 1968, and the members drifted apart, though they all remained musically active. "To the best of my memory, it was a friendly parting," Johnny Sandlin later said. "Duane and Pete went back to Florida along with Gregg [who stayed in California longer than the rest]; Paul went to Tuscaloosa, and I came back to Decatur [Alabama]."[30]

While Hour Glass did not work out for Duane Allman, Rick Hall at FAME Studio in Muscle Shoals heard about the guitarist and signed him to an artist contract. In that capacity, Allman recorded with a number of artists, including Aretha Franklin and Wilson Pickett, and reportedly talked Pickett into covering the recent Beatles hit "Hey Jude." Released in

1969, Pickett's soulful version of the song sold more than a million copies and set in motion a chain of events that led to the formation of the Allman Brothers Band. Duane Allman played on the record, which brought him a great deal of recognition in music circles, with Eric Clapton later saying, "I've never heard better rock guitar playing on an R & B record. It's the best." Jerry Wexler also took notice to the extent that he purchased the guitarist's contract from Hall. "Duane was so pale-faced, he looked like a photographic negative," Wexler later wrote in his autobiography. "He was a kick-ass good ol' boy with a beautiful personality and great feel on his ax. He played no-bullshit blues, and he phrased like the authentic black guitarists, weaving melodic segments like elaborate tapestries." Wexler wanted to promote a Duane Allman solo record, and through Wexler, Phil Walden took the reins as manager. According to Gregg Allman, Twiggs Lyndon, who worked for Walden in Macon, and later became the Allman Brothers Band's road manager, also had a hand in Walden entering the picture. "Jerry Wexler at Atlantic Records always felt that, in a way, he discovered Duane," Allman stated in his memoir, "but it was really Twiggs. Word had gotten around...so he went over there [Muscle Shoals], on his own dime, to see my brother. He came back to Phil and said, 'Dig it, man, you've got to go check out this player over there.'" Regardless of who discovered whom, the original idea was to put together a band with Duane Allman as the star attraction.[31]

Allman invited his former bandmates Paul Hornsby, Johnny Sandlin, and Pete Carr to Muscle Shoals to work on the solo effort. Also at the session were bassist Berry Oakley, whom Allman had met on the club circuit in Florida, and drummer Jai Johanny Johanson. Johanson entered the mix at the suggestion of his friend, songwriter Jackie Avery Jr., who had heard Allman play, and through his connection with Walden and some of the artists whom Walden managed. While the musicians cut several tracks at Muscle Shoals, the album never materialized, but either Wexler or Walden (or probably both) kept promoting the idea of Duane being the featured player in his own band. There was talk of reforming the old Hour Glass lineup, but Hornsby, Sandlin, and Carr were not interested. "Basically, Phil wanted to put the Hour Glass band back together, in a sense," Hornsby later told Michael Buffalo Smith. "Well, for me, Sandlin, and Carr, we had been on a virtual rollercoaster ride for the last two years, and were in the middle of looking into other musical interests. A rehash of what we had just gotten out of seemed to be walking backwards." Likewise, Sandlin later wrote in his memoir, "Duane asked Paul and me to join the band. I thought about it for a while. Paul and I talked about it, but neither one of us wanted to go on the road again. We were so burned from Liberty and the whole Los Angeles experience that we weren't ready to jump back into it."[32]

Still trying to put together a group, Allman eventually left Muscle Shoals and moved to Jacksonville, Florida, as did Jaimoe, where they made the rounds jamming with other musicians including Oakley and Dickey Betts. Betts led a band called Second Coming that included Oakley on bass and keyboardist Reese Wynans. Butch Trucks soon joined them. Trucks was a veteran of the Jacksonville club circuit who had a band called the 31st of February. According to Betts and others, Phil Walden first suggested to Duane Allman that he put together a trio with Oakley and Jaimoe, but Allman abandoned this notion after he interacted with the other musicians. "Duane started showing up and sitting in with Berry Oakley and myself, with our band in Jacksonville," Betts later said. "Berry and Duane were kind of getting used to playing with each other, getting ready to go into this new venture. As we started jamming, we all realized that Duane and I playing harmony guitars together was something that we weren't expecting to hear." After innumerable days and nights practicing together, the lineup for Allman's new band began to gel. It included Allman and Betts on guitar, Berry on bass, Wynans on keyboard, and not one but two drummers, Jaimoe and Trucks.[33]

The final element of what would become the Allman Brothers Band fell into place when Allman called his brother, Gregg, who was still in Los Angeles, and told him that the new group needed a singer. Gregg, who also played keyboards, came back to Jacksonville and replaced Wynans, who went on to have a successful music career that included induction into the Rock & Roll Hall of Fame as a member of Stevie Ray Vaughan and Double Trouble. "Duane knew that we needed to have a singer, and he knew who that needed to be, so he called his brother Gregg," Trucks later said. "Two days later we had our first rehearsal." Gregg Allman immediately accepted the invitation to join the group, though he later admitted that at first he thought it was a little "weird" that the band had two lead guitar players and two drummers.

"I beat feet over there as fast as I could to Jacksonville," he said, "and that was the Allman Brothers' start. It was March 26, 1969."[34]

With all the pieces in place, the next thing they needed was a name. The group kicked around several, including "Beelzebub," before settling on the Allman Brothers Band. According to Gregg, the group's name was a tribute to his brother's leadership. "Duane is the most powerful human I have ever known," Trucks later said. "He was the kind of person that, when he entered a room, everyone would stop and look—he had that kind of presence."[35]

Meanwhile, Phil Walden hoped that the new band would be the centerpiece of Capricorn Records and convinced the group to move to Macon. He also began putting together a house band for Capricorn, hoping to capitalize on a studio template already established in Muscle Shoals and at Stax. While Hornsby, Sandlin, and Carr had declined the offer to re-create the Hour Glass lineup, Walden was still interested in them as players and wanted them to join the Capricorn project. He was familiar with the Stax system and hoped that the trio would be the Macon label's version of Booker T. and the MGs. "[Walden] called a lot," Hornsby recalled, "and each time the deal got a little sweeter. I think what clinched it for me, though, was that Johnny Sandlin and Pete Carr had decided to accept the offer. We had always sort of stuck together. I was finally convinced, though, and 4 July, 1969, I moved to Macon." The trio added a bass player, Robert Popwell, who also knew Duane Allman. Popwell later had a stellar career playing with the Crusaders and on sessions with some of popular music's biggest stars.[36]

Despite their talent, the "house band" model did not hold up at Capricorn. Within a year or so, it was apparent that many of the groups recording with the label were self-contained units that did not need session players. Carr and Popwell moved on to pursue other opportunities while Sandlin and Hornsby stayed in Macon and ended up heavily involved in producing other artists. Both would have long, notable careers and were key figures in the Capricorn saga. Sandlin's producing credits would include several Allman Brothers efforts and Gregg Allman as a solo artist, as well as records by label notables Wet Willie, Elvin Bishop, Bonnie Bramlett, Hydra, and Cowboy, among many others. "My deal with Phil was that I wanted to produce and play on records, and we agreed that I could produce and play the drums," he later said. "Every day you never knew what would happen, and it was usually something wonderful." Hornsby played organ and piano on many Capricorn sides as he amassed his own long list of producing credits, including hits for the Marshall

Tucker Band and Charlie Daniels. When asked later how his records differed from those of Sandlin, he said, "The only thing I can point out is maybe our music backgrounds. My first influences were country.... Johnny Sandlin had more of an R & B and blues background." Both Hornsby and Sandlin left Capricorn in the mid-1970s for careers as independent producers, although they maintained a relationship with the label.[37]

Twiggs Lyndon was in charge of helping the band move to Macon, where they became Capricorn's first major act. He was the perfect wrangler for the group, having already road managed several of Walden's more high-profile clients, including Arthur Conley and Percy Sledge. Lyndon first moved them, along with their original road crew of Mike Callahan, Kim Payne, and former marine Joseph "Red Dog" Campbell, into his place on College Avenue. Campbell later became a legendary figure among Allman Brothers Band fans and a significant personality in the band's lore. Campbell later recalled that many Macon residents were shocked when the group first appeared in the neighborhood. "Nobody in Macon had long hair then," he said. "When we moved into the house down on College Street, all of us would be sitting out on the porch, and traffic would line up both ways just so people could take a look at the hippies." The accommodations were only temporary, and the group members, particularly those who were starting families, soon found places of their own.[38]

In January of 1970, Berry Oakley and his wife, Linda, rented a property at 2321 Vineville Avenue that became the domestic headquarters for the band and a home later known to fans simply as the "Big House." The structure came by its nickname honestly, as it was literally a big house capable of providing shelter to multiple families. Once the home of Nathaniel Harris, an early twentieth-century Georgia governor, it was a spacious, three-story, 6,000-square-foot Victorian home. Berry and Linda Oakley and their young daughter, Brittany, moved in, as did Duane Allman, his girlfriend, Donna Roosman, and their child, Galadrielle; and Berry's sister Candace and Gregg Allman, whom Candace was dating at the time. Other members of the Allman Brothers Band entourage also stayed there off and on. The home was a place where the band socialized, rehearsed, and bonded to an even more intimate degree. "The 'Big House,' as we all came to call it, was a place for us all to hang, but it was really Oakley's place," Gregg Allman recalled in his memoirs. "The vibe at the Big House was always good. We had a real sense of camaraderie, of family, and we would always have one big meal a day, you could count on it.... Then we would lay around and talk, and play some music on the stereo." From 1970 to 1973 the home was ground zero with regard to the Allman Brothers Band's comings and goings.[39]

Another Macon location that became important to the group was Rose Hill Cemetery, the sprawling final resting place of generations of Bibb County residents. Band members routinely visited the place to commune with nature, play their instruments, and sometimes write songs. The cemetery had an interesting history. It was designed and laid out in the 1840s by early city father Simri Rose, who had a keen interest in horticulture and botany. Rose envisioned not just a graveyard but a space that was part cemetery and part city park, decorated with perfectly placed trees, plants, and flowers. He studied the area around Macon, and chose a spot on high ground overlooking the Ocmulgee River that provided "the perfect picture of rural beauty." Rose's finished design was a masterpiece, a terraced, wooded garden complete with a large pond and five miles of carriage paths. Impressed with Rose's efforts, city officials named the place "Rose Hill" in his honor. Little wonder that the band members found it attractive. "Rose Hill is a beautiful, peaceful old place on the Ocmulgee," Dickey Betts later said. "And there was an old part that was well kept and beautiful, and had graves dating back to the 1800s. I know it sounds sappy romantic, but I would go down there day after day to the same spot and meditate and hang out and play my guitar because it was so quiet and peaceful." Betts famously titled one of his first Allman Brothers Band compositions "In Memory of Elizabeth Reed" after the name on one of the cemetery's headstones.[40]

During their early years in Macon, local African American restaurateur Louise Hudson befriended the band and became a beloved member of their extended family. With her cousin Inez Hill, Hudson owned the H & H Restaurant, a soul food place on Forsyth Street not far from the Big House. Stories of her kindness to the group are legendary around Macon. When money was hard to come by early on, she fed the band members for free, or on credit, and they never forgot it, adopting her as one of their own and forever after calling her "Mama Louise." "Money was real tight then," Gregg Allman later recalled fondly. "We were all skinny, real skinny. I guess if it hadn't been for Mama Louise, we might have never made it.... She never asked us to pay when we didn't have the money, just put it on our tab, and kept putting it on our tab, and kept putting it on our tab. She called us her boys, and we called her Mama. I'll love her till the day I die." On the Allman Brothers Band's second album, among the listed credits is a simple line that reads "Vittles: Louise."

Others later remembered H & H as being one of their safe havens in a city that was not completely comfortable with the sudden presence of an integrated band of hippies. Quoted in Alan Paul's history of the Allman Brothers Band, *One Way Out*, Hudson later recalled of the era, "Macon was just barely integrated. We didn't really have any white customers. And nobody around here had ever seen guys that looked like them. I had not. A lot of the white folks around here did not approve of them long-haired boys, or of them having a black guy with them." Based on their appearance, reaction by area whites indeed seemed mixed at best. Some were hostile, some merely curious, while others were quietly amused. Red Dog Campbell later said, "One of the only places we felt at home was down at Mama Louise's little restaurant. At the H & H, they didn't care if we were white or black or purple. Mama didn't say anything.... [S]he just fed us fried chicken and loved us." Likewise, Chuck Leavell, who joined the Allman Brothers Band in 1973, waxed philosophically when he later spoke about Hudson and her restaurant. "She felt the spirit of the times," he said. "Blacks and whites were working together, playing music together. It was almost like a religion. And Louise's cooking was a sort of soul food sacrament."[41]

Despite the early lack of personal funds, and any resistance from the surrounding community, once the Allman Brothers Band settled in Macon, their career progressed at a rapid pace. They rehearsed relentlessly at the Big House and at Capricorn's rehearsal space, and they started playing around town. Their first paid gig as the Allman Brothers Band took place on May 2, 1969, at the College Discotheque on Mulberry Street, a Victorian-era building that once housed Macon's first public library. Tickets for the event were a dollar. The group also drove to Atlanta and played free shows in Piedmont Park, where they soon developed a following. Describing these early shows, one newspaper reporter from the *Atlanta Constitution* wrote, "They play not only amplified blues-type music...but other related contemporary music—jazz or soul. It all may be classified as rock."

Their first significant performances outside the South were in the Northeast, as they prepared to record their first album. They were not an immediate hit in the region, but enthusiasm for the band grew as word spread quickly about their musicianship. "I think maybe they were playing too well in that particular era," Phil Walden later said. "It took a while for people to be educated to them. A lot of [rock] performers were doing splits and turning over backwards and throwing guitars through amplifiers and wearing gold suits, and the Allmans just stood there and played."[42]

Since the Capricorn studio in Macon was still a work in progress, the band recorded their first album, a self-titled effort, at the Atlantic Studio in New York in August of 1969, under the direction of engineer Adrian Barber. The record, along with several other early Capricorn releases, officially came out on the Atco label as part of the "Capricorn Records Series." Released the following November, *The Allman Brothers Band* included seven songs, among them "Whipping Post," which was a staple of the group's live set. While the album received some positive reviews and press, it did not sell well. Undaunted by the lack of commercial success, the musicians seemed energized by the experience and continued a rigorous touring schedule. Their reputation as a live act grew, and the crowds that came to see them play grew larger and larger. "On stage, the band is pure power and energy," one reviewer wrote. "The music is urgent but it strangely sooths. It has an obvious blues base, but what's not blues is an extremely attractive bastard child, tough and loud but gentle." The period also saw the band's first performance at the Fillmore East in New York, where they met legendary promoter Bill Graham, with whom they immediately bonded. Through the years, Graham would become one of the Allman Brothers Band's key supporters. "He was a great guy," Dickey Betts later said. "You know, either you hated Bill or you loved him. I was among the latter. He was one of the cornerstones of getting our band going."[43]

Constantly on the road, the band made plans to record their second album, *Idlewild South*, this time under the direction of veteran producer Tom Dowd. Due to logistical challenges and Dowd's own preferences, they recorded at Atlantic's Criteria Studios in Miami, as well as at Capricorn in Macon and Regent Sound Studio in New York, between February and July of 1970. "They were working 300 days a year," Dowd later said. "So they would just blow in and do some songs and blow out. That was it—in and out—just like that." Released the following September, the album included classics such as Gregg Allman's "Midnight Rider" and Betts's "In Memory of Elizabeth Reed," and it garnered positive press.

"I'm a picky eater when it comes to blues," a reviewer wrote in the *Philadelphia Daily News*, "but the new Allman Brothers album leaves me hungry for more. Not a bad track on it, so many high points that singling out one or two would be an injustice to the others." In Tampa, another critic lauded the album as "mellow, soothing, almost ethereal.... A grinding, flowing motion drifts in and around the funk and swing. The effect is, as far as I know, unprecedented. The Allman Brothers have a very unique, beautiful band." Despite the praise, the album, like its predecessor, did not do well commercially, although the positive reviews helped bolster the band's growing reputation as a live act. The connection with Dowd also led to Duane Allman's famous collaboration around the same time with Eric Clapton on *Layla and Other Assorted Love Songs* at Criteria Studios.[44]

The period also saw an abrupt change in the band's administrative support system. After a performance in Buffalo, New York, hyper-loyal road manager Twiggs Lyndon stabbed a club owner during a dispute over a $500 payment that he owed the band. The man died, and Lyndon was arrested. Later acquitted on the grounds of temporary insanity, he served time in a mental facility and had to give up his position with the band. Lyndon recommended his friend Willie Perkins as a replacement. Perkins had a background in banking and stepped right in. For him, it was quite a transition, both professionally and personally. "I knew it was the beginning of a new era for me," he recalled. "I was coming out of a bank with short hair, wearing a coat and tie. But the thing that got me there was the music. I heard that music and it reached into my soul."[45]

Not long after Perkins came on board, the band played a massive gathering just outside Macon at the Middle Georgia Raceway in Byron, Georgia. The Second Atlanta International Pop Festival (a similar event was held the previous year in Hampton, Georgia) took place July 3–5, 1970, and many people called it the "Woodstock of the South." Like Woodstock, the Byron gathering featured many high-profile entertainers, among them Jimi Hendrix, B. B. King, Johnny Winter, John Sebastian, Mountain, and Procol Harum. Logistically, it also mirrored the upstate New York event in that it drew a much larger crowd than expected, overwhelming the region and paralyzing transportation for miles in every direction. Attendance estimates vary widely between two hundred thousand and six hundred thousand, and there were so many waves of gate-crashers that not long after the festival started, it became a free event. Temperatures hovered around one hundred degrees. Drugs were rampant, as was skinny dipping in local streams, but there was little violence. After the event's first night, newspapers reported that "thousands of young people, turned on to the heady beat of rock music Friday night at the second annual Atlanta International Pop festival, unwound amid pot and perspiration."[46]

Promoters wanted to take advantage of the Allman Brothers Band's popularity in the region, so they booked the group to open the event and also to help close the show. They became the festival's unofficial host band and enjoyed hanging out and jamming with the other musicians. When the band first took the stage at the festival, the response was overwhelming, and the crowd cheered throughout their set. According to one report, "The lead singer [Gregg Allman] of the great Allman Brothers asked on Friday night that those who would like to hear some blues strike a match, and thousands of lights flickered like fireflies, the crowd roaring amazement at its own power and unity." Some viewed the scene as a coming-out party for the group, as they mixed comfortably with some of the country's rock elite. Despite complaints about the festival from state and local politicians, Willie Perkins later said that he thought the event helped warm the chilly relationship that the long-haired band had with Macon's more conservative elements. "I think that was when the city and the area finally recognized the two cultures coming together, the hippies and the hillbillies," he later said with a laugh. "The locals said, yes, these people are different, but they are not savages and aren't going to burn us out."[47]

Their next major recording project launched the Allman Brothers Band as a national act. Known for their live shows and long jams, the idea developed that the group might need a live album to showcase their talents. "The first two albums were good, but they didn't sell in massive numbers," Perkins said. "The feeling between the band, Phil Walden, and all of the people involved was that if there were a way to catch that live sound of the Allman Brothers, then that would be the way to present the band at its best." Quoted in *One Way Out*, Gregg Allman said, "We realized that we got a better sound live and that we were a live band.... And we realized that the audience was a big part of what we did, which couldn't be duplicated in a studio." Their acquaintanceship with Bill Graham and their love of the room led the group to choose the Fillmore East as the place to make the record. "There was no question about where to record the concert," Betts later recalled. "The Fillmore was the high-octane gig to play in New York—or anywhere, really."[48]

Produced by Tom Dowd, the double album, titled *At Fillmore East*, was recorded in March of 1971 and released on Capricorn the following July, peaking on the *Billboard* charts at number thirteen. It firmly established the Allman Brothers Band as a significant presence on the national music scene, with *Rolling Stone* magazine calling the group "the best damn rock and roll band this country has produced in the past five years." Blues dominated the first part of the work, including Blind Willie McTell's "Statesboro Blues" and T-Bone Walker's "Stormy Monday," with original compositions "Hot 'Lanta," "In Memory of Elizabeth Reed," and "Whipping Post" dominating sides three and four. While taking a shot at Eric Clapton and perhaps Jimmy Page and Jeff Beck, the music critic for the *Philadelphia Daily News* summed up what was the consensus of many observers at the time when he wrote "The excitement they generate in live performances manages to leak through on the recording. What's more, the record confirms Duane Allman's position as one of the finest rock guitarists ever, no matter how many British phenoms have come along." From the time of its release until today, many consider *At Fillmore East* one of the great albums of the rock era and one of the greatest live recordings of all time.[49]

While pinpointing an exact birth date is tricky, some mark the first three Allman Brothers Band albums as the genesis of a subgenre of American popular music labeled "Southern rock." Attempting to classify different styles of popular music in a definitive way has always been a flawed process, and the creation of Southern rock as a generic label was no different. Popularized during the 1970s, the term attempted to define a group of Southern bands who were prominent during the period, and whose music was a raucous mix of blues, country, and gospel, with some jazz sprinkled in for good measure. The Allman Brothers Band, Lynyrd Skynyrd, the Marshall Tucker Band, and Wet Willie were among the groups most often associated with Southern rock, but there were others, many of whom recorded with Capricorn. As a result, in years to come, fans and journalists would refer to Macon as the "cradle of Southern rock."

To use a single term to classify any musician discounts the individualism that makes an artist great, and that was what seemed to bother most of the musicians placed under the Southern rock umbrella. Members of the Allman Brothers Band, and many of their contemporaries from the South, were never comfortable with the term. "We may have inspired the

Southern rock thing, but I don't identify with it," Dickey Betts later said. "I hate the term Southern rock. I think calling us that pigeonholed us and forced people to expect a certain type of music from us." Pointing out layers of irony, Gregg Allman put it more succinctly when he once said with a smile, "Saying southern rock is like saying rock rock." Regardless of whether they liked it or not, the group was never able to divest itself of the label, and the term Southern rock never completely faded away.[50]

At Fillmore East represented the triumph that the band had hoped for, but they were not able to celebrate the achievement for very long. Just a few months after its release, tragedy struck. On October 29, 1971, Duane Allman, on a break back in Macon, died after the Harley Davidson motorcycle he was riding crashed at the corner of Hillcrest and Bartlett streets. Conflicting reports indicated that he either hit a truck that was turning in front of him, or swerved to avoid the truck and lost control of the bike. He suffered serious internal injuries and died soon afterwards at a local hospital. Duane's death was a devastating blow to the band, and especially to his brother, Gregg. The funeral took place three days later in Macon. The rest of the band attended, as did other musicians who knew Allman, including Delaney Bramlett, Thom Doucette, Mac Rebennack (Dr. John), Barry Becket, David Hood, and Jimmy Johnson. At the service, the band played several songs, and Atlantic's Jerry Wexler gave a tearful eulogy, just as he had at Otis Redding's funeral four years earlier. As was the case with Redding, Duane Allman's future as a performer seemed limitless at the time of his death. His band was on the verge of becoming wildly famous, and his reputation as a rock guitarist was stellar. He was buried in Rose Hill Cemetery.[51]

In Macon, Duane Allman's death sent shockwaves through the music community. The Allman Brothers Band's success with Capricorn had brought other musicians into the area in search of opportunity. This flood of talent lit the fuse for a cultural revolution in the city, and for all involved, Duane Allman's band was providing the foundational soundtrack for the phenomenon. "We were stunned, everybody there," Johnny Sandlin later said. "Duane was the guy.... Other bands had moved to Macon because of the Brothers, and Duane was the head Brother. There was no doubt who the bandleader was. It was Duane. Everybody focused on Duane, more than he wanted, I think." Keyboardist Chuck Leavell, who had recently come to Macon at the suggestion of Paul Hornsby, later echoed Sandlin's sentiments in his memoir, *Between Rock and a Home Place,* writing, "It was a huge blow to all of us. He was the leader, not only of the Allmans but the whole scene in Macon, and Southern rock in general. His loss was huge because he was a real figurehead. We looked up to him."[52]

The success of the Allman Brothers Band had put Macon on the map as a spot where young rock musicians might find an opportunity. By the time of Duane Allman's death, Phil Walden and Frank Fenter had established Capricorn as a label, and they were working hard to recruit artists. Cowboy, a Jacksonville band suggested by the Allmans, recorded for Capricorn early on, as did Livingston and Alex Taylor. In 1970, Capricorn released Johnny Jenkins's critically acclaimed album *Ton-Ton Macoute!*, which included session work by Duane Allman. Singer-songwriter Jonathan Edward had a top-five *Billboard* hit on Capricorn with "Sunshine."

In 1970, Capricorn signed Wet Willie, a blues-rock band out of Mobile, Alabama, that would have a solid career during the next decade. The group included Jimmy Hall on vocals and sax, his brother Jack on bass and banjo, Ricky Hirsch on guitar and mandolin, John Anthony on keyboards, and Lewis Ross on drums. "We heard about things going on in Macon, Georgia," Jimmy Hall said. "Capricorn Records and the Allman Brothers was the talk going on. We packed up our trailer and our station wagon and headed on up there." After an audition, they signed a contract, and their first album, *Wet Willie*, came out in 1971. Hall later remembered a great feeling of camaraderie among the musicians in Macon. "It was a real cooperative atmosphere," he said. "Almost like a workshop. People were interacting and learning from each other.... It was a real community feeling." When pressed to describe Wet Willie's music, Hall said, "It could be defined as rock 'n' soul, or blues 'n' roll, a mixture of rock, soul, blues and funk, with a touch of country rock."[53]

Like the Allman Brothers Band, Wet Willie grew their reputation through live performances, and they put out a live album in 1973 that sold well. "Wet Willie's approach is simple," a Nashville reviewer wrote. "They rock hard. Their lead vocalist, who doubles on alto sax, simply goes out and sings himself into exhaustion, whereupon the lead guitarist accomplishes the same, whereupon the organist picks up the baton and continues the madness."[54] They toured consistently, opening shows for the Allman Brothers Band and others. A turning point for the group came in 1974, when Capricorn released the album *Keep on Smilin'*, with a title track that became a radio staple and the band's signature song.

In homage to their blues roots, the cover of *Keep on Smilin'* featured a photograph of a blind street performer known locally in Macon as the Reverend Pearly Brown. Born in Abbeville, Georgia, in 1915, Brown grew up in Americus and attended the Georgia Academy for the Blind. He later became a minister, and because he could play guitar, accordion, and harmonica, his music became his ministry and his livelihood. He traveled extensively as a street musician, playing blues and gospel tunes. By the end of the 1950s, he was back in Americus but frequently took the bus to Macon to sing and play. During the 1960s, when interest in American folk music was on the upswing, he played at several major festivals, performed on college campuses, and in 1966 won a guitar competition at Carnegie Hall. Once the folk revival faded, he returned to Georgia, where he continued performing on the streets of Macon, and occasionally on WIBB. During a Wet Willie outdoor photo shoot, members of the group apparently recognized Brown, and a photographer snapped the picture for the album jacket. While the photo became iconic to Wet Willie fans, Brown later sued Capricorn, claiming he never gave his permission for the image's use on a commercial product.[55]

Wet Willie's recording career spanned primarily the 1970s. After *Keep on Smilin'*, they released two more albums on Capricorn before switching to Epic Records. While their recorded output dwindled, they continued touring for decades with additional musicians and in various configurations.

Another pioneering Southern rock band of the era was a group out of Spartanburg, South Carolina, called the Marshall Tucker Band. The original lineup included guitarist and vocalist Toy Caldwell, his brother Tommy Caldwell on bass, George McCorkle on rhythm guitar, vocalist Doug Gray, Jerry Eubanks on flute and tenor sax, and drummer Paul Riddle. Not long after Wet Willie signed with Capricorn, they played a Spartanburg show on the same bill with the Marshall Tucker Band and liked what they heard. Jimmy Hall recommended that they contact Phil Walden in Macon, and he told Walden about the group. Not long afterwards, the band traveled to Macon with some demo tapes, and auditioned at Grant's Lounge, a local club frequented by Capricorn's staff and artists. Johnny Sandlin remembered the occasion in his autobiography: "The first time I saw the Marshall Tucker Band, they were playing like it was an audition for us, and all the people in the [Capricorn] office were there, as were [Paul] Hornsby and I. Phil [Walden] and Frank [Fenter] really loved the band and believed in them." Hornsby, who produced the group and contributed to their records in the studio, later had a similar recollection: "Shortly after the Wet Willie band was signed at Capricorn, they played with a band in South Carolina that really impressed them. They came back and told Walden about them, and an audition gig was set up at Grant's Lounge for the Marshall Tucker Band. Phil liked what he heard."[56]

As with the Allman Brothers Band and Wet Willie, the band's first album was self-titled. Produced by Hornsby, the 1973 release, *The Marshall Tucker Band*, contained eight songs, all penned by the group's primary songsmith, Toy Caldwell. Among them was the single "Can't You See," which got a great deal of radio play. While Wet Willie leaned toward blues, the Marshall Tucker Band had more of a country flavor, highlighting that genre as a component of Southern rock. The band toured as an opening act for the Allman Brothers and headlined some of their own shows as their fan base grew. More recording followed, including their 1977 album, *Carolina Dreams*, featuring the band's most successful single "Heard It in a Love Song." The Marshall Tucker Band, like Wet Willie, remained together with multiple lineups for decades, although their time with Capricorn marked the band's golden era.

Little wonder that the Marshall Tucker Band's audition took place at Grant's Lounge. During the 1970s there was arguably no better place in Macon to hear live music. Opened in 1971 by Edward Grant, the Poplar Street bar quickly became a favorite hangout for those associated with Capricorn. Musicians drawn to Macon looking for a break, and those who were already established, performed regularly at Grant's, as did other musicians who were just passing through. "It cost a dollar to get in, but you might have a million dollar set of musicians playing up there," Willie Perkins recalled. "They were just jamming. It wasn't a gig where you went to see the Allman Brothers at Grant's Lounge. You went to Grant's Lounge thinking you might see the Marshall Tucker Band, Wet Willie, *and* the Allman Brothers." The bar was also a place for the musicians to let off steam doing what they liked to do best. According to Chuck Leavell, "Grant's was a place to jam. It could be anyone that might be in town recording, or floating through, or rehearsing. It was a welcoming place, and you could cut loose and just have fun without worrying about any particular pressure. Some of the jams were great, some were average, but it was a free-wheeling place to go, relax and groove."[57]

As Wet Willie and the Marshall Tucker Band took flight, the flood-gates opened and other musicians poured into Macon during the 1970s, all wanting to record for Capricorn. Among the artists releasing records on the label were Captain Beyond, White Witch, Duke Williams & The Extremes, the James Montgomery Band, Elvin Bishop, Eddie Henderson, Hydra, Grinderswitch, Kenny O'Dell, Kitty Wells, Bonnie Bramlett, John Hammond, Johnny Darrell, Bobby Whitlock, Travis Wammack, Dobie Gray, Billy Joe Shaver, Easy Street, Rabbitt, Fringe Benefit, and Stillwater. Paragon, the booking arm of Phil Walden's growing empire, also dealt with other popular acts, such as the Atlanta Rhythm Section. Musicians were everywhere, and new live-music venues began opening in Macon to meet the demand. "There were hundreds of musicians here," Walden later told an interviewer. "It was a real center for getting people together, I doubt we will ever reach that level again. It got kind of hip to live in Macon." The Capricorn studio was ground zero for all of this ac-tivity, a Middle Georgia oasis of creativity and musical camaraderie. Wet Willie's Jimmy Hall later told Michael Buffalo Smith, "The bands en-couraged the other bands, and the other Capricorn artists would drop in and listen to what was going on and give feedback, maybe contribute to the song. It was a real community feeling." Mark Pucci, hired as publicity director for Capricorn, told a reporter that musicians seemed to like Ma-con because "the atmosphere is so relaxed. They don't have all the periph-eral distractions of L.A. or New York. They can just settle down and play music."[58]

As the roster of artists that Walden dealt with expanded, so did the business end of the operation, and the entrepreneur hired more and more support staff. Alex Hodges, originally brought in as vice president of Wal-den Artists and Promotion, in 1970, articulated Walden's ambitious agenda to a reporter from the *Atlanta Constitution*. "Our long range out-look is that Macon, Ga....will be more than a regional music center. We want to expand music to its furthest limits, and even into television.... Our interest is in the music industry, but we're not closing the door to other opportunities." In 1972, Capricorn ended its distribution deal with Atlantic and moved to Warner Brothers. By 1975, the label was a national player in the music industry to the extent that *Fortune* magazine took no-tice and published a feature article on Walden. "In less than six years, a hip, Southern impresario named Phil Walden has built a thriving musical empire," the article read. "Recordings provide the bulk of Walden's earnings, but his other companies make profits from activities that bolster album sales. A management company, Phil Walden and Associates, Inc., guides the overall careers of Capricorn's leading performers [and] the old booking agency, now called Paragon, books appearances by most of the Capricorn artists." At the time, various reports estimated that Capricorn's acts made up almost one quarter of total record sales at Warner Brothers Records.[59]

Through Paul Hornsby's work as producer of the Marshall Tucker Band, Capricorn established a relationship with Charlie Daniels in 1974. At the time, Daniels had four albums under his belt and a hit with the novelty single "Uneasy Rider." He and his band toured with the Marshall Tucker Band, and the group invited Daniels to play fiddle on their first album. Afterwards, Daniels approach Hornsby to see if he would be interested in producing his group. "Tucker's producer was a laidback good ol' boy from Alabama named Paul Hornsby," Daniels later recalled. "I met him when I worked on Tucker's records and liked his style. He'd done a great job with Marshall Tucker's records.... I liked the thought of working at Capricorn Studios and thought perhaps Paul Hornsby was just what we needed." Hornsby produced several albums for the Charlie Daniels Band from 1974 to 1977, the most prominent being *Fire on the Mountain*, which included the hit singles "Long Haired Country Boy" and "The South's Gonna Do It." Daniels recorded *Fire on the Mountain* at the Capricorn studio, and it was released in November of 1974 on Kama Sutra Records. It became the band's first gold album, and, according to one prominent critic, "one of the most important records of the Southern rock ascendancy." Daniels later said, "It was obvious even before *Fire on the Mountain* was released that it was special. Paul Hornsby and the folks at Capricorn Studios had lived up to all expectations."[60]

While Capricorn signed more and more artists, the Allman Brothers Band remained the crown jewel of the operation. Defying predictions to the contrary, the band picked up the pieces and carried on after Duane Allman's death. In April of 1972, Capricorn released the double album *Eat a Peach*, a project they had been working on at the time of the tragedy. It was a mix of studio and live recordings featuring popular singles "Melissa," "Blue Sky," and "One Way Out." *Rolling Stone* praised the effort in no uncertain terms. "Sometimes it all seems to come down to the question of survival—and learning to live with loss," the magazine's reviewer wrote. "The Allman Brothers are still the best Goddamned band in the land.... I hope they keep playing forever." *Eat a Peach* was also the band's most successful album to date with regard to commercial viability and the record charts. "When *Eat a Peach* was released, it was the biggest thing for us yet," Gregg Allman later recalled. "It shipped gold and it was our first album to hit the Top 10. We'd been through hell, but somehow we were rolling better than ever."[61]

While they had no way of knowing it at the time, more hell was on the horizon for the Allman Brothers Band. On November 11, 1972, just over a year after Duane Allman's death, Berry Oakley crashed his motorcycle into a bus on Napier Avenue in Macon. The spot was near the site of Duane's accident. Dazed, but not showing outward sign of life-threatening injuries, Oakley turned down treatment at the scene. "He said he wasn't hurt and refused to get in an ambulance," the responding police officer reported. Instead, Oakley hitched a ride back to the Big House, where it soon became apparent that something was seriously wrong. Keyboardist Chuck Leavell was at the Big House when Oakley arrived, and later recorded the sequence of events in his memoir. "We loaded him in one of the cars and got him to the hospital as quickly as we could. The nurses or a doctor or someone came out and told us that Berry had suffered severe internal head trauma, and that he was in grave shape, but that they were going to operate and hope for the best. About a half an hour later, a doctor came out and told us that Berry had died on the operating table." As they had done the year before, the surviving band members came together to play at Oakley's funeral. He was buried in Macon next to Duane Allman at Rose Hill.[62]

Despite sustaining another severe blow, the rest of the band decided to carry on with the addition of two new players, Leavell on keyboards and bassist Lamar Williams. Born in 1949 in Gulfport, Mississippi, Williams was an old friend of Jaimoe's, and the two had played in bands together as teenagers on the Mississippi Gulf Coast, including an outfit called George Woods and the Sounds of Soul. "Jaimoe and I go back about 15 years," he told *Guitar Player* magazine in 1980. "We went to high school together and played in many of the early groups I was in before I went into the army." Leaving the military in 1970, Williams continued his music career, and after the Oakley tragedy, his old friend suggested that he audition for the position as bassist in the Allman Brothers Band. At the time, the band auditioned multiple players, but from all accounts, Williams had a stellar showing. Butch Trucks later commented that "his groove was so rock solid that absolutely no one could miss it or deny it." Likewise, Johnny Sandlin said, "I don't remember who all auditioned, but once they heard Lamar, the band discussed it and offered him the gig.... Lamar had a good melodic sense and fit right in."[63]

Chuck Leavell was born in 1952 in Birmingham, Alabama, and grew up in Tuscaloosa. While he displayed talent early on, a turning point in his life came when he attended a Ray Charles concert as a youngster with his sister Judy. "It came like a lightning bolt," he later wrote in his autobiography. "Judy had a date and free tickets to a Ray Charles concert and invited me to come along. Ray was so brilliant.... I decided that night, at the age of ten or whatever it was, that I was going to spend my life as a piano player." Like most ambitious young musicians, he played in bands as a teenager, including a group called the Misfits that appeared on local television. He later joined South Camp, a short-lived group that Paul Hornsby led after Hour Glass broke up. During that period, Leavell also did session work in Muscle Shoals, and when Capricorn opened, Hornsby suggested that his young friend move to Macon. "I was friends with Paul Hornsby," Leavell later said, "and had played in bands with him in Tuscaloosa. Paul was very much a mentor to me at that time. Then he got the call to go to Macon and join the Capricorn team as a session player and producer. That's what led up to me deciding to go and check it out."[64]

Leavell arrived in 1969 and became part of the city's blossoming music scene. He did session work at Capricorn and joined Alex Taylor's band. He also toured with Dr. John, who Phil Walden worked with for a time. After Duane Allman's death, producer Johnny Sandlin brought Leavell in to play on Gregg Allman's first solo album, *Laid Back*, an opportunity that contributed to his joining the Allman Brothers Band. According to Sandlin, "You could tell [Leavell] was going to be a star; he had that 'thing,' and still does.... I mentioned him to the band, and when the Brothers were recording [the album] *Brothers and Sisters*, they decided to try him out to add another harmony instrument. Chuck came in one night to play with the band and just stayed with them." As an artist and a fresh personality, Leavell seemed to be the tonic the band needed after going through such a rough period. "After *Eat a Peach*, we needed something," Gregg Allman later said, "and adding keyboards was the right thing to do. He started jamming with us and everybody liked him right away.... Musically, I think Chuck added a lot to the band. He put a little bit of a different sound to things, which was just what we needed." While

Leavell got along well with the band, he was surprised by the invitation to become a member. "Man, you could have knocked me over with a feather," he later remembered. "I really had no idea that they were considering adding me in as a member. I tried to maintain some sort of calm about it, but of course I accepted right away." After several weeks in the studio, Leavell, took the stage with the Allman Brothers Band at a November 2, 1972, appearance at Hofstra University in New York, just a few days before Berry Oakley's death. The show was taped for broadcast on a new late-night weekend show on ABC called *In Concert*, produced by Don Kirshner.[65]

Brothers and Sisters, the follow-up album to *Eat a Peach*, was a commercial success for the Allman Brothers Band. It included the popular songs "Ramblin' Man" and "Jessica," both penned by Dickey Betts. "Ramblin' Man," which Betts said he wrote in the kitchen of the Big House, was the band's biggest hit single. Willie Perkins later recalled, "When the song 'Ramblin' Man' came out, I was riding down the highway and you'd hear it on the radio about every twenty minutes." The tune represented a departure for the band. Thanks to Betts's musical roots, it had a distinct country flavor unlike anything they had put out before. "Jessica," which featured significant contributions from Leavell and guitarist Les Dudek, also received a good deal of airplay and became a signature concert tune. Like the rest of the album, both songs were recorded at the Capricorn studio. Johnny Sandlin shared a coproducing credit with the band, and the reviews were positive.[66]

Just before the release of *Brothers and Sisters*, the Allman Brothers Band played a massive festival in Watkins Glen, New York, on a bill that included the Grateful Dead and The Band. The event drew six hundred thousand fans, which was a testament to the popularity of Southern rock, as well as the group's conspicuous place in the youth culture of the period. As one of the event organizers stated after the show closed, "The Allman Brothers Band is the biggest group in the country right now." Walden also credited the show with bringing the enormity of the group's accomplishments to the attention of the local gentry in Macon, many of whom remained suspicious because of the band members' long hair and relaxed racial attitudes. "I think they realized for the first time how big the Allmans were when the headlines came out about Watkins Glen," he said. "I don't think the people of Macon knew what we were doing until then. They thought we booked bands for bar mitzvahs or high school proms."

Not long afterward, *Don Kirshner's Rock Concert*, a new, nationally syndicated music program, filmed an episode in Macon featuring the Allman Brothers Band, the Marshall Tucker Band, and Wet Willie. The program, titled "Saturday Night in Macon, Georgia," aired in October of 1973, further evidence of the expanding national appeal of the Allman Brothers Band and Southern rock in general.[67]

As Capricorn flourished, a performer considered by many to be the original white Southern rocker brought his act to town for a memorable engagement at the Macon Coliseum. Completed in 1968, the coliseum could seat more than seven thousand, providing the city with a venue for popular national acts, and there were few if any rock and roll acts more popular than Elvis Presley. Presley and his entourage arrived in Macon by plane just before dawn on the morning of August 15, 1972, and a police escort took him to the Macon Hilton. According to reports, at the hotel "approximately 60 local policemen, most of them off-duty and employed for security, guarded the elevator and the stairwells to ensure that no unauthorized persons reached his floor." Presley played two shows that day, one at 2:30 P.M. and one at 8:30 P.M. Ticket prices ranged from five to ten dollars but, according to the *Atlanta Constitution*, "fans gave no indication that the high prices dampened their spirits." From all accounts, the shows did not disappoint, from the opening chords of the first number, "C. C. Rider," through a generous selection of Presley classics, to the finale, which included "Dixie" and the "Battle Hymn of the Republic." According to the *Macon News*, "The audience came from all over Georgia and from distant states like Michigan and Tennessee. There were a mixture of male and female, young and old." Once the later show ended, a limousine took Presley and his group back to the hotel, and they quickly departed for the next show in Jacksonville, Florida. Presley would make three more appearances in Macon, performing in 1975, 1976, and 1977, less than three months before his death.[68]

During the mid-1970s, Macon could also boast a connection with Paul McCartney. After the breakup of the Beatles, McCartney formed a new band with his wife, Linda, that they called Wings, and began touring and recording. In the process, they met trombone player Tony Dorsey, who became the band's horn arranger. Dorsey was from Houma, Louisiana, and he studied music at Southern University in Baton Rouge, home of one of the premier African American marching bands in the nation. Dorsey later recalled that at the school he "met a lot of tremendously good musicians from New Orleans. They sort of pushed me, prodded me, embarrassed me into getting better." In addition to playing the trombone, he was also a skilled arranger. After a stint in the air force, where he was in the air force band, he found work at Allan Toussaint's Sea-Saint studio in New Orleans, and Philly Groove Records in Philadelphia. He came to Macon around 1970, where he was associated with Capricorn. During this period, he mingled with other Capricorn artists and played and toured with Clarence Carter, Johnnie Taylor, and Joe Tex.

It was apparently Dorsey's work with Joe Tex, along with recommendations from other musicians, that placed him on McCartney's radar. The former Beatle asked Dorsey to do horn arrangements in the studio, and hired him to lead the Wings horn section on tour. "Basically, the gist of the conversation," Dorsey said, "was that [McCartney's] music was a little white, and he wanted to get a little more soul." In addition to Dorsey on trombone, the Wings horn lineup included Steve Howard, Thaddeus Richard, and Howie Casey, who was an old acquaintance of McCartney's from Liverpool. "Tony played trombone," Howard later told an interviewer. "He had originally played with Joe Tex, and the way that he got the gig with Wings was that Paul had heard some stuff that he had arranged on that Joe Tex album, and said 'I love that.... Get me that.... [F]ind out who that guy is and get me in touch with him!'" Dorsey was with Wings from 1975 until the band broke up in 1980, contributing to the studio LPs *Venus and Mars*, *Wings at the Speed of Sound*, *Back to the Egg*, and the live album *Wings over America*.[69]

In addition to his musical work, Dorsey contributed to Wings by suggesting that McCartney hire transplanted Maconite Joe English as his drummer. English was a New Yorker who had played with a band called the Jam Factory, touring as an opening act for some of the era's biggest names, including Hot Tuna, Sly and the Family Stone, Janis Joplin, and Jimi Hendrix. The band eventually relocated to Florida, and then moved to Georgia before breaking up. While he was waiting for something to happen, English played local gigs in Macon and hung out with members of the Capricorn crowd. With little going on, he moved into a small place on some property that the Allman Brothers owned outside of the city at Juliette. "I ended up on the Allman Brothers farm," he later said. "I was hanging out with Jaimoe and had no band, playing little club dates in Macon." In 1975, McCartney needed a replacement for drummer Geoff Britton, who had recently left Wings, and Dorsey, who also knew Jaimoe, suggested English for the position. "Tony Dorsey was from Macon, and he told Paul about me," English later said. In what could only be described as a miraculous stroke of luck and timing, English got the job and stayed with Wings until 1977, when he abruptly left the group. "I enjoyed it and learned a lot," he said, "but I got tired of the months and months sitting in recording studios. I wanted to come home and see if I could make it as Joe English and not on [the association with] Paul McCartney." English returned to Middle Georgia and eventually joined Sea Level, a band that Chuck Leavell put together.[70]

The success and growing popularity of the Allman Brothers Band continued to generate heady times at Capricorn. Many hailed Phil Walden as a genius, and Macon's reputation as a music city soared. Gregg Allman watched it all happen and later remarked, "Apparently our success was also Macon's. Not only were the Allman Brothers getting bigger, but Macon was getting bigger. People from all over the world were coming to Macon.... There were clubs all over town." For several years during the 1970s, Walden hosted an annual picnic that drew music industry movers and shakers from all over the country, as well as personalities ranging from artist Andy Warhol to future president Jimmy Carter. "You never knew who might be there," Chuck Leavell later remembered. "So many famous people...along with those of us that lived in Macon and worked at Capricorn, musicians, executives, booking agents, record promoters or other staff members. There were jams all day, performances by artists on the label. Great food, and of course lots of libations and other things going on." In 1976, the popular British music program *The Old Grey Whistle Test* sent correspondents to Macon to document the event.[71]

During this period, a journalist from the *Atlanta Journal Constitution* wrote a lengthy article on Walden and the Allman Brothers and how the small, conservative city of Macon was an unusual setting for a thriving rock and roll empire. In it he described the Capricorn offices:

The offices of Capricorn Records, which may well be the largest independent record company in the world, are housed in a newly-remodeled, stark white building whose facade is a series of modernistic angles. It is directly across the street from Macon city hall, where policemen in uniforms come and go. The traffic in and out of Capricorn's doors is also uniformed: the T-shirt-and-embroidered-and-patched-jeans uniform, a hangover from the heyday of street people. The only incongruity is the occasional businessman's briefcase that the denimed and bearded young businessman totes into Capricorn. For all the free-form atmosphere inside—the stereos blasting in every office, the pointedly beautiful young secretaries, the anything-goes mode of dress, the wild, speedo graphics in earth tones on the office wall—it is a business, an efficient and well run and successful business at that.[72]

As his businesses expanded, Walden took on the trappings of a wealthy entrepreneur. According to press reports, these included "a Rolls Royce Silver Cloud, a Mercedes Benz sports car, a contemporary house nestled on nine acres of wooded land in Macon, a weekend house on Lake Sinclair, and a large collection of modern art including originals by Picasso, Max Ernst, Dali, Chagall, Andrew Wyeth, and Gaugin." He also opened a nightclub called Uncle Sam's that became another hangout for Capricorn musicians. Among the bands that played there frequently were Roundhouse and Stillwater.[73]

Roundhouse was a group out of Warner Robins, about twenty miles south of Macon. Their mid-seventies lineup included guitarists Bruce Brookshire and Rick Skelton, John Samuelson on bass, Eddie Stone on keyboards, and drummer Herman Nixon. They gravitated toward Macon and played in local clubs, touring as the opening act for several Capricorn bands as well as other national acts such as Ted Nugent and Bob Seger. They were regulars at Phil Walden's club, which, like Grant's Lounge, was a haven for local musicians. "There was a club in Macon that Phil Walden owned," Eddie Stone later recalled. "They had a lot of big bands in there, but it was also a playground for Capricorn artists. We were the house band out there. Stillwater was [also] the house band. We rotated out." Roundhouse hung together and, after changing their name to Doc Holiday, recorded with A&M Records in the early 1980s.[74]

Stillwater was also a Warner Robins band. Its original lineup included guitarists Michael Causey, Bobby Golden, and Rob Roy Walker, vocalist Jimmy Hall (not to be confused with the Jimmy Hall who performed with Wet Willie), David Heck and Sebie Lacey on drums, Al Scarborough on bass, and keyboardist Bob Spearman. Like other musicians from the region, they knew that Capricorn in Macon was a potential ticket to bigger things, and they started hanging around the city taking local gigs. The band's popularity soared when they started playing Uncle Sam's, and the executives at the record label noticed. "We knew if we could get a job playing Uncle Sam's we could get some eyes on us," Sebie Lacey said at the time, "so we kept pounding on the door. Once we got the job, the place was packed all the time. It got to the point where the people at Capricorn said 'What's going on? What are these guys doing to get these crowds?' After a while they signed us." Stillwater recorded two albums with Capricorn, a self-titled effort in 1977 and *I Reserve the Right* the following year, and their popular single "Mindbender" received considerable airplay. The band broke up in the early 1980s, though they later reconvened for another album.[75]

The zenith of Phil Walden's success at Capricorn coincided with the rise to national prominence of Georgia governor and Democratic presidential candidate Jimmy Carter. Introduced by a mutual friend in 1971, Carter and Phil Walden hit it off, and Carter later came to Macon to tour the Capricorn operation. Walden was one of Carter's earliest supporters and helped him raise money during the early stages of his presidential campaign by organizing benefit concerts featuring Capricorn artists, including the Allman Brothers Band. At the time, a *Washington Post* reporter wrote, "Virtually the entire roster of Capricorn Records, a Georgia-based company which dominates the immensely popular style of music that has come to be called 'Southern rock,' has announced for former Georgia governor Jimmy Carter." The relationship between Carter and Walden was mutually beneficial as Carter courted the youth vote and Walden worked to gain national respectability for what he had built in Macon. During an appearance at a Providence, Rhode Island, fundraising gig headlined by the Allman Brothers Band in late 1975, Carter told the cheering crowd, "Anyone who doesn't want a president who likes this kind of music and who is proud of his friendship with the people who make that music can go and vote for somebody else." While Carter ultimately won the election, his association with Walden was not without controversy. Republicans dubbed it the "Capricorn connection," and as drug issues within the Allman Brothers Band escalated, the group's ties to Carter drew greater public scrutiny.[76]

For the Allman Brothers Band, the popularity of *Brothers and Sisters*, the Watkins Glen show, the appearance on *Don Kirshner's Rock Concert*, the growing national acceptance of Southern rock, and their association with Jimmy Carter should have represented a series of great triumphs that would carry the band forward, but that was not the case. Despite greater popularity than they could have ever imagined, and regardless of the presence of two new members who provided a musical breath of fresh air for the group, everything they had worked to accomplish was on the verge of unravelling.

The rise and fall of the Allman Brothers Band during the 1970s has been well chronicled, though some of the stories of their decline as a group differ slightly, depending on who is telling the tale and when. In the end, there were a number of interrelated reasons that explain why the group lost its way, many of which were not unique to the band or anyone else in the entertainment business. Their original communal existence could not withstand the burdens and responsibilities of mass popularity, the daily push and pull of trying to maintain personal lives as thousands of fans clamored to touch the hems of their robes. The pressures of sudden fame were enormous. Their trip from obscurity to the pinnacle of rock and roll success was short and the g-forces powerful. The sudden burst of riches also complicated matters. "We had five years at the top," Gregg Allman later said, "and then, bam, it was all over. We had spent so much money it was unbelievable." As time wore on, and the Allman Brothers Band generated more income, questions arose over royalties, expenses, and Phil Walden's dual role as the group's manager and their label owner, which seemed to be a significant conflict of interest. Adding to the general chaos of the band's existence were their private excesses, which included substance abuse. On top of all of these things, the sudden deaths of Duane Allman and Berry Oakley left emotional scars that never faded. If anything, the band's ability to carry on at all after those tragedies was a testament to their fortitude and dedication to their craft.

By the mid-1970s, the fabric of the Allman Brothers Band had already frayed. Both Gregg Allman and Dickey Betts had released solo records as the band began working on the album that became *Win, Lose or Draw*, a lukewarm offering that did well in the charts but seemed to lack the energy of previous efforts. A major distraction developed in early 1975 when Allman met the entertainment superstar Cher, whom he later married and divorced. From all accounts, Cher did her best not to intrude on the band's work, but her status as an A-list personality meant that she and Allman drew an army of paparazzi wherever they went. Allman also spent a significant amount of time with Cher in California, which disrupted the band's recording process. Around that same time, the authorities in Macon began taking notice of the many rumors about the band's drug use.

Allman in particular was the focus of their attention much of the time, as was his personal manager/handler John C. "Scooter" Herring. In a messy, highly publicized trial, Allman testified against Herring in exchange for immunity, and Herring went to prison. Herring was well liked within the Allman Brothers bubble, and many in and around the band saw Allman's testimony as a betrayal.[77]

"Gregg and the whole band were at odds," Johnny Sandlin later wrote. "Feelings were strained because Gregg had testified against Scooter, sending him to prison....Everyone blamed Gregg for what happened." At the time, Dickey Betts told a reporter from *Creem* magazine that the Herring affair was simply the final straw in a process that had been well underway for some time. "[The trial] kind of brought the whole thing to a climax," he said. "The financial thing was terrible as well. But I think we could have solved the financial thing, and I think we could have solved the personal thing that resulted in Gregg moving out of the South and into a new lifestyle [with Cher]. But when the Scooter Herring thing fell on top of that, everybody just threw up their hands." For his part, Allman later lamented in his memoir, "There ain't one thing or person alone that broke up the Allman Brothers. It was everything and everyone. Scooter, my [solo] recording *Laid Back*, my living in L.A.—they were just easy excuses, ways of talking around the unavoidable truth: that none of us knew when or how to walk away." In *One Way Out*, Jaimoe may have summed up the situation best when he opined, "It had to end. We went through two deaths and the only thing that kept us from going crazy was the fact that we had something to do, something very intense to fill our time. If not, it could have really been a mess. What happened was, it just became a mess later on."[78]

In 1976, the Allman Brothers Band splintered, with Betts, Trucks, and Jaimoe claiming that they would never again take the stage with Allman. Lawsuits by the band against Capricorn came later as the world that they had built crumbled. Time eventually tempered some of the hard feelings, but the original magic they conjured on the banks of the Ocmulgee River was lost forever. Desperate to keep their flagship band relevant, Capricorn released *Wipe the Windows, Check the Oil, Dollar Gas*, a live compilation, in late 1976. Two years later the band—minus Chuck Leavell and Lamar Williams—reunited to record a decently received album titled *Enlightened Rouges*, released in February of 1979. The album included contributions by new members Dan Tolar and David Goldflies as well as other musicians, including Johnny Lundahl, Joe Lala, Bonnie Bramlett, Jim Essery, and Mimi Hart. It was the group's last title on the original Capricorn label.

With various lineups, the Allman Brothers Band toured and recorded off and on for decades and remained a popular live draw. While their golden years were part of their past, they maintained an extremely loyal fan base and remain one of the most respected American bands of all time. In 1995, the band was inducted into the Rock & Roll Hall of Fame, and in 2012 they received the Grammy Lifetime Achievement Award. The Allman Brothers Band played their final show on October 28, 2014, at the Beacon Theater in New York. Today in Macon, the Big House, which served as the cradle of the band's original sound and spirit, is a museum honoring the group that attracts fans from all over the world.

As the Allman Brothers Band crumbled, Jaimoe, Chuck Leavell, and Lamar Williams sometimes found themselves in the studio waiting for the other principals to show up for a recording session. Unwilling to remain idle, and almost always in the mood to play, they channeled their creative energy into what became a successful side project, a "band within the band" that they eventually called Sea Level. Johnny Sandlin, who witnessed the acrimony of the era, later recalled, "There seemed to be hard feelings all the way around even though there were never hard feelings around Chuck, Jaimoe and Lamar. In fact, the three of them used to come into the studio at whatever time we'd set and start jamming." They informally called their trio "We Three" and even made some demos and a few public appearances. They also got in a great deal of practice at sound checks before Allman Brothers shows. "Nobody wanted to do sound checks," Jaimoe remembered. "We were the only ones who would get together and play before a concert to get the acoustical feel of the hall." In his memoir, Leavell traced the origins of the group to an impromptu show in Hartford, Connecticut, in 1974, where they entertained an anxious crowd of Allman Brothers Band fans as they waited for a tardy Gregg Allman and Dickey Betts to appear for the gig.[79]

With the breakup of the Allman Brothers Band, the trio added guitarist Jimmy Nalls to the lineup and formed a band. Nalls was an old friend of Leavell's who had toured with Alex Taylor and Dr. John. The new group took the name Sea Level, a pun based on Leavell's name, "C. Leavell." They started touring, signed with Capricorn, and began working on their debut album, *Sea Level*, which came out in 1977. Some labeled the group's music jazz fusion, or a "blend of jazz and more traditional Southern rock," but the reality was more complex. "The music of Sea Level has lots of different flavors," Leavell said. "Jaimoe and Lamar are from Mississippi and I'm from Alabama, so there's a lot of R & B influence in the band. There's rock 'n' roll, and of course a little middle-of-the-road kind of jazz." Their first album received good press, with one reviewer calling it a "conspicuously creative album" that was "a testimony to what Leavell, Jaimoe, and Williams brought to the [Allman Brothers Band] that put the South on the contemporary music map."[80]

More positive reviews followed, as did several lineup changes. The group added guitarist Davis Causey and multi-talented instrumentalist and vocalist Randall Bramblett in 1977. Around the same time, drummer George Weaver replaced Jaimoe, who developed back problems and grew tired of the grind. Weaver never quite fit in and stayed with the group for only a short time. Joe English, who had recently left his gig with Paul McCartney and Wings, replaced Weaver, and percussionist Matt Greeley signed on for a brief period toward the end of the band's run. Over its four-year life span, Sea Level put out four albums with Capricorn and, after the label folded, one with Arista before breaking up. The band also attracted many fans. Asked about the experience later on, Jimmy Nalls summed up what a lot of fans probably felt when he said, "Gosh, it was quite a ride. We had a great band. I think we cut a lot of new ground. I think maybe the band was a little ahead of its time.... We sort of jumped on the old horse and rode it 'til it stopped." Leavell moved on to great success as one of rock's premier keyboardists. He has played with many of the world's greatest musicians, and since the 1980s has toured with the Rolling Stones as their principal pianist and musical director. He speaks fondly of Sea Level whenever anyone asks about the group. "I loved that band," he once said. "That period is a very special memory to me. I'm very proud of what we did. We were a slamming group."[81]

The breakup of the Allman Brothers Band signaled the beginning of the end of Phil Walden's music empire. In many ways, the demise of Capricorn mirrored the demise of the group, with the weight of its own success eventually crushing the label. Excess in the form of drugs and lavish spending ate away at Capricorn's reputation. "We probably all thought we were God," Walden later said. "Money is a strange thing. Add a little applause, start reading a few press clippings about yourself, and all of a sudden you don't know who you are." As quickly as the label had risen to prominence, it suffered a spectacular crash. Other labels poached Capricorn acts, and by the end of the 1970s the formative momentum of Southern rock as a cultural force was waning. Disco and punk had taken the record market in new directions that left Capricorn on the outside looking in. The label also spent what some thought was too much money developing new, unproven talent.[82]

In what Walden later remembered as "an unfortunate decision, a terrible decision," Capricorn ended its distribution deal with Warners and moved to PolyGram Records in 1977. In the process, PolyGram lent Capricorn a significant amount of money to keep going, and two years later, with the record industry experiencing a recession, demanded repayment. With its financial option disappearing, Capricorn filed for bankruptcy. "It was one of the worst moments in my life when I had to seek protection through bankruptcy," Walden later said. "I'm a guy that has no small amount of pride in what he's accomplished.... I've never had failure in my game plan." According to published reports, PolyGram eventually received significant assets "including master tapes and copyrights" as settlement of millions in defaulted loans, while other creditors agreed to take a piece of a special fund "to pay about $20 million in claims over the next seven years." Walden retained title to the offices and studio, but with that settlement Capricorn Records was finished in Macon. While its influence would resonate for decades, in the end the label was a phenomenon of the 1970s.[83]

The Capricorn bankruptcy exacted a great personal toll on Phil Walden and Frank Fenter. Though his drive and ambition seemed to survive the ordeal intact, Walden spent several years struggling with drugs and alcohol. From all accounts, Fenter weathered the debacle with his trademark optimism. He set up a production company, and several years later he and Walden tried to revive the label. The project fell apart after Fenter died prematurely from a massive heart attack on July 21, 1983. He was only forty-seven years old. "Frank Fenter is my friend, my confidant, and my running partner," Walden said in his eulogy. "Frank and I shared a walk on the mountaintop. The view was beautiful. The air was heady. It was euphoric." While Walden relaunched Capricorn during the 1990s in Nashville and Atlanta, and kept the new venture afloat for several years, the label would forever be associated with Macon.

Walden died in 2006 after battling cancer. His obituary appeared in newspapers across the country. All paid tribute to his "colorful life," "boyish enthusiasm," and "roller coaster career." They noted his relationships with Otis Redding and the Allman Brothers Band as well as his role in establishing Capricorn Records as "the citadel of Southern rock." He was definitely one of the most interesting characters in Macon's history, and one of the most controversial. Many hailed him as a genius, a visionary, and an ever-confident entrepreneur. Others viewed him as a quick-talking operator. Still others were never comfortable with his friendships with African American artists during an era when Macon was still a black and white city, or the way he later unleashed "hippies" on the community. Regardless of what anyone felt about him, there was no debate that he permanently altered Macon's culture. "I'm a Capricorn," he once said, "and they're strong-willed and patient. They've got the determination to get where they want to go."[84]

Epilogue

"I once saw three men from Brazil drop to their knees and cry in front of Duane's 1957 Goldtop. The 'Layla' guitar."[1]

—Richard Brent
Executive Director,
Big House Museum

As of this book's release—more than forty years removed from the demise of Capricorn's original incarnation—Macon remains a vibrant music city. Locals revel in their culture, as do thousands of tourists who are drawn to the area every year. The mood of the city was especially celebratory in December of 2019, with the grand reopening of the old Capricorn studio as a state-of-the-art recording facility christened Mercer Music at Capricorn. It was the culmination of a project led by Mercer University, in partnership with the historic preservation and revitalization concern New-Town Macon, Sierra Development, and Southern Pine Plantations, that resurrected one of the city's most famous landmarks, the historic real estate that housed the Capricorn studio during the 1970s. The finished product was a spacious, "multi-purpose music venue in downtown Macon" that all involved hoped would "leverage Macon's music heritage to create Macon's music future." Included in the almost 20,000-square-foot complex are a commercial recording studio in the same space where the Allman Brothers Band, Marshall Tucker, Wet Willie, and many other bands laid down tracks during Capricorn's golden era; a dozen rehearsal rooms; a museum; offices; and conference rooms. Most locals agree that the project could not have turned out better. "We do have a strong campaign to get the word out that Capricorn is back," Rob Evans, the venue's chief engineer and studio manager, said at the time of the reopening. "We plan to network with many musicians and producers.... This icon is back on the map, and that alone is a reason to come [to Macon]."[2]

While the new Mercer Music at Capricorn complex certainly provides a reason for those interested in America's music history to visit the
city, there are other reasons as well. The sights and sounds of contemporary Macon's musical heritage are all around. A commercial venture, Rock
Candy Tours, founded in 2011 by Alan Walden's daughter Jessica and
her husband Jamie Weatherford, gives popular tours of historic sites related to Macon music. While being part of the Walden clan gives the
owners a unique perspective on the city's heritage related to the Otis Redding and Capricorn eras, tours also include sites dating from earlier and
later periods, highlighting "the homes, offices, crash pads, and favorite
haunts of some of southern music's most legendary players, as well as the
backstage cast of characters who played a crucial role in their catapult to
fame."[3]

Macon's airwaves also took a progressive turn in 2016 when partners
Wes Griffith, Brad Evans, and Rob Evans purchased Macon-based 100.9
WNEX-FM and rebranded it as "100.9 The Creek." The new owners
crafted a format designed to feature "Americana & roots music, classic
blues, country, rock n' roll, and soul" with a distinctly Macon perspective,
including many of the artists who made Macon famous as a music city.
Steering away from "canned" programming, the station pushes live, on-
air personalities with local connections and special programming targeting
central Georgia as well as the online-streaming world beyond. "Everybody
is just kind of coming out of the woodwork to support our station," co-
owner Brad Evans said when the station launched. "We're going to live
and breathe our region."[4]

Macon has been able to parlay its generationally consistent parade of
talent into a robust tourist industry, with various public and private enti-
ties working tirelessly and with great success to promote the city's music
heritage. The Historic Macon Foundation, a preservation organization,
along with Visit Macon, which is charged with marketing Bibb County
as a tourist destination, and Rock Candy Tours worked together to create
the Macon Music Trail in 2019. Those following the trail see monuments
to the city's musical past, from the home where Sidney Lanier, one of
Macon's earliest music celebrities, was born in 1842, to the historic
Douglass Theatre, a hub of the city's African American entertainment district for decades. The Grand Opera House and the City Auditorium,
along with the Douglass, still host major music events, and after touring
the Mercer Music at Capricorn complex, visitors can relax and soak in the

ambience at Grant's Lounge, where so many Capricorn artists once performed. Little Richard's childhood home has been restored, and Ann's Tic Toc Lounge, where the singer got his start, is now an upscale restaurant called the Tic Toc Room. In addition to these more prominent sites, there are dozens of nooks and crannies, hidden alleyways, and properties, both rustic and remodeled, where significant events occurred.[5]

More than half a century after his death, Otis Redding is still a formidable presence in Macon. His music is timeless, as is his cultural imprint on the community. Unlike Little Richard, who left town, and James Brown, who only passed through, Redding chose to live in the Macon area even after he became famous, cementing his status as Middle Georgia's favorite musical son. While his family made their home in Macon, and statues and murals pay tribute to him, his greatest tangible legacy is probably the educational foundation that bears his name. Created in 2007, the Otis Redding Foundation's stated goals are "to empower, enrich, and motivate all young people through programs involving music, writing and instrumentation." It sponsors scholarships and a diverse range of programs that have had a positive impact on countless young lives. These include music camps and private instruction along with traveling performance groups that allow young people showcase their talents. While Redding's widow, Zelma, created the foundation many years after his death, it represents an extension of the singer's own philanthropic zeal and lifetime commitment to his community. "Otis was providing young people with scholarships in 1963 with the emergence of his success," she said. "And through the Otis Redding Foundation, we continue his dream to empower all young people with an education."[6]

The long shadow of the Allman Brothers Band still provides pleasant shade for Macon, and the band's current following is perhaps even stronger than it was during the 1970s. Thousands of fans, representing two and sometimes three generations, descend on the city every year to visit sites associated with their favorite group. They eat at H & H Restaurant, where the struggling band once survived on the charity of "Mama Louise," and seek out places such as the Library Ballroom, formerly known as the College Discotheque, where the band played their first ticketed show in 1969. Each year in Macon, the Georgia Allman Brothers Band Association (GABBA), a nonprofit group dedicated to preserving and promoting the band's legacy, organizes "GABBAfest," a major music festival that draws fans from all over the world.

With regard to Allman Brothers Band "holy sites" in Macon, two stand out: the Vineville Avenue home known as the Big House, where the band lived communally, and Rose Hill Cemetery, where Duane Allman, Gregg Allman, Berry Oakley, and Butch Trucks are buried. Restored to its early 1970s appearance and containing a vast array of artifacts, the Big House Museum is the epicenter of Allman Brothers Band tourism, attracting around twenty thousand visitors every year. Some have been die-hard fans for decades while others are recent converts. "Allman Brothers fans old and new come from all over the world to visit with us," says Richard Brent, the museum's executive director. "What I am most proud of is that we get visitors who know nothing about the Allman Brothers Band, and [they] leave here blown away with what they have just seen. I once saw three men from Brazil drop to their knees and cry in front of Duane's 1957 Goldtop. The 'Layla' guitar." Many fans are equally emotional but more reflective when they visit Rose Hill Cemetery, where the biological Allman siblings and their musical brothers rest in a specially designed section meticulously tended by volunteers from GABBA.[7]

Of course, there are many individuals with direct connections to Macon's musical past who are still very much among the living in the city. Alan Walden still regales visitors with tales from the Redding and Capricorn eras, and Newton Collier still dispenses his encyclopedic knowledge of Macon's history to all interested parties. Willie Perkins, former manager of the Allman Brothers Band, provides firsthand accounts of life at the Big House and beyond, and legendary producer Paul Hornsby still runs his own operation, Muscadine Recording Studio, on Vineville Avenue. Legendary guitarist Robert Lee Coleman still commands respect on-stage, where he proves time and again that he is one the best guitarists the city ever produced. In the modern era, if there is a patron saint of Macon's music scene, it might be Chuck Leavell. Forever associated with Macon, the Allman Brothers Band, and Sea Level, Leavell lives in nearby Twiggs County and remains a beloved figure on the city's music scene. In addition to solo projects and his work with the Rolling Stones, he has recorded with almost every major figure in American popular music over the last fifty years. In the process, he also established a reputation for himself as one of the country's great environmentalists.[8]

Twenty-first-century Macon remains fixated on its musical history, but not simply as a function of nostalgia, community pride, or the tourist dollars that the city's heritage brings in. The interest is much deeper, with the historical record forming a bedrock that supports the area's ongoing cultural evolution. In Macon's case, the past is not necessarily prologue, but rather the initial chapters of a book that will never quite be finished, or the first notes of a song with an infinite number of verses. If there is indeed something in the water in Macon that conjures musical prowess, or creates a warm tipsiness based in music appreciation, there are certainly many in the city who still draw water from the well.

Notes

INTRODUCTION
[1] Atlanta Constitution, March 11, 2001.
[2] Ibid.

CHAPTER 1
[1] *A Wilderness Still the Cradle of Nature: Frontier Georgia, A Documentary History*, ed. Edward J. Cashin (Savannah, GA: Beehive Press, 1994) 118.

[2] Macon *Messenger*, December 10, 1824; *A Guide to Macon's Architectural and Historical Heritage*, ed. John J. McKay Jr. (Macon, GA: The Middle Georgia Historical Society, 1972) 11–12; Ida Young, Julius Gholson, Clara Nell Hargrove, *A History of Macon, Georgia, 1823–1949* (Macon, GA: Lyon Marshall and Brooks, 1950) 39–50.

[3] Macon *Telegraph*, July 9, 1827, July 11, 1829; Young et al., *History of Macon*, 59.

[4] Raoul F. Camus, "A Source for Early American Band Music: John Beach's Selection of Airs, Marches, &c," *Notes* 38/4 (1982): 792–94; Gilbert Chase, *America's Music: From the Pilgrims to the Present* (Urbana: University of Illinois Press, 1987) 126; Willi Apel, *Harvard Dictionary of Music* (Cambridge, MA: Belknap Press of Harvard University) 529.

[5] Macon *Telegraph*, July 23, 1827; *A Collection of National English Airs, Consisting of the Ancient Song, Ballad and Dance Tunes, Interspersed with Remarks and Anecdote*, ed. W. Chappell (London: W. Chappell, 1840) 129. For more on the Cumming-McDuffie rivalry, see Joseph B. Cumming, "The Cumming-McDuffie Duels," *The Georgia Historical Quarterly* 44/1 (1960): 18–40.

[6] Macon *Telegraph*, July 11, 1836, July 28, 1836; Macon Volunteers, *By-Laws of the Macon Volunteers, Organized 23rd April, 1825, Reorganized 8th October, 1831* (Macon, GA: C. R. Hanlester, 1839) 10–11.

[7] Macon *Telegraph*, August 21, 1827, March 3, 1840, December 21, 1841, October 18, 1842.

[8] Ibid., January 2, 1829, January 31, 1829, April 24, 1830, October 10, 1843; Young et al., *History of Macon*, 59–62.

[9] Macon *Telegraph*, May 26, 1828, September 29, 1836; "Theatre-Royale," *Edinburgh Dramatic Review* 185/4 (May 26, 1823): 144; Solomon Smith, *The*

Theatrical Journey—Work and Recollections of Sol Smith (Philadelphia: T. B. Petersen, 1854) 128.

[10] Macon *Telegraph*, February 7, 1829, November 20, 1830, April 13, 1837; *History of the First Presbyterian Church, Macon, Georgia, 1826–1990*, comp. Harriet Fincher Comer (Macon, GA: Williams-Rowland Printing Co., 1990) 1–5; H. Lewis Batts and Rollin S. Armour, *History of the First Baptist Church of Christ, Macon Georgia, 1826–1990* (Macon, GA: For the Church, 1991) 9–11; Young et al., *History of Macon*, 99–101; Erskine Clarke, *Wrestlin' Jacob: A Portrait of Religion in Antebellum Georgia and the Carolina Low Country* (Tuscaloosa: University of Alabama Press, 2000) 130.

[11] John Campbell Butler, *Historical Record of Macon and Central Georgia, Containing Many Interesting and Valuable Reminiscences of the Whole State, Including Many Incidents and Facts Never Before Published and of Great Historical Value* (Macon, GA: J. W. Burke and Co., 1879) 290; James Silk Buckingham, *The Slave States of America*, vol. 1 (London: Fisher, Son, and Co., 1842) 194; James H. Stone, "Economic Conditions in Macon, Georgia in the 1830's," *The Georgia Historical Quarterly* 54/2 (1970): 214; John A. Eisterhold, "Commercial, Financial, and Industrial Macon, Georgia, During the 1840s." *The Georgia Historical Quarterly* 53/4 (1969): 426.

[12] Mary Levin Koch, "Entertaining the Public: Music and Drama in Antebellum Georgia," *The Georgia Historical Quarterly* 68/4 (Winter 1984): 517; *A Dictionary of Music and Musicians*, vol. 3, ed. George Grove (New York: MacMillan and Co., 1889) 512; Macon *Telegraph*, September 5, 1837; New Orleans *Times-Picayune*, September 1, 1840; Louisville (KY) *Courier Journal*, August 16, 1836; John Edward Cox, *Musical Recollections of the Last Half-Century* (London: Tinsley Brothers, 1872) 189; Katherine K. Preston, *Opera on the Road: Traveling Opera Troupes in the United States, 1825–60* (Urbana: University of Illinois Press, 1993) 33.

[13] Macon *Telegraph*, May 27, 1845, January 27, 1846; *Brooklyn Daily Eagle*, January 13, 1845; *Baltimore Daily Commercial*, December 29, 1846; Benjamin Franklin Perry, *Letters of Governor Benjamin Franklin Perry to His Wife* (Greenville, SC: Shannon and Co., 1890) 62.

[14] Macon *Telegraph*, April 14, 1846; New Orleans *Times-Picayune*, May 22, 1846, May 26, 1846; Holly Spring (MS) Guard, April 25, 1846; Richmond (VA) Enquirer, February 3, 1846; *The Anglo American, A Journal of Literature, News, Politics, Drama, Fine Arts, Etc.*, vol. III, ed. A. D. Paterson (New York: E. L. Garvin, 1844) 165; Vera Brodsky Lawrence, *Strong on Music: The New York Music Scene in the Days of George Templeton Strong*, vol. I (Chicago: University of Chicago Press, 1988) 275.

[15] *Georgia Telegraph*, February 13, 1849; *New Orleans Crescent*, April 3, 1848; Koch, "Entertaining the Public" 517–20; John Weeks Moore, *A Dictionary of Musical Information* (Boston: Oliver Ditson and Co., 1876) 144–45.

[16] *Georgia Telegraph*, June 18, 1850; *Buffalo (NY) Daily Republic*, September 1, 1851; George Whitney Martin, *Verdi in America: Oberto through Rigoletto* (Rochester, NY: University of Rochester Press, 2011) 368; Preston, *Opera on the Road*, 230–32.

[17] *Washington (DC) Union*, February 4, 1853; *Georgia Telegraph*, November 18, 1851, November 25, 1851, May 11, 1852. For more on Teresa Parodi and antebellum opera in the United States, see Isaac Clark Pray, *Teresa Parodi and the Italian Opera* (New York: William B. Parsons, 1851).

[18] Macon *Telegraph*, December 19, 1833, January 8, 1839, February 5, 1839, September 24, 1839, April 29, 1845; Nashville *Tennessean*, July 3, 1846; Walter E. Steinhaus, "Music in the Cultural Life in Macon, 1823–1900," (PhD Dissertation, Florida State University, 1973) 19–21.

[19] 1850 United States Census, Bibb County, Georgia; 1860 United States Census, Laurens County, South Carolina; Macon *Telegraph*, January 15, 1850, August 17, 1852, September 14, 1852. There is conflicting information on Grimme's exact birthplace. According to 1860 census records, he was born in Brunswick, although an obituary printed in the Danville, Kentucky, *Advocate* on March 13, 1905, stated that his birthplace was Hanover.

[20] *Georgia Telegraph*, June 28, 1853; 1850 United States Census, Bibb County, Georgia; 1860 United States Census, Bibb County, Georgia.

[21] *Georgia Telegraph*, January 25, 1853, February 22, 1853; Hartford (CT) *Courant*, October 2, 1852, October 4, 1852; Brattleboro (VT) *Eagle*, September 9, 1852; Boston *Daily Atlas*, February 5, 1855.

[22] Carolyn L. Harrell, *Kith and Kin: Portrait of a Southern Family, 1630–1934* (Macon, GA: Mercer University Press, 1984) 81; Lucian Lamar Knight, *Georgia's Landmarks, Memorials, and Legends*, vol. II (Atlanta: Byrd Printing Co., 1913) 826; Samuel Luttrell Akers, *The First Hundred Years of Wesleyan College, 1836–1936* (New York: Beehive Press, 1976) 27.

[23] Harrell, *Kith and Kin*, 71–96; Charleston (SC) *Courier*, January 6, 1845.

[24] *Georgia Telegraph*, July 23, 1850.

[25] Ibid., July, 20, 1852; Candace Bailey, *Music and the Southern Belle: From Accomplished Lady to Confederate Composer* (Carbondale: Southern Illinois University Press, 2010) 74–80.

[26] Robert W. Johannsen, *To the Halls of Montezumas: The Mexican War in the American Imagination* (New York: Oxford University Press, 1985) 232–35.

[27] Candace Bailey, *Music and the Southern Bell: From Accomplished Lady to Confederate Composer*, 74–80.

[28] Harrell, *Kith and Kin*, 71–96; Charleston (SC) *Courier*, January 6, 1845; Athens (GA) *Banner*, February 2, 1842.

[29] *Georgia Telegraph*, June 15, 1852, September 23, 1852, November 29, 1853, December 15, 1857, December 22, 1857; Tallahassee *Floridian and Journal*,

February 26, 1853; Mattie Croker Thomas Thompson, *History of Barbour County, Alabama* (Eufaula, AL: Privately Printed, 1939) 277.

[30] *Georgia Telegraph*, November 16, 1852, January 11, 1853, March 2, 1860, November 23, 1860; 1860 United States Census, Bibb County, Georgia; 1870 United States Census, Bibb County, Georgia.

[31] *Memoirs of Richard H. Clark*, ed. Lollie Belle Wylie (Atlanta: Franklin Printing and Publishing, 1898) 206; Lena E. Jackson and Aubrey Starke, "New Light on the Ancestry of Sidney Lanier," *The Virginia Magazine of History and Biography* 43/2 (April 1935): 165–68; 1820 United States Census, Bibb County, Georgia; 1830 United States Census, Bibb County, Georgia; 1840 United States Census, Bibb County, Georgia; 1850 United States Census, Bibb County, Georgia.

[32] *Georgia Telegraph*, November 6, 1855; Edwin Mims, *Sidney Lanier* (New York: Houghton, Mifflin and Co., 1905) 17; George Herbert Clark, "Some Early Letters and Reminiscences of Sidney Lanier," *The Independent* LXI (July–December 1906): 1093; Aubrey H. Starke, "Sidney Lanier as a Musician," *The Musical Quarterly* 20/4 (October 1934): 36–37, 385; Milton Harlow Northrup, "Some Early Recollections of Sidney Lanier," *Atlanta Constitution*, October 8, 1899.

[33] Starke, "Sidney Lanier," 385; *African American Music: An Introduction*, eds. Mellonee V. Burnim and Portia K Maultsby (New York: Routledge, 2014) 18.

[34] Starke, "Sidney Lanier," 36–37. Jane S. Gabin, *A Living Minstrelsy: The Poetry and Music of Sidney Lanier* (Macon, GA: Mercer University Press, 1985) 8–12; Samuel Gibbs French, *Two Wars: An Autobiography of Gen. Samuel G. French* (Nashville, TN: Confederate Veteran, 1901) 157; John J. Barry, "Father Tabb (1845–1909)," *The Irish Monthly* 73/862 (April 1945): 142.

[35] Philadelphia *Times*, September 9, 1881; *New York Times*, September 9, 1881; *Atlanta Constitution*, November 23, 1881.

[36] *Georgia Telegraph*, April 13, 1852, May 14, 1854; *Buffalo (NY) Daily Republic*, January 7, 1848; *The Anglo American* 7/1 (1846): 168; *The World's Best Music: Famous Songs and Those Who Made Them*, vol. 1, eds. Frederick Dean, Reginald DeKoven, Helen Kendrick Johnson, and Gerrit Smith (New York: The University Society, 1904) 110.

[37] *Georgia Telegraph*, April 22, 1956; *Richmond (VA) Dispatch*, May 8, 1856, May 9, 1856. For general information on Ole Bull, see Camilla Cai and Einar Haugen, *Ole Bull: Norway's Romantic Musician and Cosmopolitan Patriot* (Madison: University of Wisconsin Press, 1993).

[38] Ida Young, Julius Gholson, Clara Nell Hargrove. *A History of Macon, Georgia, 1823–1949*, Young et al., *History of Macon*: 164–65.

[39] *Georgia Telegraph*, March 5, 1844, February 3, 1852, May 26, 1857; Shreveport (LA) *South-Westerner*, May 26, 1857.

[40] Henry Louis Gates Jr., *The Signifying Monkey: A Theory of African American Literary Criticism* (New York: Oxford University Press, 1988) 1–12, 110–12; Eric Lott, Love and Theft: Blackface Minstrelsy and the American Working Class (New

York: Oxford University Press, 1993), 4–5; Margaret McKee and Fred Chisenhall, *Beale Black & Blue: Life and Music on Black America's Main Street* (Baton Rouge: Louisiana State University Press, 1993) 195; Edward L. Ayers, *The Promise of the New South: Life After Reconstruction* (New York: Oxford University Press, 1992) 376–77; Ted Gioia, *Delta Blues: The Life and Times of Mississippi Masters Who Revolutionized American Music* (New York: W. W. Norton & Co., 2008) 26.

[41] Jim Crow, *American: Selected Songs and Plays,* ed. W. T. Lhamon (Cambridge, MA: Harvard University Press, 2003) xxx; Lott, *Love and Theft,* 5, 94; Francis Davis, *The History of the Blues: The Roots, the Music, the People: From Charley Patton to Robert Cray* (New York: Hyperion, 1995) 37; Nick Tosches, *Country: The Twisted Roots of Rock and Roll* (New York: Da Capo Press, 1985) 109–10; Ben Wynne, *In Tune: Charley Patton, Jimmie Rodgers and the Roots of American Music* (Baton Rouge: Louisiana State University Press, 2014) 57.

[42] *Georgia Telegraph,* November 6, 1850, October 14, 1851, February 8, 1853, November 10, 1857, December 27, 1859; *Buffalo (NY) Commercial,* July 6, 1850; Frank Dumont, "The Golden Age of Minstrelsy," in *Burnt Cork and Tambourines: A Source Book for Negro Minstrelsy,* ed. William L. Stout (Rockville, MD: Wildside Press, 2007) 203.

[43] Edward Le Roy Rice, *Monarchs of Minstrelsy, from "Daddy" Rice to Date* (New York: Kenny Publishing Co., 1911) 72, 86; Macon *Telegraph,* January 14, 1861; *Mississippi Free Trader,* February 20, 1860.

[44] T. Allston Brown, "The Early History of Negro Minstrelsy," in *Burnt Cork and Tambourines: A Source Book for Negro Minstrelsy,* ed. William L. Stout (Rockville, MD: Wildside Press, 2007) , 53; Rice, *Monarchs of Minstrelsy,* 19–21; Richard Crawford, *America's Musical Life: A History* (New York: W. W. Norton & Co., 2001) 212; Macon *Telegraph,* January 5, 1861, January 3, 1863; *Wilmington (NC) Daily Herald,* December 14, 1860; Cleveland (OH) *Plain Dealer,* September 26, 1855; *Providence (RI) Evening Press,* December 18, 1860.

[45] Gerhard Kubik, *Africa and the Blues* (Jackson: University Press of Mississippi, 1999) 26; Barbara Wilcots, "African-American Folk Culture," in *The Companion to Southern Literature: Themes. Genres, Places, People, Movements and Motifs,* eds. Joseph M. Flora, Lucinda H. MacKethan, and Todd W. Taylor (Baton Rouge: Louisiana State University Press, 2002) 8; Robert Palmer, *Deep Blues* (New York: Penguin Books, 1981) 33.

[46] James Oliver Horton and Lois E. Horton, *Slavery and the Making of America* (New York: Oxford University Press, 2005) 125; John W. Blassingame, *The Slave Community: Plantation Life in the Antebellum South* (New York: Oxford University Press, 1979) 122–25; Lawrence W. Levine, *Black Culture and Black Consciousness: Afro-American Folk Thought from Slavery to Freedom* (New York: Oxford University Press, 1977) 296–98; Catherine Silk and John Silk, *Racism and Anti-Racism in American Popular Culture: Portrayals of African-Americans in Fiction and Film* (Manchester, UK: Manchester University Press, 1990) 8–9; William W.

Freehling, *The Road to Disunion: Secessionists at Bay, 1776–1854* (New York: Oxford University Press, 1990) 84–86; R. A. Lawson, *Jim Crow's Counterculture: The Blues and Black Southerners, 1890–1945* (Baton Rouge: Louisiana State University Press, 2010) ix–xi; Macon *Telegraph*, April 2, 1850.

⁴⁷ Silk and Silk, *Racism and Anti-Racism in American Popular Culture*, 8–9; Andrew E. Taslitz, *Reconstructing the Fourth Amendment: A History of Search and Seizure, 1789–1868* (New York: New York University Press, 2006) 92, 98; Freehling, *The Road to Disunion*, 84–86; Lawson, *Jim Crow's Counterculture*, ix–xi.; Albert J. Raboteau, *Slave Religion: The Invisible Institution in the South* (New York: Oxford University Press, 2004) 311–12; Blassingame, *The Slave Community*, 137–147; Houston A. Baker Jr., *Long Black Song: Essays in Black American Literature and Culture* (Charlottesville: University Press of Virginia, 1972) 12–13; Dena J. Epstein, *Sinful Tunes and Spirituals: Black Folk Music to the Civil War* (Champaign: University of Illinois Press, 2003) 130.

⁴⁸ Macon *Telegraph*, February 11, 1832, March 20, 1849; *America in the Fifties: Letters of Fredrika Bremer*, ed. Adolph Benson (New York: The American-Scandinavian Foundation, 1924) 115; Edward Alfred Pollard, *The Southern Spy* (Washington: Henry Polkinhorn, 1859) 21–23.

⁴⁹ Macon *Telegraph*, August 30, 1860; *African American Music*, eds. Burnim and Maultsby, 18; *Selections from Sidney Lanier: Prose and Verse*, ed. Henry W. Lanier (New York: Charles Scribner's Sons, 1916) 100–101; Carl Engle, "Music of the Gypsies," *The Musical Times and Singing Class Circular* 21 (July 1, 1880): 333.

⁵⁰ Paul A. Cimbala, "Black Musicians from Slavery to Freedom," *Journal of Negro History* 80/1 (Winter 1995): 15–29.

⁵¹ Giles Oakley, *The Devil's Music: A History of the Blues* (Da Capo Press, 1997) 15; For a good treatment of the history of the violin, see David Schoenbaum, *The Violin: A Social History of the World's Most Versatile Instrument* (New York: W. W. Norton & Co., 2012); Chris Goertzen, *Southern Fiddlers and Fiddle Contests* (Jackson: University Press of Mississippi, 2008) 7; Karen Linn, *That Half-Barbaric Twang: The Banjo in American Popular Culture* (Champaign: University of Illinois Press, 1991) 1, 75–76; Thomas Jefferson, *Notes on the State of Virginia by Thomas Jefferson* (Richmond, VA: J. W. Randolph, 1853) 15; Gerhard Kubik, *Africa and the Blues* (Jackson: University Press of Mississippi, 1999) 8.

⁵² *New York Herald*, May 26, 1889; *Atlanta Constitution*, January 19, 1885.

⁵³ Macon *Telegraph*, April 22, 1856, January 20, 1857.

⁵⁴ Ibid., July 28, 1863, March 26, 1880; Augusta (GA) *Daily Constitutionalist*, July 30, 1862; 1880 United States Census, Mortality Schedule, Bibb County, Georgia.

⁵⁵ *Georgia Telegraph*, December 22, 1857. For general biographical information on "Blind Tom" Wiggins, see Geneva Handy Southall, *Blind Tom, The Black Pianist-Composer: Continually Enslaved* (Lanham, MD: Scarecrow Press,

2002) and Deirdre O'Connell, *The Ballad of Blind Tom, Slave Pianist: America's Lost Musical Genius* (New York: Overlook Press, 2009).

[56] *Georgia Telegraph*, February 9, 1858; 1860 United States Census, Bibb County, Georgia.

[57] *Georgia Telegraph*, February 2, 1858, February 9, 1858. Ian G. Hominick, "Sigismund Thalberg (1812–1871) Forgotten Piano Virtuoso: His Career and Musical Contributions" (PhD Dissertation, Ohio State University, 1991) 38–39.

[58] *Georgia Telegraph*, November 30, 1858.

[59] Ibid., August 3, 1860.

[60] Richard W. Iobst, *Civil War Macon: The History of a Confederate City* (Macon, GA: Mercer University Press, 1999) 1–7; Macon *Telegraph*, April 7, 1860.

[61] Iobst, *Civil War Macon*, 88–90; Macon *Telegraph*, May 24, 1861, June 12, 1861, April 18, 1862.

[62] Macon *Telegraph*, July 13, 1863, February 24, 1864, July 15, 1864; Mobile (AL) *Advertiser and Register*, June 14, 1863; Bailey, *Music and the Southern Belle*, 59;

[63] Macon *Telegraph*, July 15, 1864; New Orleans *Times-Picayune*, August 12, 1861; E. Lawrence Abel, *Singing the New Nation: How Music Shaped the Confederacy, 1861–1865* (Mechanicsburg, PA: Stackpole Books, 2000) 52–67.

[64] *Georgia Telegraph*, June 21, 1861, July 6, 1861; Iobst, *Civil War Macon*, 88–89; *A Hundred Years of Music in America: An Account of Musical Efforts in America*, ed. W. S. B. Matthews (Philadelphia: Theodore Presser, 1900) 76–77.

[65] *The Musical Courier* 23/1 (July 1, 1891): 310; *Our War Songs: North and South* (Cleveland, OH: S. Brainards' Sons, 1887) 20.

[66] Macon *Telegraph*, March 24, 1865; *The Illustrated Sporting and Dramatic News* II (October 3, 1875–March 27, 1875): 371.

CHAPTER 2

[1] Macon *Telegraph*, May 21, 1866.

[2] "Macon, Bibb County, Georgia," *Report of the Social Statistics of Cities: Southern and Western States*, comp. George E. Waring Jr. (Washington, DC: Government Printing Office, 1887) 169–72; Macon *Telegraph*, May 21, 1866. Andrew W. Manis, *Macon in Black and White: An Unutterable Separation in the American Century* (Macon, GA: Mercer University Press and the Tubman African American Museum, 2004) 15–22.

[3] Macon *Telegraph*, January 27, 1866, February 14, 1866, March 7, 1866, March 9, 1866.

[4] Ibid., July 6, 1865, January 6, 1902; *Atlanta Constitution*, January 19, 1885; *New York Herald*, January 6, 1902. There are some variations of the names of the original Georgia Minstrels in later published sources. For instance, Aleck Jacobs is sometimes listed as "Alex" and Andrew Gospel is listed in some later accounts as "Andrew Wood," apparently because a physician named Wood owned him before

the Civil War. Similarly, Henry Fields may be a man who is listed in some sources as Henry Ayers. As for William H. Lee, he is listed in some sources as having achieved the rank of captain during the Civil War, while other state that he was mustered out at Macon as a sergeant.

[5] David Monod, *The Soul of Pleasure: Sentiment and Sensation in Nineteenth-Century American Mass Entertainment* (Ithaca, NY: Cornell University Press, 2016) 208; Cleveland *Daily Leader*, October 24, 1865, October 25, 1865; Fremont (OH) *Weekly Journal*, October 13, 1865; Buffalo (NY) *Daily Courier*, November 11, 1865.

[6] Monod, *The Soul of Pleasure*, 208; Eileen Southern, *The Music of Black Americans: A History* 3rd ed. (New York: W. W. Norton and Co., 1997) 232; *The Cambridge History of American Music*, ed. David Nichols (Cambridge, UK: Cambridge University Press, 1998) 131; Macon *Telegraph*, January 20, 1918; *New York Herald*, May 26, 1889.

[7] Macon *Telegraph*, August 2, 1866, October 29, 1866, September 24, 1866.

[8] Ibid., December 8, 1869.

[9] Ibid., August 2, 1866, January 8, 1869, January 28, 1869; Atlanta *Constitution*, January 22, 1869.

[10] Macon *Telegraph*, July 2, 1869, May 16, 1873, June 5, 1877, June 12, 1877, May 15, 1878.

[11] Journal of the Senate of the State of Georgia at the Annual Session of the General Assembly, Commencing at Atlanta, January 14, 1874 (Atlanta: J. H. Estill, 1874) 249; Georgia Civil War Correspondence, Adjutant General, Letterbooks, 1860, 1909, 22/1/1/, Incoming Correspondence, 1861–1914, 22/1/17, Georgia State Archives, Morrow, Georgia; Ancestry.com; US Passport Applications 1795–1925, accessed May 24, 2018; Raleigh (NC) *Spirit of the Age*, March 22, 1855; *Baltimore Sun*, September 7, 1857; *Richmond (VA) Enquirer*, August 5, 1859.

[12] Macon *Telegraph*, September 8, 1879, May 24, 1882, June 20, 1896, June 23, 1913.

[13] Macon *Telegraph*, July 4, 1886, March 23, 1894, November 2, 1896; *Atlanta Constitution*, May 16, 1901; *The Bulletin of the Catholic Laymen's Association of Georgia*, February 21, 1942.

[14] Macon *Telegraph*, April 22, 1889, April 15, 1906, May 10, 1914. *The Bulletin of the Catholic Laymen's Association of Georgia*, February 21, 1942.

[15] *Savannah (GA) Daily Advertiser*, October 11, 1874; Macon *Telegraph*, April 5, 1874, April 12, 1874, April 16, 1874. Octavia Hensel was the stage and pen name of Mary Alice Ives Seymour (1837–1897). For more information on her life and career, see Francis Elizabeth Willard and Mary Ashton Rice Livermore, *A Woman of the Century: Fourteen Hundred-Seventy Biographical Sketches Accompanied by Portraits of Leading American Women in All Walks of Life* (New York: Charles Wells Moulton, 1893) 294–95.

[16] Macon *Telegraph*, December 13, 1874, April 2, 1880, March 17, 1898, March 15, 1903, April 4, 1903; *Boston Globe*, December 2, 1893.

[17] Steinhaus, "Music in the Cultural Life in Macon, 1823–1900," 102.

[18] Macon *Telegraph*, September 10, 1880, July, 17, 1897.

[19] Ibid., December 31, 1873.

[20] Ibid., March 13, 1874, April 3, 1875, April 12, 1876, January 16, 1880, September 18, 1918, November 11, 1920.

[21] Ibid., March 11, 1874.

[22] Ibid., May 28, 1874, March 7, 1882.

[23] Steinhaus, "Music in the Cultural Life in Macon, 1823–1900," 94–95; Macon *Telegraph*, March 1, 1870, April 1, 1873, October 20, 1874, October 25, 1877, October 26, 1877, March 22, 1886, September 9, 1887, April 23, 1891, January 6, 1896.

[24] Macon *Telegraph*, December 6, 1877, January 11, 1878, January 27, 1878, January 29, 1878, April 28, 1878, June 6, 1878, June 18, 1878, January 6, 1902.

[25] Ibid., November 5, 1873, July 27, 1878, July 21, 1880, November 9, 1880, November 25, 1902; *Atlanta Constitution*, October 6, 1930.

[26] Rice, *Monarchs of Minstrelsy*, 283; Press Club of Chicago, *The Scoop* 4/1 (January 2, 1915): 298; Macon *Telegraph*, December 2, 1879, January 6, 1902, October 29, 1911, December 27, 1911, January 22, 1919, June 1, 1923, May 5, 1924; *Charlotte (NC) News*, March 10, 1920, April 2, 1920; *Cleveland (OH) Plain Dealer*, August 5, 1886; *Chicago Tribune*, December 14, 1936; *New York Times*, December 14, 1936.

[27] Macon *Telegraph*, March 21, 1871, December 10, 1878.

[28] Steinhaus, "Music in the Cultural Life in Macon, 1823–1900," 89–91; Macon *Telegraph*, January 16, 1880, May 25, 1884, September 23, 1884, September 26, 1884.

[29] Macon *Telegraph*, September 19, 1884, September 23, 1884.

[30] Steinhaus, "Music in the Cultural Life in Macon, 1823–1900," 95–96; Macon *Telegraph*, August 17, 1871, August 20, 1880, January 14, 1886, January 17, 1888.

[31] Interstate Directory Company, *Directory of the City of Macon and County Gazetteer of Bibb County for 1884* (Atlanta: H. H. Dickson, 1884) 334; Macon *Telegraph*, September 23, 1883, March 17, 1895, August 21, 1897, August 22, 1897.

[32] Macon *Telegraph*, April 4, 1880, June 22, 1880, May 21, 1880, June 22, 1880, April 22, 1885; *Scientific American* (February 28, 1891): 130.

[33] United States Department of the Interior, National Park Service, National Register of Historic Places Registration Form, Ingleside Historic District, Macon, Bibb County, Georgia, 16; Macon *Telegraph*, May 31, 1907; *Atlanta Constitution*, August 17, 1917.

[34] Macon *Telegraph*, August 26, 1883, November 20, 1883, June 24, 1894, May 9, 1904; *Atlanta Constitution*, June 12, 1887, March 23, 1900.

[35] Wesleyan Female College, *Annual Catalogue of Wesleyan Female College, Macon, Georgia, 1899–1900* (Atlanta: Foote and Davies Co., 1900) 6, 42; Macon *Telegraph*, August 13, 1899.

[36] Harrell, *Kith and Kin*, 87; Macon *Telegraph*, August 13, 1899, July 5, 1903, July 12, 1903, August 13, 1903, September 3, 1905, September 5, 1905.

[37] Macon *Telegraph*, August 12, 1894, February 19, 1895, February 21, 1895, August 7, 1896, July 15, 1902.

[38] *Tampa (FL) Tribune*, December 13, 1907; *Paducah (KY) Sun*, October 19, 1907; *Atlanta Constitution*, December 16, 1946.

[39] "Bobby Burns Meets Many Former 11:45s," *Billboard* 58/52 (December 28, 1946): 65; R. L. Polk and Co., *Polk's Macon (Bibb County, Ga.) City Directory, 1946–1947* (Richmond, VA: R. L. Polk and Co., 1946) 206; *Atlanta Constitution*, December 16, 1946. The article on Dan Holt's death that appears in the *Atlanta Constitution* on December 16, 1946, lists his first name as David rather than Daniel, which is apparently an error on the part of the newspaper.

[40] Steinhaus, "Music in the Cultural Life in Macon, 1823–1900," 94–95; Macon *Telegraph*, February 10, 1895, June 7, 1897, August 13, 1897, July 24, 1898, September 11, 1898, December 12, 1898.

[41] Macon *Telegraph*, April 17, 1896, August 15, 1897, October 21, 1897, January 4, 1898, February 3, 1898.

[42] Ibid., August 17, 1896, August 18, 1896, August 19, 1898, August 14, 1897, November 16, 1897, June 19, 1901; *Atlanta Constitution*, November 21, 1897.

[43] Wesleyan Female College, *Annual Catalogue of Wesleyan Female College and Wesleyan Conservatory of Music*, Macon, Georgia 1904–1905 (Atlanta: Foote and Davies Co., 1905) 7, 56–57; Macon *Telegraph*, February 25, 1903.

[44] Inger Winther Scobie, *Center Stage: Helen Gahagan Douglas, A Life* (New York: Oxford University Press, 1992) 60–62; *The Nebraska Teacher* 20 (September 1917): 168–75; Macon *Telegraph*, September 22, 1900, February 25, 1903.

[45] Macon *Telegraph*, December 11, 1904.

[46] *Atlanta Constitution*, April 7, 1905; St. Louis Post-Dispatch, June 14, 1935; Los Angeles Times, June 14, 1935; The Nebraska Teacher 20 (September 1917): 175.

[47] United States Census, 1880, Pawnee County, Kansas; *Lincoln (NE) Journal-Star*, May 8, 1897; *Larned (KS) Eagle-Optic*, August 9, 1895.

[48] *Lincoln (NE) Journal-Star*, May 8, 1897; *Atlanta Constitution*, March 26, 1905, April 14, 1905; Macon *Telegraph*, December 11, 1904; *Danville (VA) Bee*, June 9, 1924; *Musical America* 24/24 (October 14, 1916) 121.

[49] United States Department of the Interior, National Park Service, National Register of Historic Places Registration Form, Grand Opera House, Macon, Bibb County, Georgia, 2–3; Macon *Telegraph*, January 16, 1904, September 4, 1904, January 2, 1905, January 22, 1905, February 3, 1905.

[50] Lynn Abbott and Doug Seroff, *Out of Sight: The Rise of African American Popular Music, 1889–1895* (Jackson: University Press of Mississippi, 2002) 438; Frank Cullen, *Vaudeville Old and New: An Encyclopedia of Variety Performances in America, vol. 1* (New York: Routledge, 2006) 116. Macon *Telegraph*, January 20, 1895, January 25, 1900; *Atlanta Constitution*, April 15, 1900; New York Age, December 30, 1909.

[51] Macon *Telegraph*, April 22, 1856, February 11, 1873, July 28, 1874, July 3, 1885.

[52] Ibid., December 12, 1906, June 1, 1907, May 15, 1918.

[53] Ibid., June 21, 1895, April 21, 1896, March 30, 1918, April 11, 1918, April 2, 1920.

[54] Court Carnet, *Cuttin' Up: How Early Jazz Got America's Ear* (Lawrence: University of Kansas Press, 2009) 16; Susan Curtis, *Dancing to a Black Man's Tune: A Life of Scott Joplin* (Columbia: University of Missouri Press, 1994) 68–71; Emily Epstein Landau, *Spectacular Wickedness: Sex, Race, and Memory in Storyville, New Orleans* (Baton Rouge: Louisiana State University Press, 2013) 19–29.

[55] David A. Jasen and Gene Jones, *That American Rag: The Story of Ragtime from Coast to Coast* (New York: Schirmer Books, 2000) 169–70. Macon *Telegraph*, July, 31, 1908, February 21, 1909.

[56] Macon *Telegraph*, November 17, 1912, November 24, 1912; *Macon News*, November 1, 1942; Macon Morning Music Club History, Subject Files, Middle Georgia Archives, Washington Memorial Library, Macon, Georgia.

[57] Macon Morning Music Club History, Subject Files, Middle Georgia Archives; Macon *Telegraph*, June 8, 1913, December 12, 1915; Dorothy Blount Lamar, *When All Is Said and Done* (Athens: University of Georgia Press, 1952) 252.

[58] Macon Morning Music Club History, Subject Files, Middle Georgia Archives.

[59] C. H. Douglass, "Managing a Negro Theater," *Report of the 16th Annual Convention of the Negro Business League* (Bethesda, MD: University Publications of America, 1994) 184–88.

[60] Lynn Abbott and Doug Seroff, *The Emergence of the Blues in African American Vaudeville: 1899–1926* (Jackson: University Press of Mississippi, 2017) 28–32.

[61] Ibid.; Lynn Abbott and Doug Seroff, *Ragged but Right, Black Travelling Shows, "Coon Songs" and the Dark Pathway to Blues and Jazz* (Jackson: University Press of Mississippi, 2007) 292–300, 377; Macon *Telegraph*, June 4, 1905.

[62] C. H. Douglass, "Managing a Negro Theater," Report of the 16th Annual Convention of the Negro Business League, 184–88.

[63] Ibid.; Abbott and Seroff, *Emergence of the Blues*, 289–95.

[64] John Strausbaugh, *Black Like You: Blackface, Whiteface, Insult & Imitation in American Popular Culture* (New York: Penguin Group, 2006) 138–39; Christine Acham, *Revolution Televised: Prime Time and the Struggle for Black Power* (University of Minnesota Press, 2004) xii–xiv; Lynn Abbot and Doug Seroff, *"They Cert'ly*

Sound Good to Me': Sheet Music, Southern Vaudeville, and the Commercial Ascendancy of the Blues," in Ramblin on My Mind: New Perspectives of the Blues, ed. David Evans (Champaign: University of Illinois Press, 2008) 49–50.

[65] Manis, *Macon Black and White*, 63–66; Macon *Telegraph*, July 30, 1922, July 31, 1922, August 1, 1922, August 2, 1922, August 3, 1922; *Augusta Chronicle*, July 30, 1922; *Atlanta Constitution*, August 3, 1922; *Tampa (FL) Tribune*, August 2, 1922, August 3, 1922; *Greenville (SC) News*, August 2, 1922.

[66] Andrew M. Manis, *Macon Black and White*, 63–66;

[67] Abbott and Seroff, *Emergence of the Blues*, 30–31.

[68] Abbott and Seroff, *Ragged but Right*, 353; *Billboard* (October 17, 1942): 27.

[69] Doris Lanier, "Early Chautauqua in Georgia," *Journal of American Culture* 11/3 (Fall 1988): 14–16; Macon *Telegraph*, July 13, 1903, April 1, 1905.

[70] Macon *Telegraph*, April 24, 1914, June 21, 1914; *Musical Courier*.

[71] Macon *Telegraph*, September 3, 1912, November 9, 1912, March 5, 1913, September 19, 1913, December 14, 1913, January 1, 1914, May 19, 1915, May 23, 1915; Atlanta *Constitution*, June 27, 1915, November 30, 1935.

CHAPTER 3

[1] Macon *Telegraph*, March 21, 1912, January 31, 1919, May 2, 1920, July 11, 1920.

[2] *Mercer Cluster*, March 31, 1922.

[3] Macon *Telegraph*, August 17, 1918, November 19, 1922; *Mercer Cluster*, March 31, 1922, November 17, 1922; University of Oregon, *General Registry of the University of Oregon, 1873–1910* (Eugene: University of Oregon, 1911) 29.

[4] *Mercer Cluster*, November 10, 1922, April 10, 1925, May 2, 1925; *Atlanta Constitution*, March 8, 1925. Mercer University, *Mercer University Bulletin*, 1926–1927 (Macon, GA: The J. W. Burke Company, 1927) 35.

[5] *Atlanta Constitution*, April 17, 1930, September 23, 1937; *Greenville (SC) News*, April 12, 1936; Nashville *Tennessean*, April 19, 1936; *Greenwood (MS) Commonwealth*, May 22, 1937; *McComb (MS) Enterprise-Journal*, June 10, 1938.

[6] William Christopher Handy, *Father of the Blues: An Autobiography* (New York: Da Capo Press, 1969) 93–94; Ellis Cashmore, *The Black Culture Industry* (New York: Routledge, 1997) 37.

[7] Linda Dahl, *Stormy Weather: The Music and Lives of a Century of Jazzwomen* (New York: Pantheon Books, 1984) 111–18; Chip Deffaa, *Voices of the Jazz Age: Profiles of Eight Vintage Jazzmen* (Champaign: University of Illinois Press, 1992) 6–12. For further information on Gertrude "Ma" Rainey, see Sandra R. Lieb, *Mother of the Blues: A Study of Ma Rainey* (Amherst: University of Massachusetts Press, 1981); Russell Sanjek, *American Popular Music and Its Business: The First Four Hundred Years*, vol. II (New York: Oxford University Press, 1988) 31; and Scott Yanow, *Jazz on Record: The First Sixty Years* (San Francisco: Backbeat Books, 2003) 14–15.

[8] Len Kunstadt, "The Lucille Hegamin Story, Part 1" *Record Research* 39 (November 1961): 3–5. The Freeman-Harper-Muse stock company was formed by George Freeman, Leonard Harper, and Clarence Muse in Jacksonville, Florida, in 1912. For more information, see Bernard L. Peterson Jr., *The African American Theater Directory, 1916–1960: A Comprehensive Guide to Early Black Theater Organizations, Companies, Theaters, and Performing Groups* (Westport, CT: Greenwood Press, 1997) 74.

[9] Linda Dahl, *Stormy Weather: The Music and Lives of a Century of Jazzwomen* (New York: Limelight Editions, 1984), 106–108; Kunstadt, "Hegamin, Part 1," 4–7.

[10] *Encyclopedia of the Harlem Renaissance*, vol. 1, eds. Cary D. Wintz and Paul Finkelman (New York: Routledge, 2004) 550; Kunstadt, "Hegamin, Part 1," 4–7; *Pittsburgh Press*, August 21, 1921; *Montgomery (AL) Advertiser*, May 29, 1921.

[11] Kunstadt, "Hegamin, Part 1," 4–7; Len Kunstadt, "The Lucille Hegamin Story, Part 2," *Record Research* 40 (January 1962): 3–4; *The Music Trades* 26/22 (November 26, 1921): 27; *Brooklyn (NY) Daily Eagle*, May 23, 1922; Glen Falls (NY) *Post Star*, August 22, 1922; *Mauch Chunk (PA) Times-News*, August 3, 1921.

[12] Len Kunstadt, "The Lucille Hegamin Story, Part 3" *Record Research* 41 (February 1962): 4–5; Len Kunstadt, "The Lucille Hegamin Story, Part 4" *Record Research* 43 (May 1962): 6–7. While Bill and Lucille Hegamin split during the 1920s, their divorce may not have been legally formalized until 1938. For more information, see: *China Monthly Review* 84 (May 1938): 261.

[13] *Encyclopedia of the Harlem Renaissance*, vol. 1, 550; Len Kunstadt, "Lucille Hegamin's Last Performance," *Record Research* 104 (March 1970): 3; Scott Yanow, *Classic Jazz* (San Francisco: Back Beat Books, 2001) 101.

[14] Peterson Jr., African American Theater Directory, 74; Bernard L. Peterson Jr., *A Century of Musicals in Black and White: An Encyclopedia of Musical Stage Works By, About, or Involving African Americans* (Westport, CT: Greenwood Press, 1993) 332; New York Age, September 9, 1915.

[15] *New York Age*, March 26, 1921, May 27, 1922; *Uniontown (PA) Morning Herald*, September 24, 1920; *Baltimore Afro-American*, June 24, 1921, March 7, 1924, August 14, 1926; *Muncie (IN) Evening Press*, August 10, 1921, Washington (DC) *Evening Star*, June 11, 1922; *Pittsburgh Courier*, August 16, 1924; *Atlanta Constitution*, July 1, 1925, July 5, 1925; *Encyclopedia of the Harlem Renaissance*, vol. 2, eds. Cary D. Wintz and Paul Finkelman (New York: Routledge, 2004) 796–97. There are conflicting records related to the age of Lula Whidby (whose first name is occasionally listed as "Lulu"). Various census records indicate that she was born in 1892, 1893, and 1898. Her death certificate states that she died August 4, 1926, at the age of twenty-eight. For more information, see United States Census, Bibb County, Georgia, 1900, 1910, 1920; "Lula Whidby," Certificate of Death, Commonwealth of Virginia, August 4, 1926.

[16] While the date of death on Whidby's death certificate is likely accurate, the document contains errors that seem to indicate that the informant had limited knowledge of her background. It states that she was born in Macon, Georgia, but lists the name of her father incorrectly and no name for her mother. Whidby's last name is also misspelled "Whitby" on the document. See "Lula Whidby," Certificate of Death, Commonwealth of Virginia, August 4, 1926; *Baltimore Afro-American*, August 14, 1926.

[17] Bill C. Malone, *Country Music, U.S.A.* (Austin: University of Texas Press, 1968) 14–15.

[18] Ibid., 4; Norm Cohen, *Long Steel Rail: The Railroad in American Folksong*, 2nd ed. (Champaign: University of Illinois Press, 2000) 26.

[19] Joseph Harris, *The Ballad and Oral Literature* (Cambridge, MA: Harvard University Press, 1991) 46–47; David Evans, *Big Road Blues: Tradition and Creativity in Folk Blues* (New York: Da Capo Press, 1987) 44–45.

[20] United States Census, 1900, Bibb County, Georgia; United States Census, 1910, Bibb County, Georgia; United States Census, 1920, Bibb County, Georgia; Macon *Telegraph*, August 25, 1920; *Charlotte (NC) Observer*, February 6, 1921; St. Petersburg (FL) *Tampa Bay Times*, March 20, 1921; *Columbus (GA) Daily Enquirer*, May 15, 1921.

[21] Richard Carlin, *Country Music: A Biographical Dictionary* (New York: Routledge, 2003) 264.

[22] Charles R. Townsend, *San Antonio Rose: The Life and Music of Bob Wills* (Urbana: University of Illinois Press, 1986) 59; Nick Tosches, "The Strange and Hermetical Case of Emmett Miller," *The Journal of Country Music* 17 (1995): 39–47; Carlin, *Country Music*, 264.

[23] Tosches, "Emmett Miller," 39–47; Nick Tosches, *Where Dead Voices Gather* (New York: Little Brown and Company, 2001) 293; Carlin, *Country Music*, 264; Macon *Telegraph*, March 31, 1962.

[24] Jo Nardolillo, *All Things Strings: An Illustrated Dictionary* (New York: Rowen and Littlefield, 2014) 90; Mark Brend, *Strange Sounds: Offbeat Instruments and Sonic Experiments in Pop* (San Francisco: Backbeat Books, 2005) 115–16; Tony Russell, *Country Music Originals: The Legends and the Lost* (New York, Oxford University Press, 2004) 55–57.

[25] South Georgia Highballers, "Bibb County Grind," Okeh Records, New York City, 1927.

[26] Tony Russell, *Country Music Recordings: A Discography* (New York: Oxford University Press, 2004) 859–60; Ross Laird and Brian Rust, *Discography of Okeh Records, 1918–1934* (Westport, CT: Praeger, 2004) 12; *Atlanta Constitution*, March 22, 1927, October 2, 1927, October 8, 1927; Macon *Telegraph*, January 20, 1928.

[27] Augusta (GA) *Chronical*, June 20, 1908.

[28] *Atlanta Constitution*, October 22, 1915; *Stars of Country Music: Uncle Dave Macon to Johnny Rodriguez*, eds. Bill C. Malone and Judith McCulloh (Urbana: University of Illinois Press, 1975) 29–30; *Exploring Roots Music: Twenty Years of the JEMF Quarterly*, ed. Nolan Porterfield (Lanham, MD: Scarecrow Press, 2004) 143–45.

[29] Michael Gray, *Hand Me My Travelin' Shoes: In Search of Blind Willie McTell* (Chicago: Chicago Review Press, 2009) 42, 115, 148, 163,168, 169, 172.

[30] Ibid., 168, 169, 172; Alan Paul, *One Way Out: The Inside Story of the Allman Brothers Band* (New York: St. Martin's Griffin, 2014) 5–6. Musician Taj Mahal covered "Statesboro Blues" in 1968, and it was apparently this version of McTell's song that inspired members of the Allman Brothers Band.

[31] United States Census, Bibb County, Georgia, 1850; United States Census, Bibb County, Georgia, 1860, United States Census, Bibb County, Georgia, 1870; United States Census, Bibb County, Georgia, 1880; United States Census, Bibb County, Georgia, 1900; United States Census, Bibb County, Georgia, 1910; United States, Selective Service System. *World War I Selective Service System Draft Registration Cards, 1917–1918*. Washington, DC: National Archives and Records Administration, Registration County: Bibb County, Georgia Registration, Roll: *1557085*; R. L. Polk and Co., *Macon City Directory, 1914*, vol. 10 (Detroit: R. L. Polk and Co., 1914) 540; Macon *Telegraph*, September 16, 1912, January 1, 1928; Library of Congress, *Catalogue of Copyright Entries, Part 3: Musical Publications*, vol. 2 (Washington, DC: Government Printing Office, 1916) 1583; Georgia Adjutant General's Office. World War I Statements of Service Cards. Georgia State Archives, Morrow, Georgia.

[32] Macon *Telegraph*, December 26, 1920, January 1, 1928; *Paxton (IL) Record*, November 29, 1923; Library of Congress, *Catalogue of Copyright Entries, Part 3: Musical Publications*, vol. 18, part 2, nos. 8–13 (Washington, DC: Government Printing Office, 1924) 1418.

[33] New York State Census, 1925; R. L. Polk and Co., *Jacksonville City Directory*, 1929 (Detroit: R. L. Polk and Co., 1929) 631; United States Census, Harrison County, Mississippi, 1940; *Biloxi (MS) Daily Herald*, February 10, 1943; Historical Register of National Homes for Disabled Volunteer Soldiers, 1866–1938; (National Archives Microfilm Publication M1749, 282 rolls); Records of the Department of Veterans Affairs, Record Group 15; National Archives, Washington, DC; Interment Control Forms, 1928–1962. Interment Control Forms, A1 2110–B. Records of the Office of the Quartermaster General, 1774–1985, Record Group 92. The National Archives at College Park, College Park, Maryland.

[34] United States Department of the Interior, National Park Service, National Register of Historic Places Registration Form, Municipal Auditorium, Macon, Bibb County, Georgia, 2–4; Macon *Telegraph*, April 6, 1922; *Atlanta Constitution*, March 15, 1920, December 7, 1924, August 24, 1925, November 23, 1925.

[35] United States Department of the Interior, National Park Service, National Register of Historic Places Registration Form, Municipal Auditorium, Macon, Bibb County, Georgia, 2; Macon *Telegraph*, August 9, 2014; *Atlanta Constitution*, November 8, 1925.

[36] *Atlanta Constitution*, December 25, 1927, January 1, 1928, January 7, 1928, January 15, 1928; Perry (GA) *Houston Home Journal*, December 22, 1927.

[37] Macon *Telegraph*, June 4, 1907, June 23, 1917, August 19, 1922, August 22, 1922, August 24, 1922; *Miami News*, March 3, 1914; *Atlanta Constitution*, November 21, 1916, October 7, 1924; *Richmond (VA) Times Dispatch*, April 14, 1922; *Hickory (NC) Daily Record*, September 18, 1922.

[38] *Atlanta Constitution*, October 7, 1924, January 13, 1926; Macon *Telegraph*, September 13, 1922; *Oakland (CA) Tribune*, January 14, 1926; *McAllen (TX) Daily Press*, September 4, 1935.

[39] *Pittsburgh Courier*, April 19, 1941.

[40] Macon *Telegraph*, April 14, 1939, April 16, 1939, April 7, 1940, April 4, 1941.

[41] Abbott and Seroff, *Ragged but Right*, 353: *Billboard* (October 17, 1942): 27; *Macon News*, October 4, 1942.

[42] Brooklyn (NY) *Daily Eagle*, October 30, 1949; *Pensacola (FL) News Journal*, January 11, 1914; *Dayton (OH) Herald*, October 3, 1934.

[43] *Pittsburgh Press*, March 6, 1932; *Chicago Tribune*, January 30, 1955; *Honolulu Star-Bulletin*, January 28, 1933.

[44] Karen L. Cox, *Dreaming of Dixie: How the South Was Created in American Popular Culture* (Chapel Hill: University of North Carolina Press, 2011) 71–71; Honolulu Star-Bulletin, January 28, 1933; *Atlanta Constitution*, February 20, 1948; Chicago Tribune, January 1, 1937.

[45] *Georgia Biographical Dictionary*, 1999–2000, vol. 1 (St. Clair Shores, MI: Somerset Publishers, 1999) 416–18; *Atlanta Constitution*, February 20, 1948; *Miami News*, November 20, 1952; New York *Daily News*, October 21, 1951, April 17, 1955; *Chicago Tribune*, January 9, 1949, January 30, 1955; Scranton (PA) *Times Tribune*, January 25, 1955; *Los Angeles Times*, February 25, 1992; Allentown (PA) *Morning Call*, November 7, 1995.

[46] *Macon News*, November 21, 1940, January 27, 1946, November 8, 1946.

[47] Ibid., January 27, 1946, November 8, 1946; Macon *Telegraph*, April 6, 2011; Rochester (NY) *Democrat and Chronicle*, January 24, 1944.

[48] Macon *Telegraph*, April 6, 2011.

[49] Macon *Telegraph*, January 25, 1946; Michael Whorf, *America's Popular Song Lyricists: Oral Histories, 1920s–1960s* (Jefferson, NC: McFarland and Company, 2012) 79.

[50] Macon *Telegraph*, January 27, 1946, January 12, 1947, January 19, 1947; St. Petersburg (FL) *Tampa Bay Times*, July 21, 1946.

[51] Macon *Telegraph,* March 23, 1947; *Jackson (TN) Sun,* March 12, 1947; *St. Joseph (MO) Journal,* March 7, 1947; *Atlanta Constitution,* June 4, 1950; New York *Daily News,* March 27, 1949; *Tampa (FL) Tribune,* June 26, 1950; *Miami News,* June 11, 1949, September 11, 1951, November 1, 1956, December 7, 1957, August 22, 1958.

[52] United States Census, Bibb County, Georgia, 1920; United States Census, Cuyahoga County, Ohio, 1930; *Cincinnati (OH) Enquirer,* October 12, 1933; Larry Kemp, *Modern Jazz Trumpet Legends* (Pittsburgh: RoseDog Books, 2018) 164–65; Scott Yanow, *Trumpet Kings: The Players Who Shaped the Sound of Jazz Trumpet* (San Francisco: Backbeat Books, 2001) 55–56.

[53] *Honolulu Advertiser,* February 22, 1945; Kemp, *Modern Jazz,* 164–65; Yanow, *Trumpet Kings,* 55–56; Buck Clayton, *Buck Clayton's Jazz World* (Oxford, UK: Bayou Press, Ltd., 1986) 173.

[54] Mercer University, Catalogue 1909–1910 and Announcements, 1910–1911, Mercer University, Macon, Georgia (Atlanta: The Index Printing Company, 1910) 68.

[55] Blakeley (GA) *Early County News,* March 22, 1923; *Mercer Cluster,* October 14, 1921, April 21, 1922, October 17, 1924.

[56] Pi Kappa Phi, "The Star and Lamp of Pi Kappa Phi," 35/2 (August, 1949): 23; Wesleyan College (Macon, GA) *Watchtower,* May 1, 1931.

[57] Buffalo (NY) Commercial, February 3, 1892; Buffalo Morning Express and Illustrated Buffalo Express, May 3, 1893.

[58] Ibid.; Washington Post, March 7, 1907; Asheville (NC) *Citizen-Times,* January 6, 1906; *International Who's Who in Music and Musical Gazetteer: A Contemporary Biographical Dictionary and a Record of the World's Musical Activity,* ed. Cesar Saerchinger (New York: Current Literature Publishing Company, 1914) 397.

[59] Macon *Telegraph,* May 30, 1914; *Atlanta Constitution,* January 21, 1906; *Musical Courier, A Weekly Journal* 72/1 (January 6, 1916): 64. The reference to Maerz taking "a great fancy to Macon" as a young man might be a reference to an appearance he made in the area with Rosa Linde's Great Opera Company in 1906.

[60] *International Who's Who in Music and Musical Gazetteer,* 397; *Musical America,* 31/3 (November 15, 1919): 111; Macon *Telegraph,* April 5, 1922.

[61] Macon *Telegraph,* April 5, 1922.

[62] George David Anderson, "A City Comes of Age: An Urban Study of Macon, Georgia During the 1920s" (Master's Thesis, Georgia College, 1975) 44; *Atlanta Constitution,* January 30, 1932, March 2, 1932, May 29, 1932, July 14, 1940.

[63] Titus Brown, "A New England Missionary and African-American Education in Macon: Raymond G. Von Tobel at Ballard Normal School, 1908–1935," *The Georgia Historical Quarterly* 82/2 (Summer 1998): 290–94.

[64] *Macon's Black Heritage: The Untold Story* (Macon, GA: Tubman African American Museum, 1997) 67–69; United States Census, Bibb County, Georgia, 1900, 1910, 1920, 1930.

[65] Macon *Telegraph*, November 1, 1948, June 9, 1950; *Macon's Black Heritage*, 67–69.

[66] *Asbury Park (NJ) Press*, August 23, 1923, July 23, 1927, July 27, 1928, April 11, 1932, March 22, 1953, August 28, 1955; Abbott and Seroff, *Emergence of the Blues*, 306. Various birth years can be found in records pertaining to Reece DuPree, but his World War I draft registration card, which he signed in 1918 while living in New York, stated that his date of birth was July 18, 1881.

[67] *Billboard* 54/9 (February 28, 1942): 9; *Billboard* 56/11 (March 11, 1944): 11; Abbott and Seroff, *Emergence of the Blues*, 306–307.

[68] *Mercer Cluster*, February 10, 1939; *Billboard* 55/49 (December 4, 1943).

[69] Macon *Telegraph*, September 6, 1938.

[70] Lawrence McClellan Jr., *The Later Swing Era, 1942 to 1955* (Westport, CT: Greenwood Press, 2004) 5; *The Cambridge Companion to Blues and Gospel Music*, ed. Allan Moore (Cambridge, UK: Cambridge University Press, 2003) 93.

[71] Macon *Telegraph*, January 15, 1933, July 17, 1933, July 19, 1933, July 17, 1940, July 24, 1940, July 25, 1940; Manis, *Macon Black and White*, 113.

[72] Newport News (VA) *Daily Press*, January 29, 1951.

[73] Philadelphia *Daily News*, May 13, 1963; Preston Lauterbach, *The Chitlin Circuit and the Road to Rock 'n' Roll* (New York: W. W. Norton & Co., 2011) 149.

[74] James H. Cone, *The Spirituals and the Blues: An Interpretation* (New York: Seabury Press, 1971) 5.

[75] Macon *Telegraph*, November 16, 1906, August 23, 1909, August 25, 1912, September 21, 1914, July 4, 1916; *Savannah (GA) Tribune*, May 16, 1908; *Atlanta Constitution*, January 18, 1906; Baltimore *Afro-American*, August 29, 1925; United States Census, Bibb County, Georgia, 1910, 1920, 1930.

[76] Macon *Telegraph*, November 4, 1935, November 5, 1935.

[77] Fort Valley State College, *The Peachite* 3/3 (June 1, 1945): 12; *Chicago Defender*, January 29, 1938; *Pittsburgh Courier*, January 29, 1938, March 29, 1938, November 7, 1959, March 19, 1960; *Norfolk (VA) New Journal and Guide*, March 22, 1941, January 15, 1944, June 10, 1944; *Atlanta Daily World*, March 25, 1938.

[78] *More Than Precious Memories: The Rhetoric of Southern Gospel Music*, eds. Michael P. Graves and David Fillingim (Macon, GA: Mercer University Press, 2004) 10; Don Cusic, *The Sound of Light: A History of Gospel and Christian Music* (Milwaukee, WI: Hal Leonard Corporation, 1990) 154–56. James R. Goff, *Close Harmony: A History of Southern Gospel* (Chapel Hill: University of North Carolina Press, 2002) 198–200.

[79] *Macon News*, March 28, 1943; Macon *Telegraph*, May 13, 1946.

[80] *Macon News*, December 19, 1941, March 28, 1943; Macon *Telegraph* November 29, 1942.

[81] Macon *Telegraph*, September 17, 1978; *Macon News*, December 30, 1951.

[82] Macon *Telegraph*, September 17, 1978, October 10, 2013.

[83] Ibid., September 17, 1978.

[84] Ibid., March 9, 1946, December 6, 1947, May 10, 1992.

[85] Ibid., May 10, 1992; Shreveport (LA) *Times*, July 23, 1948; *Marshall (TX) News*, April 29, 1948; *Camden (AR) News*, August 11, 1948; Bonnye Stuart, *It Happened in Louisiana: Remarkable Events That Shaped History* (Lanham, MD: Rowman & Littlefield, 2015) 116–19; Tracey E. W. Laird, *Louisiana Hayride: Radio and Roots Music Along the Red River* (New York: Oxford University Press, 2005) 8–9; Ron Yule, *Louisiana Fiddlers* (Jackson: University Press of Mississippi, 2009) 307–308.

[86] Macon *Telegraph*, May 10, 1992. While the Mercer Brothers radio program ran primarily on WMAZ, through the years it also aired on WIBB, WNEX, and WDEN.

[87] Wayne W. Daniel, *Pickin' on Peachtree: A History of Country Music in Atlanta, Georgia* (Urbana: University of Illinois Press, 1990) 200–201.

[88] United States Census, Bibb County, Georgia, 1920, 1930; *Macon News*, March 29, 1928; Macon *Telegraph*, January 19, 1987.

[89] Macon *Telegraph*, May 3, 1936, January 19, 1987.

[90] Ibid., May 22, 1940, October 14, 1940, October 16, 1940, April 20, 1945, April 22, 1945, November 23, 1950; *Macon News*, November 5, 1940.

[91] Robert K. Oermann, "'Peanut' Faircloth Passes," *Music Row*, March 22, 2010. https://musicrow.com/2010/03/peanut-faircloth-passes/, accessed July 2, 2019; Macon *Telegraph*, February 27, 1948, February 15, 1950; *Aiken (SC) Standard*, October 13, 1953; Zanesville (OH) *Times Recorder*, July 19, 1964.

[92] *Macon News*, November 5, 1952, February 28, 1977; Macon *Telegraph*, March 5, 1952; *Cowboy Songs* 1/14 (March 1953): 15.

[93] Brian Turpen, *Ramblin' Man: Short Stories from the Life of Hank Williams* (Many, LA: Old Paths, New Dreams Publishing, 2007) 132. For the full interview, see Lilly's Vintage Country Music, "Hank Williams Hadacol Interview from September, 1951," https://www.youtube.com/watch?v=QHJwPbJpfCA&feature=share, accessed July 1, 2019.

[94] Macon *Telegraph*, June 21, 1991.

[95] Georgia Tech Technique, May 13, 1949.

[96] *Macon News*, December 31, 1950; *Macon News*, April 9, 1952.

[97] Macon *Telegraph*, October 20, 1978.

[98] Ibid., February 6, 2001.

CHAPTER 4

[1] *Macon News*, March 4, 1971.

[2] Jonathan Gould, *Otis Redding: An Unfinished Life* (New York: Crown Archetype, 2017) 72; Charles White, *The Life and Times of Little Richard: The Quasar of Rock and Roll* (New York: Harmony Books, 1984) 40.

[3] Lauterbach, *Chitlin Circuit*, 218. The National Archives at Fort Worth, Texas; *WWII Draft Registration Cards for Georgia, 10/16/1940–03/31/1947*; Record

Group: *Records of the Selective Service System*, 147. United States Census, Washington County, Georgia, 1920; Macon *Telegraph*, June 14, 1935, October 6, 1935, June 4, 1949.

[4] Macon *Telegraph*, June 22, 1941, June 26, 1941, June 30, 1941, July 13, 1947, July 4, 1941.

[5] Ibid., March 27, 1942, April 2, 1942, April 5, 1942, March 25, 1988. Milt Dimmons interview, on file at the Middle Georgia Archives at the Washington Memorial Library, Macon, Georgia.

[6] John Hartley Fox, *King of the Queen City: The Story of King Records* (Urbana: University of Illinois Press, 2009) 89.

[7] Clint Brantley interview, on file at the Middle Georgia Archives at the Washington Memorial Library, Macon, Georgia; Percy Welch interview, on file at the Middle Georgia Archives at the Washington Memorial Library, Macon, Georgia.

[8] United States Census, Bibb County, Georgia, 1920, 1940; Macon *Telegraph*, June 9, 1950, *Macon News*, March 4, 1971.

[9] *Macon News*, July 31, 1939, August 2, 1939, July 3, 1942, May 23, 1943, March 4, 1971.

[10] Ibid., March 4, 1971; Scott Freeman, *Otis!: The Otis Redding Story* (New York: St. Martin's Press, 2001) 18; Newton Collier, interview by author, September 8, 2018, Macon, Georgia (referred to henceforth as Collier, September 8, 2018).

[11] *Macon News*, July 3, 1942; Collier, September 8, 2018.

[12] *Macon News*, July 3, 1942, March 4, 1971; Macon *Telegraph*, June 9, 1950; *Pittsburgh Courier*, September 19, 1959; Collier, September 8, 2018; Freeman, *Otis!*, 13.

[13] *Macon News*, March 4, 1971.

[14] The National Archives at Fort Worth, Texas; *WWII Draft Registration Cards for Georgia, 10/16/1940–03/31/1947*; Record Group: *Records of the Selective Service System*, 147; *Macon News*, December 23, 1974; Macon *Telegraph*, June 30, 1942, August 9, 1944; United States Census, Bibb County, Georgia, 1930, 1940.

[15] *Macon News*, August 27, 1944, August 17, 1945, September 29, 1946, September 25, 1947; Macon *Telegraph*, October 23, 1946, March 22, 1947.

[16] Lauterbach, *Chitlin Circuit*, 245–46; R. J. Smith, *The One: The Life and Times of James Brown* (New York: Gotham Books, 2012) 111–12; Clint Brantley interview, on file at the Middle Georgia Archives at the Washington Memorial Library; *Indianapolis (IN) Recorder*, June 30, 1956; *Greenville (SC) News* December 24, 1961.

[17] Glenn C. Altschuler, *All Shook Up: How Rock 'n' Roll Changed America* (New York: Oxford University Press, 2003) 35.

[18] David Dalton, "Little Richard: Child of God," *Rolling Stone* (May 28, 1970): 28–34.

[19] White, *Little Richard*, 16–17; *New York Times*, December 8, 1992.

[20] Clint Brantley interview, on file at the Middle Georgia Archives at the Washington Memorial Library, Macon, Georgia; David Kirby, *Little Richard and the Birth of Rock 'n' Roll* (New York: Continuum International Publishing Group, 2009) 43.

[21] Arnold Shaw, *Honkers and Shouters: The Golden Years of Rhythm and Blues* (New York: Macmillan, 1978) 191; Dalton, "Little Richard," 28–34.

[22] White, *Little Richard*, 21–22; *New York Times*, December 8, 1992.

[23] White, *Little Richard*, 26–27; *Atlanta Constitution*, August 10, 1979; St. Petersburg (FL) *Tampa Bay Times*, July 22, 1956.

[24] Milt Dimmons interview, on file at the Middle Georgia Archives at the Washington Memorial Library, Macon, Georgia; Percy Welch interview, on file at the Middle Georgia Archives at the Washington Memorial Library, Macon, Georgia.

[25] Dalton, "Little Richard," 28–34; White, *Little Richard*, 14–16.

[26] Little Richard, interview by Tom Snyder, January 14, 1997, *The Late Late Show* (CBS); *Washington Post*, May 28, 1999; Parke Puterbaugh, "Little Richard: 'I Am the Architect of Rock & Roll,'" *Rolling Stone* (April 19, 1990): 51–53; Dalton, "Little Richard," 28–34.

[27] Puterbaugh, "Little Richard," 51–53; Dalton, "Little Richard," 28–34; Kirby, *Little Richard*, 109.

[28] White, *Little Richard*, 25–27; Lauterbach, *Chitlin Circuit*, 151.

[29] White, *Little Richard*, 29–30; Eric S. LeBlanc and Bob Eagle, *Blues: A Regional Experience* (Santa Barbara, CA: Praeger Publishers, 2013) 289–90; 304.

[30] Little Richard, interview by Tom Snyder, January 14, 1997, *The Late Late Show* (CBS); Little Richard, interview by Bill Boggs on *Midday* on WNEW-TV, New York, first broadcast October 17, 1984.

[31] Dalton, "Little Richard," 28–34; Macon *Telegraph*, September 23, 1990.

[32] Little Richard, interview by Tom Snyder, January 14, 1997, *The Late Late Show* (CBS); White, *Little Richard*, 32–33; Macon *Telegraph*, February 22, 1952, February 23, 1952; *Macon News*, February 22, 1952, June 5, 1952.

[33] White, *Little Richard*, 37–39; Bill Greensmith, Mike Rowe, and Mark Camarigg, *Blues Unlimited: Essential Interviews from the Original Blues Magazine* (Champaign: University of Illinois Press, 2015) 352.

[34] Charles Connor with Ziv Bitton, *Keep a Knockin': The Story of a Legendary Drummer* (Grapevine, TX: Waldorf Publishing, 2015) 17–20.

[35] *Rock & Roll*, episode 1, "Renegades: Lloyd Price," documentary directed by David Espar and Robert Levi (Boston, WBHG, London, BBC, 1995); *Music Cultures in the United States: An Introduction*, ed. Ellen Koskoff (New York: Routledge, 2005) 232.

[36] *Rock & Roll*, episode 1, "Renegades: Richard Penniman," documentary directed by David Espar and Robert Levi (Boston, WBHG, London, BBC, 1995); *Macon News*, April 3, 1955, May 1, 1955, May 8, 1955, August 21, 1955.

[37] A copy of the arrest report for the incident in question can be found in the Georgia Music Hall of Fame Collection, series 1, box 20, files 14–17 (Little Richard) Hargrett Rare Book and Manuscript Library, University of Georgia, Athens, Georgia.

[38] *Rock & Roll*, episode 1, "Renegades: Richard Penniman," documentary directed by David Espar and Robert Levi (Boston, WBHG, London, BBC, 1995); Kirby, *Little Richard*, 111.

[39] Puterbaugh, "Little Richard," 51.

[40] *Macon News*, December 11, 1955, December 25, 1955.

[41] Smith, *James Brown*, 67–68.

[42] Ibid., 7–9, 22–23; James Brown with Bruce Tucker, *James Brown: The Godfather of Soul, an Autobiography* (New York: Thunder's Mouth Press, 1986) 3–4; *Polk's Augusta (Richmond County, GA) City Directory, 1947–1948*, vol. 39 (Richmond, VA: R. L. Polk and Co., 1948) 84; *Polk's Augusta (Richmond County, GA) City Directory, 1949*, vol. 40 (Richmond, VA: R. L. Polk and Co., 1949) 90.

[43] Don Rhodes, Say It Loud!: My Memories of James Brown, Soul Brother No. 1 (Guilford, CT: Lyons Press, 2009) 8–10.

[44] Smith, *James Brown*, 7–9, 22–24; *Mr. Dynamite: The Rise of James Brown*, documentary directed by Alex Gibney (West Hollywood, CA: Jagged Films in association with Inaudible Films, Imagine Entertainment and Jigsaw Prods., 2014).

[45] Michael Goldberg, "James Brown: Wrestling with the Devil," *Rolling Stone* (April 6, 1989); *Mr. Dynamite: The Rise of James Brown*, documentary directed by Alex Gibney (West Hollywood, CA: Jagged Films in association with Inaudible Films, Imagine Entertainment and Jigsaw Prods., 2014).

[46] Smith, *James Brown*, 25–27; Rhodes, *Say It Loud!*, 10–12.

[47] Brown, *James Brown*, 17–19.

[48] James McBride, *Kill 'Em and Leave: Searching for James Brown and the American Soul* (New York: Spiegel & Grau, 2016) 74; Smith, *James Brown*, 28–31; Rhodes, *Say It Loud!*, 10–12; Brown, James Brown, 22.

[49] John Chilton, *Let the Good Times Roll: The Story of Louis Jordan and His Music* (Ann Arbor: University of Michigan Press, 1994) 109–12; *Atlanta Constitution*, December 9, 1977; Brown, *James Brown*, 23.

[50] Horace Clarence Boyer, *The Golden Age of Gospel* (Urbana and Chicago: University of Illinois Press, 1995) 52–54; Smith, *James Brown*, 47–53.

[51] Smith, *James Brown*, 54–60.

[52] Rhodes, *Say It Loud!*, 10–12; *Mr. Dynamite: The Rise of James Brown*, documentary directed by Alex Gibney (West Hollywood, CA: Jagged Films in association with Inaudible Films, Imagine Entertainment and Jigsaw Prods., 2014).

[53] Smith, *James Brown*, 50–52; Clint Brantley interview, on file at the Middle Georgia Archives at the Washington Memorial Library, Macon, Georgia; Brown, *James Brown*, 68–69.

[54] *Mr. Dynamite: The Rise of James Brown*, documentary directed by Alex Gibney (West Hollywood, CA: Jagged Films in association with Inaudible Films, Imagine Entertainment and Jigsaw Prods., 2014); Macon *Telegraph*, February 2, 1987.

[55] Clint Brantley interview, on file at the Middle Georgia Archives at the Washington Memorial Library, Macon, Georgia; Brown, *James Brown*, 69–70; Fred J. Hay, "Music Box Meets the Toccoa Band: The Godfather of Soul in Appalachia," *Black Music Research Journal* 23/1–2 (Spring–Autumn 2003): 124–25.

[56] Clint Brantley interview, on file at the Middle Georgia Archives at the Washington Memorial Library, Macon, Georgia; Macon *Telegraph*, November 19, 1955, November 20, 1955.

[57] James Brown with Bruce Tucker, *James Brown: The Godfather of Soul, an Autobiography* Brown, *James Brown*, 69–70; Macon *Telegraph*, November 6, 1955.

[58] Smith, *James Brown*, 69–70; *Encyclopedia of the Blues*, ed. Gerard Herzhaft (Fayetteville: University of Arkansas Press, 1992) 437–38; Clint Brantley interview, on file at the Middle Georgia Archives at the Washington Memorial Library, Macon, Georgia.

[59] *Atlanta Journal-Constitution*, June 15, 2009.

[60] Fox, *King Records*, 89–92.

[61] Ibid., 90–93.

[62] *Billboard* (April 7, 1956); Smith, *James Brown*, 75–76.

[63] *Greenville (SC) News*, November 2, 2003; Smith, *James Brown*, 80–82.

[64] Fox, *King Records*, 164–67; Smith, *James Brown*, 85–86; *Macon Telegraph*, March 30, 2012.

[65] Brown, *James Brown*, 90–93.

[66] Ibid.; Smith, *James Brown*, 85–86; *Macon News*, July 2, 1961.

[67] Collier, September 8, 2018.

[68] Ibid.; *James Brown*, 120–22; Smith, *James Brown*, 123–24; Freeman, *Otis!*, 70–71; Candice Dyer, *Street Singers, Soul Shakers, Rebels with a Cause: Music from Macon* (Macon, GA: Indigo Custom Publishing, 2008) 57.

[69] Gaylord Fields, "Live at the Apollo," *Rolling Stone* (June 30, 2008).

[70] Macon *Telegraph*, July 11, 1986.

[71] *Macon News*, May 21, 1951; *February Annals* (February 1950) St. Peter Claver School, Macon, GA. The document is a page from a log/diary of events related to the school, a copy of which was provided to the author by Dr. Debi Hamlin, daughter of Lewis Hamlin Jr.; *Mission Fields at Home, Magazine of the Sisters of the Blessed Sacrament* XVIII (October 1951): 5.

[72] Macon *Telegraph*, April 1, 1947, August 10, 1947, June 16, 1948, July 14, 1957, July 17, 1960, August 7, 1960, July 11, 1986.

[73] Ibid., July 11, 1986.

[74] Smith, *James Brown*, 115–17.

[75] Ibid.

[76] Macon *Telegraph*, July 11, 1986.

[77] Ibid., May 23, 1950, May 25, 1958, May 30, 1998, May 31, 1998, October 24, 2014.

[78] Ibid., May 24, 1955, February 5, 1979, May 30, 1998, July 8, 2008.

[79] Ibid., May 25, 1958, May 30, 1998, May 31, 1998, January 12, 2012.

[80] Ibid., May 25, 1958, May 30, 1998, May 31, 1998, February 28, 2002, September 17, 2015.

[81] Ibid., May 23, 1950, May 25, 1958, May 30, 1998, May 31, 1998, February 28, 2002, October 24, 2014.

[82] Ibid., May 25, 1958, May 30, 1998, May 31, 1998, February 28, 2002, January 12, 2012.

[83] *Macon News*, December 31, 1950; Macon *Telegraph*, January 27, 1957, March 4, 2003, July 15, 2015.

[84] Ibid., August 21, 1957, November 25, 1957, May 18, 1958; Macon *Telegraph*, March 16, 1959; *The Cash Box* 19/20 (February 1, 1958): 46.

[85] *Macon News*, May 18, 1958; *Pittsburgh Courier*, October 4, 1958.

[86] *Macon News*, May 18, 1958; Macon *Telegraph*, August 26, 1998, April 11, 2005.

[87] Macon *Telegraph*, February 10, 1960, February 28, 2002, January 12, 2012; *Pittsburgh Courier*, February 27, 1960.

[88] Macon *Telegraph*, February 10, 1960, February 28, 2002, January 12, 2012, October 24, 2014; *Pittsburgh Courier*, February 27, 1960.

[89] *Macon News*, August 21, 1953; Macon *Telegraph*, June 9, 1995; *Broadcast Telecasting Yearbook*, 1953–1954 (Broadcasting Publications, Inc.) 100.

[90] Macon *Telegraph*, September 27, 1953, October 13, 2013; *Macon News*, October 29, 1953, October 22, 1958.

[91] Macon *Telegraph*, September 17, 1978.

[92] Ibid., October 23, 1958, September 17, 1978, July 6, 1987; *Billboard* (March 3, 1956): 73.

[93] *Macon News*, October 19, 1958, October 22, 1958.

[94] Macon *Telegraph*, July 9, 2008; *Tifton Gazette*, October 18, 2001.

[95] Macon *Telegraph*, July 6, 1987, January 7, 2002.

[96] Ibid., October 28, 1956, November 25, 1956, September 19, 1957, August 7, 2002; *Atlanta Constitution*, February 21, 1959.

[97] Macon *Telegraph*, November 15, 1956, March 9, 1958, August 7, 2002.

[98] Ibid., March 9, 1958, October 26, 1958; *Atlanta Constitution*, February 21, 1959. All quotes from Jane Darnell and Homer Scarborough come from an interesting internet radio program called *John Talk Radio*, created by John H. Darlington. Darlington interviewed Darnell and Scarborough on November 22, 2014. On August 25, 2019, the author retrieved the interview at

https://www.blogtalkradio.com/john-darlington/2014/11/22/homer-scarborough-and-jane-darnell-keel-interview. The interview will be referenced hereafter as Darnell and Scarborough interview, November 22, 2014.

[99] Darnell and Scarborough interview, November 22, 2014; Macon *Telegraph*, July 8, 1960, November 5, 1962, August 7, 2002.

[100] *Macon News*, August 9, 1942, September 13, 1942, June 12, 1949, October 30, 1977; Macon *Telegraph*, October 31, 1981.

[101] *Macon News*, May 10, 1954, March 24, 1957, February 28, 1960, July 2, 1961.

[102] Ibid., July 2, 1961, April 8, 1962.

[103] Ibid., August 21, 1958, June 12, 1964; Macon *Telegraph*, January 28, 2006, September 14, 2013, September 11, 2016, August 31, 2017; Stanley Heard Brobston, *Daddy Sang Lead: The History and Performance Practice of White Southern Gospel Music* (New York: Vantage Press, 2006) 261–62.

[104] Macon *Telegraph*, June 24, 1953, January 16, 1955, June 12, 1955, November 20, 1960.

[105] *Macon News*, November 13, 1949, September 12, 1954; Cusic, *The Sound of Light*, 202; James R. Goff, *Close Harmony: A History of Southern Gospel*, 202–203.

[106] Forsyth (GA) *Monroe County Reporter*, February 20, 2015; *Macon News*, December 30, 1979; Tim Gardner, "Naomi Sego Reader: She Is a Legend," *Singing News* (July 2001): 58–61.

[107] Forsyth (GA) *Monroe County Reporter*, February 20, 2015.

CHAPTER 5

[1] Jim Delehant, "Otis Redding: 'Soul Survivor,'" *Hit Parader* (August, 1967): 56–57.

[2] The National Archives at Fort Worth, Texas; *WWII Draft Registration Cards for Georgia, 10/16/1940–03/31/1947*; Record Group: *Records of the Selective Service System*, 147; National Archives and Records Administration. Electronic Army Serial Number Merged File, 1938–1946 (archival database); World War II Army Enlistment Records; Records of the National Archives and Records Administration, Record Group 64; National Archives at College Park. College Park, Maryland; United States Census, Bibb County, Georgia, 1930; *Macon News*, October 17, 1945; Macon *Telegraph*, September 12, 1990; Percy Welch interview, on file at the Middle Georgia Archives at the Washington Memorial Library, Macon, Georgia.

[3] Charles Shaar Murray, *Boogie Man: The Adventures of John Lee Hooker in the American Twentieth Century* (New York: St. Martin's Press, 2000) 157–58.

[4] Percy Welch interview, on file at the Middle Georgia Archives at the Washington Memorial Library, Macon, Georgia; Macon *Telegraph*, March 11, 1984, February 15, 2004. Dyer, *Music from Macon*, 131–33.

[5] Macon *Telegraph*, May 7, 1965, January 13, 1984, March 11, 1984; *Macon News*, January 31, 1954, February 11, May 3, 1954, July 25, 1965, October 7, 1966; Dyer, *Music from Macon*, 132; Steve Turner, *Trouble Man: The Life and Death of Marvin Gaye* (New York: Echo Press, 2000) 41.

[6] Macon *Telegraph*, August 25, 1989, March 16, 1990; Charles Reynolds, interview by author, September 8, 2018, Macon, Georgia (referred to henceforth as Reynolds, September 8, 2018).

[7] Macon *Telegraph*, April 26, 1991, February 13, 2004, February 15, 2004.

[8] Ibid., February 13, 2004, February 15, 2004.

[9] Tut Underwood, "Eddie Kirkland: The Energy Man," *Living Blues* 111 (October 1993): 15–17; St. Petersburg (FL) *Tampa Bay Times*, February 20, 1983.

[10] Underwood, "Eddie Kirkland," 15–17; St. Petersburg (FL) *Tampa Bay Times*, February 20, 1983; (London, UK) *The Daily Telegraph*, March 8, 2011.

[11] Underwood, "Eddie Kirkland," 17–19; Murray, *Boogie Man*, 140–42.

[12] *Macon News*, February 21, 1954, April 11, 1954, May 21, 1954, October 26, 1957, January 9, 1964; *Atlanta Constitution*, April 2, 1989; St. Petersburg (FL) *Tampa Bay Times*, February 20, 1983; Rob Bowman, *Soulsville, U.S.A.: The Story of Stax Records* (London, UK: Schirmer Trade, 2010) 45–47.

[13] St. Petersburg (FL) *Tampa Bay Times*, February 20, 1983; *New York Times*, April 1, 1988; Underwood, "Eddie Kirkland," 17–21.

[14] Macon *Telegraph*, March 1, 2011; *Ocala (FL) Star-Banner*, August 19, 2010; St. Petersburg (FL) *Tampa Bay Times*, February 20, 1983.

[15] *All Music Guide to the Blues: The Definitive Guide to the Blues*, 3rd ed., eds. Vladimir Bogdanov, Chris Woodstra, and Stephen Thomas Erlewine (San Francisco: Backbeat Books, 2003) 282; Johnny Jenkins, interview by Brad Evans, "It's a Mean Ole World," *11th Hour* 251 (November 16–30, 2012; first published in June 2004): https://issuu.com/meg11hour/docs/macon11-16-12, accessed December 19, 2020; *Macon News*, June 30, 1970.

[16] *Macon News*, August 3, 1957, August 18, 1957, December 22, 1957, March 23, 1958, April 4, 1958, November 16, 1958, June 7, 1959. Charles Abrams's alias, "Pat Teacake," appears here spelled as it was in contemporary ads for the band that appeared in the *Macon News* and Macon *Telegraph*. Alternate spellings, including "Pat T. Cake" and "Patty Cake," appear in other published material. His band was sometimes referred to as Pat Teacake and His Mighty Panthers, and by other slightly different variations.

[17] *Macon News*, January 9, 1958.

[18] There is a good bit of internet static related to the rumor that Jimi Hendrix had a Macon connection. Quotes from Eddie Kirkland and Percy Welch related to Hendrix and Macon are attributed to the original booklet that accompanied the 1994 Jimi Hendrix compact disc titled *Blues*, a collection of previously released and unreleased blues songs. The booklet included in later editions did not mention

Macon. The quote from Arthur Ponder comes from a June 29, 2006, obituary of Jenkins that appeared in the Macon *Telegraph*; *Billboard* (September 20, 1947).

[19] *Macon News*, June 7, 1970, June 30, 1970. United States Census, Knox County, TN, 1900.

[20] Jeff Todd Titon, *Early Downhome Blues: A Musical and Cultural Analysis*, 2nd ed. (Chapel Hill: University of North Carolina Press, 1994) 52; Harry Shapiro and Caesar Glebbeek, *Jimi Hendrix: Electric Gypsy* (New York: St. Martin's Griffin, 1995) 44; James E. Perone, *Listen to the Blues: Exploring a Musical Genre* (Santa Barbara, CA: Greenwood Press, 2019) 126.

[21] Jann S. Wenner and Baron Wolman, "Jimi Hendrix on Early Influences, 'Axis' and More," *Rolling Stone* (March 9, 1968); Ben Fong-Torres, *The Rolling Stone Rock 'n' Roll Reader* (New York: Bantam Books, 1974) 289.

[22] Jenkins interview, "It's a Mean Ole World"; Macon *Telegraph*, June 29, 2006.

[23] Peter Guralnick, *Sweet Soul Music: Rhythm and Blues and the Southern Dream of Freedom* (New York: Little, Brown and Company, 1986) 136.

[24] Steven Roby and Brad Schreiber, Becoming Jimi Hendrix: From Southern Crossroads to Psychedelic London, the Untold Story of a Musical Genius (Cambridge, MA: Da Capo Press, 2010) 96; David Moskowitz, The Words and Music of Jimi Hendrix (Santa Barbara, CA: Praeger, 2010) 5.

[25] Macon *Telegraph*, June 29, 2006; *Billboard* (June 29, 2006).

[26] London *The Guardian*, September 15, 2006; Mark Ribowsky, *Dreams to Remember: Otis Redding, Stax Records, and the Transformation of Southern Soul* (New York: Liveright Publishing Corp., 2015) 33–34; Freeman, *Otis!*, 27–28.

[27] Guralnick, *Sweet Soul Music*, 136–37; Freeman, *Otis!*, 27–28.

[28] Jenkins interview, "It's a Mean Ole World," 12–17.

[29] Robert Gordon, *Respect Yourself: Stax Records and the Soul Explosion* (New York: Bloomsbury, 2013) 73; *Billboard* (August 28, 1962); Jerry Wexler and David Ritz, *Rhythm and the Blues: A Life in American Music* (New York: St. Martin's Press, 1993) 168, 194.

[30] Freeman, *Otis!*, 74–77; Gould, *Otis Redding*, 207–10.

[31] Macon *Telegraph*, October 12, 1962, October 21, 1962, December 13, 1964, June 8, 1965, March 21, 1967, March 30, 1967; *Macon News*, June 30, 1970.

[32] *Lost in the Groves: Scram's Capricorn Guide to the Music You Missed*, eds. Kim Cooper and David Smay (New York: Routledge, 2005) 91; *CMJ Music News* 52 (December 1997): 58; Macon *Telegraph*, September 8, 1996, November 22, 1996, June 29, 2006; *New York Times*, June 30, 2006; *Detroit Free Press*, July 17, 1970.

[33] Tyson Blue, "Phil Walden: The Man Who Made Macon Music," Georgia Music Hall of Fame Collection, series 1, box 26, files 3–8 (Phil Walden) Hargrett

Rare Book and Manuscript Library, University of Georgia, Athens, Georgia; Steve Walburn, "Phil Walden: The Flip Side," *Atlanta Magazine* (August 1993): 37.

[34] Robert Sam Anson, "Will Phil Walden Rise Again?" *Esquire* (June 1980): 38–40; Wexler and Ritz, *Rhythm and the Blues*, 197; Ribowsky, *Otis Redding, Stax Records*, 38.

[35] Gould, *Otis Redding*, 148–49; Guralnick, *Sweet Soul Music*, 136.

[36] Tyson Blue, "Phil Walden: The Man Who Made Macon Music," Georgia Music Hall of Fame Collection, Series 1, Box 26, files 3–8 (Phil Walden) Blue, "Phil Walden," series 1, box 26, files 3–8.

[37] Gould, *Otis Redding*, 170–71; Michael Buffalo Smith, *Capricorn Rising: Conversations in Southern Rock* (Macon, GA: Mercer University Press, 2016) 114; *Macon News*, June 16, 1963.

[38] Hamilton Jordan, *A Boy from Georgia: Coming of Age in the Segregated South* (Athens: University of Georgia Press, 2015) 100–102.

[39] Jordan, Coming of Age, 101; Mark Kemp, Dixie Lullaby: A Story of Music, Race, and New Beginnings in a New South (New York: Free Press, 2004) 9.

[40] Macon *Telegraph*, June 29, 2006; Ribowsky, *Otis Redding, Stax Records*, 38; Freeman, *Otis!*, 90–91; Mark Kemp, *Dixie Lullaby*, 9.

[41] *Billboard* (April 24, 2006); Steve Walburn, "Phil Walden: The Flip Side," *Atlanta Magazine* (August, 1993): 106; Charlie Gillett, "Phil Walden," *Rock's Backpages Audio* (1971). https://www.rocksbackpages.com/Library/Artist/phil-walden, accessed October 29, 2019.

[42] Kemp, Dixie Lullaby, 9.

[43] Macon *Telegraph*, May 1, 1955; Gould, *Otis Redding*, 77.

[44] Delehant, "Otis Redding," 56–57; Gould, *Otis Redding*, 67–68; Freeman, *Otis!*, 10–12.

[45] Stanley Booth, *Red Hot and Blue: Fifty Years of Writing about Music, Memphis, and Motherf**kers* (Chicago: Chicago Review Press, 2019) 67–68.

[46] *Macon News*, June 6, 1948, June 20, 1948; Gould, *Otis Redding*, 117–18.

[47] Booth, *Red Hot and Blue*, 69–72.

[48] White, Little Richard, 97–98; Gould, Otis Redding, 117–18; Freeman, *Otis!*, 12–15; *Macon News*, September 14, 1958, November 16, 1958, November 23, 1958, February 6, 1959, July 31, 1959.

[49] Freeman, *Otis!*, 52, 63.

[50] Gould, *Otis Redding*, 163–68; Freeman, *Otis!*, 54–56; Macon *Telegraph*, August 14, 1960.

[51] *Macon News*, August 10, 1958, October 5, 1958; Macon *Telegraph*, October 14, 2012.

[52] Wayne Pierce, interview by author, August 10, 2019; Unpublished, undated written statement by Bobby Smith. Copy in the possession of the author; Macon *Telegraph*, December 14, 2017. Leon Kennington, email correspondence with author, November 3, 2019.

[53] Leon Kennington, email correspondence with author, November 3, 2019.

[54] *Orlando Sentinel*, December 26, 2004; Ibid.

[55] Gould, *Otis Redding*, 184–87.

[56] Wayne Pierce, interview by author, August 10, 2019; Unpublished, undated written statement by Bobby Smith. Copy in the possession of the author; Ribowsky, *Otis Redding, Stax Records*, 51–56; Freeman, *Otis!*, 74.

[57] Gould, *Otis Redding*, 186–87.

[58] Macon *Telegraph*, July 1, 1962, July 22, 1962, February 3, 1987.

[59] Wayne Pierce, interview by author, August 10, 2019; Guralnick, *Sweet Soul Music*, 140.

[60] *New York Times*, November 27, 2017.

[61] *American Bandstand*, season 10, episode 19, "Otis Redding," aired January 21, 1967, on the American Broadcasting Company (ABC).

[62] Bowman, *Soulsville, U.S.A.*, 41; Gould, Otis Redding, 188; Guralnick, *Sweet Soul Music*, 152; Macon *Telegraph*, February 3, 1987; Freeman, *Otis!*, 75.

[63] Macon *Telegraph*, September 8, 1996; Gould, *Otis Redding*, 210.

[64] Freeman, *Otis!*, 75–78. Freeman's book quotes most of the witnesses who were at the Stax studio on the day of Redding's audition.

[65] Wayne Pierce, interview by author, August 10, 2019; Gould, *Otis Redding*, 225.

[66] Macon *Telegraph*, February 3, 1987.

[67] Freeman, *Otis!*, 85; Macon *Telegraph*, February 3, 1987.

[68] Macon *Telegraph*, October 14, 2012; Nashville *Tennessean*, August 13, 1969; *Atlanta Constitution*, September 15, 1975; *Billboard*, February 12, 1972.

[69] Bowman, *Soulsville, U.S.A.*, 46; Gordon, *Respect Yourself*, 409; Macon *Telegraph*, June 14, 1963.

[70] Blue, "Phil Walden," series 1, box 26, files 3–8; Smith, *Capricorn Rising*, 115.

[71] Macon *Telegraph*, September 10, 1963.

[72] Gould, *Otis Redding*, 244; Montgomery (AL) *Alabama Journal*, June 30, 1964; Lafayette (LA) *Daily Advertiser*, May 29, 1964; Staunton (VA) *News Leader*, October 21, 1964; Macon *Telegraph*, July 12, 1964.

[73] Guralnick, *Sweet Soul Music*, 150; Steve Sullivan, *Encyclopedia of Great Popular Song Recordings*, vols. 3 and 4 (New York: Rowman & Littlefield, 2017) 393; Macon *Telegraph*, February 3, 1987.

[74] Gould, *Otis Redding*, 294; Guralnick, *Sweet Soul Music*, 150; Freeman, *Otis!*, 140–41. Andrew Grant Jackson, *1965: The Most Revolutionary Year in Music* (New York: Thomas Dunne Books, 2015) 144.

[75] Smith, *Capricorn Rising*, 116; Gould, *Otis Redding*, 292.

[76] *Los Angeles Times*, March 31, 1966, April 1, 1966, April 2, 1966; *Santa Cruz (CA) Sentinel*, January 24, 1966; *Pasadena (CA) Independent*, December 18, 1965.

[77] *Melody Maker*, December 16, 1967; *Rolling Stone Presents Twenty Years of Rock & Roll*, featuring George Harrison, aired November 24, 1987, on the American Broadcasting Company (ABC).

[78] Wexler and Ritz, *Rhythm and the Blues*, 198; *San Francisco Examiner*, June 16, 1967; *Indianapolis (IN) News*, August 30, 1967; *Rolling Stone* (December 10, 2017) https://www.rollingstone.com/music/music-features/inside-otis-reddings-final-masterpiece-sittin-on-the-dock-of-the-bay-122170/, accessed November 20, 2019.

[79] Madison (WI) *Capital Times*, December 11, 1967; *Chicago Tribune*, December 11, 1967; *Atlanta Constitution*, December 11, 1967.

[80] Macon *Telegraph*, December 11, 1967; *Macon News*, December 11, 1967, December 16, 1967, December 23, 1967.

[81] Macon *Telegraph*, December 19, 1967; *Los Angeles Times*, December 19, 1967.

[82] Charlie Gillett, "Phil Walden." (1971) Rock's Backpages. Accessed November 11, 2019; Gillett, "Phil Walden," *Rock's Backpages*. Smith, *Capricorn Rising*, 116–17; *Chicago Defender*, December 28, 1967, quoted in Jonathan Gould, *Otis Redding: An Unfinished Life*, 444.

[83] Bowman, *Soulsville, U.S.A.*, 134. *Bluesblast Magazine* (October 20, 2017) http://www.bluesblastmagazine.com, accessed November 12, 2019.

[84] Baltimore (MD) *Evening Sun*, January 19, 1989; *St. Louis Post-Dispatch*, January 20, 1989; Macon *Telegraph*, June 17, 1993.

[85] Keith Richards, "Planet Rock Interview," https://www.keithrichards.com, accessed November 12, 2019 (emphasis mine).

CHAPTER 6

[1] Paul Hornsby, "'Capricorn Was a Place Where the Lightning Struck:' Mercer Works to Renovate Macon's Historic Studio," WMAZ-TV, Macon, Georgia, originally broadcast February 10, 2019.

[2] Guralnick, *Sweet Soul Music*, 135–36; Macon *Telegraph*, July 5, 1959, September 24, 1964, January 31, 1965, July 5, 1965, June 28, 1968.

[3] Bowman, *Soulsville, U.S.A.*, 46; Gordon, *Respect Yourself*, 409; Macon *Telegraph*, July 5, 1959, June 10, 1989.

[4] *Macon News*, December 2, 1962, October 5, 1963, March 7, 1965, March 18, 1966, April 17, 1966, July 2, 1969; Macon *Telegraph*, February 2, 1987.

[5] *Macon News*, August 30, 1964, September 10, 1965, September 11, 1965, October 27, 1965, January 26, 1966, March 4, 1966, March 12, 1966, December 24, 1966, August 17, 1967, August 18, 1967, October 21, 1967, December 7, 1967, December 8, 1968, January 3, 1969.

[6] Dyer, Music from Macon, 135.

[7] *Macon News*, August 22, 1964, May 7, 1967, May 4, 1972, March 6, 1980; Macon *Telegraph*, January 4, 2017; Syracuse (NY) *Post-Standard*, May 14, 1977;

Brad Evans, "Calvin Arline: A Legendary Bassline," *11th Hour*, 283 (March 14–28, 2014) 27.

[8] *Macon News*, August 8, 1964, April 17, 1967, August 30, 1967, September 16, 1967, March 21, 1969, April 7, 1969, April 14, 1969; Macon *Telegraph*, February 3, 1987; *Atlanta Constitution*, February 2, 1997.

[9] Macon *Telegraph*, September 22, 1965, April 11, 1969, February 2, 1987, May 2, 2008; Mark Coltrain, "A Conversation with Robert Lee Coleman," *Living Blues* 233 (September–October 2014) 38–40; Dyer, *Music from Macon*, 66–67.

[10] Collier, September 8, 2018; Macon *Telegraph*, November 15, 1991.

[11] Collier, September 8, 2018; *Macon News*, September 30, 1958.

[12] Macon *Telegraph*, November 15, 1991, April 20, 2008; Collier, September 8, 2018.

[13] *Chicago Tribune*, July 19, 1991.

[14] *Miami News*, August 16, 1968.

[15] For information and quotes on the 1968 NATRA convention in Miami, see: Brian Ward, *Just My Soul Responding: Rhythm and Blues, Black Consciousness, and Race Relations* (Berkeley: University of California Press, 1998) 433–34; William Barlow, *Voice Over: The Making of Black Radio* (Philadelphia: Temple University Press, 1999) 223–24; Rickey Vincent, *Party Music: The Inside Story of the Black Panthers' Band and How Black Power Changed Soul Music* (Chicago: Lawrence Hill Books, 2013) 161; Nelson George, "Black Beauty, Black Confusion (1965–1970)," ed. Floyd W. Hayes III, in *The Turbulent Voyage: Readings in African American Studies* (New York: Collegiate Press, 2000) 214; Randy Poe, *Skydog: The Duane Allman Story* (New York: Backbeat Books, 2006) 141; Gould, *Otis Redding*, 464; *Miami News*, August 16, 1968.

[16] Ben Edmonds, "Snapshots of the South: The Allman Brothers and Capricorn Records," *Creem* (November, 1972) 39–40. Smith, *Capricorn Rising*, 114–17.

[17] Smith, Capricorn Rising, 117.

[18] Duner-Fenter, "Frank Fenter," series 1, box 8, file 103.

[19] London *Record Mirror*, December 24, 1966; *Billboard* (September 17, 1966); Ahmet Ertegun interview, https://www.youtube.com/watch?v=zfC26KHTCQ4, accessed January 7, 2020.

[20] Clive Selwood, *All the Moves (But None of the Licks): Secrets of the Record Business* (London, UK: Peter Owen Publishers, 2014) 89.

[21] Gould, *Otis Redding*, 354–60; Paul Anderson, *Mods: The New Religion* (London UK: Omnibus Press, 2014) 285–300; London *Record Mirror*, December 24, 1966; *Billboard* (May 25, 1968).

[22] Ahmet Ertegun interview.

[23] Candice Dyer, "Frank Fenter: The Man Who Might Have Saved Capricorn," *11th Hour* 8/4 (May 6–19, 2010): 20; Anathalee G. Sandlin, *Johnny Sandlin's Musical Odyssey: A Never-Ending Groove* (Macon, GA: Mercer University Press, 2012) 79.

[24] Duner-Fenter, "Frank Fenter," series 1, box 8, file 103.

[25] Poe, *Skydog*, 1–9; Gregg Allman with Alan Light, *My Cross to Bear* (New York: William Morrow, 2012) 9–11; Scott Freeman, *Midnight Riders: The Story of the Allman Brothers Band* (New York: Little Brown and Company, 1995) 5–6.

[26] Hartford (CT) *Courant*, February 27, 2008; *Miami New Times*, March 20, 2019; Poe, *Skydog*, 94–95.

[27] Andy Lee White and John M. Williams, *Atlanta Pop in the 50s, 60s, and 70s: The Magic of Bill Lowery* (Charleston, SC: History Press, 2019) 106–107; Poe, *Skydog*, 71–72.

[28] Dickey Betts interview, "Rock Influences," https://www.youtube.com/watch?v=pjTwU9cMrKg, accessed January 13, 2019; Smith, *Capricorn Rising*, 114–17.

[29] Poe, *Skydog*, 71–72; Smith, *Capricorn Rising*, 114–17.

[30] Smith, *Capricorn Rising*, 100–103; Sandlin, *Johnny Sandlin*, 65–68.

[31] Damian Fanelli, "Eric Clapton: I've Never Heard Better Rock Guitar Playing," *Guitar World*, August 26, 2019, https://www.guitarworld.com/artists/listen-eric-clapton-s-favorite-rb-guitar-solo-duane-allman-guests-wilson-picketts-cover-hey-jude, accessed February 1, 2020; Jerry Wexler, *Rhythm and Blues: A Life in American Music* (New York: Alfred A. Knopf, 1993) 225–26; Allman and Light, *My Cross to Bear*, 114–15; Henry Woodhead, "Making It Big in Macon with Those Good Ol' Georgia Blues," *Atlanta Journal and Constitution Magazine* (March 3, 1974): 8–9, 22–27; Alan Paul, *One Way Out: The Inside History of the Allman Brothers Band* (New York: St. Martin's Press, 2014) 1–3.

[32] Poe, *Skydog*, 94–95; Smith, *Capricorn Rising*, 101–105; Sandlin, *Johnny Sandlin*, 65–68.

[33] "Duane Allman: The Complete 1981 Dickey Betts Interview," https://www.duaneallman.info/jasobrecht/dickeybetts/the1981dickeybettsinterview.htm, accessed February 10, 2020; Paul, *One Way Out*, 17–23; Poe, *Skydog*, 107–108.

[34] Paul, *One Way Out*, 28; "Duane Allman: The Complete 1981 Dickey Betts Interview."

[35] Paul, *One Way Out*, 30; Poe, *Skydog*, 109; Smith, *Capricorn Rising*, 20.

[36] Smith, *Capricorn Rising*, 104–106.

[37] Ibid., 88–89; Sandlin, *Johnny Sandlin*, 195–99. Paul Hornsby, interview by Luc Brunot, http://www.sweethomemusic.fr/Interviews/HornsbyUS.php, accessed February 23, 2020.

[38] Paul, *One Way Out*, 30; Poe, *Skydog*, 242–43; John T. Edge, "Mama Tried," *Oxford American*, 34 (July/August 2000) https://www.oxfordamerican.org/magazine/item/1228–mama–tried/, accessed January 30, 2020.

[39] Willie Perkins, *No Saints, No Saviors: My Years with the Allman Brothers Band* (Macon, GA: Mercer University Press, 2005) 13; Allman and Light, *My Cross to Bear*, 149.

[40] *Dictionary of Georgia Biography*, vol. II, eds. Kenneth Coleman and Charles Stephen Gurr (Athens: University of Georgia Press, 1983) 850–51; Paul, *One Way Out*, 46.

[41] *Atlanta Constitution*, May 9, 1993, March 22, 2001, May 18, 2007; Edge, "Mama Tried."

[42] Atlanta Constitution, March 3, 1974.

[43] *Tampa (FL) Tribune*, November 28, 1969; Poe, *Skydog*, 123–26; Corbin Reiff, "Allman Brothers Band's Legendary 1971 Fillmore East Run: An Oral History," *Rolling Stone* (March 11, 2016) https://www.rollingstone.com/music/music-features/allman-brothers-bands-legendary-1971-fillmore-east-run-an-oral-history-240779/, accessed December 18, 2019.

[44] *Philadelphia Daily News*, October 29, 1970; Poe, Skydog, 157–61.

[45] *Troy (NY) Record*, May 7, 1970; Paul, *One Way Out*, 242–43; Willie Perkins, interview by author, October 17, 2018.

[46] *Lincoln (NE) Star*, July 5, 1970; Bob Schinder and Andy Schwartz, *Icons of Rock: An Encyclopedia of the Legends Who Changed Music Forever*, vol. 1 (Westport, CT: Greenwood Press, 2008) 250.

[47] *Charlotte (NC) Observer*, July 26, 1970; Willie Perkins, interview by author, October 17, 2018.

[48] Paul, *One Way Out*, 116–26; Willie Perkins, interview by author, October 17, 2018.

[49] Rolling Stone (August 19, 1971); *Philadelphia Inquirer* July 31, 1971; John Glatt, *Live at the Fillmore East and West: Getting Backstage and Personal with Rock's Greatest Legends* (Lanham, MD: Rowman & Littlefield, 2016) 269, 354–55.

[50] Paul, *One Way Out*, 232; Nashville *Tennessean*, July 1, 1999; Willie Perkins, interview by author, October 17, 2018.

[51] *Atlanta Constitution*, October 30, 1971, October 31, 1971, December 10, 1971; Poe, *Skydog*, 210–12; Paul, *One Way Out*, 156–64; Wexler, *Rhythm and Blues*, 256–58.

[52] Sandlin, *Johnny Sandlin*, 128; Chuck Leavell, *Between Rock and a Home Place* (Mercer University Press, 2004) 88–91.

[53] Jimmy Hall interview, "Rock Influences," https://www.youtube.com/watch?v=3OahniOGJts, accessed January 29, 2020; Smith, *Capricorn Rising*, 133.

[54] Nashville *Tennessean*, December 17, 1972.

[55] Macon *Telegraph*, September 11, 2010; *Atlanta Constitution*, February 18, 1977; *Sacramento (CA) Bee*, October 3, 1974; *Tampa (FL) Tribune*, October 1, 1974.

[56] Nashville *Tennessean*, April 8, 1973; Smith, *Capricorn Rising*, 106–107; Sandlin, *Johnny Sandlin*, 107.

[57] Willie Perkins, interview by author, October 17, 2018; Chuck Leavell, email correspondence with author, October 8, 2019.

⁵⁸ *Billboard* (August 17, 1974): 60–61; Jackson (MS) *Clarion-Ledger,* November 24, 1983; *Anderson (IN) Herald,* June 11, 1975; Smith, *Capricorn Rising,* 133–36; Dyer, *Music from Macon,* 258–77.

⁵⁹ *Atlanta Constitution,* May 17, 1970, August 13, 1977; Louis Kraar, "How Phil Walden Turns Rock into Gold," *Fortune* (September 1975) 107.

⁶⁰ Smith, *Capricorn Rising,* 108–109; Charlie Daniels, *Never Look at the Empty Seats: A Memoir* (Nashville, TN: W. Publishing, 2017) 103–104, 107; *Detroit Free Press,* December 8, 1974.

⁶¹ Tony Glover, "Eat a Peach: Allman Brothers Band Album Review," *Rolling Stone,* April 13, 1972, https://www.rollingstone.com/music/music-album-reviews/eat-a-peach-249573/, accessed December 14, 2019; Allman and Light, *My Cross to Bear,* 210.

⁶² St. Petersburg (FL) *Tampa Bay Times,* November 13, 1972; *Boston Globe,* November 13, 1972; *Tampa (FL) Tribune,* November 13, 1972; Leavell, *Between Rock and a Home Place,* 101.

⁶³ Jim Schwartz, "Sea Level: Rock, Funk, and Blues from the South," Hittin' the Web with the Allman Brothers Band, https://www.hittintheweb.com/modules.php?op=modload&name=userpage&file=content&page_id=23, accessed December 10, 2019; Paul, *One Way Out,* 199; Sandlin, *Johnny Sandlin,* 142–43.

⁶⁴ Leavell, *Between Rock and a Home Place,* 45–46, 51–54, 59–60; Chuck Leavell, email correspondence with author, October 8, 2019.

⁶⁵ Sandlin, *Johnny Sandlin,* 139; Allman and Light, *My Cross to Bear,* 219; Leavell, *Between Rock and a Home Place,* 95; *Los Angeles Times,* September 4, 1973.

⁶⁶ Willie Perkins, interview by author, October 17, 2018; *Los Angeles Times,* September 4, 1973; Paul, *One Way Out,* 201–207. Les Dudek later claimed that he cowrote "Jessica" with Dickey Betts, and all of the involved parties chimed in on the issue in the pages of Alan Paul's book listed here.

⁶⁷ *Bennington (VT) Banner,* September 12, 1973; *Ithaca (NY) Journal,* July 27, 1973; *Boston Globe,* July 30, 1973; *Atlanta Constitution,* March 3, 1974; Marley Brant, *Join Together: Forty Years of the Rock Music Festival* (New York: Hal Leonard Corporation, 2008) 130–33; *Billboard* (September 8, 1973); *San Bernardino County (CA) Sun,* September 30, 1973.

⁶⁸ *Macon News,* April 16, 1972; *Atlanta Constitution,* April 16, 1972.

⁶⁹ Mary Webb, "Musician Returns to Houma for Southdown Reunion," April 1, 2001, https://www.houmatoday.com/article/DA/20010401/News/608094806/HC, accessed November 30, 2019; *Macon Telegraph,* June 14, 1996; Steve Howard interview, *The Paul McCartney Project,* https://www.the-paulmccartney-project.com/artist/steve-howard/, accessed December 1, 2019.

⁷⁰ *Atlanta Constitution,* May 27, 1978. Scott K. Fish, "How Joe English Got the Gig with Paul McCartney," August 4, 2015, https://scottkfish.com/2015/08/04/how-joe-english-got-the-gig-with-paul-mccartney/, accessed December 7,

2019; *Grand Junction (CO) Daily Sentinel*, August 12, 1978; Garry McGee, *Band on the Run: A History of Paul McCartney and Wings* (New York: Taylor Trade Publishing, 2003) 75–76, 85.

[71] *Atlanta Constitution*, August 19, 1977, September 3, 1977, August 26, 1978, September 7, 1978, September 28, 1978; *Billboard* (August 17, 1974), *Billboard* (August 16, 1975), *Billboard* (November 22, 1986); *Tampa (FL) Tribune*, September 9, 1977; Chuck Leavell, email correspondence with author, October 8, 2019.

[72] *Atlanta Constitution*, March 3, 1974.

[73] Ibid.

[74] Michael Buffalo Smith, "Like a Rolling Stone: A Visit with Former Doc Holliday Member, and Current Solo Star, Eddie Stone," Swampland.com, http://swampland.com/articles/view/title:eddie_stone, accessed January 14, 2020; *Pensacola (FL) News Journal*, March 3, 1975.

[75] *Atlanta Constitution*, July 30, 1977; Pensacola (FL) News Journal, September 12, 1977.

[76] *Miami Herald*, August 29, 1976; *Atlanta Constitution*, November 4, 1976; *Philadelphia Inquirer*, February 15, 1976; Austin (TX) *American-Statesman*, February 15, 1976; Patrick Anderson, *Electing Jimmy Carter: The Campaign of 1976* (Baton Rouge: Louisiana State University Press, 1994) 75–76; Jordon, *Coming of Age*, 105–106.

[77] Allman and Light, *My Cross to Bear*, 267–74; Paul, *One Way Out*, 237–38; Sandlin, *Johnny Sandlin*, 237–41.

[78] Robert Duncan, "Rhett Butler After The Fall: Dickey Betts Brushes Himself Off...," *Creem* (March 1977) https://www.rocksbackpages.com/Library/Article/rhett-butler-after-the-fall-dickey-betts-brushes-himself-off, accessed February 21, 2020; Allman and Light, *My Cross to Bear*, 275; Paul, *One Way Out*, 239; Sandlin, *Johnny Sandlin*, 185–87, 194.

[79] Sandlin, *Johnny Sandlin*, 187; *El Paso (TX) Times*, August 14, 1976.

[80] Chuck Leavell, *Between Rock and a Home Place*, 144–47; *Atlanta Constitution*, June 25, 1977; Allentown (NJ) *Messenger-Press*, January 13, 1977; *Anniston (AL) Star*, May 21, 1977.

[81] Smith, *Capricorn Rising*, 46; Chuck Leavell, *Between Rock and a Home Place*, 144–50.

[82] Macon *Telegraph*, November 7, 1983; *Greenwood (SC) Index-Journal*, November 24, 1983; *Atlanta Constitution*, October 5, 1979, November 23, 1979; *Billboard* (December 8, 1979); Sandlin, *Johnny Sandlin*, 197.

[83] Macon *Telegraph*, November 7, 1983.

[84] *Atlanta Constitution*, April 26, 2006; *Los Angeles Times*, April 25, 2006; *Pittsburg Post-Gazette*, April 25, 2006; Macon *Telegraph*, November 7, 1983.

EPILOGUE

[1] Richard Brent, email correspondence with author, October 16, 2019.

[2] Macon *Telegraph*, March 9, 2020; *Atlanta Constitution*, December 1, 2019.

[3] Rock Candy Tours, www.rockcandytours.com; Macon *Telegraph*, May 31, 2020.

[4] Macon *Telegraph*, July 21, 2016, May 31, 2020.

[5] Macon Music Trail, www.maconmusictrail.com.

[6] Otis Redding Foundation, www.otisreddingfoundation.org; *Atlanta Journal Constitution*, April 3, 2016.

[7] Georgia Allman Brothers Band Association, www.gabbafest.org; The Big House, www.thebighousemuseum.com; Richard Brent, email correspondence with author, October 16, 2019.

[8] *Atlanta Journal Constitution*, January 20, 1994; *Jackson (TN) Sun*, July 1, 2001; Chuck Leavell, www.chuckleavell.com.

Sources

PRIMARY SOURCES
COLLECTIONS
Center for Popular Music, James E. Walker Library, Middle Tennessee State University. Murfreesboro, Tennessee.
Georgia Civil War Correspondence, Adjutant General. Letterbooks, 1860, 1909, 22/1/1/. Incoming Correspondence, 1861–1914, 22/1/17. Georgia State Archives. Morrow, Georgia.
Georgia Music Hall of Fame Collection, Hargrett Rare Book and Manuscript Library, University of Georgia. Athens, Georgia.
Middle Georgia Archives, Washington Memorial Library. Macon, Georgia.
Otis Redding Collection, Library and Archives, Rock & Roll Hall of Fame and Museum. Cleveland, Ohio.

PUBLISHED PRIMARY SOURCES
Allman, Gregg, with Alan Light. *My Cross to Bear*. New York: William Morrow, 2012.
America in the Fifties: Letters of Fredrika Bremer. Edited by Adolph Benson. New York: The American-Scandinavian Foundation, 1924.
Ancestry.com, *U.S. Passport Applications 1795–1925*. https://www.ancestry.com/search/collections/1174/. Accessed May 24, 2018.
The Anglo American, A Journal of Literature, News, Politics, Drama, Fine Arts, Etc. Volume III. Edited by A. D. Paterson. New York: E. L. Garvin, 1844.
Annual Catalogue of Wesleyan Female College, Macon, Georgia, 1899–1900. Atlanta: Foote and Davies Co., 1900.
Annual Catalogue of Wesleyan Female College and Wesleyan Conservatory of Music, Macon, Georgia 1904–1905. Atlanta: Foote and Davies Company, 1905.
Broadcast Telecasting Yearbook, 1953–1954. Broadcasting Publications, Inc.
Brown, James, with Bruce Tucker. *James Brown: The Godfather of Soul, an Autobiography*. New York: Thunder's Mouth Press, 1986.
Buckingham, James Silk. *The Slave States of America*. Volume 1. London: Fisher, Son, and Co., 1842.

Butler, John Campbell. *Historical Record of Macon and Central Georgia, Containing Many Interesting and Valuable Reminiscences of the Whole State, Including Many Incidents and Facts Never Before Published and of Great Historical Value*. Macon, GA: J. W. Burke and Co., 1879.

By-Laws of the Macon Volunteers, Organized 23rd April, 1825, Reorganized 8th October, 1831. Macon Volunteers. Macon, GA: C. R. Hanlester, 1839.

Catalogue 1909–1910 and Announcements, 1910–1911. Mercer University, Macon, Georgia. Atlanta: Index Printing Company, 1910.

China Monthly Review 84 (May 1938).

Clark, George Herbert. "Some Early Letters and Reminiscences of Sidney Lanier" in *The Independent* LXI (July–December 1906).

Clerepret (pseudonym). *Teresa Parodi and the Italian Opera*. New York: William B. Parsons, 1851.

A Collection of National English Airs, Consisting of the Ancient Song, Ballad and Dance Tunes, Interspersed with Remarks and Anecdote. Edited by W. Chappell. London: W. Chappell, 1840.

Coltrain, Mark. "A Conversation with Robert Lee Coleman." *Living Blues* 233 (September–October 2014): 38–42.

Connor, Charles, with Ziv Bitton. *Keep a Knockin': The Story of a Legendary Drummer*. Grapevine, TX: Waldorf Publishing, 2015.

Cox, John Edward. *Musical Recollections of the Last Half-Century*. London: Tinsley Brothers, 1872.

Dalton, David. "Little Richard: Child of God" in *Rolling Stone* (May 28, 1970): 28–34.

Daniels, Charlie. *Never Look at the Empty Seats: A Memoir*. Nashville, TN: W Publishing, 2017.

Directory of the City of Macon and County Gazetteer of Bibb County for 1884. Interstate Directory Company. Atlanta: H. H. Dickson, 1884.

Douglass, C. H. "Managing a Negro Theater," *Report of the 16th Annual Convention of the Negro Business League*. Bethesda, MD: University Publications of America, 1994.

February Annals, February 1950. St. Peter Claver School, Macon, GA.

French, Samuel Gibbs. *Two Wars: An Autobiography of Gen. Samuel G. French*. Nashville, TN: Confederate Veteran, 1901.

General Registry of the University of Oregon, 1873–1910. Eugene: University of Oregon, 1911.

Greensmith, Bill, Mike Rowe, and Mark Camarigg. *Blues Unlimited: Essential Interviews from the Original Blues Magazine*. Champaign: University of Illinois Press, 2015.

Handy, William Christopher. *Father of the Blues: An Autobiography*. New York: Da Capo Press, 1969.

Illustrated Sporting and Dramatic News II (October 3, 1875–March 27, 1875).

International Who's Who in Music and Musical Gazetteer: A Contemporary Biographical Dictionary and a Record of the World's Musical Activity. Edited by Cesar Saerchinger. New York: Current Literature Publishing Company, 1914.

Jacksonville City Directory, 1929. Detroit: R. L. Polk and Company, 1929.

Jefferson, Thomas. *Notes on the State of Virginia*. Richmond, VA: J. W. Randolph, 1853.

Jordon, Hamilton. *A Boy from Georgia: Coming of Age in the Segregated South*. Athens: University of Georgia Press, 2015.

Lamar, Dorothy Blount. *When All Is Said and Done*. Athens: University of Georgia Press, 1952.

Leavell, Chuck. *Between Rock and a Home Place*. Macon, GA: Mercer University Press, 2004.

Macon City Directory, 1914. Volume 10. Detroit: R. L. Polk and Company, 1914.

Memoirs of Richard H. Clark. Edited by Lollie Belle Wylie. Atlanta: Franklin Printing and Publishing Company, 1898.

Mercer University Bulletin, 1926–1927. Macon, GA: J. W. Burke Company, 1927.

Mission Fields at Home, Magazine of the Sisters of the Blessed Sacrament. XVIII (October 1951).

Musical Courier, A Weekly Journal 23/1 (July 1, 1891).

Musical Courier, A Weekly Journal 72/1 (January 6, 1916).

Music Trades 26/22 (November 26, 1921).

Northrup, Milton Harlow. "Some Early Recollections of Sidney Lanier." *Atlanta Constitution* (October 8, 1899).

Our War Songs: North and South. Edited by S. Brainard's Sons. Cleveland, OH: S. Brainard's Sons, 1887.

Perkins, Willie. *No Saints, No Saviors: My Years with the Allman Brothers Band*. Macon, GA: Mercer University Press, 2005.

Perry, Benjamin Franklin. *Letters of Governor Benjamin Franklin Perry to His Wife*. Greenville, SC: Shannon and Co., 1890.

Pi Kappa Phi. *The Star and Lamp of Pi Kappa Phi* 35/2 (August 1949).

Polk's Augusta (Richmond County, GA) *City Directory, 1947–1948*. Volume 39. Richmond, VA: R. L. Polk and Company, 1948.

Polk's Augusta (Richmond County, GA) *City Directory, 1949*. Volume 40. Richmond, VA: R. L. Polk and Company, 1949.

Polk's Macon (Bibb County, GA) *City Directory, 1946–1947*. Richmond, VA: R. L. Polk and Co., 1946.

Pollard, Edward Alfred. *The Southern Spy*. Washington, DC: Henry Polkinhorn, 1859.

Puterbaugh, Parke. "Little Richard: 'I Am the Architect of Rock & Roll'" in *Rolling Stone* (April 19, 1990): 51–53.

Reiff, Corbin. "Allman Brothers Band's Legendary 1971 Fillmore East Run: An Oral History" in *Rolling Stone* (March 11, 2016). https://www.rollingstone.com/music/music-features/allman-brothers-bands-legendary-1971-fillmore-east-run-an-oral-history-240779/. Accessed December 18, 2019.

Sandlin, Anathalee G. *Johnny Sandlin's Musical Odyssey: A Never-Ending Groove*. Macon, GA: Mercer University Press, 2012.

Selections from Sidney Lanier: Prose and Verse. Edited by Henry W. Lanier. New York: Charles Scribner's Sons, 1916.

Selwood, Clive. *All the Moves (But None of the Licks): Secrets of the Record Business*. London: Peter Owen Publishers, 2014.

Smith, Solomon. *The Theatrical Journey—Work and Recollections of Sol Smith*. Philadelphia: T. B. Petersen, 1854.

"Theatre-Royale." *Edinburgh Dramatic Review* 4/185 (May 26, 1823).

Wexler, Jerry and David Ritz. *Rhythm and the Blues: A Life in American Music*. New York: St. Martin's Press, 1993.

White, Charles. *The Life and Times of Little Richard: The Quasar of Rock and Roll*. New York: Harmony Books, 1984.

The World's Best Music: Famous Songs and Those Who Made Them. Volume 1. Edited by Frederick Dean, Reginald DeKoven, Helen Kendrick Johnson, and Gerrit Smith. New York: The University Society, 1904.

GOVERNMENT SOURCES

Catalogue of Copyright Entries, Part 3: Musical Publications. Volume 2. Library of Congress. Washington, DC: Government Printing Office, 1916.

Catalogue of Copyright Entries, Part 3: Musical Publications. Volume 18, part 2, nos. 8–13. Washington, DC: Government Printing Office, 1924.

Death Certificate for Lula Whidby, August 4, 1926. Commonwealth of Virginia.

Georgia Adjutant General's Office. World War I Statements of Service Cards. Georgia State Archives, Morrow, Georgia.

Historical Register of National Homes for Disabled Volunteer Soldiers, 1866–1938. National Archives Microfilm Publication M1749.

Sources

Interment Control Forms, 1928–1962. Interment Control Forms, A1 2110-B. Records of the Office of the Quartermaster General, 1774–1985. Record Group 92. National Archives at College Park, Maryland.

Journal of the Senate of the State of Georgia at the Annual Session of the General Assembly, Commencing at Atlanta, January 14, 1874. Atlanta: J. H. Estill, 1874.

"Macon, Bibb County, Georgia." *Report of the Social Statistics of Cities: Southern and Western States.* Compiled by George E. Waring. Washington, DC: Government Printing Office, 1887.

Records of the Department of Veterans Affairs. Record Group 15. National Archives, Washington, DC.

United States Census 1820: Bibb County, Georgia.

United States Census 1840: Bibb County, Georgia.

United States Census 1850: Bibb County, Georgia.

United States Census 1860: Bibb County, Georgia.

United States Census 1860: Laurens, County, South Carolina.

United States Census 1870: Bibb County, Georgia.

United States Census 1880: Bibb County, Georgia.

United States Census 1880: Pawnee County, Kansas.

United States Census 1900: Bibb County, Georgia.

United States Census 1900: Knox County, Tennessee.

United States Census 1910: Bibb County, Georgia.

United States Census 1920: Bibb County, Georgia.

United States Census 1920: Washington County, Georgia.

United States Census 1925: New York State.

United States Census 1930: Bibb County, Georgia.

United States Census 1930: Cuyahoga County, Ohio.

United States Census 1940: Bibb County, Georgia.

United States Census 1940: Harrison County, Mississippi.

United States Census 1940: Washington County, Georgia.

United States Department of the Interior, National Park Service, National Register of Historic Places Registration Form. Grand Opera House, Macon, Bibb County, Georgia.

United States Department of the Interior, National Park Service, National Register of Historic Places Registration Form. Ingleside Historic District, Macon, Bibb County, Georgia.

United States Department of the Interior, National Park Service, National Register of Historic Places Registration Form. Municipal Auditorium, Macon, Bibb County, Georgia.

United States Selective Service System, World War I Selective Service System Draft Registration Cards, 1917–1918. Washington, DC: National Archives and Records Administration, Registration, County: Bibb County, Georgia, Registration. Roll: 1557085.

United States Selective Service System, WWII Draft Registration Cards for Georgia, 10/16/1940–03/31/1947; Record Group: Records of the Selective Service System, 147. National Archives Branch. Fort Worth, Texas.

United States World War II Army Enlistment Records, National Archives and Records Administration, Record Group 64; National Archives at College Park, Maryland.

NEWSPAPERS AND MAGAZINE

Aiken (SC) Standard

Allentown (NJ) *Messenger-Press*

Allentown (PA) *Morning Call*

Anniston (AL) Star

Asbury Park (NJ) Press

Asheville (NC) Citizen-Times

Atlanta Constitution

Atlanta Daily World

Augusta (GA) Chronicle

Augusta (GA) *Daily Constitutionalist*

Austin (TX) American-Statesman

Baltimore Afro-American

Baltimore Daily Commercial

Baltimore Sun

Bennington (VT) Banner

Billboard

Biloxi (MS) Daily Herald

Blakeley (GA) *Early County News*

Bluesblast

Boston *Daily Atlas*

Boston Globe

Brattleboro (VT) *Eagle*
Brooklyn (NY) Daily Eagle
Buffalo (NY) Commercial
Buffalo (NY) Daily Courier
Buffalo (NY) Daily Republic
Camden (AR) News
Cashbox
Charleston (SC) *Courier*
Charlotte (NC) Observer
Chicago Tribune
Cincinnati (OH) Inquirer
Cleveland (OH) *Daily Leader*
Cleveland (OH) *Plain Dealer*
CMJ Music News
Columbus (GA) Daily Enquirer
Creem
Danville (KY) Advocate
Danville (VA) Bee
Dayton (OH) Herald
Detroit Free Press
Fort Valley State College (Fort Valley, GA) *Peachite*
Fremont (OH) *Weekly Journal*
Glen Falls (NY) *Post Star*
Grand Junction (CO) Daily Sentinel
Greenwood (SC) Index-Journal,
Greenville (SC) News
Greenwood (MS) Commonwealth
Hartford (CT) *Courant*
Hickory (NC) Daily Record
Hit Parader
Holly Spring (MS) Guard

Honolulu (HI) Advertiser
Honolulu (HI) Star-Bulletin
Indianapolis (IN) Recorder
Ithaca (NY) Journal
Jackson (MS) Clarion-Ledger
Jackson (TN) Sun
Lafayette (LA) *Daily Advertiser*
Larned (KS) Eagle-Optic
Lincoln (NE) Journal-Star
Living Blues
London *Daily Telegraph*
London *Record Mirror*
London *The Guardian*
Los Angeles Times
Louisville (KY) *Courier Journal*
Macon (GA) Messenger
Macon (GA) News
Macon (GA) *Telegraph*
Madison (WI) *Capital Times*
Marshall (TX) News
Mauch Chunk (PA) Times-News
McAllen (TX) Daily Press
McComb (MS) Enterprise-Journal
Melody Maker
Mercer University (Macon, GA) *Cluster*
Miami Herald
Miami New Times
Miami News
Mobile (AL) *Advertiser and Register*
Monroe County (GA) Reporter
Montgomery (AL) Advertiser

Montgomery (AL) *Alabama Journal*
Muncie (IN) Evening Press
Musical America
Nashville (TN) *Tennessean*
Natchez (MS) *Mississippi Free Trader*
Nebraska Teacher
New Orleans Crescent
New Orleans *Times Picayune*
Newport News (VA) Daily Press
New York Age
New York Herald
New York Times
Norfolk (VA) New Journal and Guide
Oakland (CA) Tribune
Ocala (FL) Star-Banner
Orlando (FL) Sentinel
Paducah (KY) Sun
Pasadena (CA) Independent
Paxton (IL) Record
Pensacola (FL) News Journal
Perry (GA) *Houston Home Journal*
Philadelphia *Daily News*
Philadelphia Inquirer
Philadelphia *Times*
Pittsburgh Courier
Pittsburg Post-Gazette
Pittsburgh Press
Providence (RI) Evening Press
Raleigh (NC) *Spirit of the Age*
Richmond (VA) Enquirer
Richmond (VA) Times Dispatch

Rochester (NY) *Democrat and Chronicle*

Sacramento (CA) Bee

San Bernardino County (CA) Sun

San Francisco Examiner

Santa Cruz (CA) Sentinel

Savannah (GA) Daily Advertiser

Savannah (GA) Tribune

Scientific American

Scranton (PA) *Times Tribune*

Shreveport (LA) *South-Westerner*

Shreveport (LA) *Times*

Staunton (VA) *News Leader*

St. Joseph (MO) Journal

St. Louis (MO) Post-Dispatch

St. Petersburg (FL) *Tampa Bay Times*

Syracuse (NY) *Post-Standard*

Tallahassee (FL) *Floridian and Journal*

Tampa (FL) Tribune

Tifton (GA) Gazette

Uniontown (PA) Morning Herald

Washington (DC) *Evening Star*

Washington (DC) Post

Washington (DC) Union

Wesleyan College (Macon, GA) *Watchtower*

Wilmington (NC) Daily Herald

TELEVISION, FILM, AND ELECTRONIC MEDIA

Betts, Dickey. Interview. "Duane Allman: The Complete 1981 Dickey Betts Interview." Jas Obrecht Music Archive. http://jasobrecht.com/duane-allman-1981-dickey-betts-interview/. Accessed February 10, 2020.

Sources

Betts, Dickey. Interview. "Rock Influences," November 4, 1984. https://www.youtube.com/watch?v=pjTwU9cMrKg. Accessed January 13, 2019.

Brown, James. Interview. *Mr. Dynamite: The Rise of James Brown.* Documentary film directed by Alex Gibney. West Hollywood, CA: Jagged Films in association with Inaudible Films, Imagine Entertainment and Jigsaw Prods., 2014.

Ertegun, Ahmet. Interview. https://www.youtube.com/watch?v=zfC26KHTCQ4. Accessed January 7, 2020.

Hall, Jimmy. Interview. "Rock Influences." https://www.youtube.com/watch?v=3OahniOGJts. Accessed January 29, 2020.

Harrison, George. Interview. *Rolling Stone Presents Twenty Years of Rock & Roll.* Television documentary directed by Malcolm Leo, aired November 24, 1987, on ABC.

Hornsby, Paul. Interview. "'Capricorn Was a Place Where the Lightning Struck': Mercer Works to Renovate Macon's Historic Studio." WMAZ-TV, Macon, Georgia. Aired February 10, 2019.

Hornsby, Paul. Interview with Luc Brunot. http://www.sweethomemusic.fr/Interviews/HornsbyUS.php. Accessed February 23, 2020.

Howard, Steve. Interview. *The Paul McCartney Project.* https://www.thepaulmccartney-project.com/interview/interview-steve-howard/. Accessed December 1, 2019.

Penniman, Richard. Interview with Bill Boggs. *Midday.* WNEW-TV. New York. Aired October 17, 1984.

Penniman, Richard. Interview with Tom Snyder. *The Late Late Show.* CBS. Aired January 14, 1997.

Penniman, Richard. Interview. "Renegades," *Rock & Roll.* Documentary, episode 1, directed by David Espar and Robert Levi. Boston, WBHG; London, BBC, 1995.

Price, Lloyd. Interview. "Renegades," *Rock & Roll,* Documentary, episode 1, directed by David Espar and Robert Levi. Boston, WBHG; London, BBC, 1995.

Redding, Otis. Interview. *American Bandstand.* Aired January 21, 1967, on ABC.

Richards, Keith. Interview. "Planet Rock Interview," https://www.keithrichards.com. Accessed November 12, 2019.

Scarborough, Homer, and Jane Darnell Keel. Interview. "Homer Scarborough and Jane Darnell Keel." John Talk Radio.

https://www.blogtalkradio.com/john-darlington/2014/11/22/homer-scar-borough-and-jane-darnell-keel-interview. Accessed August 20, 2019.

Walden, Phil. Interview with Charlie Gillett. "Phil Walden." *Rock's Backpages Audio* (1971). "Rock's Backpages." http: www.rocksbackpages.com/Library/Article/phil-walden-1971. Accessed October 29, 2019.

Williams, Hank. Interview. "Hank Williams Hadacol Interview from September, 1951." Lilly's Vintage Country Music. https://www.youtube.com/watch?v=yKhWoR05-tc. Accessed July 1, 2019.

AUTHOR INTERVIEWS/CONVERSATIONS
Newton Collier
Robin Duner-Fenter (Telephone)
Candice Dyer
Paul Hornsby (Telephone)
Leon Kennington (Telephone)
Willie Perkins
Wayne Pierce
Charles Reynolds
Jared Wright

EMAIL CORRESPONDENCE
Virginia Blake
Richard Brent
Larry Brumley
John H. Darlington
Shawna Dooley
Peter Guralnick
Dr. Debi Hamlin
Bob Konrad
Chuck Leavell
Kristin Oren

Ben Sandifer
Michael Buffalo Smith
Jessica Walden

SECONDARY SOURCES

BOOKS AND ARTICLES

Abbott, Lynn and Doug Seroff. *The Emergence of the Blues in African American Vaudeville: 1899–1926.* Jackson: University Press of Mississippi, 2017.

_____. *Out of Sight: The Rise of African American Popular Music, 1889–1895.* Jackson: University Press of Mississippi, 2002.

_____. *Ragged but Right, Black Travelling Shows, "Coon Songs" and the Dark Pathway to Blues and Jazz.* Jackson: University Press of Mississippi, 2007.

Abel, E. Lawrence. *Singing the New Nation: How Music Shaped the Confederacy, 1861–1865.* Mechanicsburg, PA: Stackpole Books, 2000.

Acham, Christine. *Revolution Televised: Prime Time and the Struggle for Black Power.* Minneapolis: University of Minnesota Press, 2004.

African American Music: An Introduction. Edited by Mellonee V. Burnim and Portia K Maultsby. New York: Routledge, 2014.

Akers, Samuel Luttrell. *The First Hundred Years of Wesleyan College, 1836–1936.* New York: Beehive Press, 1976.

All Music Guide to the Blues: The Definitive Guide to the Blues. 3rd edition. Edited by Vladimir Bogdanov, Chris Woodstra, and Stephen Thomas Erlewine. San Francisco: Backbeat Books, 2003.

Altschuler, Glenn C. *All Shook Up: How Rock 'n' Roll Changed America.* New York: Oxford University Press, 2003.

Anderson, Patrick. *Electing Jimmy Carter: The Campaign of 1976.* Baton Rouge: Louisiana State University Press, 1994.

Anderson, Paul. *Mods: The New Religion.* London: Omnibus Press, 2014.

Anson, Robert Sam. "Will Phil Walden Rise Again?" *Esquire* (June 1980): 38–44.

Apel, Willi. *Harvard Dictionary of Music.* Cambridge, MA: Belknap Press of Harvard University, 1970.

Ayers, Edward L. *The Promise of the New South: Life After Reconstruction.* New York: Oxford University Press, 1992.

Bailey, Candace. *Music and the Southern Belle: From Accomplished Lady to Confederate Composer.* Carbondale: Southern Illinois University Press, 2010.

Baker, Houston A., Jr. *Long Black Song: Essays in Black American Literature and Culture*. Charlottesville: University Press of Virginia, 1972.

Barlow, William. *Voice Over: The Making of Black Radio*. Philadelphia: Temple University Press, 1999.

Barry, John H. "Father Tabb (1845–1909)." *The Irish Monthly* 73/862 (April 1945): 141–47.

Batts, H. Lewis and Rollin S. Armour. *History of the First Baptist Church of Christ, Macon Georgia, 1826–1990*. Macon, GA: For the Church, 1991.

Blassingame, John W. *The Slave Community: Plantation Life in the Antebellum South*. New York: Oxford University Press, 1979.

Booth, Stanley. *Red Hot and Blue: Fifty Years of Writing about Music, Memphis, and Motherf**kers*. Chicago: Chicago Review Press, 2019.

Bowman, Rob. *Soulsville, U.S.A.: The Story of Stax Records*. London: Schirmer Trade, 2010.

Boyer, Horace Clarence. *The Golden Age of Gospel*. Urbana and Chicago: University of Illinois Press, 1995.

Brant, Marley. *Join Together: Forty Years of the Rock Music Festival*. New York: Hal Leonard Corporation, 2008.

Brend, Mark. *Strange Sounds: Offbeat Instruments and Sonic Experiments in Pop*. San Francisco: Backbeat Books, 2005.

Brobston, Stanley Heard. *Daddy Sang Lead: The History and Performance Practice of White Southern Gospel Music*. New York: Vantage Press, 2006.

Brown, Titus. "A New England Missionary and African-American Education in Macon: Raymond G. Von Tobel at Ballard Normal School, 1908–1935." *The Georgia Historical Quarterly* 82/2 (Summer 1998): 283–304.

Bulletin of the Catholic Laymen's Association of Georgia, February 21, 1942.

Burnt Cork and Tambourines: A Source Book for Negro Minstrelsy. Edited by William L. Slout. Rockville, MD: Wildside Press, 2007.

Cai, Camilla and Einar Haugen. *Ole Bull: Norway's Romantic Musician and Cosmopolitan Patriot*. Madison: University of Wisconsin Press, 1993.

The Cambridge Companion to Blues and Gospel Music. Edited by Allan Moore. Cambridge, UK: Cambridge University Press, 2003.

The Cambridge History of American Music. Edited by David Nichols. Cambridge, UK: Cambridge University Press, 1998.

Camus, Raoul F. "A Source for Early American Band Music: John Beach's Selection of Airs, Marches, &c." Notes 38, no. 4 (1982): 792–94.

Carlin, Richard. *Country Music: A Biographical Dictionary*. New York: Routledge, 2003.

Carney, Court. *Cuttin' Up: How Early Jazz got America's Ear*. Lawrence: University of Kansas Press, 2009.

Cashmore, Ellis. *The Black Culture Industry*. New York: Routledge, 1997.

Chase, Gilbert. *America's Music: From the Pilgrims to the Present*. Urbana: University of Illinois Press, 1987.

Chilton, John. *Let the Good Times Roll: The Story of Louis Jordan and His Music*. Ann Arbor: University of Michigan Press, 1994.

Cimbala, Paul A. "Black Musicians from Slavery to Freedom." *Journal of Negro History* 80/1 (Winter 1995): 15–29.

Clarke, Erskine. *Wrestlin' Jacob: A Portrait of Religion in Antebellum Georgia and the Carolina Low Country*. Tuscaloosa: University of Alabama Press, 2000.

Clayton, Buck. *Buck Clayton's Jazz World*. Oxford, UK: Bayou Press, 1986.

Cohen, Norm. *Long Steel Rail: The Railroad in American Folksong*. 2nd edition. Champaign: University of Illinois Press, 2000.

The Companion to Southern Literature: Themes. Genres, Places, People, Movements and Motifs. Edited by Joseph M. Flora, Lucinda H. MacKethan, and Todd W. Taylor. Baton Rouge: Louisiana State University Press, 2002.

Cone, James M. *The Spirituals and the Blues: An Interpretation*. New York: Seabury Press, 1971.

Cowboy Songs 1/14 (March, 1953).

Cox, Karen L. *Dreaming of Dixie: How the South Was Created in American Popular Culture*. Chapel Hill: University of North Carolina Press, 2011.

Crawford, Richard. *America's Musical Life: A History*. New York: W. W. Norton and Co., 2001.

Cullen, Frank. *Vaudeville Old and New: An Encyclopedia of Variety Performances in America*. Volume 1. New York: Routledge, 2006.

Cumming, Joseph B. "The Cumming-McDuffie Duels." *The Georgia Historical Quarterly* 44/1 (1960): 18–40.

Curtis, Susan. *Dancing to a Black Man's Tune: A Life of Scott Joplin*. Columbia: University of Missouri Press, 1994.

Cusic, Don. *The Sound of Light: A History of Gospel and Christian Music*. Milwaukee, WI: Hal Leonard Corporation, 1990.

Dahl, Linda. *Stormy Weather: The Music and Lives of a Century of Jazzwomen*. New York: Pantheon Books, 1984.

Daniel, Wayne W. *Pickin' on Peachtree: A History of Country Music in Atlanta, Georgia*. Urbana: University of Illinois Press, 1990.

Davis, Francis. *The History of the Blues: The Roots, the Music, the People from Charley Patton to Robert Cray*. New York: Hyperion, 1995.

Deffaa, Chip. *Voices of the Jazz Age: Profiles of Eight Vintage Jazzmen*. Champaign: University of Illinois Press, 1992.

Delehant, Jim. "Otis Redding: 'Soul Survivor.'" *Hit Parader* (August 1967): 56–57.

Dictionary of Georgia Biography. Volume II. Edited by Kenneth Coleman and Charles Stephen Gurr. Athens: University of Georgia Press, 1983.

A Dictionary of Music and Musicians. Volume 3. Edited by George Grove. New York: MacMillan and Co., 1889.

Duncan, Robert. "Rhett Butler After the Fall: Dickey Betts Brushes Himself Off..." *Creem* (March 1977). "Rock's Backpages." http://www.rocksback-pages.com/Library/Article/rhett-butler-after-the-fall-dickey-betts-brushes-himself-off. Accessed February 21, 2020.

Dyer, Candice. "Frank Fenter: The Man Who Might Have Saved Capricorn," *11th Hour* 8/4 (May 6–19, 2010): 20–24.

_____. *Street Singers, Soul Shakers, Rebels with a Cause: Music from Macon.* Macon, GA: Indigo Custom Publishing, 2008.

Eagle, Bob and Eric S. LeBlanc. *Blues: A Regional Experience.* Santa Barbara, CA: Praeger Publishers, 2013.

Edge, John T. "Mama Tried." *Oxford American* 34 (July/August 2000). https://www.oxfordamerican.org/magazine/item/1228-mama-tried/. Accessed January 30, 2020.

Edmonds, Ben. "Snapshots of the South: The Allman Brothers and Capricorn Records." *Creem* (November 1972): 39–40.

Eisterhold, John A. "Commercial, Financial, and Industrial Macon, Georgia, During the 1840s." *The Georgia Historical Quarterly* 53/4 (1969).

Encyclopedia of the Blues. Edited by Gerard Herzhaft. Fayetteville: University of Arkansas Press, 1992.

Encyclopedia of the Harlem Renaissance. Volumes 1 and 2. Edited by Cary D. Wintz and Paul Finkelman. New York: Routledge, 2004.

Engle, Carl. "Music of the Gypsies." *The Musical Times and Singing Class Circular* 21 (July 1, 1880): 331–38.

Epstein, Dena J. *Sinful Tunes and Spirituals: Black Folk Music to the Civil War.* Champaign: University of Illinois Press, 2003.

Evans, Brad. "Calvin Arline: A Legendary Bassline," *11th Hour* 283 (March 14–28, 2014): 29–30.

_____. "It's a Mean Ole World," *11th Hour* 251 (November 16–30, 2012; first published in June 2004).

Evans, David. *Big Road Blues: Tradition and Creativity in Folk Blues.* New York: Da Capo Press, 1987.

Exploring Roots Music: Twenty Years of the JEMF Quarterly. Edited by Nolan Porterfield. Lanham, MD: Scarecrow Press, Inc., 2004.

Fanelli, Damian. "Eric Clapton: I've Never Heard Better Rock Guitar Playing." *Guitar World* (August 26, 2019).

https://www.guitarworld.com/artists/listen-eric-clapton-s-favorite-rb-guitar-solo-duane-allman-guests-wilson-picketts-cover-hey-jude. Accessed February 1, 2020.

Fields, Gaylord. "Live at the Apollo." *Rolling Stone* (June 30, 2008). https://www.rollingstone.com/music/music-album-reviews/live-at-the-apollo-255609/. Accessed December 1, 2019.

Fish, Scott K. "How Joe English Got the Gig with Paul McCartney." August 4, 2015. https://scottkfish.com/2015/08/04/how-joe-english-got-the-gig-with-paul-mccartney/. Accessed December 7, 2019.

Fong-Torres, Ben. *The Rolling Stone Rock 'n' Roll Reader.* New York: Bantam Books, 1974.

Fox, John Hartley. *King of the Queen City: The Story of King Records.* Urbana: University of Illinois Press, 2009.

Freehling, William W. *The Road to Disunion: Secessionists at Bay, 1776–1854.* New York: Oxford University Press, 1990.

Freeman, Scott. *Midnight Riders: The Story of the Allman Brothers Band.* New York: Little, Brown and Company, 1995.

_____. *Otis!: The Otis Redding Story.* New York: St. Martin's Press, 2001.

Gabin, Jane S. *A Living Minstrelsy: The Poetry and Music of Sidney Lanier.* Macon, GA: Mercer University Press, 1985.

Gardner, Tim. "Naomi Sego Reader: She Is a Legend." *Singing News* (July 2001): 58–61.

Gates, Henry Louis, Jr. *The Signifying Monkey: A Theory of African American Literary Criticism.* New York: Oxford University Press, 1988.

Georgia Biographical Dictionary, 1999–2000. Volume 1. St. Clair Shores, MI: Somerset Publishers, Inc., 1999.

Gioia, Ted. *Delta Blues: The Life and Times of Mississippi Masters Who Revolutionized American Music.* New York: W. W. Norton & Company, 2008.

Glatt, John. *Live at the Fillmore East and West: Getting Backstage and Personal with Rock's Greatest Legends.* Lanham, MD: Rowman & Littlefield, 2016.

Glover, Tom. "Eat a Peach: Allman Brothers Band Album Review." *Rolling Stone* (April 13, 1972). https://www.rollingstone.com/music/music-album-reviews/eat-a-peach-249573/. Accessed December 14, 2019.

Goertzen, Chris. *Southern Fiddlers and Fiddle Contests.* Jackson: University Press of Mississippi, 2008.

Goff, James R. *Close Harmony: A History of Southern Gospel.* Chapel Hill: University of North Carolina Press, 2002.

Goldberg, Michael. "James Brown: Wrestling with the Devil." *Rolling Stone* (April 6, 1989). https://www.rollingstone.com/music/music-news/james-brown-wrestling-with-the-devil-49247/. Accessed December 18, 2019.

Gordon, Robert. *Respect Yourself: Stax Records and the Soul Explosion*. New York: Bloomsbury, 2013.

Gould, Jonathan. *Otis Redding: An Unfinished Life*. New York: Crown Archetype, 2017.

Gray, Michael. *Hand Me My Travelin' Shoes: In Search of Blind Willie McTell*. Chicago: Chicago Review Press, 2009.

A Guide to Macon's Architectural and Historical Heritage. Edited by John McKay Jr. Macon, GA: Middle Georgia Historical, Society, 1972.

Guralnick, Peter. *Sweet Soul Music: Rhythm and Blues and the Southern Dream of Freedom*. New York: Little, Brown and Company, 1986.

Harrell, Carolyn L. *Kith and Kin: Portrait of a Southern Family, 1630–1934*. Macon, GA: Mercer University Press, 1984.

Harris, Joseph. *The Ballad and Oral Literature*. Cambridge, MA: Harvard University Press, 1991.

Hay, Fred J. "Music Box Meets the Toccoa Band: The Godfather of Soul in Appalachia." *Black Music Research Journal* 23/1–2 (Spring–Autumn 2003): 103–33.

History of the First Presbyterian Church, Macon, Georgia, 1826–1990. Compiled by Harriet Fincher Comer. Macon, GA: Williams-Rowland Printing Co., 1990.

Horton, James Oliver and Lois E. Horton. *Slavery and the Making of America*. New York: Oxford University Press, 2005.

A Hundred Years of Music in America: An Account of Musical Efforts in America. Edited by W. S. B. Matthews. Philadelphia: Theodore Presser, 1900.

Iobst, Richard W. *Civil War Macon: The History of a Confederate City*. Macon, GA: Mercer University Press, 1999.

Jackson, Andrew Grant. *1965: The Most Revolutionary Year in Music*. New York: Thomas Dunne Books, 2015.

Jackson, Lena E. and Aubrey Starke. "New Light on the Ancestry of Sidney Lanier." *The Virginia Magazine of History and Biography* 43/2 (April 1935): 165–68.

Jasen, David A. and Gene Jones. *That American Rag: The Story of Ragtime from Coast to Coast*. New York: Schirmer Books, 2000.

Jim Crow, American: Selected Songs and Plays. Edited by W. T. Lhamon. Cambridge, MA: Harvard University Press, 2003.

Johannsen, Robert W. *To the Halls of Montezumas: The Mexican War in the American Imagination*. New York: Oxford University Press, 1985.

Kemp, Larry. *Modern Jazz Trumpet Legends*. Pittsburgh: RoseDog Books, 2018.

Kemp, Mark. *Dixie Lullaby: A Story of Music, Race, and New Beginnings in a New South*. New York: Free Press, 2004.

Kirby, David. *Little Richard and the Birth of Rock 'N' Roll*. New York: Continuum International Publishing Group, 2009.

Knight, Lucian Lamar. *Georgia's Landmarks, Memorials, and Legends*. Volume II. Atlanta: Byrd Printing Co., 1913.

Koch, Mary Levin. "Entertaining the Public: Music and Drama in Antebellum Georgia." *The Georgia Historical Quarterly* 68/4 (Winter 1984).

Kraar, Louis. "How Phil Walden Turns Rock into Gold." *Fortune* (September 1975): 107–12.

Kubik, Gerhard. *Africa and the Blues*. Jackson: University Press of Mississippi, 1999.

Kunstadt, Len. "The Lucille Hegamin Story, Part 1." *Record Research* 39 (November 1961).

_____. "The Lucille Hegamin Story, Part 2." *Record Research* 40 (January 1962).

_____. "The Lucille Hegamin Story, Part 3." *Record Research* 41 (February 1962).

_____. "The Lucille Hegamin Story, Part 4." *Record Research* 43 (May 1962).

_____. "Lucille Hegamin's Last Performance." *Record Research* 104 (March 1970).

Laird, Ross and Brian Rust. *Discography of Okeh Records, 1918–1934*. Westport, CT: Praeger, 2004.

Laird, Tracey E. W. *Louisiana Hayride: Radio and Roots Music Along the Red River*. New York: Oxford University Press, 2005.

Landau, Emily Epstein. *Spectacular Wickedness: Sex, Race, and Memory in Storyville, New Orleans*. Baton Rouge: Louisiana State University Press, 2013.

Lanier, Doris. "Early Chautauqua in Georgia." *Journal of American Culture* 11/3 (Fall 1988).

Lauterbach, Preston. *The Chitlin Circuit and the Road to Rock and Roll*. New York: W. W. Norton and Company, 2011.

Lawrence, Vera Brodsky. *Strong on Music: The New York Music Scene in the Days of George Templeton Strong*. Volume I. Chicago: University of Chicago Press, 1988.

Lawson, R. A. *Jim Crow's Counterculture: The Blues and Black Southerners, 1890–1945*. Baton Rouge: Louisiana State University Press, 2010.

Levine, Lawrence W. *Black Culture and Black Consciousness: Afro-American Folk Thought from Slavery to Freedom*. New York: Oxford University Press, 1977.

Lieb, Sandra R. *Mother of the Blues: A Study of Ma Rainey*. Amherst: University of Massachusetts Press, 1981.

Linn, Karen. *That Half-Barbaric Twang: The Banjo in American Popular Culture*. Champaign: University of Illinois Press, 1991.

Lost in the Groves: Scram's Capricorn Guide to the Music You Missed. Edited by Kim Cooper and David Smay. New York: Routledge, 2005.

Lott, Eric. *Love and Theft: Blackface Minstrelsy and the American Working Class.* New York: Oxford University Press, 1993.

Macon's Black Heritage: The Untold Story. Macon, GA: Tubman African American Museum, 1997.

Manis, Andrew W. *Macon in Black and White: An Unutterable Separation in the American Century.* Macon, GA: Mercer University Press and the Tubman African American Museum, 2004.

Martin, George Whitney. *Verdi in America: Oberto Through Rigoletto.* Rochester, NY: University of Rochester Press, 2011.

McBride, James. *Kill 'Em and Leave: Searching for James Brown and the American Soul.* New York: Spiegel & Grau, 2016.

McClellan, Lawrence, Jr. *The Later Swing Era, 1942 to 1955.* Westport, CT: Greenwood Press, 2004.

McGee, Garry. *Band on the Run: A History of Paul McCartney and Wings.* New York: Taylor Trade Publishing, 2003.

McKee, Margaret and Fred Chisenhall. *Beale Black & Blue: Life and Music on Black America's Main Street.* Baton Rouge: Louisiana State University Press, 1993.

Mims, Edwin. *Sidney Lanier.* New York: Houghton, Mifflin and Co., 1905.

Monod, David. *The Soul of Pleasure: The Soul of Pleasure: Sentiment and Sensation in Nineteenth-Century American Mass Entertainment.* Ithaca, NY: Cornell University Press, 2016.

Moore, John Weeks. *A Dictionary of Musical Information.* Boston: Oliver Ditson and Co., 1876.

More Than Precious Memories: The Rhetoric of Southern Gospel Music. Edited by Michael P. Graves and David Fillingim. Macon, GA: Mercer University Press, 2004.

Moskowitz, David. *The Words and Music of Jimi Hendrix.* Santa Barbara, CA: Praeger, 2010.

Murray, Charles Shaar. *Boogie Man: The Adventures of John Lee Hooker in the American Twentieth Century.* New York: St. Martin's Press, 2000.

Music Cultures in the United States: An Introduction. Edited by Ellen Koskoff. New York: Routledge, 2005.

Nardolillo, Jo. *All Things Strings: An Illustrated Dictionary.* New York: Rowen and Littlefield, 2014.

Oakley, Giles. *The Devil's Music: A History of the Blues.* De Capo Press, Inc., 1997.

O'Connell, Deirdre. *The Ballad of Blind Tom, Slave Pianist: America's Lost Musical Genius*. New York: Overlook Press, 2009.

Oermann, Robert K. "'Peanut' Faircloth Passes." *Music Row* (March 22, 2010). https://musicrow.com/2010/03/peanut-faircloth-passes/. Accessed July 2, 2019.

Palmer, Robert. *Deep Blues*. New York: Penguin Books, 1981.

Paul, Alan. *One Way Out: The Inside Story of the Allman Brothers Band*. New York: St. Martin's Griffin, 2014.

Perone, James E. *Listen to the Blues: Exploring a Musical Genre*. Santa Barbara, CA: Greenwood Press, 2019.

Peterson, Bernard L., Jr. *The African American Theater Directory, 1916–1960: A Comprehensive Guide to Early Black Theater Organizations, Companies, Theaters, and Performing Groups*. Westport, CT: Greenwood Press, 1997.

_____. *A Century of Musicals in Black and White: An Encyclopedia of Musical Stage Works by, About, or Involving African Americans*. Westport, CT: Greenwood Press, 1993.

Poe, Randy. *Skydog: The Duane Allman Story*. New York: Backbeat Books, 2006.

Preston, Katherine A. *Opera on the Road: Traveling Opera Troupes in the United States, 1825–60*. Urbana: University of Illinois Press, 1993.

Raboteau, Albert J. *Slave Religion: The Invisible Institution in the South*. New York: Oxford University Press, 2004.

Ramblin on My Mind: New Perspectives of the Blues. Edited by David Evans. Champaign: University of Illinois Press, 2008.

Rhodes, Don. *Say It Loud!: My Memories of James Brown, Soul Brother No. 1*. Guilford, CT: Lyons Press, 2009.

Ribowsky, Mark. *Dreams to Remember: Otis Redding, Stax Records, and the Transformation of Southern Soul*. New York: Liveright Publishing Corp., 2015.

Rice, Edward Le Roy. *Monarchs of Minstrelsy, from "Daddy" Rice to Date*. New York: Kenny Publishing Co., 1911.

Roby, Steven and Brad Schreiber. *Becoming Jimi Hendrix: From Southern Crossroads to Psychedelic London, the Untold Story of a Musical Genius*. Cambridge, MA: Da Capo Press, 2010.

Russell, Tony. *Country Music Originals: The Legends and the Lost*. New York, Oxford University Press, 2004.

_____. *Country Music Recordings: A Discography*. New York: Oxford University Press, 2004.

Sanjek, Russell. *American Popular Music and Its Business: The First Four Hundred Years*. Volume II. New York: Oxford University Press, 1988.

Schinder, Bob and Andy Schwartz. *Icons of Rock: An Encyclopedia of the Legends Who Changed Music Forever.* Volume 1. Westport, CT: Greenwood Press, 2008.

Schoenbaum, David. *The Violin: A Social History of the World's Most Versatile Instrument.* New York: W. W. Norton & Company, 2012.

Schwartz, Jim. "Sea Level: Rock, Funk, and Blues from the South." *Hittin' the Net with the Allman Brothers Band.* http://www.allmanbrothersband.com/modules.php?op=modload&name=userpage&file=content&page_id=23. Accessed December 10, 2019.

Scobie, Inger Winther. *Center Stage: Helen Gahagan Douglas, A Life.* New York: Oxford University Press, 1992.

Shapiro, Harry and Caesar Glebbeek. *Jimi Hendrix: Electric Gypsy.* New York: St. Martin's Griffin, 1995.

Shaw, Arnold. *Honkers and Shouters: The Golden Years of Rhythm and Blues.* New York: Macmillan, 1978.

Silk, Catherine and John Silk. *Racism and Anti-Racism in American Popular Culture: Portrayals of African-Americans in Fiction and Film.* Manchester, UK: Manchester University Press, 1990.

Smith, Michael Buffalo. *Capricorn Rising: Conversations in Southern Rock.* Macon, GA: Mercer University Press, 2016.

_____. "Like a Rolling Stone: A Visit with Former Doc Holliday Member, and Current Solo Star, Eddie Stone." http://swampland.com/articles/view/title:eddie_stone. Accessed January 14, 2020.

Smith, R. J. *The One: The Life and Times of James Brown.* New York: Gotham Books, 2012.

Southall, Geneva Handy. *Blind Tom, the Black Pianist-Composer: Continually Enslaved.* Lanham, MD: Scarecrow Press, 2002.

Starke, Aubrey H. "Sidney Lanier as a Musician." *The Musical Quarterly* 20/4 (October 1934).

Stars of Country Music: Uncle Dave Macon to Johnny Rodriguez. Edited by Bill C. Malone and Judith McCulloh. Urbana: University of Illinois Press, 1975.

Stone, James M. "Economic Conditions in Macon, Georgia in the 1830's." *The Georgia Historical Quarterly* 54/2 (1970).

Strausbaugh, John. *Black Like You: Blackface, Whiteface, Insult & Imitation in American Popular Culture.* New York: Penguin, 2006.

Stuart, Bonnye. *It Happened in Louisiana: Remarkable Events that Shaped History.* Lanham, MD: Rowman & Littlefield, 2015.

Sullivan, Steve. *Encyclopedia of Great Popular Song Recordings.* Volumes 3 and 4. New York: Rowman & Littlefield, 2017.

Taslitz, Andrew E. *Reconstructing the Fourth Amendment: A History of Search and Seizure, 1789–1868*. New York: New York University Press, 2006.

Thompson, Mattie Croker Thomas. *History of Barbour County, Alabama*. Eufaula, AL: Privately Printed, 1939.

Titon, Jeff Todd. *Early Downhome Blues: A Musical and Cultural Analysis*. 2nd edition. Chapel Hill: University of North Carolina Press, 1994.

Tosches, Nick. *Country: The Twisted Roots of Rock and Roll*. New York: Da Capo Press, 1985.

_____. "The Strange and Hermetical Case of Emmett Miller." *The Journal of Country Music* 17 (1995): 39–47.

_____. *Where Dead Voices Gather*. New York: Little, Brown and Company, 2001.

Townsend, Charles R. *San Antonio Rose: The Life and Music of Bob Wills*. Urbana: University of Illinois Press, 1986.

The Turbulent Voyage: Readings in African American Studies. Edited by Floyd W. Hayes III. New York: Collegiate Press, 2000.

Turner, Steve. *Trouble Man: The Life and Death of Marvin Gaye*. New York: Echo Press, 2000.

Turpen, Brian. *Ramblin' Man: Short Stories from the Life of Hank Williams*. Many, LA: Old Paths, New Dreams Publishing, 2007.

Underwood, Tut. "Eddie Kirkland: The Energy Man." *Living Blues*. 111 (October 1993): 15–19.

Vincent, Rickey. *Party Music: The Inside Story of the Black Panthers' Band and How Black Power Changed Soul Music*. Chicago: Lawrence Hill Books, 2013.

Walburn, Steve. "Phil Walden: The Flip Side." *Atlanta Magazine* (August 1993): 36–40.

Ward, Brian. *Just My Soul Responding: Rhythm and Blues, Black Consciousness, and Race Relations*. Berkeley: University of California Press, 1998.

Webb, Mary. "Musician Returns to Houma for Southdown Reunion." April 1, 2001. https://www.houmatoday.com/article/DA/20010401/News/60809 4806/HC. Accessed November 30, 2019.

Wenner, Jann S. and Baron Wolman. "Jimi Hendrix On Early Influences, 'Axis' and More." *Rolling Stone* (March 9, 1968). https://www.rollingstone.com/music/music-news/jimi-hendrix-on-early-influences-axis-and-more-203924/. Accessed November 26, 2019.

White, Andy Lee and John M. Williams. *Atlanta Pop in the 50s, 60s, and 70s: The Magic of Bill Lowery*. Charleston, SC: History Press, 2019.

Whorf, Michael. *America's Popular Song Lyricists: Oral Histories, 1920s–1960s*. Jefferson, NC: McFarland and Company, 2012.

A Wilderness Still the Cradle of Nature: Frontier Georgia, A Documentary History. Edited by Edward J. Cashin. Savannah, GA: Beehive Press 1994.

Willard, Francis Elizabeth and Mary Ashton Rice Livermore. *A Woman of the Century: Fourteen Hundred-Seventy Biographical Sketches Accompanied by Portraits of Leading American Women in All Walks of Life.* New York: Charles Wells Moulton, 1893.

Woodhead, Henry. "Making It Big in Macon with Those Good Ol' Georgia Blues." *Atlanta Journal and Constitution Magazine* (March 3, 1974): 8–9, 22–27.

Wynne, Ben. *In Tune: Charley Patton, Jimmie Rodgers and the Roots of American Music.* Baton Rouge: Louisiana State University Press, 2014.

Yanow, Scott. *Classic Jazz.* San Francisco: Back Beat Books, 2001.

_____. *Jazz on Record: The First Sixty Years.* San Francisco: Backbeat Books, 2003.

_____. *Trumpet Kings: The Players Who Shaped the Sound of Jazz Trumpet.* San Francisco: Backbeat Books, 2001.

Young, Ida, Julius Gholson, and Clara Nell Hargrove. *A History of Macon, Georgia, 1823–1949.* Macon, GA: Lyon Marshall and Brooks, 1950.

Yule, Ron. *Louisiana Fiddlers.* Jackson: University Press of Mississippi, 2009.

THESES AND DISSERTATION

Anderson, George David. "A City Comes of Age: An Urban Study of Macon, Georgia during the 1920s." MA Thesis, Georgia College, 1975.

Hominick, Ian G. "Sigismund Thalberg (1812–1871) Forgotten Piano Virtuoso: His Career and Musical Contributions." PhD Dissertation, Ohio State University, 1991.

Steinhaus, Walter E. "Music in the Cultural Life in Macon, 1823–1900." PhD Dissertation, Florida State University, 1973.

WEBSITES

The Big House. https://thebighousemuseum.com/the-house/.

Chuck Leavell. https://www.chuckleavell.com/.

Georgia Allman Brothers Band Association. http://www.gabbafest.org/.

Macon Music Trail. https://www.maconmusictrail.com/.

Otis Redding Foundation. https://otisreddingfoundation.org/.

Rock Candy Tours. https://www.rockcandytours.com/.

Index

Index

Index

Index

Index

Index

Index

MUSIC AND THE AMERICAN SOUTH

Michael Buffalo Smith, *From Macon to Jacksonville: More Conversations in Southern Rock*, with a Foreword by Charlie Starr

Michael Buffalo Smith, *The Road Goes on Forever: Fifty Years of The Allman Brothers Band Music (1969–2019)*, with a Foreword Chuck Leavell

Doug Kershaw, *The Ragin' Cajun: Memoir of a Louisiana Man*, with Cathie Pelletier

Don Reid, *The Music of The Statler Brothers: An Anthology*, with a Foreword by Bill and Gloria Gaither

Paul Hornsby, Fix it in the Mix: A Memoir with Michael Buffalo Smith